JANE'S
WARSAW PA
MERCHANT SHIPS
Recognition Handbook

Compiled by David Greenman and
Lt-Cdr E C Talbot-Booth, RD, RNR

JANE'S TRANSPORT PRESS

"Jane's" is a registered trade mark

Copyright © 1987 Jane's Publishing Company Limited

First published in the United Kingdom in 1987 by
Jane's Publishing Company Limited
238 City Road, London EC1V 2PU, England

Distributed in the USA and its dependencies by
Jane's Publishing Inc, 4th Floor, 115 Fifth Avenue, New York, NY 10003, USA

ISBN 0 7106 0455 6

All rights reserved. No part of this publication may be reproduced, stored in a retrieval system,
transmitted in any form by any means electrical, mechanical or photocopied, recorded or otherwise
without the prior permission of the publisher.

Whilst every care has been taken in the compilation of this publication to ensure its accuracy at the
time of going to press the publishers cannot be held responsible for any errors or omissions.

Furthermore no responsibility for loss occasioned to any person acting or refraining from action as
a result from use of any material in this publication can be accepted by the editor and/or authors or
publisher.

Computer typesetting by Method Limited, Epping, Essex

Printed in the United Kingdom by
Butler & Tanner Ltd
Frome and London

CONTENTS

Introduction   7

Member Countries of the Warsaw Pact   9
  Union of Soviet Socialist Republics   13
  Bulgaria   21
  Czechoslovakia   22
  German Democratic Republic   23
  Hungary   24
  Poland   25
  Romania   28

Merchant and Fishing Fleet Funnel Designs   29

Recognition System   34

Explanatory Notes   42

Abbreviations   44

Ship Drawings   47

Indexes   210

INTRODUCTION

The Warsaw Pact and COMECON

The Treaty of Friendship and Mutual Assistance, known as the Warsaw Pact, was formed in 1955 by the following signatories: Albania, Bulgaria, Czechoslovakia, East Germany (German Democratic Republic), Hungary, Poland, Romania and the USSR. Albania withdrew from the Pact in 1968. The Pact's function is primarily military and the Commander-in-Chief of its forces is always a Soviet Marshal. This, combined with the fact that all the signatories are Soviet satellites, clearly indicates that the USSR has the most significant influence on the group. NATO may be regarded as the western equivalent of the Warsaw Pact.

The economic and trade interests of the Soviet bloc are represented by COMECON, an acronym for the Council for Mutual Economic Assistance, also known as CMEA. Formed in 1949, it was initially concerned with land-links and short-sea shipping but, with the addition of Cuba in 1972, and more recently of Viet-Nam, more deep-sea trade is now involved. The other members are the USSR and the Warsaw Pact countries. In 1986 the COMECON merchant fleet represented almost 12 per cent of the world fleet of significant merchant ships, in terms of numbers of ships, only Japan having more vessels (*Lloyd's Register of Shipping Statistical Tables 1986*). The percentage of Warsaw Pact merchant ships would only be marginally lower as its vessels form about 95 per cent of the COMECON fleet. The fleet grew by 1.2 million gross tons over the three-year period 1984–86; while the merchant fleet of the NATO countries dropped by 30 million gross tons over the same period. Another significant fact, particularly from a military point of view, is that 40 per cent of NATO merchant ships are flagged-out.

Soviet shipping

The expansion of the Soviet merchant fleet has slowed down in the last few years and the average age of its ships has increased from 9.5 years in 1975 to 14 years in 1987. In the Five Year Plan period which ended in 1985, the Soviet merchant fleet increased by 8.6 per cent in terms of deadweight tonnage and stood at 20 million tons. During the current five years, the Soviets intend to acquire an aggregate deadweight of 2.6 million tons. They have been particularly active in the second-hand market in recent years, especially in the purchase of medium-sized bulk carriers. Recently it has been noted with interest that the Soviets intend to make their major national shipping lines, ports and shipyards more financially independent and to put them onto a more commercial footing. It will be interesting to see how this affects the growth and performance of their fleet.

Although the preliminary sections of this book contain certain information which may be regarded as more 'intelligence' than 'recognition' material, the drawings section is entirely concerned with recognition. To this end, the information given beneath the drawings has been limited to the essential facts, and names of sister ships etc have been omitted. However, all these names appear in the alphabetical index except for some of the very large classes of smaller fishing craft etc. Even the total numbers of vessels in the classes have been omitted as these may vary considerably over a short period and become misleading. If sisters of similar ships exist under flags other than Warsaw Pact this information is also excluded for similar reasons. The numbering system used is the same as in *Jane's Merchant Ships 1987–88*, ie, a drawing which has already appeared in JMS keeps the same number, and additional drawings have been given numbers which put them into their correct position in the drawings section of JMS. This means that the numbers are in numerical order although there may be large gaps between some. Readers with access to JMS will thus be able easily to check with that publication for more detailed information. However, this facility does not devalue this book for the person without JMS, as the latter provides *extra* information and not essential *recognition* information.

The drawings cover most sea-going vessels and, although there is no particular cut-off point, there are very few vessels illustrated of less than 30 metres (98 feet) overall length. Only certain dredgers are included as they are considered to be principally harbour craft. Many of those which have been included have other functions such as pollution control.

MEMBER COUNTRIES OF THE WARSAW PACT
'WARPAC'

The Warsaw Pact or 'Treaty of Friendship and Mutual Assistance' came into existence in 1955.

It comprises the following countries, all of which possess merchant fleets:

People's Republic of Bulgaria
Czechoslovak Socialist Republic
German Democratic Republic (DDR)
Hungarian People's Republic
Polish People's Republic
Socialist Republic of Romania
Union of Soviet Socialist Republics

Albania was originally a member but withdrew in 1968. It remains uncertain whether it will reconsider its position following the death of Enver Hoxha, but it would seem unlikely.

MERCHANT (CIVIL) ENSIGNS

The Soviet Ensign is in the proportion of 2 to 1, the rest approximately 3 to 2. The abbreviation given after the country name is that used throughout the book.

1. Union of Soviet Socialist Republics (Ru) – Red star, outlined in yellow.

2. Czechoslovakia (Cz).

3. Poland (Pd) – White eagle.

4. Bulgaria (Bu) – Badge principally yellow (cornsheaves, lion in circle). Red star above.

5. Hungary (Hu).

6. German Democratic Republic (DDR) – Bottom stripe more gold than yellow. Device is yellow cornsheaves outlined in black, bound in 5 places near base with ribbons of black, red and yellow. Gold device (divider and hammer) in centre.

7. Romania (Rm) – Blue section rather brighter than normal blue. Complex central device indicating yellow cornsheaves, green mountains, yellow sun, blue sky and oil rig, with small red star above. Badge resting on 3 ribbons in national colours, blue, yellow and red (horizontally).

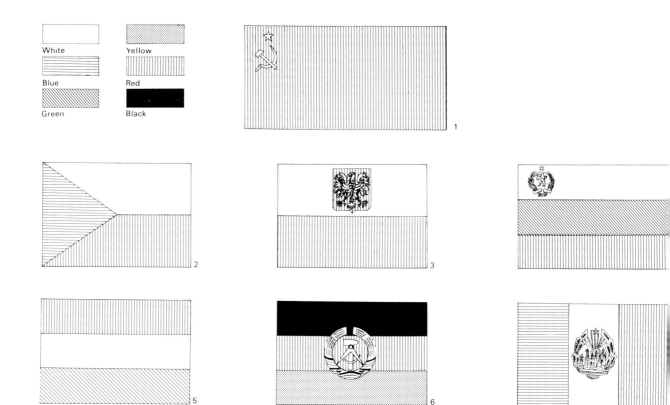

White

Yellow

Blue

Red

Green

Black

1

2

3

5

6

10

Warsaw Pact Merchant Fleets
(Vessels of 100 grt and above)

	Bulgaria	Czecho-slovakia	Germany, Democratic Republic	Hungary	Poland	Romania	USSR	Total
Oil Tankers	20		8		20	11	412	471
Oil/Chemical Tankers					4			4
Chemical Tankers			3				2	5
Liquid Gas Carriers			1				11	12
Bulk/Oil (OBO)			2				13	15
Bulk and Ore	36	6	18		86	66	168	380
General Cargo	60	14	147	22	177	207	1574	2201
Passenger/Cargo	3					1	12	16
Container Ships	2		9				54	65
Passenger/Ferries	16		16		30	2	250	314
Supply Ships			3		4	4	59	70
Tugs	18		12		69	44	455	598
Dredgers			5		5	5	43	58
Livestock Carriers						3		3
Icebreakers			1		1		37	39
Research Ships	1		6		4	1	178	190
Fish Factories/ Fish Carriers	6		8		13	11	526	564
Trawlers (including factory trawlers)	32		130		312	50	2815	3339
Miscellaneous	11		34		24	21	110	200
Total	205	20	403	22	749	426	6719	8544

Total tonnage: 33 800 000 grt; 34 900 000 dwt

Extracted with permission from *Lloyd's Register of Shipping Statistical Tables 1986.*

Warsaw Pact Vessels on Order (at March 1987)
(Vessels of 1000 dwt and over, excluding fishing craft)

	Bulgaria	Czecho-slovakia	Germany, Democratic Republic	Hungary	Poland	Romania	USSR	Total
General Cargo	4	4	2		16	6	65	97
Container			5		3	2	2	12
Tanker	6					11	32	49
Bulk		4	1		13	2	6	26
Passenger			3		2	1	10	16
Ro-Ro	2				5		11	18
Reefer							7	7
OBO					2			2
Offshore							29	29
Miscellaneous							22	22
Total	12	8	11		41	22	184	278

Reproduced with permission from Fairplay Information Systems Ltd.

Note: These figures do not carry on from the list of Warsaw Pact vessels in service given on page 11.

UNION OF SOVIET SOCIALIST REPUBLICS

MERCHANT FLEET

This is the fifth largest fleet in the world and is made up of the following types, excluding the fishing fleet which is shown separately (1986 figures).

Bulk/Oil (OBO)	13
Bulk and Ore Carriers	168
Cable Ships	13
Cargo/Passenger	12
Chemical Tankers	2
Container Ships/ Barge Carriers	54
Dredgers	43
General Cargo	1574
Icebreakers	37
Liquefied Gas Carriers	11
Passenger/Ferries	250
Research and Survey	178
Supply Ships/Tenders	59
Tankers	412
Tugs	455
Miscellaneous	97

Approximate Total (100 grt and over): 6726 ships of 24 960 000 grt, 28 150 000 dwt (including fishing craft)

The Soviet Merchant Fleet – MORFLOT

Administration

Management of the merchant fleet is vested in the Ministry of the Merchant Fleet in Moscow, which in itself is under the direct control of the Council of Ministers, the nation's supreme governing body. The Ministry is also responsible for port operations, maintenance of repair yards, planning and research. Shipbuilding yards come under the Ministry of Transport Construction.

The Moscow Ministry acts as a holding company for the operating companies located in the major ports. Originally designated SOVTORGFLOT, it was re-designated MORFLOT in the early 1960s when the former organisation was broken down into regional groupings.

Shipping Companies

There are 16 shipping companies and each is responsible for port operations, repair yards, tugs, lighters and navigational aids in its area. Additionally, each conducts training schools and is responsible for personnel welfare both ashore and afloat.

The companies are arranged under their Regional groupings, listing some of the regular lines operated, although altogether there are now some 140–150 such lines in operation.

The full Soviet title of each company has the prefix 'USSR–', but for clarity this is omitted.

SEVZAPFLOT (North-West Shipping State Corporation)
1. **Baltic Shipping Company** (Leningrad).

   Many lines operated, including:
   Balt-America Line – South America

Balt-Atlantic Line – Europe, New York, Philadelphia and Baltimore
Baltic-Australia Line
Baltic-East Africa Line – East African ports via Suez
Baltic-Pacific Line – Central America and west coast of South America
New Zealand Line
Rotterdam-Leningrad Line
2. **Estonian Shipping Company** (Tallinn)
 Balt-Levant Line – Benghazi, Beirut, Latakia and Alexandria
 Uni-Africa Line – West Africa
3. **Latvian Shipping Company** (Riga)
4. **Lithuanian Shipping Company** (Klaipeda)
5. **Murmansk Shipping Company** (Murmansk)
 Arctic Line USSR – Europe, eastern Canada and the Great Lakes
6. **Northern Shipping Company** (Arkhangelsk)

YUZHFLOT (South Shipping State Corporation)
7. **Azov Shipping Company** (Zhdanov)
8. **Black Sea Shipping Company** (Odessa)
 Odessa-Ocean Line – Malaysia and Singapore
9. **Caspian Shipping Company** (Baku)
 Caspian-Volgo-Balt Line – Iran and Afghanistan
10. **Georgian Shipping Company** (Batumi)
11. **Novorossiysk Shipping Company** (Novorossiysk)
12. **Soviet-Danube Shipping Company** (Izmail)
 Passenger craft on the Danube

DALFLOT (Far-Eastern Shipping State Corporation)
13. **Far-Eastern Shipping Company** (Vladivostok)
 'FESCO' Line
 'FESCO'-Pacific Line
 Nakhodka-Japan Line
14. **Kamchatka Shipping Company** (Petropavlovsk)
15. **Primorski Shipping Company** (Nakhodka)
16. **Sakhalin Shipping Company** (Kholmsk)

In addition to the above, there is another Corporation known as the Aral Sea Shipping Company (or sometimes the Central Asian Shipping Company), but this is entirely internal and does not operate under MORFLOT control.

A number of other Government Ministries operate ships outside MORFLOT control, including the Ministry of Geology, Ministry of Gas, Ministry of Shipbuilding, Hydrometeorological Service, Academy of Science, and Schools of Marine Engineering.

USSR-Leningrad High School of Marine Engineers (Leningrad) – about 6 vessels of around 6000 tons.
USSR-Odessa High School of Marine Engineers (Odessa) – about 6 vessels of around 6000 tons.
USSR-'KASPNEFTEFLOT' (Petropavlovsk-Kamchatsky) – a very large fleet of about 200-ton passenger ferries, a few larger ones and a considerable fleet of fairly large tugs.
USSR-MORTRANSPORT (Kaliningrad) – about 20 cargo vessels, largely Fish Carriers of up to 13 000 tons.
USSR-North Eastern Department – approximately 20 vessels, mostly for general cargoes.

FISHING FLEET
Fish Carriers and Fish Factories

100 – 499 grt	50
500 – 999 grt	88
1000 – 1999 grt	20
2000 – 3999 grt	88
4000 grt and above	280

Approximate Total (100 grt and over): 526 ships of
3 160 000 grt.

Trawlers (including factory trawlers)

100 – 499 grt	870
500 – 999 grt	781
1000 – 1999 grt	245
2000 – 3999 grt	868
4000 grt and above	51

Approximate Total (100 grt and over): 2815 ships of
3 700 000 grt.

These totals omit the large numbers of small coastal craft,
seiners, inshore and Caspian vessels.

The enormous Soviet fishing fleet is administered by the
Ministry of the Fishing Fleet, and operated by numerous
Combines and Administrations, the principal large groups
being:

USSR-'AZCHERRYBA' (Novorossiysk)
USSR-'DALRYBA' (Vladivostok)
USSR-'KASPRYBA' (Astrakhan)
USSR-'SEVRYBA' (Murmansk)
USSR-'ZAPRYBA' (Kaliningrad)

Fishing Vessel Identification Markings
Pendant numbers The number usually appears on either
the hull or superstructure in large characters, on both port
and starboard side of the ship. It consists of two alphabetical
(Cyrillic) characters followed by three or four numerals. By
using the alphabetical characters, the ship type and base
area can be determined.

The first letter (here shown with English transliteration)
indicates the base area as follows:

A	(A)	Arkhangelskaya oblast	Northern fleet
V	(B)	Karelskaya ASSR	Northern fleet
E	(E)	Estonskaya SSR	Baltic fleet
Ф	(F)	Krymskaya oblast	Black Sea fleet
Г	(G)	Gruzinskaya SSR	Black Sea fleet
K	(K)	Kaliningradskaya oblast	Baltic fleet
X	(Kh)	Khabarovskiy Kray	Pacific fleet
Л	(L)	Litovskaya SSR	Baltic fleet
M	(M)	Murmanskaya oblast	Northern fleet
Н	(N)	Leningradskaya oblast	Baltic fleet
П	(P)	Primorskiy Kray	Pacific fleet
Р	(R)	Latviyskaya SSR	Baltic fleet
C	(S)	Sakhalinskaya oblast	Pacific fleet
Т	(T)	Kamchatskaya oblast	Pacific fleet
B	(V)	Krasnodarskiy Kray	Black Sea fleet
Я	(Ya)	Odesskaya oblast	Black Sea fleet

The second letter indicates the specific ship type. The
majority of the alphabet is taken up with differentiating

fishing vessel types, but some are reserved for other support ships directly subordinate to the fishing fleets. For example:

Ч (Ch) Tug
Н (N)   Tanker
П (P)   Factory/Mother ship
Р (R)   Fisheries support ship
У (U)   Training ship

Call signs   On Soviet vessels these are given on either the funnel or the superstructure, usually in small letters.

INLAND WATERWAYS

It is frequently forgotten that the Soviet Union has the most highly developed and the longest network of canals, rivers and lakes in the world and that these play an important role in naval strategy and operations. There are in this vast territory about 1 800 000 miles (2 900 000 km) of rivers and some 2000 lakes.

Along these arteries, together with the canals, it is estimated that about 6000 million tons of cargo is transported annually and there are stated to be over 300 regular passenger lines in operation.

Vessels are able to provide a continuous service from Britain and northern Europe to Iranian ports on the Caspian Sea by way of Leningrad, canals and the River Volga, and from the Mediterranean and Black Sea through the Sea of Azov and the Volgo-Don Canal. Leningrad is linked to the White Sea at Soroka and destroyers and seagoing merchant ships increasingly make the passage. A fleet of icebreakers

of all sizes prolong navigation on many of the vast rivers and keep open the Northern route round Siberia to the Pacific.

A long-cherished dream of some of the Tsars has materialised by the construction of the so-called Volga Cascade, which, by the building of seven hydro-electric power blocks complete with barrages and locks, links the Volga system by means of canals with the outside world. There have been three major cuts: the Baltic-White Sea Canal (opened in 1933); the Volgo-Balt Canal (opened in 1964 as a modernised pre-revolution plan); and the Volgo-Don Canal (opened in 1952). This has enabled ships of a certain structural character to venture from the inland waterway system into the open deep sea.

Typical Sea/River Ships

Class	Length overall	Draught	Grt	Speed
'Baltiyskiy'	96 m (315 ft)	3.15 m (10 ft 4 in)	1865	10 kt
'Inzhener Belov'	120.1 m (394 ft)	4.5 m (14 ft 9 in)	3398	11.5 kt
'Vasiliy Shukshin'	117 m (384 ft)	4.5 m (14 ft 9 in)	4417	13.2 kt

The 'Baltiyskiy' class deep sea/river traders were the first to pass Leningrad into the Baltic. 'Inzhener Belov' was the prototype of the UK-Europe-Caspian service. The 'Vasiliy Shukshin' class has been built in the 'Oka' yard south of Moscow.

Soviet sources state that the following are the principal services in operation:

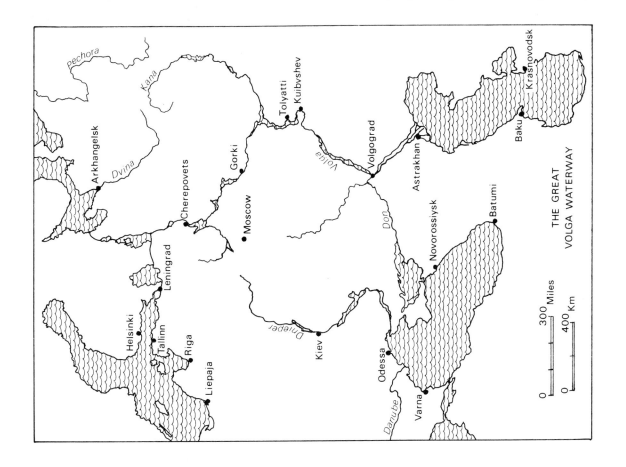

THE GREAT
VOLGA WATERWAY

Pechora

Kana

Arkhangelsk

Dvina

Cherepovets

Gorki

Tolyatti

Kuibyshev

Volgograd

Volga

Astrakhan

Baku

Krasnovodsk

Moscow

Don

Novorossiysk

Batumi

Leningrad

Helsinki

Tallinn

Riga

Liepaja

Dnieper

Kiev

Odessa

Varna

Danube

300 Miles

400 Km

0

0

Cherepovets–Varna	Steel
Tolyatti–Europe	Cars
Arkhangelsk–London	Timber
Baku–Finland and Scandinavia	Crude oil
Krasnovodsk–Denmark	Salt
Sea of Azov–Stralsund	Steel

RIVER AND SEA/RIVER COMPANIES

All the companies are prefixed with the letters 'USSR–', but for the sake of clarity these are omitted from the following list.

Amur River Shipping Company (Nikolayevsk-na-Amure)
Dnepr River Shipping Company (Kherson)
Joint Volga River Shipping Company (Astrakhan)
North Western River Shipping Company (Leningrad)
Northern River Shipping Company (Arkhangelsk)
Volga-Don River Shipping Company (Odessa)
Western River Shipping Company (Kaliningrad)
White Sea-Onega Shipping Company (Petrozavodsk)

USSR-'Volgotanker' (Naberejnaia Leitenanta)
A fleet of over 30 sea/river type Ore/Oil sisterships of 2700 grt, trading largely with European or North African ports.

Built over a decade, 1972–1982, they all bear the name 'Nefterudovoz' followed by consecutive numbers starting with 8M. Most are registered at Astrakhan.

COLOURING

There would appear to be numerous variations that do not confirm to a general pattern of colouring and what follows must be accepted with reserve.
Hulls: Passenger Ships, Survey and Research Vessels and Training Ships: White, although some large liners have black with a white band.
All other craft: Black or varying shades of grey.

Some vessels have their service name in large letters along the hull, usually in Roman characters:
eg BALTGULF, RINELA LINE etc.
Salvage Tugs: Frequently have the word 'SPASSATEL' (Rescue or salvage) in large Cyrillic characters on hull.
Fishing Fleet: Almost invariably have grey hulls except small, inshore trawlers or seiners.
Boot-topping: Usually green for white or grey ships. Red or red with white dividing-line for black ships
Superstructure and Boats: All white with white or orange boats
Masts, Kingposts, Cranes: Usually white, grey or a distinctive bright yellow

NAMES

In Cyrillic characters on either bow, on quarter or round the counter.

In Roman letters on bridge-board, but names may sometimes be abbreviated, *eg* N. PETROVSKY or PETROV-SKY alone for NIKOLAY PETROVSKIY.

The transliteration from the Cyrillic characters in the Soviet Register does not always read the same as Western transliteration.

Principal Ports of Registry
White Sea
АРХАНГЭЛЬСК	Arkhangelsk
МУРМАНСК	Murmansk

Baltic Sea
КАЛИНИНГРАД	Kaliningrad
КЛАИПЭДА	Klaipeda
ЛЭНИНГРАД	Leningrad
РИГА	Riga
ТАЛЛИНН	Tallinn
ВЭНТСПИЛС	Ventspils

Black Sea
ИЖМАИЛ	Izmail
НОВОРОССЫСК	Novorossiysk
ОДЭССА	Odessa
СЭВАСТОПОЛЬ	Sevastopol
ЖДАНОВ	Zhdanov

Far East-Pacific
НАХОДКА	Nakhodka
ПЭТРОПАВЛОВСК	Petropavlovsk
ВЛАДИВОСТОК	Vladivostok
ЮЖНО-САХАЛИНСК	Yuzhno-Sakhalinsk

Russian (Cyrillic) Alphabet
The Russian alphabet was introduced into certain Slav districts by the Greek monk, St Cyril, during the ninth century, hence the similarities with both ancient and modern Greek. Some of the 32 characters of the modern alphabet correspond to those of the Roman alphabet, some appear to be the same but have a different sound, while the remainder are entirely different.

As shown in the table, the characters are not in alphabetical sequence but in 'recognition' order, those bearing a visual resemblance being shown consecutively.

The principal difficulty lies in the widely varying transliteration systems employed in different countries. Even the bridge-boards may not be consistent. That adopted throughout this book is the one in current use in British Registry books.

Another difficulty is that the name on a vessel may be seen during poor weather conditions, or while rust or chips on the paintwork conceal or mutilate a vital 'tail' to a character, thus rendering transliteration more difficult.

А	A or AR	**С**	S	**Ю**	YU	**У** U
Д	D	**Е**	Ye as in 'Yet'	**Р**	R	**И** I (i)
Л	L	**Ё**	YO	**Ц**	TS	**Й** OY
В	V	**Н**	N	**Ш**	SH	**П** P
Б	B or BAR	**К**	K	**Щ**	SHCH	**Г** G
Ъ **Ь**	} mute	**М**	M	**Х**	KH	**Я** YA
		О	O	**Ж**	ZH	**З** Z
Ы	i as in 'it'	**Ф**	F	**Ч**	CH	**Э** E as in 'Met'

BULGARIA

MERCHANT FLEET (1986)

Bulk/Ore	36
General Cargo	60
Cargo/Passenger	3
Container Ships	2
Dredgers	2
Passenger/Ferries	16
Tankers	20
Tugs	18
Research	1
Miscellaneous	11

Approximate total: 200 ships of 1 400 000 grt, 2 000 000 dwt (including fishing craft)

In 1970 the shipowning and shipbuilding industries were re-organised and control of building and deployment centralised under the Bulgarski Turgovski Flot.

SHIPPING COMPANIES

Navigation Maritime Bulgare (NAVBULGAR) (Varna)
Tankers were formerly under a separate company known as Bulgarski Tanker Flot – (BULET) but all are now under the Bulgare management.

General Cargo Vessels, Bulk Carriers, Tankers and Cargo/Training ships

Colouring

Hulls: Mostly grey, some black. Training ships, white.
Boot-topping: Usually green
Upperworks and Boats: Mostly white, but some bulkers have stone colour with orange boats
Masts, Kingposts, Cranes: Stone, yellow or white

Names

On bows: In Cyrillic characters, frequently with Roman characters below.
On quarters or round stern: Cyrillic only with port of registry beneath.
On bridge-boards: In Roman characters.

FISHING FLEET

Bulgaria has a deep water fleet of vessels, built by and purchased from the USSR, East Germany and Poland, and this is usually employed in conjunction with the fishing activities of these countries.

Fish Carriers (over 4000 grt)	5
Stern Trawling Factory Ships (2000 – 3999 grt)	29

Approximate Total: 100 000 grt

Okeansky Ribolov (Ocean Fishing) (Burgas)
Trawlers/Fish Factories and Fish Carriers

Colouring
Hull: Grey
Boot-topping: Green
Upperworks and Boats: White
Masts, Kingposts: Stone or yellow

Principal Ports of Registry

БУРГАСЬ Burgas
ВАРНА   Varna

Bulgarian Alphabet
The Bulgarian alphabet has the following additions to the standard Cyrillic form:

Ь U
Ж U
Ђ E

CZECHOSLOVAKIA

MERCHANT FLEET (1986)

Bulk and Ore	6
General Cargo	14

Approximate Total: 20 ships of 198 000 grt, 300 000 dwt

SHIPPING COMPANIES
Czechoslovak Ocean Shipping (International Joint-Stock Co) (Československa Namorni Spolcnest) (Prague)
General Cargo Ships and Bulk Carriers

Czechoslovak Danube Navigation National Enterprise (Československa Plavba Dunajska) (Bratislava)
General Cargo Ships

Colouring
Hulls: Grey or black
Boot-topping: Green or black
Upperworks and Boats: White. Boats sometimes orange
Masts, Kingposts: White

GERMAN DEMOCRATIC REPUBLIC

MERCHANT FLEET (1986)

Bulk/Oil	2
Bulk and Ore	18
Chemical Tankers	3
General Cargo	147
Container Ships	9
Dredgers	5
Icebreakers	1
Liquid Gas Carriers	1
Passenger/Ferries	16
Tankers	8
Tugs	12
Supply Ships	3
Research Ships	6
Miscellaneous	34

Approximate Total: 265 ships of 1 356 000 grt, 1 800 000 dwt

SHIPPING COMPANIES

Deutfracht/Seereederei (VEB Deutfracht/Seereederei) (Rostock)
General Cargo, Bulk Carriers, Ro-Ro and Tankers
Colouring
Hulls: Mostly grey. Reefers, white
Boot-topping: Green or red
Upperworks and Boats: White. Boats may be orange
Masts, Kingposts, Cranes: Cream, yellow or stone

Deutsche Reichsbahn (German State Railway) (Sassnitz)
Passenger Ferries
Colouring
Hulls: White

Bagger Bugsier VEB (Dredge, Tug and Salvage Co) (Rostock)
Dredgers, Tugs, Barges

FISHING FLEET (1986)

Fish Carriers and Fish Factories

2000 – 3999 grt	3
4000 grt and above	5

Approximate Total (100 grt and over): 8 ships of 50 000 grt

Trawlers (including factory trawlers)

100 – 499 grt	63
500 – 999 grt	46
1000 – 1999 grt	1
2000 – 3999 grt	20

Approximate Total (100 grt and over): 130 ships of 104 000 grt

FISHING COMPANIES

Rostock Fischkombinat (Rostock)
Stern Trawling Factory Ships and Fish Carriers

Sassnitz Fischfang VEB (Sassnitz)
Large fleet of small Fish Factory Ships and Trawlers

Pendant Numbers
The three-letter alpha prefix denotes homeport:
    ROS   Rostock
    SAS   Sassnitz
    STR   Stralsund
    WIS   Wismar

These letters are followed by three or four numerals. The pendant number usually appears on the superstructure and may also appear on the bows. A call sign may also be seen on the bridge.

HUNGARY

MERCHANT FLEET (1986)
            General Cargo   22

Total: 22 ships of 86 000 grt, 122 000 dwt

Hungarian Shipping Co Ltd – MAHART (Magyar Hajosai RT)
(Budapest)
General Cargo Vessels up to about 12 000 grt

Colouring
Hulls: Mostly grey
Boot-topping: Green
Upperworks, Masts, Kingposts, Boats: White. Boats may be orange

POLAND

MERCHANT FLEET (1986)

Bulk/Ore	86
General Cargo	177
Chemical Tankers	4
Dredgers	5
Icebreakers	1
Passenger/Ferries	30
Tankers	20
Tugs etc	69
Supply Ships	4
Research Ships	4
Miscellaneous	24

Approximate Total (100 grt and over): 424 ships of 3 150 000 grt, 4 700 000 dwt

SHIPPING COMPANIES

Polish Ocean Lines (POL) (Polskie Linie Oceaniczne) (Gdynia)
Passenger/Ferries, General Cargo, Ro-Ro
Colouring
Hulls: Passenger ships, white; others light grey or black
Boot-topping: Green
Upperworks: White
Masts, Kingposts, Cranes: White or pale yellow

Polish Steamship Co (PZM) (Polska Zegluga Morska) (Szczecin)
Bulk Carriers. Also Managers for Anglo-Polish Shipping Venture (Polsko-Brytijskie Przedsiewziecie Zeglugowe Spoikal)
Bulkers and General Cargo vessels

Colouring
Hulls: Black or grey
Boot-topping: Red or black

Polish Baltic Shipping Company (PZB) (Polska Zegluga Baltycka) (Kolobrzeg)
Passenger/Ferries, General Cargo
Colouring
Hulls: Passenger ships, white. Cargo vessels, grey

Chinese-Polish Joint Stock Shipping Company (Chinsko-Polskie Towarzystwo Okretowe SA) (Gdynia)

Polish Shipping Association (Polskie Towarzystwo Okretowe) (Gdynia)
General Cargo

Polish Shipping Company (Zegluga Polska Spolka Akcyjna) (Szczecin)
General Cargo, Bulk Carriers, Tankers

Polish Ship Salvage Company (Polskie Ratownictwo Okretowe) (Gdynia)
Tugs, Salvage Craft etc

Gdanskie Przedsiebiorstwo (Gdanskie Przedsiebiorstwo Obrotu Produktami Naftowymi) (CPN) (Gdansk)
Small Tankers

Szczecinskie Przedsiebiorstwo (Szczecinskie Przedsiebiorstwo Obrotu Produktami Naftowymi) (CPN) (Szczecin)
Small Tankers

Morski Instytut Rybacki (MIR) (Sea Fisheries Institute) (Gdynia)
Research Ships
Colouring
Hulls: White

There are also a considerable number of Research, Survey and Training ships and these are white-painted overall.

FISHING FLEET (1986)
Fish Carriers and Fish Factories

2000 – 3999 grt	4
4000 grt and above	9

Approximate Total: (100 grt and over): 13 ships of 86 000 grt

Trawlers (including factory trawlers)

100 – 499 grt	213
500 – 999 grt	18
1000 – 1999 grt	23
2000 – 3999 grt	56

Approximate Total (100 grt and over): 312 ships of 218 000 grt

FISHING COMPANIES
Dalmor Deep Sea Fishing Enterprise (Przedsiebiorstwo Polowow Dalekomorskich i Uslug Rybackich 'Dalmor') (Gdynia)
Fish Factory/Stern Trawlers

Gryf Deep Sea Fishing Enterprise (Przedsiebiorstwo Polowow Dalekomorskich i Uslug Rybackich 'Gryf') (Szczecin)
Fish Factory/Stern Trawlers

Odra Deep Sea Fishing Enterprise (Przedsiebiorstwo Polowow Dalekomorskich i Uslug Rybackich 'Odra') (Swinoujscie)
Fish Factory/Stern Trawlers and smaller fishing craft

Transocean Fishing Enterprise (Przedsiebiorstwo Przentyslowo-Uslugowe Rybolowstwa Morskiego 'Transocean') (Szczecin)
Fish Carriers and Fish Factory Ships

Pendant numbers
The three-letter alpha prefix denotes homeport:

DAR	Darlowo
GDY	Gdynia
HEL	Hel
KOL	Kolobrzeg
SWI	Swinoujscie
SZN	Szczecin
WLA	Wladyslawowo
UST	Ustka

The letters are followed by three or four numerals. The pendant number normally appears on the bows. This may be repeated on the superstructure where the call sign may also be seen.

Principal Ports of Registry
Gdynia
Szczecin

ROMANIA

MERCHANT FLEET (1986)

Bulk and Ore	66
General Cargo	207
Cargo/Passenger	1
Dredgers	5
Passenger/Ferries	2
Tankers	11
Tugs, etc	44
Research Ships	1
Livestock Carriers	3
Supply Ships	4
Miscellaneous	21

Approximate Total (100 grt and over): 369 ships of 3 000 000 grt, 4 800 000 dwt

SHIPPING COMPANIES

NAVROM (Romanian Maritime Navigation) (Bucharest)
General Cargo Vessels, Tankers and Bulk Carriers
Colouring
Hulls: Grey or black
Boot-topping: Green or red
Upperworks: White
Masts, Kingposts and Cranes: Stone or white

NAVLOMAR (Bucharest)
Managers for BATAM (Baza De Aprovizionare Tehnico Materiala)
General Cargo Vessels and Tankers

FISHING FLEET (1986)

Fish Carriers and Fish Factories
4000 grt and over	11

Approximate Total (100 grt and over): 11 ships of 88 000 grt

Trawlers

100 – 499 grt	7
2000 – 3999 grt	43

Approximate Total (100 grt and above): 50 ships of 132 000 grt

NAVROM Tulcea (Ministerul Industrei Alimentare – NAVROM Tulcea) (Managers for Fishing Industry) (Tulcea)
Deep Sea Fish Factory Stern Trawlers and Fish Carriers
Colouring
As for NAVROM ships

Principal Ports of Registry
Constanţa
Braila

FUNNEL DESIGNS

Arranged in recognition order of basic funnel colour alphabetically – Black, Blue, Green, Red, White, Yellow (covering varying shades from deep cream to golden brown).

1. Czechoslovak Ocean Shipping (Cz)
   Some ships

2. Czechoslovak Danube Navigation (Cz)
   Danube

3. Ministerul Industrei Alimentare – NAVROM Tulcea (Rm)
   Deep sea fishing fleet

4. USSR (Ru)
   Older ships

5. USSR (Ru)
   Fishing fleets

6. Polish Steamship Co (Pd)
   Some funnels may be very dark blue, not black

7. Hungarian Shipping Co – MAHART (Hu)

8. Sea Fisheries Institute (Pd)
   Pale blue funnel

9. 'Dalmor' Deep Sea Fishing Enterprise (Pd)

10. Transocean Fishing Enterprise (Pd)
    Inner circle may sometimes be black

11. VEB Deutfracht/Seereederei (DDR)
    Passenger ships and Reefers

12. VEB Deutfracht/Seereederei (DDR)
    Some ships

13. NAVROM – Romanian Maritime Navigation & NAVROM Tulcea (Rm)

14. USSR (Ru)
    Passenger ships and some Survey vessels

15. USSR (Ru)
    Some passenger ships

16. USSR (Ru)
    Some passenger ships

17. USSR (Ru)
    Fishing fleets (alternative to 5)

18. Gdanskie Naftowymi – 'CPN' (Pd)
    Tanker fleet. Deep golden brown funnels

19. Czechoslovak Ocean Shipping (Cz)
    Alternative to 1. Bright yellow funnels

20. Navigation Maritime Bulgare – NAVBULGAR (Bu)
    Dark buff funnels

21. Ocean Fishing Fleet (Bu)
    Funnel insignia may sometimes be yellow. Dark buff funnel

22. Chinese-Polish Joint Stock Shipping Company (Pd)

23. Polish Ocean Lines (Pd)
    Deep cream funnels

24. Polish Baltic Shipping Company (Pd)
    Deep cream funnel, prongs of trident blue

25. 'Gryf' Deep Sea Fishing Enterprise (Pd)
    Basic funnel colour sometimes black

26. VEB Deutfracht/Seereederei (DDR)
    Alternative to 11

27. VEB Deutfracht/Seereederei (DDR)
    Alternative to 12

28. 'Odra' Deep Sea Fishing Enterprise (Pd)

1

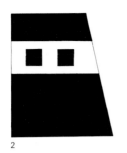

2

3

4

5

6

7

8

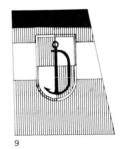

9

10

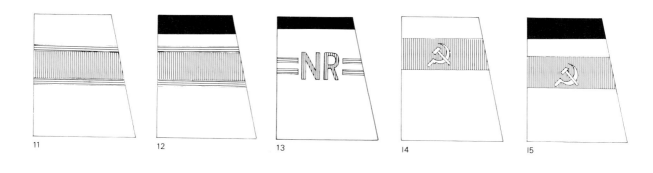

11   12   13   14   15

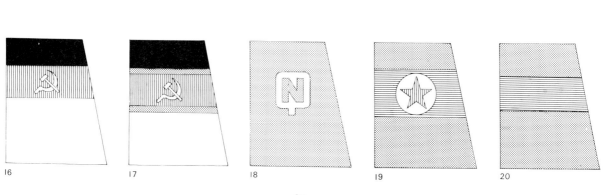

16   17   18   19   20

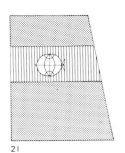

21

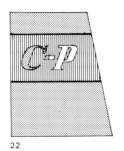

22

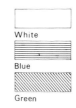
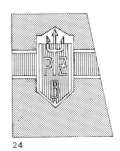

23

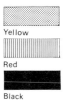
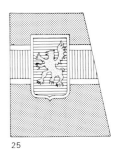

24

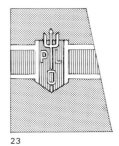

25

26

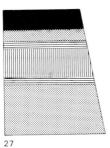

27

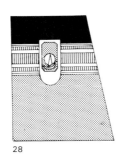

28

White	Yellow
Blue	Red
Green	Black

THE RECOGNITION SYSTEM

The system used in this book is designed to identify either individual ships or a group of very similar or identical ships.

The basis of the system is the noting of three features:
1. The PROFILE, defined as the funnel position (amidships or aft) and the arrangement of the superstructure.
2. The SEQUENCE, defined as the noting of certain prescribed features on the ship in the order in which they occur.
3. The HULL FORM, defined as the arrangement and number of castles, or islands, on the hull.

These features are reported in a simple abbreviated form which is described in the following pages, along with a fuller description of the coding features.

An important fact to remember is that, although many standard nautical terms are used in the system, they are often defined in a very different way. The term hull form is a good example of this. Technically, it refers to the actual shape of the hull, but, in the recognition system, it is the arrangement of islands. All the features used in the system are classified purely by *appearance* and *never by function*. This is one reason why many everyday nautical terms, such as mast or kingpost, have been re-defined for the purposes of the recognition system.

To gain a thorough knowledge of the system it is essential to go through the pages of this manual slowly and in strict order. Learn the definitions and the methods as they are set out and, more importantly, apply them when coding a vessel. Although this may seem unnecessarily pedantic, the appearance of different ships can vary so much that it is left, finally, to the judgement of the observer to decide how a particular vessel should be coded.

The number of elements in the system has deliberately been kept to a minimum, in order to make it easily memorable. In the sequence, for example, there are only six classifications: kingpost, mast, crane, funnel, gantry and ramp. With the abundance of ships and the increasing diversity in design it is often very difficult to classify these features. By following the prescribed method it should be possible to decide on a classification but, if it is impossible to decide, the solution is to try an *alternative sequence*. Alternative codings can also be applied to the profile and the hull form. Many of the vessels in this book appear under two, or sometimes more, codings.

It is important to remember that a ship is always coded from a broadside view. It may therefore be necessary to re-assess certain features if a ship is not seen broadside on.

THE PROFILE

The profile consists of two separate elements: the funnel position (amidships or aft) and the arrangement of the superstructure.

It is very important that the two elements (funnel and superstructure) are considered independently. In other words, after the funnel position has been decided it must be ignored when deciding the superstructure arrangement.

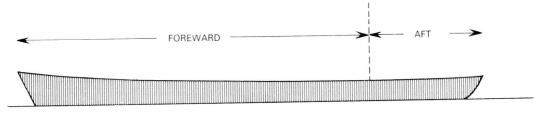

FOREWARD — AFT

FUNNEL POSITION

Funnel position

There are two positions: amidships and aft. Note that the ¾-aft position is regarded as funnel amidships if *any part* of the funnel touches the ¾-aft line. Remember that the terms 'amidships' and 'aft' may be defined differently when used in another context.

Superstructure

For the purposes of classifying a ship's profile, the superstructure is the main bulk of accommodation, bridge, engine-room casing etc. Smaller structures, such as mast houses, docking bridges and islands, are not considered as superstructure. Although there can be confusion between islands and superstructure (this is also mentioned in the section on hull form), islands appear as integral parts of the hull although they are raised above the upper deck.

Determining the profile

There are *five* profiles in the system. They are reported as P1, P2, P3, P4 and P5.

The first two profiles, P1 and P2, have the funnel amidships and the other profiles, P3, P4 and P5, have the funnel aft. Having decided whether the funnel is amidships or aft, the observer then looks at the superstructure to determine the actual profile.

IMPORTANT NOTE. The superstructure is analysed in a different way in the two groups of profiles. In the funnel-amidships group it is the number of blocks of superstructure that determines the profile, regardless of where that superstructure is situated. In the funnel-aft profiles, however, the distinguishing feature is the position of the bridge-front (foreward, amidships or aft) that determines the profile. The number of blocks of superstructure is irrelevant.

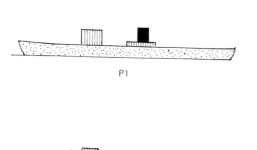

P1

P2

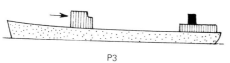

P3

P3

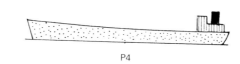

P4

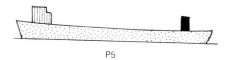

P5

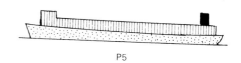

P5

Problems in positioning the funnel or superstructure accurately

As the observer normally has to judge by eye where the ¾-aft line falls on a ship, it may be very difficult to decide exactly where the funnel or bridge-front falls. If the observer is undecided the answer is, as stated previously, *try alternative profiles.*

THE SEQUENCE

Defined as the noting of certain prescribed features on the ship in the order in which they occur (working foreward to aft).

There are six features which are coded as follows:

Kingpost	K	Funnel	F
Mast	M	Gantry	N
Crane	C	Ramp	R

Apart from the mast and the kingpost, which will be dealt with separately, all these features can be easily identified. It is important to remember that with all cargo gear it is the upright part and not the lifting device, derrick, jib etc, which is considered the principal feature.

The following drawings give the basic shapes of the sequence features. The funnel is normally a prominent and obvious feature, and it has not been illustrated.

Cranes

Although they can be very similar to kingposts, cranes differ principally by the fact that they have a *width* as well as height, whereas the kingpost is merely an upright pole. Very small cranes, such as those installed to handle small lifeboats or liferafts, are usually too small to code.

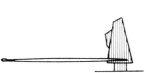
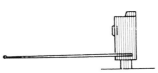
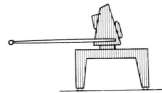
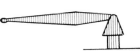

Gantries

As the drawings show, there are a wide variety of designs although the commonest is the one which gives the appearance of a goalpost from the side. A crane mounted on a gantry is always coded C.

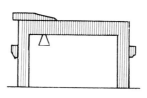

Ramps

Only the increasingly numerous quarter and stern slewing ramps. The conventional type of stern ramp will simply appear as an upright if it rises above the upper deck or superstructure and may be coded as K or M, according to its height. Codeable ramps can be seen occasionally in the foreward parts of some vessels.

QUARTER RAMP

SLEWING RAMP

Superimposed features

If one coding feature is mounted on another the topmost feature is always coded first; eg a mast from a funnel is coded MF and a mast from a ramp is coded MR.

Masts and Kingposts

Masts and kingposts must be considered together as they are both basically upright poles. They are distinguished by their relative heights. Do not take into account any additions to the upright, such as derricks or a gaff, for example, when deciding upon a classification. The radar mast from the bridge and a mast from the funnel are *always* coded M, if heavy enough to code. As with all the features in the sequence, it is important to forget their technical function and only remember how they are defined within the coding system. In some older vessels, kingposts are often arranged in pairs. These are coded as a *single* K, as a ship is always coded from a complete broadside view, which must be approximated if the vessel is not actually seen broadside. This applies to every aspect of the coding system.

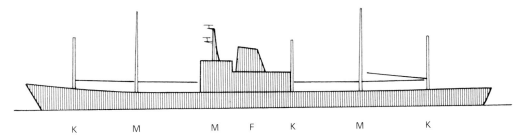

K   M   M   F   K   M   K

HULL FORM

Defined as the arrangement of castles or islands, on the hull. The reported method is simple: the castles are numbered 1—forecastle, 2—midcastle, 3—poop and the letter H is placed before the numerals, eg H13, H2. A flush-decked vessel is simply reported as H.

There are a number of possible combinations, the following illustrations show the main ones.

It is sometimes difficult to distinguish islands from superstructure. Islands can be simply defined as structures

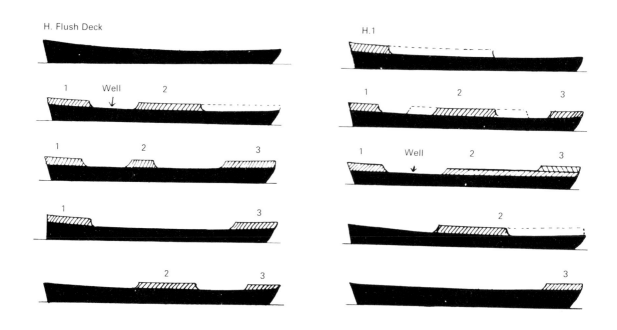

H. Flush Deck

H.1

1   Well   2

1   2   3

1   2   3

1   Well   2   3

1   3

2

2   3

3

which stand proud from the upperdeck although incorporated into the hull. They always appear solid although they may have windows. Problems can arise when superstructure is built out practically to the hull sides and can, perhaps, only be identified by openings such as large windows. Passenger ships can be particularly difficult in this respect. The height of an island is normally about the same as one deck of superstructure, about 8 feet. However, there are exceptions. The modern ro-ro ship, for example, often has several decks above the upper-deck which are solidly plated and meet the sides of the hull. They give the appearance of very high islands and should be coded as such.

Other confusions in hull forms

As can be seen from the drawings of hull forms shown previously, the length of island can vary considerably. A forecastle may extend almost to the stern of a vessel but it is still reported as H1 although it may seem to be combined with a midcastle. The same would apply to a midcastle which runs into a poop, it is coded H2. This is only the case, however, if the island begins on, or forward of, the amidships line. If it begins abaft of amidships it is regarded as a poop, H3. If an island begins near the stem but *not at it*, it cannot be regarded as a forecastle but must be a midcastle, H2. Although the islands are called forecastle and midcastle, this does not necessarily indicate their position on the hull. The only definite rules that can be made are that the forecastle must *begin at the stem* and the poop must *end at, or very near, the stern.*

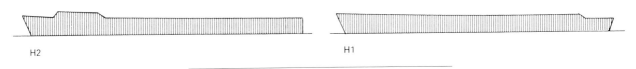

H2

H1

Do not confuse islands with *bulwark plating*. Plating is only about half the height of an average island and should be easily distinguished.

Long hances often disguise an island and may give the impression of slightly exaggerated sheer. A hull of this type must be regarded as flush-decked, H.

FORECASTLE

H

41

Another problem is the *trunk-deck*, a common feature on smaller tankers. If a vessel with a trunk-deck is seen silhouetted it may appear to be flush-decked. If the trunk-deck can be seen the islands should be coded, even though the trunk may be the same height as the islands.

EXPLANATORY NOTES
FOR SHIP DRAWING SECTION

Drawings. Most of the drawings are to a scale of 1 inch = 200 feet (1:2400). Certain smaller vessels are drawn to a standard length of 1⅛ inches and their overall length at a scale of 1:2400 is indicated by a line drawn just below the waterline. The majority of drawings show the port side but a starboard view is sometimes given where more information exists for that side.

The drawings are arranged in *five sections*, corresponding to the five profiles, P1–P5.

Within these main sections the drawings are arranged in *alphabetical order of sequence*. This simply means that the sequence is regarded in the same way as words in a dictionary, eg the following sequences are in alphabetical order: C_2F, C_2FK, C_2MF. Vessels with twin funnels, ie funnels side-by-side, are coded as *single funnelled ships*, as only one funnel can be seen in the broadside view. Note that rather than repeat letters in the sequence that fall consecutively, a small number after the letter indicates the number of repetitions, eg KKKMFKK is shown as K_3MFK_2.

Within a particular sequence the drawings are further divided into hull forms. These are arranged in numerical order thus—H, H1, H12, H123, H13, H2, H23, H3.

After having divided and sub-divided the drawings, one may still have several vessels with the same sequence and hull form. These groups are not very large as a rule, so we have made their arrangement conform to general guidelines rather than to strict rules. In most cases we have taken the coded features (masts, kingposts, funnel, etc) and their positioning as the initial distinguishing feature. Explained simply, this means that a vessel with its first coded feature at No 2 on the grid would precede another with its first feature at No 6, and so on. If this system has, however, tended to split up two practically identical vessels which only vary by the positioning of one or two features, we have remained flexible. The type of vessel and size has also been taken into account.

As an aid to identification we have marked certain coded features on the drawings. Masts can be assumed to be on the centre line and kingposts in pairs if they are not marked. If they do not conform to this pattern they are marked (CL for centre line or small silhouettes for goalpost, bi-pod, etc). Tripods are not always indicated as they may be obvious from the drawing.

On a vessel which has a line of, for example, centre-line

kingposts, the first post only is marked and the remainder simply arrowed. If there is a combination of features, any that are marked with an arrow only are the same as the last feature foreward of them that was fully identified.

Text beneath drawings. This list follows the same order as the text.

Coding: profile, sequence and hull form, respectively.

Drawing number: The numbers used are those which appear in *Jane's Merchant Ships 1987–88* for the vessels which appear in that publication. All additional drawings have numbers which correctly place them in the drawing section of JMS. An occasional number may be duplicated where no gap existed in JMS, but these are never drawing numbers, only numbers for sisters/similar ships.

Name: The name given cannot be assumed to be the class name unless stated. In some cases an individual name and a class name may both be given. A problem with classes can be the existence of a builder's designation as well as a class name, see drawing number 28600 for example. Names that have been transliterated, ie Russian and Bulgarian, use the spellings given in Lloyd's Register. See pages 20 and 22 for transliteration of the Cyrillic alphabet.

Flag/country of build: Abbreviated form (see page 44).

Year of build/major alteration or completion: Example: 1956/65/72 (completed 1956, rebuilt 1965, further rebuilding 1972).

Type of vessel: Abbreviated form (see pages 44 and 45). Where a vessel has more than one function, a combination of abbreviations is used (eg Tk/Ch—oil tanker/chemical tanker).

Tonnage: GRT to nearest 100 tons. Smaller tonnages are shown exact. Other tonnages shown if the grt is unavailable are dwt (deadweight) and dspl (full displacement). For open/closed shelterdeck vessels both tonnages are shown.

Dimensions: Length overall × maximum draught. Stated in metres and taken to the nearest centimetre. Imperial measurements (to the nearest hundredth of a foot) follow in brackets. Open/closed shelterdeck vessels have both draughts. Length between perpendiculars (bp) is given if overall length is not available.

Machinery: Abbreviated form (see page 45).

Speed: Service speed, unless otherwise indicated, in knots.

Remarks: Special features, details of rebuilding, etc.

Variants: This section indicates the existence of sisters or similar ships and the flags under which they operate. The flags are in abbreviated form (see list on page 44).

ABBREVIATIONS

Flag and Country of Build Abbreviations

These indicate the ensign worn at the time of compilation of the book, and country of build. It is not necessarily the same as nationality of owners.

Ar	Argentina		In	India
Be	Belgium		It	Italy
Br	Britain and British Dependencies		Ja	Japan
Bu	Bulgaria		Ne	Netherlands
Bz	Brazil		No	Norway
Ca	Canada		Pd	Poland
Cz	Czechoslovakia		Po	Portugal
DDR	German Democratic Republic (East)		Rm	Romania
De	Denmark		Ru	USSR
Fi	Finland		Sg	Singapore
Fr	France		Sp	Spain
FRG	Federal Republic of Germany (West)		Sw	Sweden
Ge	Germany—pre 1945		Tu	Turkey
Gr	Greece		Tw	Taiwan
Hu	Hungary		Ys	Yugoslavia

Abbreviations of Ship Types

Vessels of more than one function will have a combination of abbreviations from this list separated by an oblique stroke (e.g. C/HL).

A	Auxiliary		C	General Dry Cargo Ship
B	Bulk Carrier		Cbl	Cable Ship
Bg	Barge Carrier		Ch	Chemical Tanker
BO	Bulk/Oil Carrier		Con	Container ship
BT	Buoy Tender		CP	Cargo Passenger Ship (up to 12 passengers)
BWC	Bulk Carrier—Wood Chip		CS	Crane Ship

D	Dredger		RoPF	Ro/Ro Passenger Ferry
Dk	Dock Ship		RS	Research Ship (including hydrographic, oceanographic, etc)
DS	Drilling Ship			
F	Ferry (probably carrying unberthed passengers)		RT	Replenishment Tanker (Naval)
FA	Fleet Auxiliary		Sal	Salvage Vessel
FC	Fish Carrier		Spt	Support Ship (Naval)
FF	Fish Factory		SS	Stern Trawler
Fg	Fishing Craft		SSDC	Semi-Submersible Deck Cargo Ship
Fire	Fire-fighting Vessel		ST/S	Stern Trawler/Sealer
FT	Stern Trawling Factory Ship		Sub S	Submersible Support Ship
FV	Fishing Vessel		TB	Bitumen Tanker
HL	Heavy Lift Vessel		TC	Timber Carrier
Hosp	Hospital Ship		TF	Train Ferry
IB	Ice Breaker		Tg	Tug
IC	Intelligence Collector		Tk	Oil and Oil Products Tanker
LC	Landing Craft		Trlr	Trawler
LGC	Liquefied Gas Carrier		TS	Training Ship
MSS	Missile Support Ship		VO	Vegetable Oil Tanker
MTV	Missile Tracking Vessel		WF	Whale Factory Ship
O	Ore Carrier		WT	Wine Tanker
OBO	Ore/Bulk/Oil			
OO	Ore/Oil			

D   Dredger
Dk   Dock Ship
DS   Drilling Ship
F   Ferry (probably carrying unberthed passengers)
FA   Fleet Auxiliary
FC   Fish Carrier
FF   Fish Factory
Fg   Fishing Craft
Fire   Fire-fighting Vessel
FT   Stern Trawling Factory Ship
FV   Fishing Vessel
HL   Heavy Lift Vessel
Hosp   Hospital Ship
IB   Ice Breaker
IC   Intelligence Collector
LC   Landing Craft
LGC   Liquefied Gas Carrier
MSS   Missile Support Ship
MTV   Missile Tracking Vessel
O   Ore Carrier
OBO   Ore/Bulk/Oil
OO   Ore/Oil
ORSV   Oil Rig Supply Vessel
OSS   Offshore Support Ship
P   Passenger Ship
PC   Passenger Cargo Ship (over 12 passengers)
Poll   Pollution Control Vessel
R   Cargo Vessel with large Refrigerated Capacity
Riv   River Craft
Rmt   Replenishment Ship (Naval)
RoC   Ro/Ro Cargo Ship
RoPCF   Ro/Ro Passenger Car Ferry

RoPF   Ro/Ro Passenger Ferry
RS   Research Ship (including hydrographic, oceanographic, etc)
RT   Replenishment Tanker (Naval)
Sal   Salvage Vessel
Spt   Support Ship (Naval)
SS   Stern Trawler
SSDC   Semi-Submersible Deck Cargo Ship
ST/S   Stern Trawler/Sealer
Sub S   Submersible Support Ship
TB   Bitumen Tanker
TC   Timber Carrier
TF   Train Ferry
Tg   Tug
Tk   Oil and Oil Products Tanker
Trlr   Trawler
TS   Training Ship
VO   Vegetable Oil Tanker
WF   Whale Factory Ship
WT   Wine Tanker

Abbreviations of Engine Types

D-E   Diesel Electric
GT   Gas Turbine
M   Motor Vessel
R   Reciprocating
T   Turbine

All vessels are single screw unless otherwise stated:

TS   Twin Screw
TrS   Triple Screw
QS   Quadruple Screw

SHIP DRAWINGS

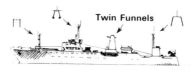

P1   KMFK/KMFM; H1

00140: ADMIRAL GOLOVKO Ru/Ru 1975; FT; 4500; 112.81 × 6.52
(370.11 × 21.39); M; 17. Sisters (Ru flag).

P1   KM₂F; H13

00240: YULIUS FUCHIK Ru/Fi 1978; Bg/Con; 22800/35900; 266.45
× —/11 (874.18 × —/36.09); TSM; 20; May be spelt **JULIUS
FUCIK**. Sister (Ru flag).

P1   KM₂FMK; H

00250: KOSMONAUT PAVEL BELYAEV Ru/Ru 1963/77; RS; 5500;
123.15 × 6.71 (404 × 22.01); M; 14.75; Converted from cargo ship
1977. Sisters (Ru flag).

P1   MFM; H2

00280: ANATOLIY ZHELEZNYAKOV Ru/It 1984; Bg; 9100; 154.01
× 4.3 (505.28 × 14.11); TSM; —. Sister (Ru flag).

P1   MKFM; H

00330: ALEKSANDROVSK Ru/Fi 1960; C; 5400; 139 × 7.9 (457 × 28); M; 14.5. Sisters (Ru flag).

P1   MKFM; H

00340: ALAPAYEVSK Ru/Fi 1960; C; 5400; 139 × 7.9 (457 × 26); M; 16; Now broken up. Sister (Ru flag).

P1   MKFM; H

00350: TAUYSK Ru/FRG 1956; R; 3800; 110.6 × 7 (363 × 23); M; 15.

P1   MK₃FKM; H/H1

00850: IZHEVSK Ru/Fi 1958; C; 5500; 139.4 × 7.86 (457.35 × 25.79); M; 16; May have been broken up.

P1   MKNF; H12

00965: ALEKSEY KOSYGIN Ru/Ru 1984; Bg/IB/Con; 37500; 262.82 × 11.65 (862.27 × 38.22); TSM; 18.4. Sisters (Ru flag).

49

Twin Funnels

P1   M₂F; H

00967: BORIS POLEVOY Ru/Fi 1984; Bg/RoC/Dk; 10700; 158.91 × 4.3 (521.36 × 14.11); TSM; 13.5; Can carry containers (855 TEU). Stern ramp. Sister (Ru flag).

P1   M₂KFM; H

01020: ALAPAYEVSK Ru/Fi 1961; C; 5400; 139.2 × 7.9 (457 × 25.8); M; 14.5; Now broken up. Sister (Ru flag).

P2   C₃M₂FC; H1

01070: BELORETSK Ru/De 1962; C; 10500; 160.3 × 9.6 (526 × 31.7); M; 18.5. Sisters (Ru flag); Similar (Ru flag).

P2   C₂KCMFC; H13

01100: PYATIDYESYATILETIYE KOMSOMOLA Ru/Ru 1968; C; 3900/5600; 129.9 × 7.8 (426 × 25.7); M; 16.5; 'Kaliningrad' type. Also known as **50 LETIYE KOMSOMOLA**.

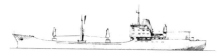

P2   CKCMFC; H13

01380: 'KALININGRAD' type —/Ru 1969; C; 3900/5600; 129 × 6.55/7.83 (426 × 21.49/25.69); M; 16; There are 2 types—the earlier ones having cranes by the foremast. Sisters (Ru & Rm flags).

P2   CMC₂MFC; H1

01540: OTRADNOE Ru/Ja 1964; C; 11100; 157 × 9.4 (518 × 30.9); M; 18; Cranes abreast foremast. Sisters (Ru flag).

P2   CMC₂MFC₂MC; H13

01560: AKADEMIK SHIMANSKIY Ru/Ru 1964; C; 7400/11200; 170 × 8.25/9.75 (558 × 27.07/32); T; 18. Sisters (Ru flag). Ships vary slightly. Some have lighter masts or masts from funnel and some have gas turbine machinery.

P2   CMCMFC; H13

01640: 'KALININGRAD' type —/Ru 1969; C; 3900/5600; 129 × 6.55/7.83 (426 × 21.49/25.69); M; 16; There are 2 types—the earlier ones having cranes by the foremast. Sisters (Ru & Rm flags).

P2   CMF; H1

01733: 'MOMA' class Ru/Pd 1967-72; RS; 1600 Dspl; 73.3 × 3.9 (240.5 × 12.8); TSM; 17; Variations: some have superstructure extended into well-deck and crane removed. Some operated as intelligence collectors (AGIs) by Ru Navy. Sisters (Ru, Bu & Pd flags).

P2   CMF; H1

01736: 'SAMARA' class Ru/Pd 1962-64; RS; 1270 Dspl; 59 × 3.8 (193.5 × 12.5); TSM; 15; Operated by Ru Navy. Some have crane removed. Sisters (Ru flag).

P2   CMFC; H

01750: ALEKSANDR PUSHKIN Ru/DDR 1965; P; 19900; 176 × 8 (577 × 26.1); TSM; 20.5. Similar (Ru flag).

P2   *CMFM; H*

01935: ANTONINA NEZHDANOVA Ru/Ys 1978; P; 3900; 100.01 × 4.65 (328 × 15.26); TSM; 17.25. Sisters (Ru flag).

P2   *CMFM; H*

01960: YUNOST Ru/Bu 1964; P; 1000; 64 × 3 (211 × 10); M; 13. Sisters (Ru flag), one is a training ship.

P2   *CMFM; H*

01980: GEORGI DIMITROV Bu/Bu 1957; P; 900; 62.7 × 3 (206 × 10); M; 12. Sister (Bu flag).

P2   *CMFM; H1*

02060: KAPITAN SOROKIN Ru/Fi 1977; IB; 10600; 131.88 × 8.5 (432.68 × 27.89); Trs D-E; 19; Helicopter deck. Sister (Ru flag); similar – sloping funnel top and stepped bridge-front (Ru flag).

P2   *CMFM; H1*

02070: MOSKVA Ru/Fi 1960; IB; 9400; 122 × 10.7 (401 × 35.6); TrS D-E; 18; Helicopter deck and 2 helicopters. Sisters (Ru flag).

P2   *CMFM; H1*

02080: KAPITAN M IZMAYLOV Ru/Fi 1976; IB/Sal; 1400; 56.3 × 4.2 (184 × 14); TS D-E; 14. Sisters (Ru flag).

P2   CMFM; H13

02105: VENTA Ru/DDR —; Spt; 3400; 103.97 × 6.58 (341.1 × 21.6); M; 12.5; Built in late 1950s. Used for missile support. Converted from cargo vessel of 'Levant' or 'Kovel' type 1974 or 75. Sister (Ru flag).

P2   CMFM; H2

02110: INGUL Ru/Fi 1962; Cbl; 5600; 130.41 × 5.21 (427.85 × 17.09); TS D-E; 14; 'KLASMA' class. Sister (Ru flag).

P2   CMFMC; H

02120: BAYKAL Ru/DDR 1964; P; 5200; 122.1 × 5.2 (401 × 17); TSM; 17. Similar—vary in details (Ru flag).

P2   CMFMC; H

02140: BASHKIRIYA Ru/DDR 1964; P; 5300; 122.15 × 5.27 (400.75 × 17.29); TSM; 17; May be modified like ESTONIYA—which see. Sister – troopship (Ru flag).

P2   CMFMC; H

02150: ADZHARIYA Ru/DDR 1964; P; 5300; 122 × 5.2 (401 × 17); TSM; 17; May be modified like ESTONIYA—which see.

P2   CMFMC; H

02160: ESTONIYA Ru/DDR 1960; P; 4900; 122 × 5.2 (401 × 17); TSM; 17. Sisters (Ru flag) – some have larger funnel and different type of crane – see inset – and others have taller funnel and thicker masts.

P2   CMFMC; H

02180: STEFAN BATORY Pd/Ne 1952; P; 15000; 153.3 × 8.7 (503 × 18.9); T; 16.5.

P2   CMFMC; H1

02230: KAPITAN SOROKIN Ru/Fi 1977; IB; 10600; 131.88 × 8.5 (432.68 × 27.89); TrS D-E; 19; Helicopter deck. Sister (Ru flag); similar – sloping funnel top and stepped bridge-front (Ru flag).

P2   CMFMK; H12

02270: MUSSON Ru/Pd 1967; RS; 3300; 97 × 5.2 (319 × 17.1); TSM; 16; 'B88' type. Sisters (Ru flag).

P2   CMFMN; H

02280: KATYN Ru/Fi 1973; Cbl; 6000; 130.41 × 5.75 (427.8 × 18.86); TS D-E; 14; 'KLASMA' class; also known as **KATUNJ**. Sisters (Ru flag).

P2   CM₂F; H

02340: MARIYA YERMOLOVA Ru/Ys 1974; P; 3900; 100 × 4.5 (328 × 14.1); TSM; 17. Sisters (Ru flag).

P2   CM₂F; H

02350: KOLKHIDA Ru/Ru 1961; P; 3200; 101.5 × 4 (333 × 13); TSM; 14.5; Some ships have taller funnel; Some ships may not have crane. Sisters (Ru flag).

P2   CM₂F; H

02415: ARKTIKA Ru/Ru 1974; IB; 18200; 148.0 × 11.0 (485.6 × 36.09); TrS T-E; —. Sister (Ru flag).

P2   CM₂F; H1

02417: SERGEY KRAVKOV Ru/Fi 1974; RS; 1100; 68.23 × 4.15 (223.85 × 13.62); M;13.5. Sisters—some have small crane abaft funnel (Ru flag); Similar—larger crane (Ru flag).

P2   CM₂FK; H

02460: AKADEMIK KRYLOV Ru/DDR —; RS; 9100 Dspl; 147 × — (483 × —); M; 15.

P2   KC₇MFCK; H13

02520: IRKUTSK Ru/DDR 1968; C; 4800/8500; 151 × 8.8 (497 × 29.9); M; 17. Sisters (Ru flag).

P2   KC₄MFC; H13

02670: SVETLOGORSK Ru/Ru 1970; C; 6300/8900; 152.7 × 9.3 (501 × 30.85); M; 17. Sisters (Ru flag); Similar – smaller cranes arranged in pairs (Ru flag).

P2   KC₄MFC; H13

02690: NOVGOROD Ru/Fi 1967; C; 5800/8800; 150.9 × 9 (495 × 29.5); M; 18. Sisters – some later ships have modified superstructure. Can be fitted with heavy lift derrick (Ru flag).

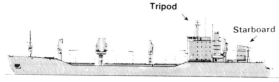

P2   KC4MFCR; H13

02724: NORILSK Ru/Fi 1982; C/Con/RoC; 18600; 174.02 × 10.52 (570.9 × 34.51); M; 17; Side ramp; 'SA 15' type. Sisters (Ru flag).

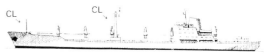

P2   KC3MC2MFC; H1

02790: KAPITAN ALEKSEYEV Ru/Ru 1971; C; 7500/11300; 169.6 × 7.8/10.0 (556.43 × 25.59/32.81); M; 18; 'Feodosiya' type. Sisters (Ru flag).

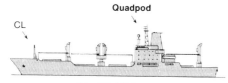

P2   KC3MFC; H1

02847: AKADEMIK N. VAVILOV Ru/De 1985; R; 9500; 138.21 × 8.2 (453.44 × 26.9); M; 20.25; Side doors (4 port—4 starboard). Sisters (Ru flag).

P2   KC3MFC; H123

02900: PERM Ru/Ru 1969; C; 4800; 122 × 7.2 (400 × 23.5); M; 14.5. Sisters (Ru flag).

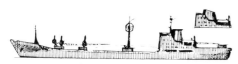

P2   KC3M2FC; H13

03040: KALININABAD Ru/Fi 1963; C; 6000/8600; 147 × 9.1 (482 × 30); M; 17. Sisters (Ru flag).

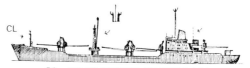

P2   KC2KC3MFC/KC2KC3MFKC; H123

03060: HARRY POLLITT Ru/DDR 1971; C; 9300; 151.5 × 9 (497 × 29.5); M; 17; Some sisters vary in details. Some have small kingpost abaft funnel as indicated in drawing. Sisters (Ru flag).

P2   KC₂KC₂MFC; H13

03110: NOVGOROD Ru/Fi 1967; C; 5800/8800; 150.9 × 9 (495 × 29.5); M; 18; Heavy lift derrick is not normally fitted. See alternative entry under KC₄MFC – No. 02690. Sisters (Ru flag).

P2   KC₂KCMFC; H1

03150: KARL MARX DDR/DDR 1971; C; 11000; 166.4 × 9.5 (546 × 31.35); M; 21.5. Sister (DDR flag).

P2   KC₂KMFC; H13

03230: RADZIONKOW Pd/Pd 1973; C; 3500/5500; 124 × 7.3 (407 × 24.1); M; 15.5; 'B432' type. Sisters (Pd flag);.

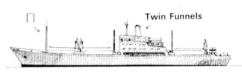

Twin Funnels

P2   KC₂KMFKC; H

03260: KULDIGA Ru/Br 1971; R; 5900; 149.3 × 8.5 (490 × 27.9); M; 21. Sisters (Ru flag).

P2   KC₂MC₃MFC; H1

03270: OMSK Ru/Ja 1961; C; 7500/10900; 155 × 9.6 (509 × 31.5); M; 17. Sisters (Ru flag).

P2   KC₂MF; H1

03400: AKADEMIK FEDOROV Ru/Fi 1987; RS; 7600 Dwt; 140 × 8.5 (459.32 × 27.89); D-E; 16; Ice breaker. Helicopter deck. Antarctic research.

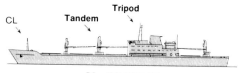

P2   *KC₂MFC; H1*

03423: KURSK Ru/Pd 1983; R; 8800; 146.62 × 8.1 (481.04 × 26.57); M; 21.75; Side doors; 'B365' type. Sisters (Ru flag).

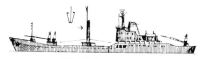

P2   *KC₂M₂FC; H13*

03620: RADZIONKOW Pd/Pd 1973; C; 3500/5500; 124 × 7.3 (407 × 24.1); M; 15.5; 'B432' type. Sisters (Pd flag).

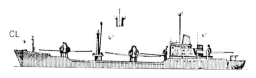

P2   *KCKC₃MFC; H13*

03650: HARRY POLLITT Ru/DDR 1971; C; 9300; 151.5 × 9 (497 × 29.5); M; 17. Sisters (Ru flag).

P2   *KCKC₂MFC; H1*

03690: WARNEMUNDE Ru/DDR 1972; C; 11000; 150.2 × 8.9 (493 × 29); M; 19.25; 'MERCATOR' type. Sisters (Ru & DDR flag).

P2   *KCKCMFK; H13*

03770: LENINSKAYA GVARDIYA Ru/Pd 1972; C; 6600; 135 × 7.5 (443 × 24.5); M; 15.5; 'B 46' type. Sisters (Ru flag).

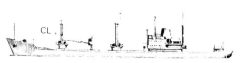

P2   *KCK₂MFM; H1*

03870: ALTENBURG DDR/DDR 1967; C; 5400/8500; 150.2 × 8.2 (493 × 26.11); M; 17; 'XD' type. Sisters (DDR flag).

P2 KCMC₂MFC; H13

03930: KLIN Ru/Fi 1964; C; 6600/9400; 147 × 9.1 (482 × 30); M; 17.5. Sisters (Ru flag).

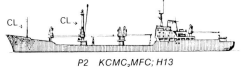

P2 KCMC₂MFC; H13

03950: SOSNOGORSK Ru/Ru 1969; C; 6800/8900; 153 × 9.1 (501 × 29.8); M; 17; Cranes abreast mast. Sisters (Ru flag).

P2 KCMCMFK; H13

04010: LENINSKAYA GVARDIYA Ru/Pd 1972; C; 6600; 135 × 7.5 (443 × 24.5); M; 15.5; 'B 46' type. Sisters (Ru flag).

P2 KCMF; H

04065: 'KAMENKA' class Ru/Pd 1968-72; RS; 700 Dspl; 53.5 × 2.6 (175.5 × 8.5); TSM; 14; Naval operated. Sisters (Ru & DDR flags).

P2 KCMF; H

04066: 'KAMENKA' class Ru/Pd 1968-72; RS; 700 Dspl; 53.5 × 2.6 (175.5 × 8.5); TSM;14; May be several of this class with this appearance—see drawing no 04065. Sister (Ru flag).

P2 KCMF; H1

04067: 'BIYA' class Ru/Pd 1972-76; RS; 750 Dspl; 55 × 2.6 (180.45 × 8.53); TSM;13. Sisters (Ru flag).

P2   KCMF; H1

04068: 'SAMARA' class Ru/Pd 1962-64; RS; 1270 Dspl; 59.0 × 3.8 (193.5 × 12.5); TSM;15; May be several in this class with this appearance—see drawing no 01736.

P2   KCMF; H12

04088: PLANETA Pd/Pd 1982; BT/RS; 750; 61.32 × 3.19 (201.18 × 10.47); TSM; —; 'B91' type. 'Finik' class. Sisters (Pd, DDR and Ru flags); Some of the Pd vessels are modified and the Ru vessels are operated as survey ships.

P2   KCMFMFC; H1

04200: 'TOMBA' class Ru/Ru 1975; Repair/FA; 5200 Dspl; 107 × 6 (351 × 20); M; —; Class of at least 3 ships operated by the Soviet Navy.

P2   KCMF; H1

04080: STROPTIVYY Ru/Fi 1979; Sal/Tg; 4200 Dspl; 69.8 × 6.5 (229 × 21.33); M; 15. Sisters (Ru flag); Similar (Ru flag).

P2   KCMFMC; H13

04180: KIROVSKLES Ru/Fi 1962; TC/C; 2900; 102 × 5.7 (335 × 18.9); M; 12.25. Sisters (Ru flag).

P2   KCMFMN; H2

04210: INGURI Ru/Fi 1978; Cbl; 6000; 130.41 × 5.75 (427.8 × 18.8); TS D-E; 14; Modified 'KLASMA' type; Others in this class may also have this sequence—see DONETS.

P2   KCM₂F; H

04215: SHOTA RUSTAVELI Ru/DDR 1968; P; 20500; 175.77 × 8.09 (576.67 × 26.54); TSM; 20.5; Ice strengthened.

P2   KCM₂F; H1

04216: FYODOR MATISEN Ru/Fi 1976; RS; 1200; 68.74 × 4.16 (225.52 × 13.65); M; 13.5; May be spelt **FEDOR MATISEN.** Sisters (Ru flag).

P2   KCM₂FC; H1

04225: AKADEMIK GAMBURTSYEV Ru/Fi 1983; RS; 1800; 71.61 × 4.5 (234.94 × 14.76); M; 12; Port side superstructure may differ. Sisters (Ru flag).

P2   KCM₂FC; H1

04226: PROFESSOR BOGOROV Ru/Fi 1976; RS; 1200; 68.76 × 4.21 (225.59 × 13.81); M;13.5. Sisters—some may have 'A' frame aft (Ru flag).

P2   KCM₂FC₂; H1

04230: WILHELM FLORIN DDR/DDR 1964; C; 5000/7700; 142.3 × 7.2 (467 × 23.7); M; 14.5. Sisters (DDR flag).

P2   KCM₂FK; H

04240: ADMIRAL VLADIMIRSKIY Ru/Pd 1975; RS; 9100 Dspl; 147 × 6.2 (483 × 20.34); M; 20. Sister (Ru flag).

P2 KCM₃FC; H1

04270: TAYMYR Ru/Fi 1988; IB; —; 150.2 × 8.1 (492.78 × 26.57); TrST; —; May be spelt **TAIMYR**. Sister (Ru flag) due in 1989.

P2 KCM₃FCK; H1

04275: AKADEMIK SHULEYKIN Ru/Fi 1982; RS; 1800; 71.61 × 4.75 (235 × 15.58); M; 12. Sisters (Ru flag); Similar – larger crane aft and larger 'A' frame (Ru flag).

P2 KFM; H1

04312: KATUN Ru/No 1983; ORSV; 1600; 67.72 × 5.95 (222.18 × 19.52); TSM; —. Sister (Ru flag).

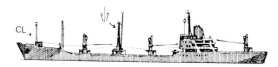

P2 K₂CKCMFC; H13

04400: HEL Pd/De 1970; C; 7700/11000; 166.7 × 9.7 (547 × 31.9); M; 20.75. Sisters (Pd flag).

P2 K₂CK₂MFM; H1

04423: ALTENBURG DDR/DDR 1967; C; 5400/8500; 150.2 × 7.26/8.2 (493 × 23.82/26.9); M; 18.5; 'XD' type. Sisters (DDR flag).

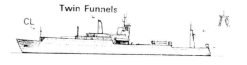

P2 K₂FM₂; H2

04520: NATALIYA KOVSHOVA Ru/Fr 1965; FT; 6300; 129 × 7 (423 × 23.1); D-E; 13.5. Sisters (Ru flag).

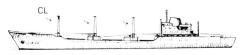

P2   K₄MFK; H13

04860: MIKOLAJ REJ Pd/Fi 1969; C; 7300/9800; 151 × 8.6/9.7 (496 × 28/32); M; 18. Sister (Pd flag).

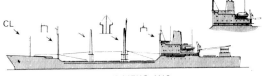

P2   K₄MFKC; H13

04910: DRESDEN DDR/DDR 1976; C/Con; 10000; 156.85 × 9.45 (514.6 × 31); M; 18.25; 'Meridian' type. Sisters (DDR flag).

P2   K₃MFK; H13

05410: VOLCHANSK Ru/DDR 1968; C; 9500; 150.8 × 8.9 (494 × 29.3); M; 16.5.

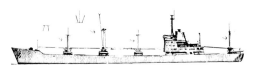

P2   K₃MFK₂; H1

05620: IGNATIY SERGEYEV Ru/Pd 1968; C; 10200; 154.5 × 9.5 (507 × 29.6); M; 16.5; 'B40/B401' type; 'Kommunist' class. Sisters (Ru & Pd flags).

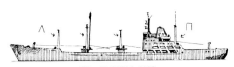

P2   K₃MFM; H13

06060: VELIKIYE LUKI Ru/DDR 1964; C; 9400; 150.6 × 8.8 (494 × 29.3); M; 16.5. Sisters (Ru flag).

P2   K₃MFM; H13

06069: COTNARI Rm/DDR 1979; C; 6200/9500; 152.63 × 7.56/9.31 (500.75 × 24.8/30.54); M; 17; 'Ozean' type. Sisters (Rm & Cz flags).

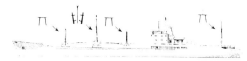

P2 K_3MFM; H13

06090: WLADYSLAW ORKAN Pd/Pd 1971; C; 6400/10100; 153.74 × —/8.97 (504.4 × —/29.43); M; 18; Modified 'B442' type. Sister (Pd flag).

P2 $K_3M_2FK_2$; H13

06142: ALBA IULIA Rm/Pd 1976; C; 5300/8100; 145.07 × 7.46/9.08 (476 × 24.47/29.79); M; 18.5; 'B478' type. Sister (Rm flag).

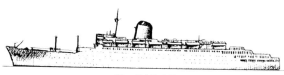

P2 K_2MF; H2

06200: LEONID SOBINOV Ru/Br 1954; P; 21400; 185 × 8.7 (608 × 28.7); TST; 20. Sister (Ru flag).

P2 K_2MFK; H1

06380: HEINZ KAPELLE DDR/DDR 1965; C; 5000/7700; 142 × 7.2/8.5 (466 × 23.6/28); M; 14.5. Similar (DDR flag).

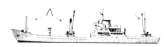

P2 K_2MFK; H13

06770: BEREZNIK Ru/Fi 1968; C/TC; 2700; 102 × 6.2 (335 × 20.2); M; 13.5; Ships vary in appearance. Sisters (Ru flag).

P2 K_2MFK; H13

06795: UNZHA Ru/Ru 1968; C/TC; 3000; 104.5 × 6.05 (343 × 19.85); M; 13.5; Some sisters have goalpost on forecastle and poop. Sisters (Ru flag).

P2 K_2MFK_2; H

06825: ABKHAZIYA Ru/DDR 1972; RS; 4800; 123.86 × 6.54 (406 × 21.46); TSM; 17.5. Sisters (Ru flag).

P2 K_2MFKMK; H1

07440: MAJOR SUCHARSKI Pd/Po 1974; C; 5800/8800; 152.97 × —/9.05 (501.87 × —/29.69); M; 18. Sister (Pd flag).

P2 K_2MFM; H

07460: DZIECI POLSKIE Pd/Po 1978; R; 3300/6400; 139.63 × 6.62/7.78 (458 × 21.72/25.52); M; 22.5; 8 side doors. 'B437' type. Completed in Poland. Sisters (Pd flag).

Twin Funnels

P2 K_2MFM; H

07470: 'ATLANTIK' type Ru/DDR; FT; 2200 approx; 82 × 5.3 (269 × 17.6); M; 14.25; Many 'Atlantik' type ships may have this appearance (see others under KMFM). Sisters (Ru flag).

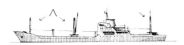

P2 K_2MFM; H13

07550: 'BEREZNIK' class Ru/Fi 1968; C/TC; 2700; 102 × 6.2 (334 × 20.4); M; 13.5; Ships vary. Radar mast often from bridge top. Similar (Ru flag).

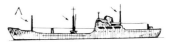

P2 K_2MFM; H13

07600: LENALES Ru/Fi 1964; C/TC; 2900; 102 × 6.2 (334 × 20.4); M; 13.75; May be other vessels of the 'BEREZNIK' class with this appearance—see No 07550.

P2   K₂MFM; H13

07610: LYONYA GOLIKOV Ru/DDR 1968; C; 3600; 105.7 × 6.8 (347 × 22.4); M; 13.75; May be other ships of this class with this sequence. See 'SHURA KOBER' class under KM₂FM.

P2   K₂MFMC; H

07620: AKADEMIK KURCHATOV Ru/DDR 1966; RS; 5500; 123.88 × 6.06 (406.43 × 19.88); TSM; 18.25. Sister (Ru flag); Similar – funnel top differs (Ru flag).

P2   K₂M₂FC; H12

07860: ANTONI GARNUSZEWSKI Pd/Pd 1974; C/TS; 6000; 122.2 × 7.4 (401 × 24.3); M; 15.75; 'B.80' type. Sisters (Pd, Bu & Rm flags).

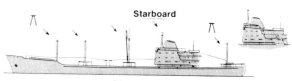

P2   K₂M₂FK; H1

07900: MINSK Ru/Pd 1964; C; 7400/9700; 155 × 7.4/9 (508 × 24.3/29.10); M; 17.25; 'B 44' type. Sisters (Ru flag) (some have modified superstructure—see inset. Some are 'B441' type:).

P2   K₂M₂FK; H13

07947: TARKHANSK Ru/Pd 1978; C/FC; 3500/5500; 123.93 × —/7.32 (406 × —/24.02); M; 15.75; 'B432' type. Sisters (Ru flag).

P2   K₂M₂FM; H13

08030: VYBORG Ru/DDR 1964; C; 5500/8500; 151 × 7.2/8.9 (494 × 23.6/29); M; 16.5. Sisters (Ru flag).

P2   KMCMF; H1

08115: AKADEMIK SERGEY KOROLOV Ru/Ru 1970; RS; 17100; 181.90 × 7.95 (597 × 26.08); M; 17.5; Space tracking.

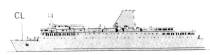

P2   KMF; H

08170: POMERANIA Pd/Pd 1978; RoPCF; 7400; 127.25 × 5.42 (417.49 × 17.78); M; 20.4; 'B490' type. Sister (Pd flag).

P2   KMF; H1

08565: NAVIGATOR Pd/Pd 1975; IC; 1700 Dspl; 67 × 4 (219.8 × 13.1); TSM; 15; Operated by Polish Navy. Sister—longer, higher forecastle (Pd flag).

P2   KMF; H1

08778: ERNST THALMANN DDR/DDR 1987; Con; 17800; 172.4 × 9.6 (565.62 × 31.5); M;17.5. Sister (DDR flag).

P2   KMF; H1

08834: ARAKS Ru/No 1977; ORSV; 498; 64.39 × 3.8 (211.25 × 12.47); TSM; 15; 'UT 704' type. Sisters (Ru flag); Similar—longer (67m – 219ft) (Ru flag); Similar—'B90' type (Pd flag).

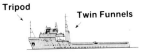

P2   KMF; H1

08846: RIONI Ru/Fi 1984; ORSV; 1600; 67.21 × 5.00 (220.51 × 16.4); TSM; 15.5. Sisters (Ru flag).

P2   KMF; H1

08849: 'SAMARA' class (modified) Ru/Pd approx 1964; RS; 1270 Dspl; 59.0 × 3.8 (193.5 × 12.5); TSM; 15. Sisters (Ru flag).

P2   KMFC; H1

09035: SB-406 Ru/Fi 1984; Tg/Sal; 2100; 67.21 × 5.4 (220.51 × 17.72); TSM; —. Sisters (Ru flag).

P2   KMFC; H12

09080: PROFESSOR SHCHYOGOLEV Ru/Pd 1970; C/TS; 6000; 122 × 7.3 (402 × 24.2); M; 15.5; 'B 80' type. Sisters (Ru flag). Some have light mast from funnel.

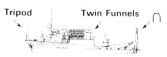

P2   KMFCK; H1

09120: SPRUT Ru/Fi 1979; OSS; 2200; 77 × 5.35 (262.62 × 17.55); TSM; 14; Helicopter deck. Radar mast and 'A' frame are hinged.

P2   KMF₂M; H

09210: PRIAMURYE Ru/Ru 1957; P; 5800; 119 × 6.7 (391 × 19); D-E; 16. Sister (Ru flag).

P2   KMFK; H

09360: GRUMANT Ru/De 1964; FT; 4700; 103 × 5.5 (337 × 18.3); M; 14; Differs from SKRYPLEV (No 09380) by having both KP's on houses. Sisters (Ru flag).

P2 KMFK; H

09380: SKRYPLEV Ru/De 1962; FT; 4700; 103 × 5.5 (337 × 18.3); M; 14. Sisters (Ru flag).

Tripod   Starboard

P2 KMFK; H1

09899: BAKERIT Ru/Fi 1986; RS/DS; 3500; 85.81 × 5.60 (281.53 × 18.37); TS D-E; —. Sister (Ru flag).

CL

P2 KMFK; H13

09995: GAMZAT TSADASA Ru/Ys 1971/80; Con; 12300; 176.23 × 9.80 (578 × 32.15); M; 17.75; Converted to container and lengthened 1980. Sisters (Ru flag).

P2 KMFK₂; H2

10250: WALTER DEHMEL DDR/DDR 1963; FT; 2900; 85.3 × 5.3 (280 × 17.6); M; 13.5. Sisters (DDR flag).

P2 KMFKM; H

10260: BURAN Pd/Pd 1972; FC; 2900/5100; 120 × —/7.3 (394 × —/24); M; 18; 'B433' type. Sisters (Pd flag).

P2 KMFKM; H1

10280: K. I. GALCZYNSKI Pd/Pd 1964; C; 5600; 145.73 × 7.65 (478.12 × 25.1); M; 16.5. Sister (Pd flag); Similar—goalpost kingpost abaft superstructure (Pd flag).

P2   *KMFKM; H1*

10350: STEFAN CZARNIECKI Pd/De 1967; CP; 6900/10200; 154 × 7.9/8.5 (504 × 26/28); M; 16. Sisters (Pd flag).

P2   *KMFKM; H2*

10535: DELTA DUNARII Rm/Pd 1968; FT; 2700; 88.02 × 5.6 (289 × 18.37); M; 13.5; 'B22' type. Sister (Rm flag).

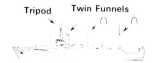

P2   *KMFKM; H2*

10540: REGULUS Pd/Pd 1976; FT; 2600; 89.06 × 5.6 (292.19 × 18.37); M; 17.75; 'B414' type. Sisters (Pd flag).

P2   *KMFKMK; H1*

10570: FRANCESCO NULLO Pd/Pd 1964; C; 5700/8600; 152.6 × 7.7/8.8 (501 × 25.4/29); M; 15.5; 'B41' type. Sister (Pd flag); Similar – larger funnels (Pd flag).

P2   *KMFKMK; H1*

10610: SIMFEROPOL Ru/Pd 1962; C; 6600/9200; 155 × 7.8/8.9 (508 × 26/29.3); M; 15; 'B43' type. Sisters (Ru flag).

P2   *KMFM; H*

10720: YANIS RAYNIS Ru/Pd 1971; R; 5200; 119.4 × 7.3 (393 × 23.11); M; 19. Sisters (Ru flag).

70

P2 KMFM; H

10740: NIKOLAY KOPERNIK Ru/Pd 1974; R; 6400; 140 × 7.7 (460 × 25.6); M; 21.75; 'B 437' type. Sisters – some have a light pole foreward (Ru & Pd flags).

P2 KMFM; H

10760: BURAN Pd/Pd 1972; FC; 2900/5100; 120 × —/7.3 (392 × —/24); M; 18; 'B 433' type. Sisters (Pd flag).

P2 KMFM; H

10780: OKAH Ru/— 1959; P; 800; 61 × — (200 × —); M;12.

P2 KMFM; H

10810: SEJWAL Pd/Pd 1968; FT; 2500; 87 × 5.3 (286 × 17.7); M; 13.5; 'B 18' type. Sisters (Pd flag).

P2 KMFM; H1

10880: SLAVA SEVASTOPOLYA Ru/De 1954; FC; 3800/5100; 124.16 × —/7.35 (407.35 × —/24.11); TSM; 17.5.

P2 KMFM; H1

11140: THEODOR STORM DDR/Be 1966; R; 5000; 135 × 6.8 (443 × 22.3); M; 21. Sister (DDR flag).

P2 KMFM; H1

11300: KOPET-DAG Ru/Ru 1970; FT; 3300; 107.5 × 6.2 (353 × 20.4); D-E; 13. Sisters (Ru flag).

P2 KMFM; H1

11333: BALAKHNA Ru/Ru 1981; FT; 3400; 103.71 × 5.8 (340 × 19.03); M; 14. Sisters (Ru flag) – some have more rake on stem and some are fishery research.

P2 KMFM; H1

11337: AQUILA Pd/Pd 1981; FT; 3700; 102.6 × 5.97 (337 × 19.59); M; 16.25; 'B407' type. Sisters (Pd flag).

P2 KMFM; H12

11380: BOROVICHI Ru/Ru 1965; RS; 5300; 122 × 4.7 (400 × 15.3); M; 15; Missile tracking vessel. Converted from cargo ship 1967. Sisters (Ru flag).

P2 KMFM; H123

11430: CHULYMLES Ru/Ru 1963; C; 4500; 122 × 6.78 (400 × 22.24); M; 14.5. Sisters (Ru flag).

P2 KMFM; H123

11460: BASKUNCHAK Ru/Ru 1964; RS; 4900; 122.1 × 4.3 (400.3 × 14); M; 15; Modified cargo vessels. Helicopter deck. Sisters (Ru flag).

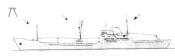

P2   KMFM; H13

11490: INDIGA Ru/Fi 1965; C/TC; 2900; 102 × 6 (334 × 19.6); M; 13.75. Sisters (Ru flag).

P2   KMFM; H2

11575: 'VISHNYA' class Ru/— —; IC; 3300 Dspl; 91 (approx) × — (298.5 × —); —;—; Two 30 mm guns foreward. Mountings for surface-to-air missiles aft.

P2   KMFM; H2

11580: PLANETA Ru/Pd 1963; FT; 2300; 83 × 5.5 (273 × 18); M; 12.5; 'B26' type (early version). Sisters (Ru flag) – some are fishery research.

P2   KMFM; H2

11610: SMOLNYY Ru/Pd 1969; FT; 2900; 8.32 × 5.5 (273 × 18); M; 11.75; 'B 26' type (later version). Sisters (Ru flag) – some have pole foremast.

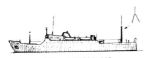

P2   KMFM; H2

11640: ANDROMEDA Pd/Pd 1964; FT; 2800; 85 × 5.5 (279 × 18); M; 12.5; 'B15' type. Sisters (Pd flag).

P2   KMFM; H2

11670: VEGA Pd/Pd 1973; FT; 2700; 88 × 5.6 (289 × 18.8); M; 15; 'B419' type. Sisters (Pd & Rm flags).

P2 KMFM; H2

11690: PROFESSOR SIEDLECKI Pd/Pd 1971; SS/RS; 2800; 89.3 × 5.5 (293 × 18); D-E; 14; 'B424' type.

Twin Funnels

P2 KMFM; H2

11695: CARINA Pd/Pd 1967; FT; 2600; 87.97 × 5.60 (289 × 18.37); M; 13; 'B22' type.

P2 KMFM; H2

11700: RETEZATUL Rm/Pd 1972; FT; 2700; 88 × 5.6 (289 × 18.4); M; 13.75; 'B22' type. Sisters (Rm & Pd flags).

P2 KMFM; H2

11720: TARUSA Ru/Ru 1974; FT; 2300; 83.27 × 5.72 (273 × 18.77); M; —. Sisters (Ru flag).

Twin Funnels

P2 KMFM; H2

11790: WLOCZNIK Pd/Pd 1975; FT; 2600; 88.58 × 5.6 (291 × 18.4); M; 17.75; 'B414' type. Sister (Pd flag).

Twin Funnels

P2 KMFM; H2

11800: 'ATLANTIK' class Ru/DDR 1966; FT; 2200; 82.1 × 5.1 (270 × 17); M; 13.5; Built 1966-1977. Sisters (Ru, Bu & Rm flags) – some are fishery research (Ru flag) and some of these have differences such as extended boat deck.

P2   KMFM; H2

11995: SSV 465 Ru/Ru —; RS; 3400 Dspl; 83.6 × 6.00 (275 × 19.69); M; 13; Based on hull of 'Mayakovskiy' class trawler.

P2   KMFMC; H

12000: AKADEMIK KOROLYOV Ru/DDR 1967; RS; 5500; 124.3 × 6 (408 × 19.11); TSM; 18.15. Sisters (Ru flag) (may vary slightly).

P2   KMFMK; H2

12230: KERCH Ru/DDR 1961; FT; 1900; 79.8 × 5.2 (262 × 17); M; 12.5; 'TROPIK' class (built 1961-1966). Similar (Ru & Bu flags) – some Ru flag vessels are fishery research.

P2   KMFMK; H2

12340: 'PUSHKIN' class (modified) Ru/FRG 1955/57; FT; 2500/3000; 84.5 × 5.5 (278 × 18); M; 12.5. Similar (Ru flag).

P2   KMFMK; H2

12360: 'MAYAKOVSKIY' class Ru/Ru 1958/59; FT; 3200; 84.7 × 5.6 (278 × 18.4); M; 13.75; Distinguished from 'Modified Mayakovskiy' class by having a pole foremast. Similar (Ru flag).

P2   KMFMK; H2

12380: 'MAYAKOVSKIY' class (modified) 1959/68; FT; 3200; 78 × 5.5 (256 × 18); M; 12. Sisters (Ru & Bu flags).

P2 KMFMK; H2

12570: AKADEMIK KNIPOVICH Ru/Ru 1964; RS; 2300; 84.7 × 5.8 (278 × 19); M; 13; 'MAYAKOVSKIY' class; both masts tripod. Similar (Ru flag).

Tripod

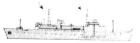

P2 KMFMK; H2

12585: ODISSEY Ru/Ru 1970; Sub S; 2800; 84.66 × 5.80 (278 × 19.03); M; 12.5; Converted from 'MAYAKOVSKIY' class trawler. May be spelt **ODISSEJ**. Shell doors in hull move apart laterally to reveal a large hold where the submersible is housed. Similar (Ru flag).

CL

P2 KMFMK; H2

12587: SSV 502 Ru/Ru —; RS; 3400 Dspl; 83.6 × 6.00 (274.3 × 19.69); M; 13; Based on hull of 'MAYAKOVSKIY' class trawler. Sisters (Ru flag).

P2 KMFMK; H2

12590: 'LESKOV' class Ru/Pd 1960/63; FT; 2800; 84.6 × 5.3 (277 × 17.6); M; 12.5; 'B 15' type. Similar (Ru flag).

P2 KMFMK; H2

12610: JUPITER Pd/Pd 1963; FT; 2300; 83 × 5.5 (272 × 18); M; 12.5; 'B 15' type. Sisters (Pd flag).

P2 KMFMK; H2

12620: BERTOLT BRECHT DDR/DDR 1959; FT; 3000; 86 × 5.3 (281 × 17.4); M; 12.5. Similar (DDR flag).

P2   KMFMK; H2

12630: WALTER DEHMEL DDR/DDR 1963; FT; 3000; 85.6 × 5.3 (281 × 17.5); M; 13.5. Sisters (DDR flag).

Twin Funnels

CL

P2   KMFR; H

12680: KAPITAN SMIRNOV Ru/Ru 1979; RoC/Con; 14300; 227.3 × 9.87 (745.74 × 32.38); TS GT/M;—; Quarter ramp. Sisters – ramp design varies (Ru flag).

CL

P2   KMFR; H1

12685: TADEUSZ KOSCIUSKO Pd/Fr 1981; RoC/Con; 30100; 200.26 × 9.52 (657 × 31.23); M; 20.75; Starboard quarter ramp. Sisters (Pd flag).

P2　KMKFKM; H1

13010: INGURLES Ru/Pd 1958; C; 9900; 154 × 8.7 (505 × 28.8); M; 16; 'B54' type. Sisters (Ru flag).

P2　KMKFM; H1

13650: 'SUPER ATLANTIK' type Ru/DDR 1972 onwards; FT; 4000; 102 × 5.2 (335 × 17); M; 15. Sisters (Ru, Rm & DDR flags) – bridge configuration differs in some Ru ships – see inset.

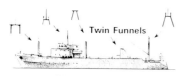

P2　KMKFM; H1

13751: Later **'SUPER ATLANTIK' type** Ru/DDR 1977 onwards; FT; 3100; 101.45 × 5.70 (333 × 18.70); M; 14.75; Differs from earlier 'Super Atlantik' principally by filled-in well abaft superstructure. Some have boats ahead of funnels (LUDWIG RENN has this feature). Sisters (Ru, DDR & Rm flag) – some Ru flag ships are fishery research.

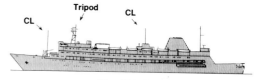

P2　KMKFM; H

13590: OB Ru/Pd 1980; Hosp; 11000 Dspl; 152 × 6.2 (498.69 × 20.34); TSM; 18; Helicopter deck and hangar. Sister (Ru flag).

P2　KMKFM; H1

13745: PRIZVANIE Ru/DDR 1979; FT/TS; 3300; 101.83 × 5.60 (334 × 18.37); M; 14.75; Modified 'Super Atlantik' type. Differs from standard design by centre-line kingpost foreward, position of boats etc. Sisters (Ru flag).

P2　KMKFM; H123

13850: MAMAIA Rm/Ru 1930; C; 4000; 112 × 7.3 (366 × 24); M; 11.

P2   KMKMFK; H13

14370: PULA Ru/Ys 1964; C; 8000/10100; 160 × 9.7 (525 × 26/32); M; 18. Sisters (Ru flag).

P2   KMKMFK₂; H1

14450: IGNATIY SERGEYEV Ru/Pd 1968; C; 10200; 154.5 × 9.5 (507 × 29.6); M; 16.5; 'B40/B401' type-'KOMMUNIST' class. Similar (Ru & Pd flags).

P2   KMKMFK₂; H13

14480: FRANCISZEK ZUBRZYCKI Pd/Pd 1973; C/Con; 7200/10100; 161 × —/9.7 (529 × —/32); M; 21; 'B438' type. Sisters (Pd flag).

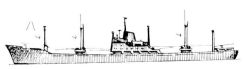

P2   KMKMFKMK; H1

14700: DIVNOGORSK Ru/Pd 1961; C; 6400; 164 × 8.8 (505 × 29); M; 16; 'B54' type.

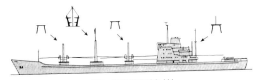

P2   KMKMFM; H1

14770: URSUS Pd/Pd 1972; C; 6400/10100; 154.7 × —/8.97 (507.55 × —/29.43); M; 17.75; 'B442' type. Sister (Pd flag).

P2   KMKMFM; H13

14800: WLADYSLAW ORKAN Pd/Pd 1971; C; 6400/10100; 154.74 × —/8.97 (504.4 × —/29.43); M; 18; Modified 'B442' type. Sister (Pd flag).

P2 KMKM₂FK₂; H1

14905: VITYAZ Ru/Pd 1981; RS; 4800; 110.93 × 5.70 (364 × 18.70); TSM; 16; 'B86' type. Sisters (Ru flag).

P2 KMKM₂FK₂; H13

14910: WLADYSLAW JAGIELLO Pd/Pd 1971; C; 5400/8100; 145.37 × 7.36/9.09 (476.94 × 24.15/29.82); M; 17.5; 'B445' type. Sisters (Pd & Hu flags) – some are 'B 474' types.

P2 KM₂F; H1

14955: AKADEMIK MSTISLAV KELDYSH Ru/Fi 1981; RS; 5500; 122.21 × 5.9 (400.95 × 19.36); TSM; 16; Inset drawing shows detail of starboard side superstructure.

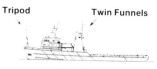

Tripod   Twin Funnels

P2 KM₂F; H1

14962: NEFTEGAZ-8 Ru/Pd 1984; ORSV; 2400; 81.39 × 4.75 (267.03 × 15.58); TSM; 15; 'B92' type. Sisters (Ru flag).

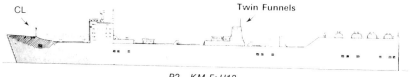

Twin Funnels

P2 KM₂F; H13

14975: YULIUS FUCHIK Ru/Fi 1978; Bg/Con; 22800/35900; 266.45 × —/11 (874.18 × —/36.09); TSM; 20; May be spelt **JULIUS FUCIK**; Deck stowage of barges indicated by dotted lines. Sister (Ru flag).

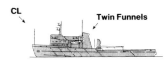

CL   Twin Funnels

P2 KM₂FC; H1

14983: NEFTEGAZ 51 Ru/Pd 1986; ORSV; 3800 approx; 81.4 × 4.75 (267.06 × 15.58); TSM; 15; 'B92/II' type. Sisters (Ru flag).

Tripod

H1 KM₂FC; H1

14986: AKADEMIK FERSMAN Ru/Pd 1986; RS; 3300; 81.87 × 5.00 (268.6 × 16.4); M; 14.5; 'B 93' type. Sisters (Ru flag).

CL

P2 KM₂FC; H1

14988: AKADEMIK OPARIN Ru/Fi 1985; RS; 2300; 75.72 × 4.5 (248.43 × 14.76); M; 15.25; Starboard side superstructure varies (see inset).

P2 KM₂FC; H12

15000: 'PROFESSOR' class Ru/Pd 1970; C/TS; 6000; 122 × 7.3 (401 × 24.2); M; —; 'B80' type; Several vessels of this class may have this sequence; Superstructure varies—see drawing no 09080. Sisters (Ru flag).

P2 KM₂FCK; H1

15003: AKADEMIK M A LAVRENTYEV Ru/Fi 1984; RS; 2300; 75.47 × 4.50 (247.60 × 14.76); M; 15.25; Port and starboard sides differ—see inset. Sisters (Ru flag).

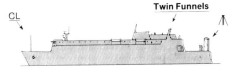

CL   Twin Funnels

P2 KM₂F₂K; H2

15040: MIKOLAJ KOPERNIK Pd/No 1974; RoC/P/TF; 2900; 125.61 × 4.50 (412.11 × 14.76); M; 18; Stern door/ramp; Side doors. Sister – stepped bridge-front (Pd flag).

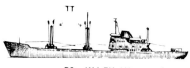

P2   KM₂FK; H1

15090: KRIVAN Cz/Pd 1970; CP; 3400/5500; 124 × 6.5/6.9 (407 × 21.6/23); M; 16; 'B455' type. Sisters (Cz flag).

P2   KM₂FK; H1

15095: AKADEMIK MSTISLAV KELDYSH Ru/Fi 1981; RS; 5500; 122.21 × 5.9 (400.95 × 19.36); TSM;16; Inset drawing shows detail of starboard side superstructure.

P2   KM₂FK; H13

15120: ALEKSANDR DOVZHENKO Ru/Rm 1965; C/TC; 2700; 100.67 × 6.00 (330 × 19.69); M; 13.75. Sisters (Ru flag).

P2   KM₂FKMK; H1

15310: MAJOR SUCHARSKI Pd/Po 1974; C; 5800/8800; 152.97 × —/9.05 (501.87 × —/29.69); M; 18. Sister (Pd flag).

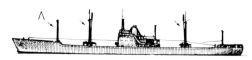

P2   KM₂FKMK; H1

15340: FRANCESCO NULLO Pd/Pd 1964; C; 5700/8600; 152.6 × 7.7/8.8 (501 × 25.4/29); M; 15.5; 'B-41' type. Sister (Pd flag); Similar – larger funnels (Pd flag).

P2   KM₂FKMK; H1

15360: PULKOWNIK DABEK Pd/Pd 1970; C; 5800/8700; 152.36 × —/9.07 (499.87 × —/29.76); M; 15.5; 'B 41' type.

P2 KM₂FM; H1

15410: HEINZ KAPELLE DDR/DDR 1965; C; 5000/7700; 142 × 7.2/8.5 (466 × 23.6/28); M; —. Similar (DDR flag).

P2 KM₂FM; H1

15420: BUCURESTI Rm/Ys 1962; C; 6700/9200; 152 × 8.1/9 (500 × 26.4/29.8); M; 14. Similar – lower superstructure (Rm flag).

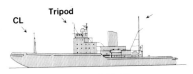

P2 KM₂FM; H1

15459: MUDYUG Ru/Fi 1982/86; IB; 7800 Dspl; 111.36 × 6.5 (365.35 × 21.33); TSM; —; New bow section 1986.

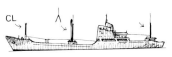

P2 KM₂FM; H13

15460: SINEGORSK Ru/DDR 1963; C; 3200; 106 × 6.6 (347 × 21.3); M; 12.5; 'Povonets' type. Sisters (Ru flag); Similar – space monitoring ship (Ru flag).

P2 KM₂FM; H13

15500: PYARNU Ru/DDR 1963; C; 3200; 106 × 6.7 (347 × 21.6); M; 13.75; 'Povonets' type. Sisters (Ru flag).

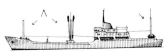

P2 KM₂FM; H13

15510: SHURA KOBER Ru/DDR 1971; C; 3600; 105.7 × 6.7 (347 × 21.6); M; 13.75; 'Pioner' type. Sisters (Ru flag).

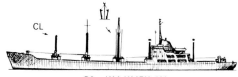

P2   KM₂KMFK; H1

15580: KRASZEWSKI Pd/De 1963; CP; 7200/10400; 153.3 × 8.3/9.1 (503 × 27.6/30); M; 16.

P2   KM₄FK₂; H13

15720: WLADYSLAW JAGIELLO Pd/Pd 1971; C; 5400/8100; 145.3 × 7.5/9 (477 × 24.6/29.11); M; 17.5; Sisters—'B 445' type (Pd flag); 'B 474' type (Hu flag).

P2   MCF; H

16000: STRAZAK-5 Pd/Pd —; Fire; 276; 37.32 × 3.1 (122.44 × 10.17); M; 14. Sisters (Pd flag).

P2   MCFMC₂; H

16140: UKRAINA Ru/De 1938; PC; 6400; 132 × 5.7 (432 × 15.9); TSM; 21.

P2   MCMF; H3

16205: NEVER Ru/Ru 1965; Trlr; 638; 54.26 × 3.68 (178 × 12.07); M; 11.5. Sisters (Ru flag).

P2   MCMFM; H1

16270: JASLO Pd/De 1967; C; 2300; 101.5 × 6 (335 × 19.8); M; 15.

P2 MF; H

16810: MAKSIM GORKIY Ru/FRG 1969; P; 25000; 194.6 × 8.3 (627 × 27); TST; 23.

P2 MF; H

16925: ARKONA DDR/FRG 1981; P; 18800; 164.34 × 6.10 (539 × 20.01); TSM; 18.

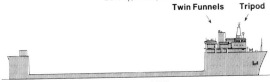

P2 MF; H13

17257: TRANSSHELF Ru/Fi 1987; SSDC; 34150 Dwt; 162 (bp) × 8.8 (531 × 28.87); —;14; Drawing is approximate.

P2 MF; H

16960: ODESSA Ru/Br 1974; P; 13800; 136.3 × 5.8 (447.6 × 19); TSM; 19.

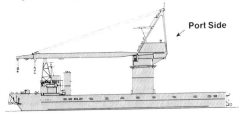

P2 MFC; H

17323: TITAN-1 Ru/Fi 1984; CS; 19800; 141.41 × 4.0 (463.94 × 13.12); TS D-E; 11; Catamaran. Funnel is on starboard side. Sister (Ru flag).

P2 MF; H2

17320: ZARNITZA Ru/DDR 1957; F; 350; 39 × 2.9 (128 × 9.7); M; 10.5.

85

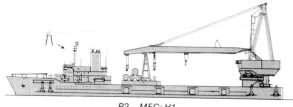

17327: STANISLAV YUDIN Ru/Fi 1985; CS; 24800; 183.2 × 8.9 (601.05 × 29.2); M; —; Helicopter deck foreward.

P2   MFC; H1

17329: JUPITER Bu/DDR 1964; Tg/IB; 500; 44.71 × 3.91 (146.69 × 12.83); TS D-E; 12.75. Sister (DDR flag).

P2   MFCK; H

17350: SPRUT Ru/Fi 1979; OSS; 2200; 77 × 5.35 (252.62 × 17.55); M; 14; Helicopter deck. Stern gantry.

P2   MF₂M; H

17480: WARNEMUNDE DDR/DDR 1962; P/TF; 6100; 136 × 4.7 (499 × 16); TSM; 18.

P2   MF₂M; H

17500: DOVATOR Ru/DDR 1955; P/Riv; 1400; 96 × 2.7 (316 × 9); M; 12. Sisters (Ru flag).

P2   MF₂M; H1

17560: PETR LEBEDEV Ru/Fi 1957; RS; 3600; 94 × 5.8 (309 × 19); M; 13.5; May be spelt **PYOTR LEBEDEV**. Sister (Ru flag).

P2   MFK; H

17580: CELTIC PRIDE Pd/Fr 1972; RoPF; 7800; 126.9 × 5.2 (416 × 17.1); TSM; 21; Bow and stern doors; chartered – Polish name is **ROGALIN**.

P2   MF; H

17634: KRAB-2 Ru/Ru 1974; Tg; 307; 41 × 2 (134.5 × 6.56); —;12; Similar—diving tenders of YELVA class operated by Ru Navy.

P2   MFK; H

17637: KAPITAN ARON Ru/Ru 1967; Fg; 169; 33.91 × 2.9 (111.25 × 9.51); M; 9.5. Sisters (Ru flag).

P2   MFK; H13

17639: BAKLAN Ru/Ja 1980; Tg; 628; 43 × 3.61 (141.08 × 11.84); TSM; —. Sister (Ru flag).

P2   MFKM; H

17660: GALATI Rm/Ja 1964; FT; 3600; 93.1 × 5 (305 × 16.3); M; 13. Sister (Rm flag).

P2   MFKM; H

17670: ERNST HAECKEL DDR/DDR 1962; RS/SS; 1600; 67.7 × 4.9 (222 × 16.1); M; 11.5.

P2   MFKM; H1

17830: FASTOV Ru/Fi 1958; C; 1700; 94.2 × 5.7 (309 × 18.7); M; 13.5. Sister (Ru flag).

P2   MFKM; H123

17920: ADMIRAL SARYCHEV Ru/Pd 1959; C; 3700; 108.3 × 6.6 (355 × 21.8); R; 12.25; 'B-31' type. Sisters (Ru flag).

P2   MFKM; H123

17940: 'B 31' type Ru/Pd —; C/B; approx 3800; 108.26 × 6.66 (355.8 × 21.85); R & LPT; approx 11.5; Several vessels in this class may be modified like this.

P2   MFKM; H2

17950: ZVYEROBOY Ru/Pd 1973; ST/S; 2000; 72.8 × 4.9 (239 × 16.2); D-E; 13; 'B-422' type. Sisters (Ru flag).

P2   MFKM; H2

17980: BODO UHSE DDR/DDR 1965; FT; 3200; 87.7 × 5.7 (288 × 18.9); M; 14. Sister (DDR flag).

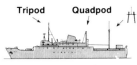

Tripod Quadpod

P2   MFKM; H2

17985: GRANITZ DDR/DDR 1965; FC; 2600; 79.79 × 5.8 (261.78 × 19.03); M; 11.75. Sister (DDR flag).

P2   MFKMK; H1

17990: MARTIN ANDERSEN NEXO DDR/FRG 1951; FF; 4800; 120.4 × 6 (395 × 19.7); M; 16.5; Converted from a cargo ship 1960.

P2   MFM; H

18090: MIKHAIL LOMONOSOV Ru/DDR 1957; RS; 3900; 102.4 × 6 (335 × 19.7); R; 13.

P2   MFM; H

18270: HAVANA Ru/FRG 1955; FC; 3100; 128.8 × 6.1 (423 × 20); M; 17; Could be called **GAVANA**. Sisters (Ru flag).

P2   MFM; H

18280: KUBA Ru/FRG 1955; FC; 3200; 130.5 × 6.1 (431 × 20); M; 16.

P2   MFM; H

18320: TSIKLON Ru/FRG 1963; FC; 4700; 135.2 × 7.2 (444 × 23.7); M; 21; Converted general cargo ship 1966. Sister (Ru flag).

P2   MFM; H

18615: AKADEMIK A. KOVALEVSKIY Ru/DDR 1949; RS; 284; 38.51 × 2.94 (126.35 × 9.65); M; 11.

Twin Funnels

P2   MFM; H

18720: NORDSEE DDR/DDR 1966; FT; 640; 48.9 × 3.5 (160.3 × 11.4); M; 12. Sisters (DDR flag).

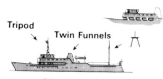

Tripod   Twin Funnels

P2   MFM; H

18740: LASKARA Pd/Pd 1968; FT; 1500; 75.6 × 5 (248 × 17); M; 14.5; 'B-29' type (later vessels have stanchions in open superstructure and more pronounced sheer foreward etc— see inset). Sisters (Pd flag).

P2   MFM; H

19985: ROSTOCK DDR/No 1977; RoPF/TF; 6100; 158.35 × 5.55 (520 × 18.21); TSM; 20.5; Stern door and 2 side doors (starboard).

P2   MFM; H

20310: SAKHALIN-1 Ru/Ru 1963; RoPF/TF; 5000; 127 × 6.2 (417 × 20.3); D-E; 18; Stern door. Sisters (Ru flag); Similar (Ru flag).

P2   MFM; H

20320: SOVIETSKIY AZERBAIDZHAN Ru/Ru 1963; RoPF/TF; 8800; 133.6 × 4.5 (438 × 15.1); TrS D-E; 14; Stern door. Sisters (Ru flag).

P2   MFM; H

20353: DMITRIY SHOSTAKOVICH Ru/Pd 1980; RoPF; 9900; 133.51 × 5.28 (438.02 × 17.32); TSM; —; 'B492' type. Sisters (Ru flag); Similar – 'B 493' type, smaller (124.8 m – 410 ft) (Ru flag).

P2   MFM; H

20370: BYELORUSSIYA Ru/Fi 1975; RoPF/P; 16600; 157 × 6.2 (516 × 20.4); TSM; 21.25; Bow, stern and side doors. Sisters (Ru flag) (one vessel has two-deck extension foreward of bridge and another is converted to cruise ship with excursion boats etc).

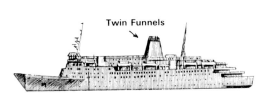

Twin Funnels

P2   MFM; H

20650: AYVAZOVSKIY Ru/Fr 1977; P; 7100; 121.49 × 4.4 (398.59 × 14.44); TSM; 18.25.

P2   MFM; H

20655: ILYCH Ru/Fi 1973; RoPCF; 12300; 128.02 × 5.92 (420.01 × 19.42); TSM; 22; Bow and stern doors.

P2   MFM; H

20731: AYU-DAG Ru/Bu 1961; RS; 900; 63.78 × 3.00 (209.25 × 9.84); M; 13; Converted from ferry. Sisters (Ru flag).

P2   MFM; H

20735: DIMITAR BLAGOEV Bu/Bu 1969; P; 1100; 68 × 5.46 (223 × 17.91); M; —. Sister (Bu flag).

P2   MFM; H

20738: KANIN Ru/Bu 1970; PC; 1100; 68 × 3.15 (223 × 10.33); TSM; 13.25. Sisters (Ru flag).

P2   MFM; H

20745: B.K. BABA ZADE Ru/Ru 1962; F; 2300; 82.4 × 3.56 (270.34 × 11.68); TS D-E; 16; May be called **K BABA ZADE**. Sister (Ru flag).

P2   MFM; H

20790: BELINSKIY Ru/DDR 1955; P/Riv; 1100; 65.2 × 2.4 (214 × 8); M; 12. Sisters (Ru flag).

P2   MFM; H

20870: YERMAK Ru/Fi 1973; IB; 12200; 135 × 11 (445 × 37); TrS D-E; 19. Sisters (Ru flag).

P2   MFM; H

20875: KAPITAN YEVDOKIMOV Ru/Fi 1983; IB; 1800; 76.5 × 2.50 (251 × 8.20); QS D-E; 13.5; River service; May be spelt **KAPITAN EVDOKIMOV**. Sisters (Ru flag); Similar (Ru flag).

P2   MFM; H

20880: PERKUN Pd/Br 1963; IB/Sal; 1200; 56.5 × 5 (185 × 16.3); TS D-E; 10.

P2   MFM; H1

21220: ARAGVI Ru/FRG 1960; R; 3600; 120.6 × 7.1 (396 × 23.3); M; 18.5. Sisters (Ru flag).

P2   MFM; H1

21240: TSIKLON Ru/FRG 1963; FC; 2100/4800; 136.02 × —/6.54 (446.26 × —/21.46); M; 21. Sisters (Ru flag).

P2   MFM; H1

21260: SCHTORM Ru/FRG 1964; R/FC; 4800; 136 × 7.1 (446.2 × 23.3); M; 21. Sisters (Ru flag).

P2   MFM; H1

21450: SHKVAL Ru/Sw 1963; R; 4200; 126.4 × 7.3 (415 × 24); M; 17.

P2   MFM; H1

21560: FALESHTY Ru/Fi 1959; C; 1700; 94.5 × 5.7 (309 × 18.7); M; 13.5. Sisters (Ru flag).

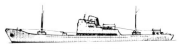

P2   MFM; H1

21580: JANA Ru/FRG 1955; FC; 3800; 111.2 × 6.2 (365 × 21); M; 14. Sisters (Ru flag).

P2   MFM; H1

21600: ZELENOGORSK Ru/Ne 1955; C/FC; 3600; 114.7 × 6.5 (377 × 18); M; 13. Sisters (Ru flag).

P2   MFM; H1

21610: AMGUEMA Ru/Ru 1962; C; 8100; 133 × 8.9 (436 × 30); D-E; 15; Polar service. Sister (Ru flag); Similar (Ru flag)— some have helicopter deck. One vessel is a research ship and has superstructure extended aft to mainmast and a helicopter deck.

P2   MFM; H1

21945: RIFT Ru/Ru 1981; RS/SS/Sub S; 780; 53.7 × 6 (176.18 × 19.69); M; 12.

P2   MFM; H1

21947: 'MIRNY' class Ru/Ru 1956-63; IC; 840; 63.4 × 4.2 (208 × 13.8); D-E; 18; Converted whalers—naval operated. Sisters (Ru flag).

P2   MFM; H1

22135: 'OREL' class Ru/Fi 1958-60; Tg/Sal; 1100; 61.3 × 3.76 (201.12 × 12.34); M; 13.5. Sisters (Ru flag).

P2   MFM; H1

22137: 'OREL' class (modified) Ru/Fi 1962-63; Tg/Sal; 1200; 61.37 × 4.71 (201.35 × 15.45); M; 15. Sisters (Ru flag).

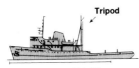

Tripod

P2   MFM; H1

22138: JANTAR Pd/Br 1958; Tg/Sal; 1200; 65.64 × 4.56 (215.35 × 14.96); M; 15.5. Sister (Pd flag).

Tripod

P2   MFM; H1

22139: 'OKHTENSKIY' class Ru/Ru approx 1958; Tg; 930 Dspl; 47.6 × 4.1 (156.1 × 13.4); D-E; 13; Mostly naval manned—approx 50 in class. Sisters (Ru flag).

P2   MFM; H1

22150: MB 18 Ru/Fi 1977; Tg; 1500; 63.51 × 5.2 (208.37 × 17.06); M; 13. Sisters (Ru flag).

Tripod

P2   MFM; H1

22154: BIZON Ru/No 1977; Tg; 645; 45.67 × 6.06 (149.84 × 19.88); M; 15.5; Twin funnels. Sister (Ru flag).

P2   MFM; H1

22155: GERAKL Ru/Ne 1974; Tg/Sal; 1700; 72.5 × 5.96 (237.86 × 19.55); M; 17; Ice strengthened. Sisters (Ru flag).

P2   MFM; H1

22159: 'PAMIR' class Ru/Sw 1959-60; Tg/Sal; 2050 Dspl; 78 × 4.1 (256 × 13.5); TSM; 17. Sisters (Ru flag)—2 are converted to intelligence collectors (AGI) and have an array of electronic equipment; extra superstructure deck and heightened funnel.

P2   MFM; H1

22160: YAGUAR Ru/Ru 1976; Tg/Sal; 2800; 92.79 × 5.8 (304.43 × 19.03); M; 18.5. Sister (Ru flag).

P2   MFM; H1

22173: PURGA Ru/Ru 1974; Tg/Sal; 1100; 58.55 × 4.67 (192.09 × 15.32); D-E; 13.25. Sisters (Ru, Pd & Bu flags); Similar—lattice tripod mainmast, taller foremast etc (Ru Navy—'SORUM' class).

P2   MFM; H1

22175: GORDYY Ru/Rm 1958; Tg; 534; 45.67 × 3.86 (149.84 × 12.66); M; 11; 'GROMOVOY' class. Sisters (Ru flag).

P2   MFM; H1

22178: ATLANT Ru/Ru 1959; Tg/Sal; 828; 52.3 × 4.59 (171.59 × 15.06); D-E; 13.5. Sisters (Ru & Rm flags).

P2   MFM; H1

22180: NIKOLAY ZUBOV Ru/Pd 1964; RS/SS; 2700 Dspl; 90 × 4.6 (295 × 15); TSM; 16.5. Sisters (Ru flag) – some are intelligence collectors.

P2   MFM; H1

22195: NEVELSKOY Ru/— —; RS; 2600 Dspl; 83 × 3.5 (272 × 11.48); M; 17; Probably built around 1960.

P2   MFM; H1

22200: KAPITAN CHECHKIN Ru/Fi 1977; IB; 1700; 77.6 × 3.25 (254.59 × 10.66); TrS D-E; 14; River Service. Sisters (Ru flag).

P2   MFM; H1

22220: DOBRINYA NIKITICH Ru/Ru 1961; IB; Approx 2300; 68 × 5.5 (223 × 18.9); TrS D-E; 13.75; May be spelt **DOBRINYA NIKITCH**. Sisters (Ru & DDR flags)—some are Naval manned.

P2   MFM; H1

22240: OTTO SCHMIDT Ru/Ru 1979; RS/IB; 2800; 73.00 × 6.62 (240 × 21.72); TS D-E; 15.

P2   MFM; H1

22250: KAPITAN M IZMAYLOV Ru/Fi 1976; IB/Sal; 1400; 56.3 × 4.2 (184 × 14); TS D-E; 14. Sisters (Ru flag).

P2   MFM; H1

22290: ANDREY I. KOROBITSIN Ru/Ru 1968; RoPCF; 1300; 55.2 × 4.6 (181.1 × 15.09); TSM; 14; May be known as **A. I. KOROBITSIN**. Sisters (Ru flag).

Tripod   Twin Funnels

P2   MFM; H1

22325: SEVER Ru/Ru 1967; RS; 1900; 71.02 × 5.02 (233 × 16.47); D-E; 13.25; Converted from stern trawler.

P2   MFM; H1

22327: ALPINIST Ru/Ru 1971; SS; 865; 53 × 4.25 (173.88 × 13.94); M; 13; Funnel on port side. Sisters (Ru flag)—some are used as intelligence collectors (AGIs) and are naval manned.

P2   MFM; H1

22330: BELONA Pd/Pd 1964; FT; 1000; 69.3 × 5 (228 × 16.7); M; 13.5; 'B-23' type. Sisters (Pd flag).

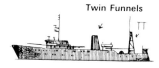

P2   MFM; H1

22350: RYBAK MORSKI Pd/Pd 1976; FT; 2600; 89 × 5.2 (292 × 17); M; 15.25; 'B-89' type. Sister (Pd flag).

P2   MFM; H12

22550: ROBERT KOCH DDR/DDR 1955; Hospital Ship; 1100; 66.1 × 4.8 (217 × 15.7); M; 14.

P2   MFM; H12

22720: SPASSK Ru/Pd —; MTV; 3800; 144.8 × 6.1 (475 × 20); TSR; 15; Converted from 'B31' type cargo vessel c 1958. Similar (Ru flag).

P2   MFM; H123

22840: YEYSK Ru/DDR 1962; C; 3200; 104.2 × 6.6 (341 × 22); M; 12.5; May be spelt **EYSK**. 'LEVANT' type or 'KOVEL' type. Sisters (Ru flag).

98

Tripod

P2   MFM; H13

23195: COTTBUS DDR/DDR 1961; Trlr; 940; 65.56 × 4.64 (215.09 × 15.22); M; 11. Sisters (DDR flag).

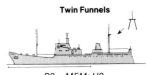

Twin Funnels

P2   MFM; H2

23305: ARNEB Ru/Ru 1973; SS; 650; 54.82 × 4.11 (179.86 × 13.48); M; 12. Sisters (Ru flag). Some have mainmast further aft.

P2   MFM; H2

23307: EISVOGEL DDR/DDR 1957; Tg/IB; 388; 39.2 × 3.55 (128.61 × 11.65); M; 12.

Twin Funnels

P2   MFM; H2

23335: TEKHUMARDI Ru/Ru 1973; RoPF; 920; 55.48 × 4.5 (182.02 × 14.76); D-E; 13.75; Bow and stern ramps. Later vessels may have no lifeboats. Sisters (Ru flag).

Twin Funnels

P2   MFM; H2

23337: KERCHENSKIY-2 Ru/Ru 1978; RoC/F; 770; 55.48 × 4.67 (182.02 × 15.32); D-E; 13.5. Sister (Ru flag).

P2   MFM; H2

23390: ZVEZDA Ru/DDR 1957; F; 350; 39.3 × 3.5 (129 × 11.4); M; 10. Sisters (Ru flag).

P2   MFM; H2

23410: RYBAK Ru/DDR 1968; SS; 1000; 63.1 × 4.8 (207 × 15.6); M;
—; 'JUNGE WELT' class. Sisters (Ru & DDR flags).

P2   MFM; H2

23440: AFALA Bu/Pd 1974; FT; 2500; 89 × 5.2 (292 × 17.3); M;
15.5; 'B-418' type. Sisters (Pd & Bu flags).

P2   MFM; H2

23474: KOLIAS Pd/Pd 1977; FT; 2400; 89.9 × 5.2 (294.95 × 17.06);
M; 16; 'B417' type. Sisters (Pd flag)—one is used for fishery
research.

P2   MFM; H2

23480: 'LUCHEGORSK' class Ru/Ru 1969; FT; 3000; 83.9 × 5.7
(275 × 19); M; 12. Sisters – some are fish carriers and some
fishery research (Ru flag).

P2   MFM; H3

23605: 'MAYAK' class Ru/Ru 1962-68; Trlr; 700; 54.3 × 3.8 (178 ×
12.47); M; 12; Inset shows starboard side of superstructure.
Sisters (Ru flag). Variations include pole foremast, short mast
from funnel, absence of lifeboats, plating round poop etc. Many
used as intelligence collectors (AGIs).

P2   MFM; H3

23607: 'OKEAN' class Ru/DDR 1959-60; Trlr; 508; 50.81 × 3.59
(166.7 × 11.78); M; 10; Starboard superstructure more open—see
inset. Sisters (Ru flag). Some used as intelligence collectors
(AGI). AGIs have variations, including extension forward of
bridge and structures on the bridge-top. One AGI has DDR flag.

P2   MFM; H3

P2   MFM; H3

23608: 'LENTRA' class Ru/DDR 1957-63; IC; 260; 39.2 × 2.8 (128.6 × 9.2); M; 11. Sisters—some modified for research and others may be fishing craft or fish carriers (Ru flag).

23609: 'LENTRA' class (modified) Ru/Ru 1957-63; IC; 330; 43.2 × 2.9 (141.7 × 9.5); M; 9. Sisters (Ru flag).

P2   MFMC; H

P2   MFMC; H1

23640: VLADIMIR KAVRAYSKIY Ru/Ru 1962; RS; 2500 Dspl; 68 × 5.5 (223 × 18.1); Tr SM; 13.75; Converted from 'Dobrynya Nikitch' class (IB); Helicopter platform aft.

23664: VOLGOGRAD Ru/Ru 1965; FC; 862; 55.12 × 3.11 (180.84 × 10.2); D-E; 10. Sisters (Ru flag).

P2   MFMC; H1

P2   MFMCN; H12

23665: SB-365 Ru/Fi 1982; Tg/Sal; 1400; 63.51 × 5.1 (208 × 16.73); TSM; 14. Sisters (Ru flag).

23685: 'SURA' or **'KIL' class** Ru/DDR 1965-78; BT/Sal; 2400; 87 × 5 (285.43 × 16.4); D-E; 12; At least 10 vessels having prefix 'Kil' (or 'Kilektor') followed by a numeral.

P2   MFMF; H

23710: WAWEL Pd/FRG 1965; RoPCF; 3800; 110.65 × 4.44 (363.02 × 14.57); TSM; 17.5; Bow door and stern door/ramp.

P2   MFMK; H

23760: BATAYSK Ru/Pd 1955; TS; 4900; 108.3 × 6.1 (355 × 21); R; 11.5; Converted from 'B-31' type cargo vessel.

P2   MFMK; H

23770: ALEKSANDR IVANOVICH VOEYKOV Ru/Ru 1959; RS; 3200; 84.7 × 5.5 (278 × 18); M; 13; Also known as **A I VOEYKOV**; Converted 'MAYAKOYSKIY' class trawler.

P2   MFMK; H

23820: LANCUT Pd/FRG 1967; RoPCF; 4400; 123.25 × 4.72 (404.36 × 15.49); TSM; 17; Bow door/ramp; Stern door;ramp; Side doors (1 port, 1 starboard).

P2   MFMK; H1

23860: PLUTON Ru/Pd 1978; RS; 2300; 82 × 4 (268.9 × 13.1); M; 18. Sisters (Ru flag).

P2   MFMK; H1

23880: NORILSK Ru/It 1951; PC; 3500; 101.9 × 5.5 (334 × 17.11); TSM; 13.

P2   MFMK; H1

23970: KAPITAN BELOUSOV Ru/Fi 1955; IB; 3700; 83.2 × 7 (273 × 23); TS D-E; 15. Sisters (Ru flag).

P2   MFMK; H123

24030: VOLGOLES Ru/Pd 1960; C/TC; 4600; 123.9 × 6.9 (406 × 22.8); M; 14.75; 'B-514' type. Similar – some are 'B 45' type (Ru flag).

P2   MFMK; H2

24145: SSV 591 Ru/Ru —; RS; 3400 Dspl; 83.6 × 6 (274 × 19.69); M; 13; Based on hull of 'MAYAKOVSKIY' class trawler. Sister (Ru flag) – has a rounded antenna cover foreward of the foremast and SSV 591 may be similarly altered.

P2   MFMK₂; H

24160: JUNGE GARDE DDR/DDR 1967; FT; 10200; 141.4 × 7.8 (464 × 25.9); D-E; 14. Sister (DDR flag).

P2   MFM₂; H

24200: EISBAR DDR/DDR 1963; SS/RS; 600; 48.87 × 4.1 (160.33 × 13.45); D-E; 10.

P2   MKF; H

24310: RODINA Ru/Pd 1979; FF; 1700/2600; 85 × —/6.0 (278.87 × —/16.96); M; 16; Helicopter deck foreward; 'B406' type. Sisters (Ru flag).

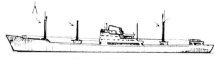

P2   MKFKM; H1

24560: SIENKIEWICZ Pd/De 1959; CP; 5300/7700; 138.7 × 7.8/8.7 (455 × 25.7/28.7); M; 16.25.

P2   MKFKM; H1

24630: PETAR BARON Bu/Br 1949; C; 7400; 139.3 × 8.4 (457 × 27.7); M; 15.

P2   MKFKM; H123

25550: 'KHASAN' class Ru/Fi 1954; C; 2600; 90.5 × 5.6 (295 × 18); R; 10. Sisters (Ru flag).

P2   MKFKM; H13

25780: VRANCEA Rm/In 1962; C; 6200/9100; 153.83 × —/8.1 (504.59 × —/26.57); M; 18.

P2   MKFKM; H13

25840: SEVERODVINSK Ru/Pd 1958; FF; 10000; 155 × 8.2 (510 × 26.11); TSR & LPT; 14.5; 'B-62' type. Sisters – some converted to fishmeal processing vessels with large housing and equipment in place of hatches 3 & 4 (Ru flag).

Twin Funnels

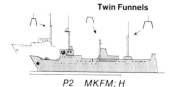

P2   MKFM; H

26210: BARENTSYEVO MORE Ru/Ru 1974; SS; 1500; 59.01 × 4,87 (193.6 × 15.98); M; 13.75; Inset shows superstructure of earlier vessels. Sisters (Ru flag).

P2 MKFM; H123

28060: 'KOLOMNA' type Ru/DDR 1956; C; 3300; 102.4 × 6.6 (335 × 21.8); R & LPT; 12.5. Sisters (Ru flag).

P2 MKFM; H13

28490: LEONID LEONIDOV Ru/Be 1957; C; 3100; 120.5 × 6.71 (395.34 × 22.01); M; 13.5.

P2 MKFM; H2

28600: 'ATLANTIK 333' type Ru/DDR 1981 onwards; FT; 1500/1900; 62.26 × 5.13 (204.27 × 16.83); M; 12.5; Also known as 'ORLYONOK' class. Twin funnels. Sisters (Ru flag).

P2 MKFMK; H1

28750: BOGDAN KHMELNITSKY Ru/Br 1954; C; 7300; 136 × 8.2 (446 × 27); R & LPT; 11.75.

P2 MKFMK; H1

28980: IVAN BABUSHKIN Ru/Be 1956; C; 1800; 101.1 × 5.8 (333 × 18.1); M; 13; Now broken up. Sisters (Ru & Bu flags).

P2 MK₂MFKMK; H13

31050: LENINSKIY KOMSOMOL Ru/Ru 1960; C; 12000; 170 × 9.7 (558 × 32); T; 19. Sister (Ru flag).

P2 MKMF; H1

31150: GEROITE NA SEVASTOPOL Bu/No 1978; RoC/TF; 9600;
185.45 × 7.42 (608.43 × 24.34); TSM; 19; Stern door. Sister (Bu
flag); Similar (Ru flag).

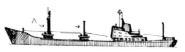

P2 MKMFK; H1

31180: GRUDZIADZ Pd/Pd 1963; C; 2900; 113.5 × 6.4 (373 × 20.2);
M; 15.5; 'B-49' type. Sister (Pd flag).

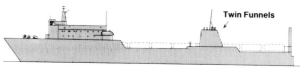

P2 MKMFK; H1

31185: MUKRAN DDR/DDR 1986; TF; 22400; 190.38 × 7.18 (624.61
× 23.56); TSM; —; Stern ramp. Sisters (Ru & DDR flags).

106

P2 MKMFM; H1

31770: LEWANT II Pd/De 1967; C; 3000; 114.5 × 6.3 (375 × 20.6); M; —. Sister (Pd flag).

P2 MKMFM; H123

31830: ARZAMAS Ru/DDR 1955; C; 3300; 102.4 × 6.6 (329 × 21.6); R & LPT; 12.5.

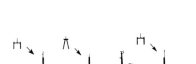

P2 MKMFM; H13

31890: MALAYA VISHERA Ru/Ru 1964; C/TC; 2900; 100.84 × 6 (331 × 19.69); M; 13. Sisters (Ru flag).

P2 M₂; H

32065: LENIN Ru/Ru 1959; IB; 14100; 134 × 10.5 (440 × 34.6); TrS T-E; 18; Nuclear-powered; New reactors fitted c. 1971.

P2 M₂; H

32080: GENERAL GAMIDOV Ru/Ru 1970; Tg/Fire; 600; 62.62 × 3.1 (205.45 × 10.17); TSM; 17. Sisters (Ru flag – naval manned – 'KATUN' class).

P2 M₂F; H

32715: WILANOW Pd/FRG 1966; RoPCF; 4000; 110.17 × 4.35 (361.45 × 14.27); TSM; 15. Similar—superstructure abaft foremast (Pd flag).

P2   M₂F; H

32890: RUGEN DDR/DDR 1972; RoPCF/F; 6500; 152 × 5.6 (500 × 18.3); TSM; 20.9; Stern and side doors.

P2   M₂F; H

32915: OSETIYA Ru/Ru 1963; P; 3200; 101.50 × 3.85 (333 × 12.63); TSM; 14.5; Rebuilt as cruise ship; BUKOVINA (see nos. 02351 and 35370) has now been modified and may be a sister of OSETIYA.

P2   M₂F; H

33015: SADKO Ru/DDR 1967; Tg; 233; 34.63 × 2.92 (113.62 × 9.58); M; 11.25. Sisters (Ru, Bu and Pd flags).

P2   M₂F; H

33017: GIRULYAY Ru/Ru 1978; SS; 282; 35.72 × 3.43 (117.19 × 11.25); M; 10.5. Sisters (Ru flag).

P2   M₂F; H1

33035: 'MOMA' class (modified) Ru/Pd 1968-72; IC; 1600 Dspl; 73.3 × 3.9 (240.5 × 12.8); TSM; 17. Sisters—one is a survey ship (Ru flag).

P2   M₂F; H1

33065: LEOPARD Ru/FRG 1977; Tg/Sal; 1000; 62.72 × 5.78 (205.77 × 18.96); TSM; 14.

P2   *M₂F; H1*

33076: NADEZHNYY Ru/Ru 1978; Fg; 455; 44.89 × 3.77 (147.28 × 12.37); M; 11.5. Sisters (Ru flag).

Tripod   Starboard

P2   *M₂F; H13*

33193: MIEDWIE Pd/Pd 1961; Trlr; 800; 61.24 × 4.42 (200.92 × 14.5); M; 12.5. Sisters (Pd flag).

P2   *M₂F; H13*

33197: HYDROMET Pd/Pd 1953/65; RS; 200; 32.57 × 2.83 (106.86 × 9.28); M; 7; Converted from side trawler 1965.

Tripod

P2   *M₂F; H13*

33198: DYUNY Ru/Bu 1971; Fg; 179; 31.7 × 2.81 (104 × 9.22); M; 9.25; 'KARELIYA' class. Sisters (Ru flag); Similar—'DALDYN' class—Ru Navy.

Twin Funnels

P2   *M₂F; H2*

33280: INOWROCLAW Pd/F 1980; RoC; 6400; 137.19 × 7.4 (450 × 24.28); TSM; 15; 2 stern doors/ramps.

P2   *M₂F; H3*

33305: RADUZHNYY Ru/Ru 1972; FC; 634; 55.0 × 4.18 (180.45 × 13.71); M;11.75. Sisters (Ru flag) (note: one may be converted to research ship).

P2 M₂FK; H12

33527: SULLEYMAN BAGIROV Ru/No 1962; RS; 800; 62.97 × 4.97 (206.59 × 16.31); M; 13; May be called **'SHELF-2'**. Converted from trawler.

Tripod   Starboard

P2 M₂FK; H13

33560: JAMNO Pd/Pd 1963; Trlr; 800; 61.24 × 4.42 (200.92 × 14.5); M;12.75. Sister (Pd flag) (note: may be others of this class with this sequence—see drawing no 33193).

P2 M₂FK; H3

33605: AKADEMIK PETROVSKIY Ru/Ru 1970; RS; 603; 54.08 × 3.67 (177.43 × 12.04); M;11.

. CL

P2 M₂FKM; H

33620: YEYSKIY LIMAN Ru/FRG 1968; R; 3400; 139 × 6.5/7.6 (456 × 21/25.2); M; 22.75. Sister (Ru flag).

P2 M₂FM; H

33870: FERDINAND FREILIGRATH DDR/Br 1967; R; 5600; 152.7 × 7.6 (501 × 25); M; 21; Also known as **F. FREILIGRATH**. Sister (DDR flag).

P2 M₂FM; H

33900: BRESTSKAYA KREPOST Ru/No 1968; FC; 4900; 139.27 × 7.92 (456.92 × 25.98); M; 22.5; Converted from reefer 1975.

P2   M₂FM; H

33910: KOTOVSKIY Ru/It 1968; R; 4100; 121.7 × 7.5 (401 × 24); M; 18. Sisters (Ru flag).

P2   M₂FM; H

33980: POLYUS Ru/DDR 1962; RS; 3900; 112 × 6 (368 × 20); D-E; 13.5.

P2   M₂FM; H

33990: BAYKAL Ru/DDR 1964; RS; 3900; 111.56 × 6 (366 × 19.69); D-E; 13.5. Sister (Ru flag).

P2   M₂FM; H1

34100: AMGUEMA Ru/Ru 1962; C; 8100; 133 × 8.9 (437 × 29); D-E; 15. Sisters (Ru flag); Similar (Ru flag) – some have helicopter deck. One vessel is a research ship and has superstructure extended aft to mainmast and helicopter deck.

P2   M₂FM; H1

34200: GERHART HAUPTMANN DDR/Br 1974; R; 4900/6700; 140.75 × 8.29/9.01 (461.78 × 27.2/29.56); M; 19. Sisters (DDR flag).

P2   M₂FM; H1

34240: NIKOLAY BURDYENKO Ru/Fr 1956; C; 3900; 129.7 × 6.8/7.5 (426 × 22.5/24.8); T; 13.75. Sisters (Ru flag).

111

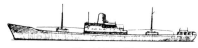

P2   M₂FM; H1

34290: SHKVAL Ru/Sw 1963; R; 4200; 126.4 × 7.3 (415 × 24); M; 17.

P2   M₂FM; H1

34330: JOHN BRINCKMAN DDR/Sw 1964; R; 4600/6300; 138.8 × —/7.9 (455 × —/25.11); M; 19. Sister (DDR flag).

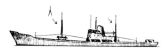

P2   M₂FM; H1

34360: SANDOMIERZ Pd/De 1966; C; 2000/3000; 99.6 × 5.7/6.3 (327 × 19/22.3); M; 12.75. Sisters (Pd flag).

P2   M₂FM; H1

34405: MAGADAN Ru/Fi 1982; IB/Tg; 5300; 92 × 6.5 (302 × 21.33); TSM; 16.5. Sister (Ru flag).

P2   M₂FM; H123

34470: YEYSK Ru/DDR 1962; C; 3200; 104.2 × 6.6 (341 × 22); M; 12.5; May be spelt **EYSK**. 'LEVANT' or 'KOVEL' type. Some ships may vary slightly. Some have large radar mast from bridge. Sisters (Ru flag).

P2   M₂FM; H2

34610: TARUSA Ru/Ru 1974; FT; 2300; 83.27 × — (273 × —); M; —. Sisters (Ru flag).

P2 M₂FMC; H

34710: ZENIT Ru/DDR 1961; TS; 4400; 104.9 × 6.2 (344 × 20); M; 13.75. Sister (Ru flag).

Twin Funnels

P2 M₂KFM; H1

34872: IVAN BOCHKOV Ru/Pd 1978; FT; 2900; 94.01 × 5.67 (308 × 18.6); M; 15.75; 'B408' type. Sisters (Ru & Pd flags); 'B408/II' version has a solid radar mast.

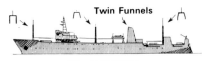

Twin Funnels

P2 M₂KFM; H1

34880: SPRUT Ru/Pd 1978; FT; 4800; 119 × 6.5 (390.42 × 21.33); M; 15. Sisters (Ru flag).

P2 M₂KMFM; H1

34960: WISMAR DDR/DDR 1968; CP; 3700/5700; 129.4 × 6.7/7.6 (424 × 22/25); M; 16; 'AFRIKA' type. Sisters (DDR flag).

P2 M₃F; H2

34985: KLYKACH Ru/Ru 1978; SS; 635; 54.8 × 4.14 (179.79 × 13.58); M; 12. Sisters (Ru flag).

Twin Funnels

P2 MN₂FM; H

35150: STAKHANOVETS KOTOV Ru/Fi 1978; RoC/Dk; 4300; 135.53 × 6.2 (444.65 × 20.34); TSM; 14.25; Stern door. Sisters (Ru flag).

P2   NCMFM; H2

35170: INGUL Ru/Fi 1962; Cbl; 5600; 130.41 × 5.2 (427.85 × 17.06); TS D-E; 14; 'KLASMA' class. Sister (Ru flag).

P2   NCMFMN; H2

35180: KATUNJ Ru/Fi 1973; Cbl; 6000; 130.41 × 5.75 (427.85 × 18.86); TS D-E; 14; May be spelt **KATYN**; 'KLASMA' class. Sisters (Ru flag).

P2   NKCMFMN; H2

35190: INGURI Ru/Fi 1978; Cbl; 6000; 130.41 × 5.75 (427.85 × 18.86); TS D-E; 14; 'KLASMA' class.

P3   CMCMF; H3

35310: KASPIY Ru/DDR 1968; FV; 1100; 65.51 × 3.61 (214.93 × 11.83); M; 10.75. Sisters (Ru flag); Similar (Ru flag).

P3   CM₂F; H

35370: KOLKHIDA Ru/Ru 1961; P; 3200; 101.5 × 4 (333 × 13); TSM; 14.5. Sisters—some ships have taller funnel; Some may not have crane (Ru flag).

P3   CM₂F; H

35390: IZUMRUD Ru/Ru 1970; RS; 3900; 99.37 × 5.4 (326 × 17.75); D-E; 13.75.

P3   KC₂MF; H3

35480: BOJNICE Cz/Hu 1966; C; 1400; 81.39 × 3.1 (267.03 × 10.16); TSM; 12. Sister (Cz flag).

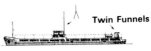

P3   KMF; H

36140: DRUZHBA SSSR-DDR Ru/DDR 1977; Riv/C/Con; —; 82 × 2.5 (269.2 × 8.57); TSM; 20.75.

P3   KMF; H123

36235: 'LUZA' class Ru/— —; Tk; 1900 Dspl; 62.5 × 4.3 (205 × 14.1); M; —; Operated by Ru Navy. Sisters (Ru flag).

P3   KMF; H123

36250: BUNKEROVSCHCHIK-3 Ru/Fi 1958; Tk; 3100; 105.11 × 6.13 (344.85 × 10.1); M; 13.5. Sisters (Ru flag).

P3   KMF; H13

36300: ZWICKAU DDR/Sw 1958; OO; 15600; 181.6 × 10.04 (596 × 32.94); M; 14.5.

P3   KMFK; H1

36390: PERELIK Bu/Ne 1958; B; 8400; 144.81 × 9.13 (475 × 29.95); M; 13.

P3   KMFK; H13

36460: ZWICKAU DDR/Sw 1958; OO; 15600; 181.6 × 10.04 (596 × 32.94); M; 14.5.

P3   KMKF; H123

36820: TOUNDYA Bu/No 1963; Tk; 26800; 213.62 × 11.76 (700.85 × 38.58); M; 15.5.

P3   KMKF; H123

36840: PRAGA Ru/Ru 1961; Tk; 20300; 202.8 × 10.99 (665.35 × 36.06); T; 17.5; May be spelt **PRAHA**. Sister (Ru flag).

P3   KMKF; H123

36890: EVENSK Ru/Fi 1963; Tk; 3400; 105.39 × 6.22 (345.77 × 20.42); M; 14. Sisters (Ru flag).

P3   KMKF; H13

37310: PLISKA Bu/Sw 1959; C; 4500; 106.41 × 7.53 (349.11 × 24.7); M; 13.5. Sister (Bu flag).

P3   KMKFK; H13

37780: TRUD Ru/Ys 1960; Tk; 17900; 192.36 × 10.24 (631.1 × 33.59); T; 16.

P3   KMK₂FK; H123

38530: PLYAVINYAS Ru/Pd 1967; Tk; 12600; 176.89 × 9.5 (580.35 × 31.17); M; 16.25; 'B-79' type. Sisters (Ru flag).

117

P3   *KMK₂FK; H123*

38580: GIORDANO BRUNO Ru/It 1964; Tk; 31300; 227.01 × 12.4
(744.78 × 39.83); M; 15.75; Also spelt **DZHORDANO BRUNO**.
Sister (Ru flag).

P3   *KMK₂FK; H123*

38610: BALDONE Ru/Pd 1963; Tk; 12600; 176.94 × 9.55 (580.51 × 31.33); M; 15.25; 'B-70' type. Sisters (Ru flag); Similar—shorter funnel and forepart of superstructure more open (Ru flag).

P3   *KMK₂MF; H123*

38950: DESNA Ru/Ru —; RT/FA; 8200; 136.5 × 7 (448.49 × 22.97); M; —; Converted from 'KAZBEK' class tanker. Sisters (Ru flag).

P3   *KM₂F; H12*

39110: CHAZHMA Ru/— 1963; MTV; 5300 Dspl; 132.8 × 6.1 (437 × 20); M; 18; Carries 1 helicopter. Similar (Ru flag).

P3   *KM₂F; H123*

39120: OLEKMA Ru/Fi 1964; RT; 3400; 105.11 × 6.22 (344.85 × 20.41); M; 13.5; Converted from tanker; May be others in this class similarly converted.

P3   KM₂F; H13

39130: BOGDAN Bu/Sw 1946; O; 8800; 149 × 8.46 (488.85 × 27.76); M; 13; Converted from ore/oil.

P3   MC₂MF; H3

39290: DRUZHBA Ru/DDR 1953; Trlr; 700; 57.26 × 2.60 (187.86 × 8.53); TS D-E; 9.25; Some sisters are fish carriers. Sisters—one converted to research (Ru flag).

P3   MCF; H123

39300: POEL DDR/DDR 1960; Tk/FA; 600 Dwt; 59.5 × 3.8 (195 × 12.5); M; 14; Type 600; operated by DDR Navy. Similar (DDR flag).

P3   MKF; H

39450: RODINA Ru/Pd 1978; FF; 1700/2600; 85 × —/6.00 (278.87 × —/19.69); M; 16; Tuna Seiner; Helicopter deck foreward; 'B406' type. Sisters (Ru flag).

P3   MK₂MF; H

39660: BAIA MARE Rm/Rm 1965; C; 2100/3100; 100.62 × 5.5/6.58 (330.12 × 18.04/21.59); M; 12.5. Sisters (Rm flag).

P3   MK₂MF; H

39670: GALATI Rm/Rm 1960; C; 2100/3100; 100.62 × 5.5/6.59 (330.12 × 18.04/21.62); M; 12.5; Heavy derrick amidships. Sisters (Rm flag).

P3   MK₂MF; H123

39960: KLAIPEDA Ru/Ru 1954; Tk; 7700; 145.5 × 8.52 (477.36 × 27.95); M; 12.25; 'KAZBEK' class.

P3   MK₂MF; H123

39970: KERCH Ru/Ru 1954; Tk; 8200; 145.5 × 8.52 (477.36 × 27.95); M; 12.25; 'KAZBEK' class. Sisters (Ru flag).

P3   MKMF; H123

40580: ANTON IVANOV Bu/Sw 1945; Tk; 8500; 147.38 × 8.51 (483.53 × 27.92); M; 13; Now converted to tanker/pollution processing—drawing shows vessel before this conversion.

P3   MKMF; H123

40660: LOKBATAN Ru/Fi 1956; Tk; 3300; 105.11 × 6.07 (344.85 × 19.91); M; 13.5.

P3   MKMKF; H

41310: ORADEA Rm/Rm 1963; C; 2100/3100; 100.62 × 5.5/6.59 (330.12 × 18.04/21.62); M; 12.5. Sisters (Rm flag).

P3   MKMK₂F; H123

41630: PRAHOVA Rm/Sw 1957; Tk; 12400; 173.41 × 9.35 (569 × 30.68); M; 13.5.

P3 M₂F; H123

42800: PEVEK Ru/Fi 1958; Tk; 3100; 105.11 × 6.13 (344.85 × 20.1); M; 13.5. Sisters (Ru flag).

P3 M₂F; H123

42960: VOLNOVAKHA Ru/Pd 1953; O; 2000; 87 × 5.36 (285.43 × 17.59); R; 9.5; 'B-30' type.

P3 M₂F; H13

43110: ZWICKAU DDR/Sw 1958; OO; 15600; 181.82 × 10.04 (595.87 × 32.91); M; 14.

P3 M₂F; H13

43300: LAMUT Ru/Ja 1959; FF; 5000; 110.27 × 5.9 (361.78 × 19.36); M; 12.5. Sister (Ru flag).

P3 M₂FK; H13

43520: AMBURAN Ru/Ge 1939; Tk; 640; 64.01 × 3.13 (210.01 × 10.27); TSM; 13.

P3 M₂FKF; H

43540: IMPULS DDR/DDR 1983; RS; 1100; 82.02 × 2.5 (269 × 8.2); TSM; 10.5.

P3   M₂KF; H123

43790: EVENSK Ru/Fi 1963; Tk; 3400; 105.39 × 6.22 (345.77 × 20.42); M; 14. Sisters (Ru flag).

P3   M₂KF; H13

44100: BOLSHEVIK KARAYEV Ru/Bu 1959; Tk; 3800; 123.5 × 4.4 (405.18 × 14.44); TSM; 10.5; Caspian Sea Service. Sisters (Ru flag)—one is a wine tanker.

P3   M₂KFK; H123

44370: ELGAVA Ru/Sw 1961; Tk; 2900; 104.88 × 6.1 (344.09 × 20.01); M; 14; May be spelt **YELGAVA**.

P3   M₂K₂F; H123

44620: LIEPAYA Ru/Ru 1960; Tk; 7600; 145.5 × 8.69 (477.36 × 28.51); M; 13. Sisters (Ru flag).

P3   M₂K₂MF; H123

44890: RAVA RUSSKAYA Ru/Ru 1960; Tk; 7700; 145.5 × 8.67 (477.36 × 28.44); M; 12.25; 'KAZBEK' class. May be others of this class with similar appearance.

P3   M₃F; H123

45110: KALININGRAD Ru/Ru 1959; FC; 5500; 130.79 × 6.72 (429.1 × 22.05); D-E; 16.5. Sisters (Ru flag).

P3   M₃F; H123

45120: YANTARNYY Ru/Ru 1964; FC; 5500; 130.92 × 6.72 (429.53 × 22.05); D-E; 16.25. Sisters (Ru flag).

P2   M₃F; H13

45210: KAMENOGORSK Ru/Ru 1957; FC; 5200; 130.92 × 7.49 (429.53 × 24.57); D-E; 18. Sisters (Ru flag); Similar—cargo ship (Ru flag).

P3   M₃KMF; H1

45270: KONSTITUTSIYA SSSR Ru/Pd 1979; FF; 15800; 178.3 × 7.2 (584.97 × 23.62); M; 14.5; 'B-670' type. Helicopter deck aft. Sisters (Ru flag).

P3   M₄FK; H1

45290: PYATIDYESYATILYETIYE SSSR Ru/Ru 1973; FF; 18500; 197.31 × 8.1 (647.34 × 26.57); M; 14.5; Also known as **50 LET SSSR**. Sisters (Ru flag).

P4   C₃MC₃MFC; H13

45350: POLTAVA Ru/Ru 1962; C; 9800; 155.68 × 9.09 (510.76 × 29.82); M; 15. Sisters (Ru flag); Similar (Hu flag).

P4   C₂MF; H13

45540: 'OSKOL' class Ru/Pd 1963/70; FA; 2500 Dspl; 90 × 4.5 (295.28 × 14.8); TSM; 16; Ru Navy.

P4   CKMF; H13

45590: MANYCH Ru/Ru 1972; A/Rmt; 7500 Dspl; 115 × 6 (377 × 20); M; —; Ru Navy. Sister (Ru flag).

P4   CMC₂MFC; H1

45630: OLA Ru/Ja 1964; C; 11100; 154.77 × 9.59 (507.78 × 31.46); M; 17.25. Sisters (Ru flag).

P4   CMCMF; H13

45680: IZHMALES Ru/Fi 1962; C; 2900; 102.32 × 5.91 (335.7 × 19.39); M; 13. Sisters (Ru flag).

P4   CMF; H

45700: 'OSKOL III' type Ru/Pd 1963/70; FA; 2500 Dspl; 90 × 4.5 (295.28 × 14.8); TSM; 16; Ru Navy.

P4   CMF; H13

45715: KODOR Ru/Ru 1962; C; 433; 49.2 × 3.26 (161.42 × 10.7); M; 10. Sisters (Ru flag).

P4   CMF; H3

45720: 'ALLIGATOR III' class Ru/Ru 1968; A/LC; 4100 Dspl; 113 × 4.4 (371 × 12); TSM; 18; Ru Navy.

P4   CMFK; H13

45730: 'AMGA' class Ru/Ru —; A/MSS; 6400 Dspl; 102 × 5.8 (361 × 19); M; 18. Sisters (Ru flag).

P4   KC$_6$MF; H1

45850: GOTHA DDR/FRG 1971; B; 24600; 203.18 × 11.6 (666.6 × 38.06); M; 16. Sister (DDR flag).

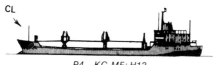

46370: LIEBENWALDE DDR/DDR 1977; C; 3500/5700; 120.61 × —/7.83 (395.7 × —/25.69); M; 16.75. Sisters (DDR flag).

P4   KC₅MF; H13

46424: KAPITAN TRUBKIN Ru/Ja 1981; B; 14600; 170.52 × 10.03 (559.45 × 32.91); M; 14.75.

P4   KC₅MFK; H1

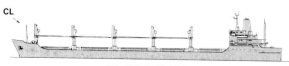

46547: PAHOM MAKARENKO Ru/Ja 1977; B; 18700; 179 × 10.95 (587.27 × 35.93); M; 15.

P4   KC₅MFK; H13

46550: KAPITAN PENKOV Ru/Ja 1981; B; 18600; 186.52 × 10.77 (611.94 × 35.33); M; —. Sister (Ru flag).

P4   KC₅MFK; H13

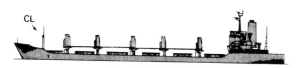

46560: VLADIMIR GAVRILOV Ru/Ja 1977; B; 20400; 177.02 × 11.16 (580.77 × 36.61); M; 15.5. Sisters (Ru flag).

P4   KC₅MFK; H13

46580: ADLER Ru/Ja 1973; B; 16400; 176.77 × 10.57 (580 × 34.68); M; 15.25. Sisters (Ru flag).

P4   KC₅MFK; H13

P4   KC₅MFK; H13

46620: YASNOYE Ru/No 1967; B; 15800; 180.3 × 10.21 (591.54 × 33.5); M; 15.

P4   KC₅MFK; H13

47070: LIEBENWALDE DDR/DDR 1977; C; 3500/5700; 120.61 × —/7.83 (395.7 × —/25.69); M; 16.75. Sisters (DDR flag).

P4   KC₄KMFK; H1

47150: MEGANOM Ru/Ja 1970; B; 15900; 170.52 × 10.06 (559.45 × 33); M; 15. Sister (Ru flag).

P4   KC₄KMFK₂; H1

47167: KAPITAN A POLKOVSKIY Ru/Ja 1978; B; 15600; 172.88 × 9.73 (567 × 31.92); M; 15.

P4   KC₄MF; H13

47540: RADAUTI Rm/Rm 1974; C; 4400/6300; 130.77 × 6.6/8.1 (429.04 × 21.65/26.57); M; 15.75. Sisters (Rm & Bu flags).

P4   KC₄MFK; H1

47674: ROMAN KARMEN Ru/Ja 1981; B/Con; 21500; 188.58 × 11.63 (618.7 × 38.16); M; 17.75. Sisters (Ru flag).

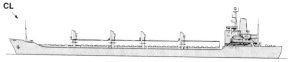

P4   KC₄MFK; H13

47860: VASILIY AZHAYEV Ru/Ja 1977; B; 20200; 180.02 × 10.89
(590.62 × 35.73); M; 15.5. Sister (Ru flag).

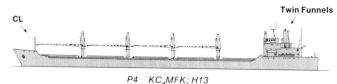

P4   KC₄MFK; H13

47939: CHERNOVTSY Ru/Bz 1983; B; 24800; 200.9 × 10.75 (659.12
× 35.27); M; 15.25.

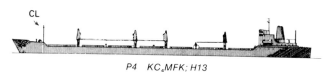

P4   KC₄MFK; H13

47990: LENINSK Ru/Sp 1975; B; 19900; 196.02 × 11.15 (643.11 ×
36.58); M; 15.25. Sister (Ru flag).

P4   KC₄MFK; H13

48150: SVILEN RUSSEV Bu/Bu 1982; B; 23100; 201.56 × 11.19
(661.29 × 36.71); M; 14.5. Sister (Bu flag); Similar (Bu & Ru flags).

P4   KC₄MFK; H13

48240: HENNIGSDORF DDR/DDR 1986; B/Con; 16800; 178.01 ×
10.9 (584 × 35.76); M; 15.75; 'OBC' type. Sisters—radar masts
may vary in design (DDR & Ru flags).

P4   KC₄MFK; H3

48380: AVDEYEVKA Ru/Ja 1977; B; 16600; 174.02 × 10.45 (570.93
× 34.28); M; 14.5.

P4   KC$_4$MFKC; H13

48383: ROJEN Bu/Bu 1978; B; 15700; 185.2 × 10.21 (607.61 × 33.5); M; 14.5. Sister (Bu flag).

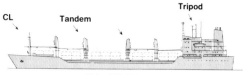

P4   KC$_4$M$_2$F; H13

48407: WARSZAWA II Pd/Pd 1986; C/Con; 11600; 149.51 × 9.14 (490.52 × 30.0); M; 16.75; 'B354' type. Sisters (Pd flag).

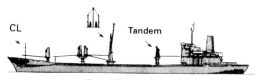

P4   KC$_3$KCMF; H1

48430: IVAN ZAGUBANSKI Bu/Ru 1975; C; 11800; 162.31 × 9.17 (532.51 × 30.09); M; 18; 'Dnepr' type. Sisters (Bu, Hu, Rm & Ru flags).

P4   KC$_3$KCMFK; H13

48480: PREDEAL Rm/Br 1966; C; 10800; 162.46 × 9.38 (533 × 30.77); M; 18.25.

P4   KC$_3$MF; H1

48650: VASILIY KOVAL Ru/De 1977; B; 25600; 182.99 × 11 (600.4 × 36.1); M; 15. Sisters (Ru flag).

P4   KC$_3$MF; H1

48660: KOPALNIA GRZYBOW Pd/Sp 1972; B; 9200; 145.01 × 8.36 (475.75 × 27.43); M; 16. Sister (Pd flag).

P4   KC₃MF; H13

48835: KOPALNIA JASTRZEBIE Pd/Br 1979; B; 11000; 158.53 × 8.38 (520 × 27.49); M; 15. Sister (Pd flag).

P4   KC₃MF; H13

48845: BERDYANSK Ru/Ja 1977; B/Con; 16700; 178.11 × 10.09 (585.35 × 35.76); M; 15.5. Sister (Ru flag).

P4   KC₃MF; H13

48860: STEPAN ARTEMENKO Ru/Ja 1977; B; 15900; 178.21 × 10.92 (584.68 × 35.83); M; 15.5. Sisters (Ru flag).

P4   KC₃MF; H13

48878: SVETLOMOR Ru/Ru 1953/79; Poll; 7600; 145.5 × 8.71 (477.36 × 28.58); TSM; 12.25; Converted from 'Kazbek' class tanker 1979.

P4   KC₃MFK; H1

49040: PIRIN Bu/Ja 1965; B; 6100; 126.02 × 7.6 (413.45 × 24.93); M; 13. Sisters (Bu flag).

P4   KC₃MFK; H13

49100: YASENYEVO Ru/No 1967; B; 15800; 180.3 × 10.21 (591.54 × 33.5); M; 15.5.

P4   KC₃MFK; H13

49160: BUZLUDJA Bu/Ja 1968; B; 9100; 139.83 × 9.26 (458.75 × 30.38); M; 15. Sisters (Bu flag).

P4   KC₃MFK; H13

49170: KAPITAN FOMIN Ru/Ja 1977; B; 19000; 179.03 × 10.95 (587.37 × 35.93); M; 15.5.

P4   KC₃MFK; H13

49210: KOPALNIA PIASECZNO Pd/Sp 1971; B; 9100; 146.72 × 8.27 (481.36 × 27.13); M; 15.5. Sister (Pd flag).

P4   KC₃MFK; H13

49240: KISHINEV Ru/Ru 1968; C (sea/river); 3600; 123.53 × 4.5 (405.28 × 14.76); TSM; 11.75. Sisters (Ru flag).

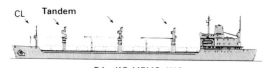

P4   KC₃MFMC; H13

49342: VIKTOR TKACHYOV Ru/DDR 1981; B/Con; 13500; 162.11 × 9.88 (532 × 32.41); M; 14.75; Ice strengthened; 'UL-ESC' type. Sisters (Ru flag).

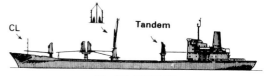

P4   KC₂KCMF; H1

49470: IVAN ZAGUBANSKI Bu/Ru 1975; C; 11800; 162.31 × 9.17 (532.51 × 30.09); M; 18; 'Dnepr' type. Sisters (Bu, Hu, Rm & Ru flags).

P4　KC₂KCMF; H13

49520: ALBA Rm/Rm 1977; C; 6100; 130.77 × 8.10 (429 × 26.57); M; 16.

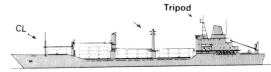

P4　KC₂KMFC; H13

49655: JACEK MALCZEWSKI Pd/Ca 1979; C/Con; 13000; 168.36 × 10.5 (552 × 34.45); M; 21.25. Sisters (Pd flag).

P4　KC₂MC₃MFC; H1

49720: OMSK Ru/Ja 1961; C; 7500/10900; 155 × 9.6 (509 × 31.5); M; 17. Sisters (Ru flag).

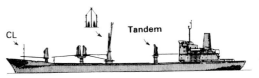

P4　KC₂MCMF; H1

49740: IVAN ZAGUBANSKI Bu/Ru 1975; C; 11800; 162.31 × 9.17 (532.51 × 30.09); M; 18; 'Dnepr' type. Sisters (Bu, Hu, Rm & Ru flags).

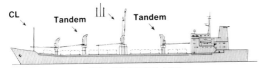

P4　KC₂MCMF; H13

49785: PEYO IAVOROV Bu/Bu 1984; C/Con; 12200; 158.88 × 9.01 (521.26 × 29.56); M; —. Sisters (Bu & Ru flags).

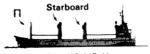

P4　KC₂MF; H

49810: ARNOLD SOMMERLING Ru/Ja 1976; C; 1600; 80.22 × 5.98 (263.19 × 19.62); M; 13.5. Sisters (Ru flag).

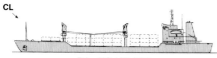

P4 KC₂MF; H13

50112: PAVLIN VINOGRADOV Ru/Pd 1987; C/Con; 4500; 131.6 × 8.8 (431.76 × 28.87); M; 14.7; 'B352' type. Sisters (Ru flag).

P4 KC₂MF; H13

50125: VARNA Bu/Sp 1987; C/Con; 7200; 123.6 × 8.0 (405.5 × 26.25); M; 14. Sister (Bu flag).

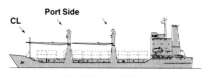

P4 KC₂MF; H13

50128: HALBERSTADT DDR/Sp 1985; Con; 6800; 122.1 × 8.01 (400.59 × 26.28); M; 14.5. Sisters (DDR flag).

P4 KC₂MF; H13

50275: 'MORSKOY 1' class Ru/Fi 1966-71; C; 1700; 87.99 × 3.31 (288.68 × 10.86); TSM; 11.75; Sea/River. Sisters (Ru flag).

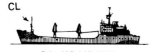

P4 KC₂MF; H13

50280: SOVIETSKIY VOIN Ru/Ru 1968; C; 1700; 82 × 5.43 (269.03 × 17.82); M; 12.75. Sisters (Ru flag).

P4 KC₂MF; H13

50440: MARLOW DDR/DDR 1971; C/Con; 300; 57.87 × 3.68 (189.96 × 12.07); M; 12; 'Boizenburg' type. Sisters (DDR flag).

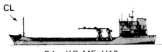

P4 KC₂MF; H13

50460: BOLESLAWIEC Pd/Br 1979; B; 3000; 95 × 6.08 (311.68 × 19.95); M; 12.25; Travelling cranes. Sisters (Pd flag)—some may not have cranes.

P4 KC₂MFC; H1

50570: 'AMUR' class Ru/Pd 1969; A/Repairs; 6400 Dspl; 115 × 5.5 (377 × 18); TSM; 18; 24 ships in class; Ru Navy.

P4 KC₂MFK; H1

50670: GRIGORIY ALEKSEYEV Ru/Ja 1974; BWC; 18400; 169.45 × 9.88 (555.94 × 32.41); M; 14.5; Travelling cranes. Sister (Ru flag).

P4 KC₂MFK; H13

50730: SOVIETSKAYA YAKUTIYA Ru/Ru 1972; C (Sea/River); 3600; 123.53 × 4.5 (405.28 × 14.76); TSM; 11.75. Sisters (Ru flag).

P4 KC₂MFK; H13

50763: VASILIY SHUKSHIN Ru/Ru 1978; C (Sea/River); 4400; 124.39 × 5.5 (408 × 18.04); TSM; 13; Has four deck cranes. Sisters (Ru flag).

P4 KC₂MFK; H13

50770: BAKU Ru/Ru 1959; C; 3400; 120.02 × 4.4 (393.77 × 14.44); TSM; 11.5; 'Caspian-Volgo-Balt' type. Sisters (Ru flag).

P4   *KC₂MFM; H13*

50900: DOLMATOVO Ru/DDR 1960; B; 6800; 139.5 × 8 (457.68 × 26.25); M; 14.25.

P4   *KC₂MFR; H13*

50908: DOBRUDJA Bu/Sp 1987; RoC/Con/C; 8800; 125.3 × 9.0 (411 × 29.53); M; 14; Angled stern ramp (starboard).

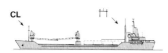

P4   *KC₂M₂F; H13*

50909: BODROG Hu/Pd 1977; C/Con; 2200; 93.53 × 5.58 (306.86 × 18.31); M; 13; 'B479' type. Sisters (Hu & Cz flags).

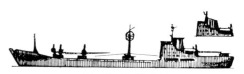

P4   *KC₂M₂FC; H13*

50910: KALININABAD Ru/Fi 1963; C; 6000/8500; 147 × 7.65/9.19 (482 × 25.1/30.15; M; 17. Sisters (Ru flag).

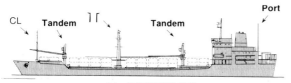

P4   *KCKCMFK; H13*

51212: ASTRAKHAN Ru/DDR 1983; RoC/C/Con; 15900; 172.32 × 10.02 (565.35 × 32.87); M; 17; Quarter door/ramp. Sisters (Ru flag).

P4   *KCK₂MF; H13*

51260: KWIDZYN Pd/Pd 1974; C; 2800; 106.38 × 5.68 (349.02 × 18.64); M; 14; 'B472' type. Sisters (Pd flag).

P4 KCKMF; H1

51370: VAYDAGHUBSKIY Ru/Fi 1986; D/Poll/Fire; 8000; 132.01 × 8.5 (433 × 27.89); TSD-E; —; Travelling crane.

P4 KCKMFC; H13

51410: DMITRIY MEDVEDYEV Ru/Ru 1983; Tk; 18500; 178.52 × 10.4 (585.7 × 34.12); M; 15. Sisters (Ru flag).

P4 KCKMFC; H2

51416: CHERNOE MORE Ru/Fr 1964; D; 5500; 120.5 × 6.32 (395.34 × 20.73); TS D-E; 14.75. Sister (Ru flag).

P4 KCMF; H

51570: POLAR DDR/DDR 1970; Sal; 385; 49.2 × 2.91 (161.42 × 9.55); —; 9.

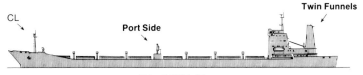

P4 KCMF; H1

51672: ION SOLTYS Ru/Ru 1976; B; 30100; 215.37 × 12.22 (706.59 × 40.09); M; 14.75; Some other vessels in this class may also have a crane amidships—see ZOYA KOSMODEMYANSKAYA no **73290**. Sisters (Ru & Bu flags); Similar—modified superstructure and kingpost between bridge and funnel (Ru flag).

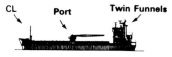

P4   KCMF; H1

51780: BALATON Hu/Sg 1979; C/Con; 1600/3300; 81.01 × 5.84/7.21 (265.78 × 19.16/23.65); M; 13; Crane may be removed. Sister (Hu flag).

P4   KCMF; H1

51910: GOGLAND Ru/Fi 1982; D; 9700; 122 × 8.02 (400.26 × 26.31); TSM; 13.75; Travelling crane.

P4   KCMF; H13

51986/1: ALEKSANDR KAVERZNEV Ru/Sw 1981; Ch; 5700; 129.65 × 6.97 (425.36 × 22.87); M; 14.25.

P4   KCMF; H13

52000: MARLOW DDR/DDR 1971; C/Con; 300; 57.87 × 3.68 (189.86 × 12.07); M; 12; 'Boizenburg' type. Sisters (DDR flag).

P4   KCMF; H13

52020: BALKHASH Ru/Ru 1969; C; 1100; 72.12 × 4.63 (236.61 × 15.19); M; 11. Sisters (Ru flag).

P4   KCMF; H13

52070: BUNA DDR/Ne 1979; Ch; 1800; 73.46 × 4.91 (241 × 16.11); M; 13. Sister (DDR flag).

138

CL

Tripod · Starboard

P4   KCMF; H13

52270: URAL Ru/Ru —; A/Spt. Nuclear; 4000 Dspl; 103 × 6 (337.92 × 19.68); M; Ru Navy.

P4   KCMFC; H13

52304: VENTSPILS Ru/Fi 1983; Tk; 5200; 113.01 × 7.2 (370.77 × 23.62); M; 14; Icebreaking. Sisters (Ru flag).

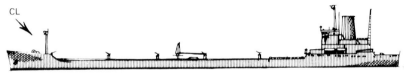

CL

P4   KCMFK; H13

52440: KHAN ASPARUKH Bu/Bu 1976; Tk; 59900; 244.48 × 15.5 (802.1 × 50.85); M; 14.5.

CL

P4   KCMFK; H13

52466: LUBOMIR Pd/Pd 1978; Tk; 1000; 64.55 × 4.7 (211.78 × 15.42); M; 11.75; 'ZB 1300' type. Sisters (Pd flag).

P4   KCMFK; H3

52605: 'MUNA' class Ru/— —; Spt; 800 Dspl; 50 × 3 (164 × 9.8); M; 10; Operated by Ru Navy—torpedo transports. Sisters (Ru flag).

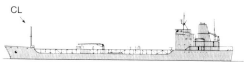

P4 KCMFKC; H13

52612/1: JOSIP BROZ TITO Ru/Ys 1984; Tk; 10900; 151.31 × 8.50 (496.42 × 27.89); M; 15; Also reported as **I. BROZ TITO**. Sisters (Ru flag).

P4 KCMFKC; H13

52616: VENTSPILS Ru/Fi 1983; Tk; 5200; 113.01 × 7.2 (370.77 × 23.62); M; 14; Icebreaking. Sisters (Ru flag).

P4 KFM; H

52745: ALI AMIROV Ru/Fr 1977; DS; 1700; 72.80 × 3.20 (239 × 10.50); TS D-E; 10.

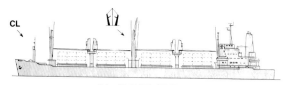

P4 K₂C₂KC₂KMF; H1

52805: PRACA Pd/Ja 1977; C/Con; 12800/19000; 171.02 × 10.9/11.5 (561.09 × 32.81/37.73); M; 17.5. Sister (Pd flag).

P4 K₂CKCMF; H13

52927: ORLIK Cz/Ys 1980; C; 6900/10400; 145.55 × 8.14/9.12 (477.53 × 26.71/29.92); M; 14.75.

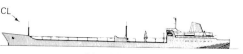

P4 K₂CMF; H13

53160: MANGYSHLAK Ru/Ru 1969; Tk; 8400; 150.02 × 8 (492 × 26.25); M; 13.5. Sisters (Ru flag).

P4   K₂CMFC; H13

53190: SCHWEDT DDR/No 1975; Tk; 33100; 211.16 × 13.22 (692.78 × 43.37); M; 17.

P4   K₄CK₂MF; H

53535: LENSOVET Ru/It 1980; LGC; 49800; 234.02 × 12 (768 × 39.37); M; 16.5. Sister (Ru flag).

P4   K₄CK₂MF; H1

53537: SMOLNYY Ru/It 1980; LGC; 25700; 197.42 × 10 (647.7 × 32.81); M; —.

P4   K₅MF; H13

54630: DONUZLAV Ru/Ja 1971; B; 19700; 185.5 × 11.15 (608.6 × 36.58); M; 14.75. Sister (Ru flag).

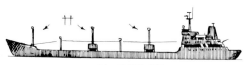

P4   K₅MF; H13

54710: NIKOLAY NOVIKOV Ru/Pd 1973; B/TC; 10200; 150.27 × 8.69 (493.01 × 28.51); M; 15; 'B-436' type. Sisters (Ru flag)—some are 'B540' type.

P4   K₅MFK; H

54870: MESTA Bu/Ja 1974; Tk; 46800; 237.01 × 12.92 (777.59 × 42.39); M; 16.5. Sister (Bu flag).

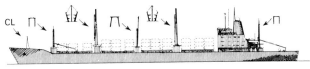

P4 K₅MFK; H1

54970: JOZEF CONRAD KORZENIOWSKI Pd/Pd 1978; C/Con; 17600; 190.28 × 9.55 (624.28 × 31.33); M; 25; 'B-467' type. Sisters (Pd flag).

P4 K₅MFK; H13

55060: DONUZLAV Ru/Ja 1971; B; 19700; 185.5 × 11.15 (608.6 × 36.58); M; 14.75. Sisters (Ru flag).

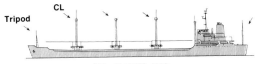

P4 K₅MFK; H13

55100: UELEN Ru/Ja 1968; B; 10000; 143.72 × 9.45 (471.52 × 31.0); M; 14.5.

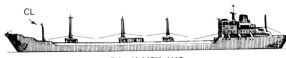

P4 K₅MFK; H13

55130: KARSKOYE MORE Ru/Fr 1972; FC; 18300; 186.8 × 7.75 (612.86 × 25.43); M; 19. Sister (Ru flag).

143

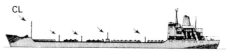

P4   K₅MFK; H13

55410: MUSALA Bu/Ja 1967; B; 9100; 139.83 × 9.26 (458.76 × 30.38); M; 14. Sisters (Bu flag).

P4   K₄MF; H1

55780: BANAT Rm/Ja 1975; Tk; 46900; 242.12 × 13.61 (794.36 × 44.65); M; 15.75. Sisters (Rm flag).

P4   K₄MF; H13

56155: BUSSEWITZ DDR/FRG 1983; LGC; 14400; 152.28 × 8.45 (499.61 × 27.72); M; 12.75.

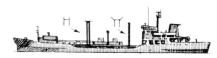

P4   K₄MF; H13

56270: DUBNA Ru/Fi 1974; RT; 6000; 130 × 7.19 (426.51 × 23.59); M; 16. Sisters (Ru flag).

144

P4 K₄MFK; H1

56480: BANAT Rm/Ja 1975; Tk; 46900; 242.12 × 13.61 (794.36 × 44.65); M; 15.75. Sisters (Rm flag).

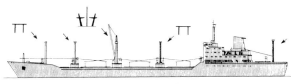

P4 K₄MFK; H13

56633: PROFESOR SZAFER Pd/Ys 1978; C/Con; 10800/16400; 180.42 × —/9.65 (592 × —/31.66); M; 22. Sisters (Pd flag).

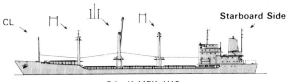

P4 K₄MFK; H13

56638: VALENTIN ZOLOTAREV Ru/DDR 1983; C/Con; 13000; 158.05 × 10.17 (518.54 × 33.37); M; 17; 'Monsun' type. Sisters (Ru & DDR flags).

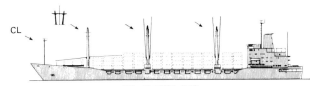

P4 K₄MFK; H13

56639: BORIS ANDREYEV Ru/Pd 1982; C/Con; 10900/15600; 176.71 × 8.63/9.99 (579.76 × 28.31/32.78); M; 18; 'B181' type. Sister (Ru flag).

P4 K₄MFK; H13

57200: DAGONYS Ru/Br 1971; B; 18600; 186.11 × 10.83 (610.6 × 35.53); M; 14.

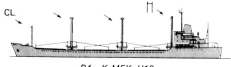

P4   K₄MFK; H13

57475: ASKOLD Ru/Ja 1972; B; 9100; 138.99 × 9.34 (456 × 30.64); M; 13.5.

P4   K₄MFK; H13

57540: BOLGRAD Ru/DDR 1969; C; 4100; 114.71 × 6.73 (376.35 × 22.08); M; 14.5. Sister (Ru flag).

P4   K₄MFK; H13

57630: LENINAKAN Ru/Ja 1964; Tk; 23100; 207.04 × 11.11 (679.27 × 36.45); M; 16.5. Sisters (Ru flag).

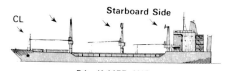

P4   K₄MFR; H13

57760: IZVESTIYA Ru/De 1978; RoC/C/Con; 8800; 132.9 × 9.43 (436.02 × 30.94); M; 16.5; 'Hamlet-Multiflex' type; quarter stern door/ramp (starboard). Sister (Ru flag).

P4   K₃MF; H

58140: KARLOVY VARY Cz/Ja 1974; B; 13600; 164.37 × 9.87 (539.27 × 32.38); M; —; 'Fortune' type.

146

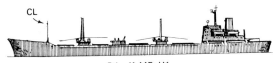

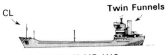

P4 K₃MF; H1

58510: PYATIDYESYATILYETIYE SSSR Ru/Ru 1973; FC; 13100; 172.12 × 8.1 (564.7 × 26.57); M; 19; Also known as **50 LET SSSR**. Sisters (Ru flag).

P4 K₃MF; H13

58730: NIEWIADOW Pd/Pd 1978; C; 1600; 84.18 × 5.73 (276.18 × 18.8); M; 14; Launched as *Ran*; 'B-431' type. Sister (Pd flag).

P4 K₃MF; H13

58995: SERGEY KIROV Ru/Rm 1983; Tk; 5900; 147.02 × 5.3 (482.35 × 17.39); TSM; 12.5. Sisters (Ru flag).

P4 K₃MF; H13

59220: FILIPP MAKHARADZE Ru/Pd 1972; B; 20300; 198.71 × 10.68 (651.93 × 35.03); M; 15; 'B-447' type. Sisters (Ru & Pd flags).

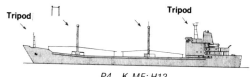

P4   K₃MF; H13

59230: SLAPY Cz/Ys 1981; C; 6900/10400; 145.55 × 8.14/9.12 (477.53 × 26.71/29.92); M; 14.75. Sisters (Cz flag).

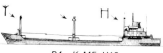

P4   K₃MF; H13

59650: KLOSTERFELDE DDR/DDR 1972; C; 3100; 104.91 × 6.39 (344.19 × 20.97); M; 14.5. Sisters (DDR flag).

p4   K₃MF; H13

59690: ZULAWY Pd/Pd 1974; FC; 8100; 151.31 × 7.4 (496.42 × 24.28); M; 19; 'B68' type. Sisters (Pd flag).

P4   K₃MFC; H13

59880: BORIS CHILIKIN Ru/Ru 1971; Rmt; 23400 Dspl; 162 × 8.6 (532 × 28.1); M; 16.5; Naval auxiliary. Similar (Ru flag).

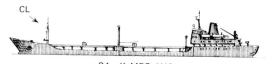

P4   K₃MFC; H13

59890: VELIKIY OKTYABR Ru/Ru 1967; Tk; 11000; 162.31 × 8.93 (532.51 × 29.3); M; 16.25. Sisters (Ru & Bu flags).

P4   K₃MFK; H1

60360: BELCHATOW Pd/Ja 1976; B; 39300; 232.37 × 13.85 (762 ×
45.44); M; 14.5. Sister (Pd flag).

Twin Funnels

P4   K₃MFK; H1

60373: OLEG KOSHEVOY Ru/Ru 1980; Tk; 4100; 125.61 × 4.2
(412.11 × 13.78); TSM; —; Sea/river service. Sisters (Ru flag).

P4   K₃MFK; H1

60484: LEOPOLD STAFF Pd/FRG 1977; C/Con; 6700/9800; 149.82
× 8.18/9.23 (491.54 × 26.84/30.28); M; 16.5; '36-L' type.

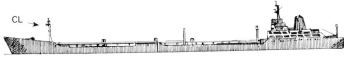

P4   K₃MFK; H123

60500: GIUSEPPE VERDI Ru/It 1964; Tk; 30300; 227.9 × 12.14
(747.7 × 39.83); M; 16; Launched as *Maria Adelaide*; May be spelt
DZHUZEPPE VERDI. Sister (Ru flag).

P4   K₃MFK; H13

60620: DAUGAVPILS Ru/Ys 1965; Tk; 15100; 186.21 × 9.84 (610.93 × 32.28); M; 17. Sisters (Ru flag).

P4   K₃MFK; H13

60660: LUBNY Ru/Ja 1964; Tk; 22100; 206.99 × 11.08 (679 × 36.35); M; 16.5. Sisters (Ru flag).

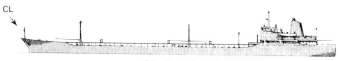

P4   K₃MFK; H13

60670: LENKORAN Ru/Ja 1962; Tk; 22500; 207.04 × 11.07 (679.27 × 36.32); M; 16.5. Sister (Ru flag).

P4   K₃MFK; H13

60680: INTERNATSIONAL Ru/Pd 1968; Tk; 13800; 177.27 × 9.37
(581.59 × 30.74); M; 16; 'B-72' type. Sisters (Ru flag).

P4   K₃MFK; H13

60720: STRUMA Bu/Sw 1966; Tk; 41000; 239.25 × 12.73 (784.94 ×
41.77); M; 14.

P4   K₃MFK; H13

60900: GEORGIY LEONIDZE Ru/Pd 1974; B; 20300; 202.34 × 10.64
(663.85 × 34.91); M; 15; 'B447' type. Sister (Ru flag).

P4 K₃MFK; H13

60971: POLAR VII Rm/Rm 1980; FC; 6100; 129.6 × 7.5 (425 × 24.61); M; 16.5. Sisters (Rm flag).

P4 K₃MFK; H13

60978: RAZBOIENI Rm/Rm 1982; C/Con; 7100/11400; 158.71 × —/9.6 (520.7 × —/31.5); M; —. Sisters (Rm flag).

P4 K₃MFK; H13

61020: RIURENI Rm/Rm 1981; C/Con; 10000; 145.09 × 10.13 (476 × 33.23); M; 15. Sisters (Rm flag).

P4 K₃MFK; H13

61090: KOPALNIA MOSZCZENICA Pd/De 1968; B; 8400; 141.71 × 8.2 (464.93 × 26.9); M; 15.25. Sisters (Pd flag).

P4 K₃MFK; H13

61100: RIZHSKIY ZALIV Ru/Fr 1969; FC; 12900; 164.62 × 7.01 (540.09 × 23); M; 17.5. Sisters (Ru flag).

P4 K₃MFK; H13

61270: PRIBOY Ru/Sw 1964; FC; 10900; 156.93 × 7.4 (514.86 × 24.28); M; 18.25. Sisters (Ru flag).

152

P4   K₃MFK; H13

61400: CRIMMITSCHAU DDR/DDR 1979; C; 9200; 149.99 × 9.05 (492.09 × 29.69); M; 17. Sisters (DDR flag).

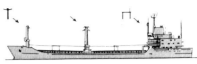

P4   K₃MFK; H13

61700: BURG DDR/DDR 1974; C; 6000; 121.75 × 7.73 (399.44 × 25.36); M; 15.5. Sisters (DDR & Ru flags).

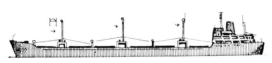

P4   K₃MFK; H13

61840: YAKHROMA Ru/No 1967; B; 13000; 166.45 × 10.17 (546.1 × 33.37); M; 15.5.

P4   K₃MFK; H13

62050: FIOLENT Ru/Tw 1973; B; 17000; 181.21 × 10.27 (594.52 × 33.69); M; 15.25.

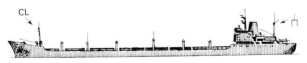

P4   K₃MFM; H13

62460: ZVENIGOROD Ru/Pd 1967; B; 16000; 187.15 × 9.54 (614 × 31.29); M; 15.5. 'B 470' type. Sisters (Ru & Pd flags).

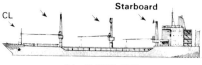

P4   K₃MFR; H13

62480: IZVESTIYA Ru/De 1978; RoC/C/Con; 8800; 132.9 × 9.43 (436.02 × 30.94); M; 16.5; Quarter stern door/ramp (starboard); 'Hamlet-Multiflex' type. Sister (Ru flag).

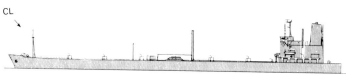

P4   K₃MKF; H

62495: ADYGEJA Ru/Ja 1982; Tk; 31800; 224.98 × 12.52 (738.12 × 41.08); M; 14.5.

P4   K₃MKFK; H13

62570: LUBNY Ru/Ja 1964; Tk; 22100; 206.99 × 11.08 (679 × 36.35); M; 16.5. Sisters (Ru flag).

P4 K₃MKFK; H13

62580: DAUGAVPILS Ru/Ys 1965; Tk; 15100; 186.21 × 9.84 (610.93 × 32.28); M; 17. Sisters (Ru flag).

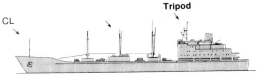

P4 K₃M₂F; H1

62671: ALMAZNYY BEREG Ru/DDR 1978; FC; 7900; 152.69 × 8 (500.95 × 26.25); M; 17; 'Kristal' type. Sisters (Ru flag); Similar—'Kristal II' type (Ru & DDR flags).

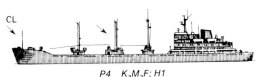

P4 K₃M₂F; H1

62680: KARL LIEBKNECHT Ru/DDR 1970; FC; 8400; 155 × 7.79 (508.53 × 25.58); M; 17.25; 'Polar' type. Sisters (Ru flag).

P4 K₃M₂F; H1

62701: ANTANAS SNECHKUS Ru/DDR 1974; FC; 8300; 152.25 × 8.17 (499.51 × 25.8); M; 17.25; Launched as *Ignalina*; 'Polar' type. Sisters—some have tripod mast (see inset) (Ru, Rm & DDR flags).

P4 K₃M₂F; H13

62730: DUBNA Ru/Fi 1974; RT; 6000; 130 × 7.19 (426.51 × 23.59); M; 16. Sisters (Ru flag).

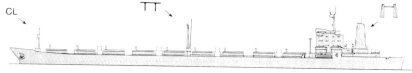

P4   K₂MF; H

63570: BORIS BUTOMA Ru/Ru 1978; BO; 63200; 258.22 × 15.65 (847.17 × 51.34); M; 15. Sisters (Ru flag).

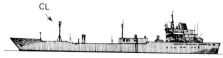

P4   K₂MF; H

63640: YURMALA Ru/FRG 1976; LGC; 9100; 139.71 × 8.22 (458.37 × 26.97); M; 16.25. Sisters (Ru flag).

P4   K₂MF; H1

63975: POBYEDA Ru/Ru 1981; Tk; 37400; 242.81 × 13.6 (796.62 × 44.62); M; 15.75. Sisters (Ru flag).

P4   K₂MF; H1

63980: KRYM Ru/Ru 1975; Tk; 88700; 295.05 × 17 (968.01 ×
55.77); T; 17; Used as production and storage vessel. Sister (Ru
flag).

P4   K₂MF; H1

63982: KAVKAZ Ru/Ru 1977; Tk; 88700; 295.21 × 17 (968.54 ×
55.77); T; 15.75. Sisters (Ru flag).

P4   K₂MF; H1

64568: KAPITAN E. EGOROV Ru/Sw 1982; OBO; 31800; 206.89 ×
12.66 (678.77 × 41.54); M; 16; May be spelt **KAPITAN YE
YEGOROV**. Sister (Ru flag).

P4   K₂MF; H13

65850: FELIKS DZIERZYNSKI Pd/Pd 1978; B; 20300; 198.18 × 11
(650.2 × 36.09); M; 15.2; 'B-517' type. Sisters (Pd flag).

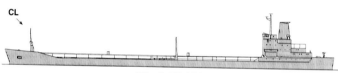

P4   K₂MF; H13

66170: GEROI SEVASTOPOLYA Ru/No 1979; Tk; 28300; 207.42 ×
12.7 (680.51 × 41.67); M; 15.25. Sisters (Ru flag).

P4   K₂MF; H13

66380: KALININGRADNEFT Ru/Fi 1978; RT/Tk; 4500; 115.53 × 6.5
(379.04 × 21.33); M; 16. Sisters (Ru flag).

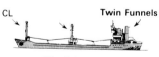

P4   K₂MF; H13

66980: JAROSLAW Pd/Pd 1979; C; 1600; 84 × 5.65 (275.59 ×
18.54); M; 14; 'B431' type.

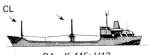

P4 K₂MF; H13

67010: ANTON GUBARYEV Ru/Rm 1974; C; 1200/2100; 88.75 × 4.15/5.2 (291.17 × 13.62/17.06); M; 13. Sisters (Ru flag).

P4 K₂MF; H13

67081: FLORA Pd/Pd 1967; C; 299; 44.76 × 3 (146.85 × 9.84); M; 9.

P4 K₂MF; H13

67170: BELOPOLYE Ru/No 1977; TB/Ch; 1500; 69.73 × 5.4 (228.77 × 17.72); M; 11.5.

P4 K₂MF; H13

67350: ROSTOK Ru/DDR 1973; C; 2900/4500; 117.79 × 5.8/6.92 (386.45 × 19.03/22.7); M; 16.5; 'POSEIDON' class. Sisters (Ru flag).

P4 K₂MF; H13

67395: 'VOLGONEFT' type Ru/Ru-Bu 1966-82; Tk; 3500; 135 × 3.50 (442.91 × 11.81); TSM; 10.5; Sea/river type. Sisters (Ru flag).

Tripod

P4   K₂MFC; H

67530: ISKAR 2 Bu/It 1974; Tk; 126400; 349 × 20 (1145 × 65.62); M; 15.

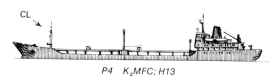

CL

P4   K₂MFC; H13

67650: VELIKIY OKTYABR Ru/Ru 1967; Tk; 11000; 162.31 × 8.93 (532.51 × 29.3); M; 16.25. Sisters (Ru & Bu flags).

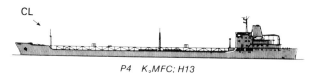

CL

P4   K₂MFC; H13

67670: ASHKHABAD Ru/Ys 1978; Tk; 15600; 183.01 × 10 (601 × 32.81); M; 16.75. Sisters (Ru flags).

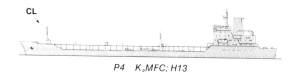

CL

P4   K₂MFC; H13

67677: TATRY Pd/Sw 1975; Tk; 18200; 170.57 × 11.07 (559.51 × 36.32); M; 15. Sister (Pd flag).

CL

P4   K₂MFC; H13

67680: KOMANDARM FEDKO Ru/Ru 1976; Tk; 18500; 178.49 × 10.4 (585.6 × 34.12); M; 15.25; Some sisters may be K₂MFKC—see No. 71433. Sisters (Ru flag).

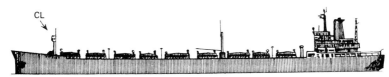

Twin Funnels

CL

P4   K₂MFC; H13

67690: FELIKS DZIERZYNSKI Pd/Pd 1978; B; 20300; 198.18 × 11 (650.2 × 36.09); M; 15.2; 'B-517' type. Sisters (Pd flag).

CL

P4   K₂MFK; H

68250: MARSHAL BUDYONNYY Ru/Pd 1975; OBO; 59600; 245.52 × 16 (805.51 × 52.49); M; 16; 'B-524' type. Sisters (Ru flag).

CL

P4   K₂MFK; H1

68560: MESTA Bu/Ja 1974; Tk; 46800; 237.01 × 12.92 (777.59 × 42.39); M; 16.5. Sister (Bu flag).

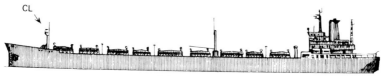

P4   K₂MFK; H1

68800: MARSHAL BUDYONNYY Ru/Pd 1975; OBO; 59600; 245.52
× 16 (805.51 × 52.49); M; 16; 'B-524' type. Sisters (Ru flag).

P4   K₂MFK; H1

68805: MARSHAL GRECHKO Ru/Pd 1978; OBO; 65800; 245.5 ×
17.5 (805.45 × 57.41); M; 14.5; 'B-527' type. Sisters (Ru flag).

P4   K₂MFK; H1

68920: ZAWRAT Pd/Ja 1975; Tk; 81200; 293 × 15.29 (961.29 ×
50.16); M; 16.25. Sisters (Pd flag).

P4 K₂MFK; H1

69310: NIKOLAY ZHUKHOV Ru/Ru 1972; C; 4000/6500; 136.81 × 6.51/7.5 (448.85 × 21.36/24.61); M; 16.5. Sisters (Ru flag).

P4 K₂MFK; H13

69725: ISKAR Bu/Ja 1966; Tk; 15900; 174 × 10.06 (571 × 33.01); M; 13.5. Sister (Bu flag).

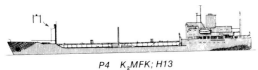

P4 K₂MFK; H13

70020: SAMOTLOR Ru/Fi 1975; Tk/IB; 12200; 160 × 9.17 (524.93 × 30.09); M; 16.25. Sisters (Ru flag).

P4 K₂MFK; H13

70165: URZHUM Ru/Gr 1983; Tk; 18300; 170.69 × 10.76 (560 × 35.3); M; 16. Sisters (Ru flag).

P4 K₂MFK; H13

70540: SYN PULKU Pd/Pd 1974; B; 20600; 199.17 × 10.63 (653.44 × 34.88); M; 15.25. 'B 447' type. Sisters (Pd flag).

P4   K₂MFK; H13

70572: MAYKOP Ru/Br 1975; Tk; 19600; 171 × 11.3 (561 × 37.07);
M; 15; Launched as *Helena K*. Sisters (Ru flag).

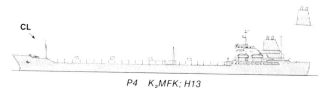

P4   K₂MFK; H13

70590: MATE ZALKA Ru/Ys 1976; Tk; 27700; 195 × 12.2 (639.76 ×
40.03); M; 17. Sisters—some have taller funnel (Ru flag).

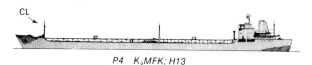

P4   K₂MFK; H13

70610: KUTAISI Ru/Ys 1976; Tk; 15700; 182.99 × 10 (600.36 ×
32.81); M; 17. Sister (Ru flag).

P4   K₂MFK; H13

70695: JENA DDR/DDR 1978; B/Con; 16000; 176.69 × 10.11 (580
× 33.17); M; 16. Sisters (DDR flag).

P4   K₂MFK; H13

70698: ZIEMIA CHELMINSKA Pd/Ar 1984; B; 16700; 180.25 × 9.85 (591.37 × 32.32); M; 14.5. Sisters (Pd flag).

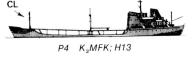

P4   K₂MFK; H13

70740: KAPITAN SHVETSOV Ru/Bu 1973; Tk; 4200; 116.08 × 6.69 (381 × 21.95); M; 14. Sisters (Ru flag).

P4   K₂MFK; H13

70760: AKTAU Ru/Fi 1967; Tk; 3500; 106.15 × 6.74 (348.26 × 22.11); M; 13.25. Sisters—some have bipod mast foreward (Ru flag).

P4   K₂MFK; H13

70800: AUSKEKLIS Ru/Fi 1970; Tk; 3500; 106.15 × 6.74 (348.26 × 22.11); M; 13.25. Sisters (Ru flag).

P4   K₂MFK; H13

70810: PRUT Ru/Fi 1971; RT; 3700; 106.08 × 6.5 (348.03 × 21.33); M; 14; Converted from oil tanker of 'Altay' class. Sisters (Ru flag).

P4   K₂MFK; H13

70955: TERRAL Pd/Pd 1980; FC; 2300; 90.99 × 5.36 (298.5 × 17.59); M; 15.5; 'B361' type. Sisters (Pd flag).

P4   K₂MFK; H13

71040: PIONER MOSKVY Ru/Ru 1973; C/Con; 4800; 130.31 × 7.36 (428 × 24.15); M; 15.5. Sisters (Ru & DDR flags).

P4   K₂MFK; H13

71310: OSTROV RUSSKIY Ru/Sw 1969; FC; 9800; 150.55 × 7.47 (494 × 24.51); M; 18.25. Sisters (Ru flag).

P4   K₂MFK; H13

71360: ROSTOK Ru/DDR 1973; C; 2900/4500; 117.79 × 5.8/6.92 (386.45 × 19.03/22.7); M; 16.5; 'POSEIDON' class. Sisters (Ru flag).

P4   K₂MFKC; H13

71433: ALEKSANDR TSULUKIDZE Ru/Ru 1978; Tk; 18500; 178.49 × 10.4 (586 × 34.12); M; 15.25; May be several in this class with this appearance—see No 67680; Kingpost abaft funnel is on port side and the crane on the starboard side. Sister (Ru flag).

P4   K₂MFR; H

71530: MAGNITOGORSK Ru/Fi 1975; RoC; 15300; 205.8 × 9.7 (675.2 × 31.82); M; 22; Stern door and angled ramp. Sisters—one has lifeboats foreward of bridge (Ru flag).

P4   K₂MK₃MFK; H13

71670: LENINSKIY LUCH Ru/Ja 1964; FF; 5000; 115.02 × 5.6 (377 × 18.37); M; 14. Sisters (Ru flag).

P4   K₂MK₂MF; H13

71680: PRIGNITZ DDR/Ne 1967; C; 4200/6100; 135.79 × 6.67/7.61 (446 × 21.88/24.97); M; 17. Sisters (DDR flag).

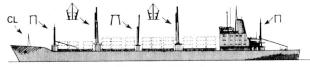

P4   K₂MKM₂FK; H1

71810: JOZEF CONRAD KORZENIOWSKI Pd/Pd 1978; C/Con; 17600; 190.28 × 9.55 (624.28 × 31.33); M; 25; 'B-467' type. Sisters (Pd flag).

P4   K₂M₂F; H1

71820: 50 LET SSSR Ru/Ru 1973; FC; 13100; 172.12 × 8.1 (564.7 × 26.57); M; 19; also known as **PYATIDYESYATILYETIYE SSSR**. Sisters (Ru flag).

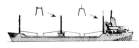

P4   K₂M₂F; H13

71900: ARTERN DDR/Pd 1971; C; 1600; 84.13 × 5.28 (276.02 × 17.32); M; 12.5; 'B431' type. Sister (DDR flag).

CL

P4   K₂M₃F; H13

72115: MAJOR HUBAL Pd/Pd 1985; B; 21500; 195.21 × 10.68 (640 × 35.04); M; —; 'B542' type. Sisters (Pd flag); similar—'B545' type (Pd flag).

P4   K₂M₃F; H13

72116: PETROSENI Rm/Rm 1968; B; 9600; 148.72 × 7.93 (487.93 × 26.02); M; 12.5.

CL   Twin Funnels

P4   KMF; H1

73290: ZOYA KOSMODEMYANSKAYA Ru/Ru 1973; B; 30100; 215.37 × 11.73 (706.59 × 38.48); M; 15.7. Sisters—some have small crane amidships (Ru & Bu flags).

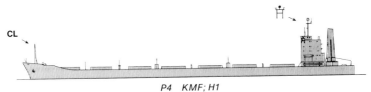

CL

P4   KMF; H1

73374: OSSOLINEUM Pd/Ar 1986; B; 35800; 224.54 × 12.40
(736.68 × 40.68); M; 14. Sister (Pd flag).

CL

P4   KMF; H1

73550: TARNOBRZEG Pd/Sw 1973; Ch; 7000; 146.11 × 7.61
(479.36 × 24.97); M; 14.5. Sisters (Pd flag).

CL   Tripod

P4   KMF; H1

73650: SYRENKA Pd/Pd 1961; Con; 1100; 72.32 × 4.5 (237.27 ×
14.76); M; 11.5; Lengthened 1978; 'B-57' type. Sold—now Sri
Lankan flag. Sister (Pd flag).

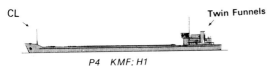

CL   Twin Funnels

P4   KMF; H1

73997: SIBIRSKIY 2101 Ru/Fi 1979; C (sea/river); 3200; 127.5 × 3
(418 × 9.84); M; 11. Sisters (Ru flag).

CL   Twin Funnels

P4   KMF; H1

74000: SIO Hu/Sg 1979; C/Con; 1600/3600; 81.01 × 5.75/7.21 (266
× 18.86/23.65); M; 13.

P4   KMF; H1

74140: NALECZOW Pd/Rm 1970; C; 1200/2000; 85.88 × 4.5/5.1
(281.76 × 14.76/16.73); M; 14. Similar (Pd flag).

P4   KMF; H13

74515: ZIEMIA KIELECKA Pd/It 1969; B; 15700; 190.48 × 10.59
(624.93 × 34.74); M; 16. Sister (Pd flag).

P4   KMF; H13

74540: FILIPP MAKHARADZE Ru/Pd 1972; B; 20300; 198.71 ×
10.68 (651.93 × 35.03); M; 15; 'B-447' type. Sisters (Ru & Pd flags).

P4   KMF; H13

74655: KOPALNIA GOTTWALD Pd/Br 1980; B; 11000; 158.73 × 8.38 (521 × 27.49); M; 14.75. Sisters (Pd flag).

P4   KMF; H13

74660: ZIEMIA BYDGOSKA Pd/Br 1967; B; 15700; 179.51 × 9.91 (588.94 × 32.51); M; 15. Sister (Pd flag).

P4   KMF; H13

74820: THALE DDR/FRG 1960; B; 14500; 171.79 × 10.28 (563.62 × 33.73); M; 14.75.

P4   KMF; H13

75170: BUNA DDR/Ne 1979; Ch; 1800; 73.46 × 4.91 (241.01 × 16.11); M; 13. Sister (DDR flag).

P4   KMF; H13

75312: KAPITAN VOOLENS Ru/Fi 1981; C/Con; 1400; 82.5 × 5.05 (270.67 × 16.57); M; —. Sisters (Ru flag).

P4   KMF; H13

75320: BOLTENHAGEN DDR/DDR 1970; C/Con; 300; 57.79 × 3.68 (189.6 × 12.07); M; 12. Sisters (DDR & Ru flags).

P4 KMF; H13

75327: HAJNOWKA Pd/Pd 1971; C/Con; 800; 59.82 × 4.2 (196 × 13.78); M; 11.5; 'B-457' type. Sisters (Pd flag).

P4 KMF; H13

75330: FRITSIS ROSIN Ru/DDR 1971; C/Con; 500; 71.07 × 3.68 (233.17 × 12.07); M; 12. Sisters (Ru & DDR flags).

P4 KMF; H13

75350: 'BALTIYSKIY' type Ru/Ru 1962-68; C (sea/river); 1900; 95.61 × 3.26 (313.68 × 10.7); TSM; 10; Most of this class of over 70 ships have the sequence KMFK—which see; Funnel heights vary.

P4 KMF; H13

75360: 'LADOGA' class Ru/Fi 1972-74; C (sea/river); 1600; 81.01 × 4.01 (265.78 × 13.16); TSM; 12. Sisters—funnels vary in shape and height (Ru flag).

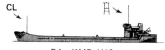

P4 KMF; H13

75380: BALTIYSKIY 101 Ru/Fi 1978; C/Con (sea/river); 2000; 95 × 4 (311.68 × 13.12); TSM; 11.5; Hinged masts. Sisters (Ru flag).

P4 KMF; H13

75392: PAVEL YABLOCHKOV Ru/Fi 1980; C/TS; 2200; 95 × 4 (311.68 × 13.12); TSM; 12.5. Sisters (Ru flag).

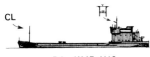

P4 KMF; H13

75400: SAYMENSKIY KANAL Ru/Fi 1978; C (sea/river); 1600; 81.01 × 4 (265.78 × 13.12); TSM; 12. Sisters (Ru flag).

P4 KMF; H13

75412: MIELEC Pd/Br 1980; B; 3000; 95 × 6.05 (312 × 19.85); M; 13.5. Sisters (Pd flag).

P4 KMF; H13

75640: KESSULAID Ru/Tu 1972; RoC/Con; 1000; 80.22 × 4.15 (263.19 × 13.62); M; 13; Stern door. Similar (Ru flag).

P4 KMF; H13

75730: ZAGLEBIE DABROWSKIE Pd/Pd 1967; B; 11000; 156.37 × 9.51 (513.02 × 31.2); M; 15.5; 'B-520' type. Sisters (Pd flag).

P4 KMF; H13

75770: TARNOW Pd/Pd 1970; O; 3800; 108.77 × 6.86 (356.86 × 22.51); M; 14; 'B-522' type. Sisters (Pd flag).

P4 KMF; H13

75790: VERILA Bu/Bu 1969; B; 7800; 134.02 × 7.48 (439.7 × 24.54); M; 13. Sisters (Bu flag).

P4 KMF; H13

76220: STAROGARD GDANSKI Pd/Sp 1971; RoC; 1000; 79.33 × 4.7 (260.27 × 15.42); M; 14; Stern door; 'Porter' type.

P4 KMF; H13

76310: ALTAIR Ru/It 1970; Tk/WT; 1200; 68.92 × 4.6 (226.12 × 15.09); M; 12. Sister (Ru flag).

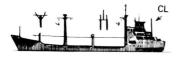

P4 KMF; H13

76580: ABRAM ARKHIPOV Ru/Fi 1973; C/TC; 3200; 97.31 × 6.7 (319.26 × 21.98); M; 14. Sisters (Ru flag).

P4 KMF; H13

76665: SNIEZKA Pd/Pd 1970; Wa; 525; 57.61 × 3.35 (189 × 10.99); M; 8.5.

P4 KMF; H13

76715: TURINSK Ru/Hu 1958; C; 1200; 70.19 × 3.83 (230.28 × 12.57); TSM; 9.5; 'Korsakov' class.. Similar (Ru flag).

P4 KMF; H3

76865: SREDETZ Bu/It 1975; RoC/P/F; 3200; 141.71 × 5.82 (464.93 × 19.09); TSM; 14.5; Stern door/ramps (1 port, 1 starboard); Ice strengthened; lengthened.

174

P4   KMF; H3

76890: ALIOT Ru/Fi 1970; WT/Ch; 3100; 93.88 × 6.5 (308.01 × 21.33); M; 14. Sisters (Ru flag).

P4   KMF; H3

76900: STAROGARD GDANSKI Pd/Sp 1971; RoC; 1000; 79.33 × 4.7 (260.27 × 15.42); M; 14; Stern door; 'Porter' type.

P4   KMF; H3

76945: DNEPR Ru/Ru 1969; FC; 1400; 72.07 × 3.6 (236.45 × 11.81); M; 12.25. Sisters (Ru flag).

P4   KMFC; H1

76984: HUTA LENINA Pd/Ja 1976; B; 36200; 223.98 × 13.35 (735 × 43.8); M; 14.5. Sisters (Pd flag).

175

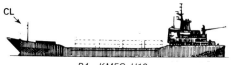

P4 KMFC; H13

77060: ALEKSANDR FADEYEV Ru/Ru 1973; Con; 6500; 130.21 × 7.5 (427 × 24.61); M; 17. Sisters (Ru flag).

P4 KMFC; H13

77080: KHUDOZHNIK FEDOROVSKIY Ru/Bu 1978; B; 15600; 185.22 × 10.1 (607.68 × 33.14); M; 15.25; This vessel may be fitted with 4 deck cranes; This could also apply to the sisterships. Sisters (Ru, Bu & Rm flags).

P4 KMFC; H13

77105: MAXHUTTE DDR/Bz 1985; B; 22500; 193.81 × 10.93 (635.86 × 35.86); M; 14.5. Sister (DDR flag).

P4 KMFCK; H13

77127: GENERAL BERLING Pd/Bu 1984; B; 23300; 198.56 × 11.2 (651.44 × 36.75); M; 14.5. Sisters (Pd & Bu flags).

176

P4   KMFK; H

77340: KHUDOZHNIK SARYAN Ru/DDR 1975; Con; 17800; 169.63
× 9.2 (556.52 × 30.18); M; 20; 'Mercur' type. Sisters (Ru flag).

P4   KMFK; H1

77398: WOLGAST DDR/Ne 1965; C; 500; 63.3 × 3.9 (207.68 ×
12.8); M; 12. Sister—converted to chemical carrier, may be
altered in appearance (DDR flag).

P4   KMFK; H1

77560: BEIUS Rm/Rm 1978; B; 32100; 219.72 × 12.4 (720.87 ×
40.68); M; 16.25. Sisters (Rm flag); Sisters—lengthened version
(239.7m—786ft) (Rm flag).

P4   KMFK; H1

77980: LYULIN Bu/Ja 1965; B; 6100; 126.02 × 7.6 (413.45 × 24.93);
M; 13. Sisters (Bu flag).

P4   KMFK; H1

78010: KAPITAN PANFILOV Ru/Ru 1975; B; 10100; 146.21 × 9.43
(479.69 × 30.94); M; 14. Sisters (Ru flag).

P4 KMFK; H1

78041: SIBIRSKIY 2113 Ru/Fi 1980; C (sea/river); 3800; 129 × 2.5 (423 × 8.2); TSM; 10. Sisters (Ru flag).

P4 KMFK; H1

78060: IVAN SKURIDIN Ru/Ru 1975; RoC/Con; 4000; 139.6 × 6.62 (458 × 21.72); M; 17; Bow door; 'Neva' type. Sisters—some have bow & stern doors (Ru flag); Sisters 12m (40ft) longer (Ru flag).

P4 KMFK; H13

78140: ZIEMIA BYDGOSKA Pd/Br 1967; B; 15700; 179.51 × 9.91 (588.94 × 32.51); M; 15. Sister (Pd flag).

P4 KMFK; H13

78290: HUTA ZGODA Pd/FRG 1974; B; 9300; 145.65 × 8.35 (477.85 × 27.4); M; 15. Sisters (Pd flag).

P4 KMFK; H13

78300: KOPALNIA PIASECZNO Pd/Sp 1971; B; 9100; 146.72 × 8.27 (481.36 × 27.13); M; 15.5. Sister (Pd flag).

Twin Funnels

P4 KMFK; H13

78355: CHKALOVSK Ru/Bz 1978; B; 23600; 200.92 × 10.76 (659.19 × 35.3); M; 15.25. Sister (Ru flag).

178

P4   KMFK; H13

78520: SOVFRACHT Ru/Ys 1967; B; 26000; 211.41 × 11.79 (693.6 × 36.68); M; 16. Similar—see inset (Ru flag).

P4   KMFK; H13

78540: ZARECHENSK Ru/Pd 1967; B; 16000; 187.12 × 9.54 (614.17 × 31.3); M; 15.5; 'B-470' type. Sisters (Ru flag); Similar (Pd flag).

P4   KMFK; H13

78580: BUCEGI Rm/Ja 1966; B; 16600; 181.13 × 9.5 (594.26 × 31.17); M; 16. Sisters (Rm flag).

P4 KMFK; H13

78680: UNIWERSYTET JAGIELLONSKI Pd/De 1971; B; 30400; 218.85 × 12.09 (718 × 39.67); M; 15.5.

P4 KMFK; H13

78730: GORLITZ DDR/Ru 1974; B; 22800; 201.38 × 11.21 (660.7 × 36.78); M; 15.75; 'Baltika' type. Sister (DDR flag); Similar (Ru flag); Similar—crane aft (DDR flag).

P4 KMFK; H13

78841: PIONIERUL Rm/Rm 1976; B; 10300; 145.12 × 10.14 (476 × 33.27); M; 15. Sisters (Rm flag).

P4 KMFK; H13

78850: MUSALA Bu/Ja 1967; B; 9100; 139.83 × 9.26 (458.76 × 30.38); M; 14. Sisters (Bu flag).

P4   KMFK; H13

78891: VLADIMIR LENORSKIY Ru/Ru 1970; O; 4200; 123.53 × 4.80
(405 × 15.75); TSM; 11.25; Hot ore carrier. Sisters (Ru flag).

P4   KMFK; H13

78980: GENERAL SWIERCZEWSKI Pd/Bu 1973; B; 23300; 201.17
× 11.2 (660.01 × 36.75); M; 17. Sisters (Pd, Bu & Ru flags).

P4   KMFK; H13

79110: UNIWERSYTET WARSZAWSKI Pd/De 1974; B; 30200;
218.83 × 12.07 (717.95 × 39.6); M; 15.5. Sister (Pd flag).

P4   KMFK; H13

79230: GEORGIY LEONIDZE Ru/Pd 1974; B; 20300; 202.34 × 10.64 (663.85 × 34.91); M; 15; 'B-447' type. Sister (Ru flag); Similar (Cz flag).

P4   KMFK; H13

79315: VOGTLAND DDR/DDR 1986; Con; 13300; 158.07 × 10.11 (518.6 × 33.17); M; 16. Sister (DDR flag).

P4   KMFK; H13

79340: SORMOVSKIY Ru/Ru 1967 onwards; C (sea/river); 2500; 114.2 × 3.42 (374.67 × 11.22); TSM; 10.5. Sisters—appearance varies, some have goalpost radar mast (Ru & Bu flags); Some VOLGO-BALT type vessels may be similar in appearance.

P4   KMFK; H13

79450: 'NEFTERUDOVOZ' type Ru/Ru 1972/77; OO (sea/river); 2700; 118.93 × 3.42 (390.19 × 11.22); TSM; 11. Sisters—some have heightened funnel (Ru flag).

P4   KMFK; H13

79500: 'BALTIYSKIY' type Ru/Ru 1962-68; C (sea/river); 1900; 96.02 × 3.26 (315.03 × 10.7); TSM; 10; Vessel illustrated is **Baltiyskiy 32**; Some have lower funnels; After kingpost omitted on some vessels. Sisters (Ru flag).

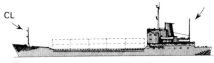

P4   KMFK; H13

79550: PIONER NAKHODKI Ru/Ru 1972; Con; 4800; 130.31 × 6.93 (427.53 × 22.74); M; 15. Sisters (Ru flag).

P4   KMFK; H13

79640: BELMEKEN Bu/Bu 1973; B; 15700; 185.2 × 9.86 (607.61 × 32.35); M; 15.15. Sisters (Bu & Pd flags).

P4   KMFK; H13

79730: ESPENHAIN DDR/DDR 1962; O; 8100; 151.87 × 8.58 (498.26 × 28.15); M; 12. Sisters (DDR flag).

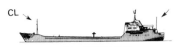

P4   KMFK; H13

79870: SUWALKI Pd/Bu 1969; C; 2400; 95.89 × 5.66 (314.6 × 18.57); M; 13. Sisters (Pd flag).

P4   KMFK; H13

79930: ABRAM ARKHIPOV Ru/Fi 1973; C/TC; 3200; 97.31 × 6.7 (319.26 × 21.98); M; 14. Sisters (Ru flag).

P4   KMFK; H13

79945: SEREBRYANKA Ru/Ru 1974; —; 3900; 122 × 4 (400.26 × 13.12); —; 11.7; May be based on 'Kishinev' type – see no. 49240.

P4   *KMFKC; H13*

79985: COLDITZ DDR/Ru 1980; B; 23100; 199.8 × 11.21 (655.5 × 36.78); M; 16.25; 'Baltika' type; crane aft is on starboard side.

P4   *KMFKC; H1*

79990: KAPITAN PANFILOV Ru/Ru 1975; B; 10100; 146.21 × 9.43 (479.69 × 30.94); M; 14. Sisters (Ru flag).

P4   *KMFKC; H13*

80000: KHUDOZHNIK FEDOROVSKIY Ru/Bu 1978; B; 15600; 185.22 × 10.1 (607.68 × 33.14); M; 15.25; This vessel may be fitted with 4 deck cranes; This could also apply to the sisterships. Sisters (Ru, Bu & Rm flags).

P4   *KMFKC; H13*

80010: BORIS LIVANOV Ru/Bu 1985; B; 15400; 184.41 × 10.21 (605 × 33.5); M; Sisters (Ru flag).

P4 KMFKC; H13

80020: HUTA ZGODA Pd/FRG 1974; B; 9300; 145.65 × 8.35 (477.85 × 27.4); M; 15. Sisters (Pd flag).

P4 KMFK₂; H13

80060: KAPITAN TOMSON Ru/Ja 1977; RoC/Con; 4600; 113.49 × 6.87 (372.34 × 22.54); M; —; Launched as *R S One*. Sister (Ru flag).

P4 KMFKR; H1

80090: INZHENIER MACHULSKIY Ru/Fi 1975; RoC/Con; 4000; 124.21 × 6.6 (407.51 × 21.65); M; 16.75; Quarter ramp; Stern door. Sisters (Ru flag); Similar—stern ramp and no extension foreward of bridge (Ru flag).

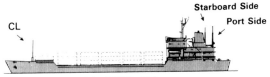

P4 KMFK₂; H13

80052: SIMON BOLIVAR Ru/Bu 1981; Con; 8700; 148.67 × 7.65 (488 × 25.1); M; 18. Sisters (Ru & Bu flags).

P4 KMFK₂; H2

80071: BAZIAS 1 Rm/Rm 1984; RoC/Con; 2800; 121.49 × 5.33 (398.59 × 17.49); TSM; 15.5; 2 stern door/ramps. Sisters (Rm flag).

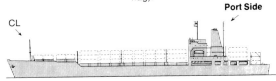

P4 KMFM; H1

80100: KAPITAN KANEVSKIY Ru/DDR 1982; Con; 17700; 173.92 × 9.82 (570.60 × 32.22); M; 20. Sisters (Ru flag).

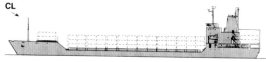

P4   KMFM; H13

80109: RUHLAND DDR/DDR 1985; Con; 13800; 165.51 × 10.05 (543 × 32.97); M; 17.75. Sisters (DDR flag).

P4   KMFM; H13

80130: ZARECHENSK Ru/Pd 1967; B; 16000; 187.12 × 9.54 (614.17 × 31.3); M; 15.5; 'B-470' type. Sisters (Ru flag); Similar (Pd flag).

P4   KMFMC; H13

80171: DMITRIY DONSKOY Ru/DDR 1977; B/Con; 13600; 162.11 × 9.88 (532 × 32.41); M; 15.25; 'UL-ESC' type. Sisters (Ru flag).

186

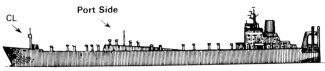

P4   KMFR; H

80200: MAGNITOGORSK Ru/Fi 1975; RoC/Con; 15700; 205.8 × 9.7 (675.2 × 31.82); M; 22; Stern door/quarter ramp. Sisters—one has lifeboats foreward of bridge-front (Ru flag).

P4   KMFR; H1

80205: POZNAN Pd/Sp 1982; RoC/Con; 18500; 199.5 × 9.52 (654.53 × 31.23); M; 18.5; Angled stern door and ramp (starboard). Sisters (Pd flag).

P4   KMFR; H1

80250: AKADEMIK ARTSIMOVICH Ru/Fr 1975; RoC/Con; 3200; 119.03 × 5.77 (390.52 × 18.93); M; 17; Angled stern door and ramp. Sisters (Ru flag).

P4   KMFR; H1

80260: SKULPTOR KONENKOV Ru/Pd 1975; RoC/Con; 18500; 181.41 × 9.64 (595.18 × 31.63); M; 20.5; Stern door/quarter ramp; 'B-481' type. Sisters (Ru flag).

P4 KMKFK; H1

80750: LEONID TELIGA Pd/FRG 1969; C; 2800/5700; 125.18 × 6.45/7.64 (410.7 × 21.16/25.07); M; 12.

P4 KMK₂MF; H13

80890: ADAM ASNYK Pd/FRG 1974; C; 7000/9600; 145.04 × 8.23/9.43 (475.85 × 27/30.94); M; 16; '36-L' type.

P4 KMK₂MF; H13

80900: PETKO R. SLAVEJNOV Bu/Ys 1968; C; 9100; 143.64 × 8.87 (471.26 × 29.1); M; 15; Launched as *Atria*. Sister (Bu flag).

P4 KMK₂MFK; H13

80920: LENKORAN Ru/Ja 1962; Tk; 22500; 207.04 × 11.07 (679.27 × 36.32); M; 16.5. Sister (Ru flag).

P4 KMKMF; H

81000: NOVY BUG Ru/Rm 1963; C; 3300; 100.59 × 6.55 (330.02 × 21.49); M; 12.5. Sisters (Ru flag).

P4 KMKMF; H13

81195: TATARSTAN Ru/Ru 1977; FC; 2400; 95.28 × 5.48 (313 × 17.98); M; 14.5. Sisters (Ru flag).

P4 KMKMF; H13

81305: CARANSEBES Rm/Rm 1964; C; 1300; 70.54 × 4.9 (231.43 × 16.08); M; 11.5. Sister (Rm flag).

P4 KMKMF; H13

81350: ZULAWY Pd/Pd 1974; FC; 8100; 151.31 × 7.4 (496.42 × 24.28); M; 19; 'B-68' type. Sisters (Pd flag).

P4 KMKMF; H13

81400: ALIOT Ru/Fi 1970; WT/Ch; 3100; 93.88 × 6.5 (308.01 × 21.33); M; 14. Sisters (Ru flag).

P4 KMKMFK; H1

81450: LEONID TELIGA Pd/FRG 1969; C; 2800/5700; 125.18 × 6.45/7.64 (410.7 × 21.16/25.07); M; 12.

P4 KMKMFK; H13

81490: PRIBOY Ru/Sw 1964; FC; 10900; 156.93 × 7.4 (514.86 × 24.28); M; 18.25. Sisters (Ru flag).

P4 KMKMFK; H13

81555: SLATINA Rm/Rm 1973; C; 2500/3500; 106.2 × 5.64/7.06 (348 × 18.5/23.16); M; 14. Sister (Rm flag).

P4 KMKM₂FK; H13

81640: ZAKOPANE Pd/Pd 1968; C; 4200/6600; 135.41 × 6.78/7.67 (444.26 × 22.24/25.16); M; 17; 'B-446' type. Sisters (Pd flag).

P4 KM₂F; H1

81860: CIECHOCINEK Pd/Rm 1970; C; 1200/2000; 85.91 × 4.5/5.1 (281.86 × 14.76/16.73); M; 14.

P4 KM₂F; H13

82110: BRAD Rm/Rm 1971; C; 2500/3500; 106.2 × —/7.06 (348.43 × —/23.16); M; 14. Sisters (Rm & Bu flags).

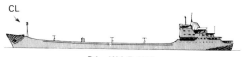

P4 KM₂F; H13

82220: URICANI Rm/Rm 1971; B; 9600; 148.72 × 7.93 (487.93 × 26.02); M; 12.5. Sisters—some have cranes and some have goalpost foreward (Rm flag).

P4   KM₂F; H13

82260: PLOCK Pd/Bu 1967; C; 2600; 95.89 × 5.64 (314.6 × 18.5); M; 12.75. Sisters—some have heavier radar mast and some have cowl-top funnel (Pd flag).

P4   KM₂FK; H13

82460: OSTROV RUSSKIY Ru/Sw 1969; FC; 9800; 150.55 × 7.47 (494 × 24.51); M; 18.25. Sisters (Ru flag).

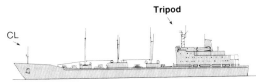

P4   KM₄F; H1

82651: KOMSOMOLETS PRIMORYA Ru/DDR 1983; FC; 7700; 152.79 × 7.45 (501.28 × 24.44); M; 17.5; 'Kristal II' type. Sisters (Ru & DDR flags).

P4   MC₄MFM; H13

83430: DUBNO Ru/DDR 1960; O; 6800; 139.5 × 8.12 (457.68 × 26.64); M; 14.25. Sisters—some may have 3 cranes (Ru flag).

P4   MC₂MF; H

83600: NORDSTERN DDR/DDR 1959; C; 539; 59.47 × 3.6 (195 × 11.81); M; 10. Sister—converted to cargo chemical carrier (DDR flag).

P4   MC₂MF; H13

83680: CHEREPOVETS Ru/Rm 1970; C; 1500; 80.27 × 4.9 (263.35 × 16.08); M; 12. Sisters—some without extra bridge level (Ru & Rm flags).

P4   MC₂MF; H13

83720: BATAK Bu/Bu 1966; C; 1300/1800; 80.65 × 4.35/5.29 (264.6 × 14.27/17.36); M; 12; Sisters (some are reported to have a 3rd crane on focsle. Some may be converted to container ships similar to ELENA—which see) (Bu flag):.

P4   MCMF; H

83930: BELLATRIX DDR/DDR 1961; C; 500; 59.47 × 3.66 (195.11 × 12.01); M; 10.

P4   MCMF; H13

84150: BALKHASH Ru/Ru 1969; C; 1100; 72.12 × 4.63 (236.61 × 15.19); M; 11. Sisters (Ru flag).

P4   MCMF; H13

84210: KITEN Bu/Bu 1960; C; 300; 49.31 × 3.09 (161.78 × 10.41); M; 9. Sister (Bu flag).

P4   MFM; H12

84330: ZVAYGZNE Ru/De 1953; FC; 1600; 70.01 × 4.31 (229.69 × 14.14); M; 10.75. Similar (Ru flag).

P4   MFM; H12

84360: KHASAN Ru/DDR 1961; FC; 2300; 82.4 × 5.15 (270.34 × 16.9); M; 11. Similar (Ru flag).

P4   MKF; H13

84460: IRTISH Ru/Sw 1951; Tk; 1100; 68.48 × 3.72 (224.67 × 12.2); M; 9. Similar (Ru flag).

P4   MKFM; H12

84510: PALEKH Ru/DDR 1959; FC; 2300; 82.4 × 5.15 (270.34 × 16.9); M; 11; May be altered in appearance.

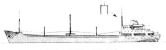

P4   MK₃MF; H1

84710: BOTEVGRAD Bu/No 1962; C; 2300; 102.77 × 6.01 (337.17 × 19.72); M; 14.

P4   MK₃MFK; H13

84810: LENINAKAN Ru/Ja 1964; Tk; 23100; 207.04 × 11.11 (679.27 × 36.45); M; 16.5. Sisters (Ru flag).

P4   MK₂MF; H13

84930: CONDOR DDR/DDR 1962; C; 1000/1700; 82.33 × 4.26/5.75 (270.11 × 13.98/18.86); M; 12. Sisters (DDR flag).

P4   MK₂MF; H13

84940: OELSA DDR/DDR 1967; C; 2500; 92.82 × 5.92 (304.53 × 19.42); M; 12.75. Sisters (DDR flag).

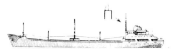

P4   MKMF; H1

85170: BOTEVGRAD Bu/No 1962; C; 2300; 102.77 × 6.01 (337.17 × 19.72); M; 14.

P4   MKMF; H1

85185: BREZA Bu/Ne 1971; C/Con; 1600; 94.7 × 5.43 (310.7 × 17.81); M; 14.

P4   MKMF; H12

85320: DALNEVOSTOCHNY Ru/Ru 1960; FC; 3200; 99.35 × 5.65 (325.95 × 18.54); D-E; 13.5. Sisters—some vary; taller funnels etc (Ru & DDR flags).

P4   MKMF; H13

85610: BIRA Ru/Ru —; —; 2100 Dspl; 75 × — (246 × —); M; 12; Probably used as a naval transport or landing craft. Sister (Ru flag).

P4 MKMF; H13

85895: KONDA Ru/Fi 1955; Tk; 1980 Dspl; 69 × 4.3 (226.4 × 14.1); M; 12; Naval manned. Sisters (Ru flag).

P4 MKMF; H13

85970: KRIPTON Ru/Ru 1964; Tk; 1800; 83.67 × 4.6 (274.51 × 15.09); M; 12.5. Sisters—some have taller funnels (Ru & Bu flags); One vessel used as supply ship by DDR Navy.

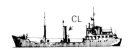

P4 MKMF; H13

86070: 'KORSAKOV' type Ru/Hu 1949-61; C; 1300; 65.97 × 3.8 (216.44 × 12.47); TSM; 9.5; The existence of some is doubtful and some have been reported as passenger/cargo; For similar vessels see no 86170. Sisters (Ru flag).

P4 MKMF; H13

86110: BUDAPEST Hu/Bu 1967; C; 3000/4500; 114 × —/7.5 (374 × —/24.61); M; 13. Sister (Hu flag).

P4 MKMF; H13

86170: OLENSK Ru/Hu 1953; C; 1200; 70.24 × 3.8 (230.45 × 12.47); TSM; 9.5. Sisters (Ru flag); Similar (Rm flag).

P4 MKMF; H13

86220: ANANYEV Ru/Hu 1960; C; 1200; 78.49 × 4.1 (257.51 × 13.45); M; 10.75; Some have taller funnels and other smaller differences; For later ships in this class see KEKHRA—M₂F. Sisters (Ru flag).

P4   MKMFK; H13

86420: EISENHUTTENSTADT DDR/Sw 1960; OO; 23400; 199.65 ×
11.38 (655 × 37.34); M; 14.5.

P4   MKMFK; H13

86470: KEGUMS Ru/Ja 1965; LGC; 3500; 96.53 × 5.02 (316.7 ×
16.47); M; 13.75. Sister (Ru flag).

P4   MKMFK; H13

86540: OZERNOYE Ru/Pd 1962; Tk; 1300; 75.62 × 4.74 (248.1 ×
15.55); M; 12.5; 'B-74' type. Sisters (Ru flag).

P4   M₂F; H

86824: KAPITAN ZBIGNIEW SZYMANSKI Pd/Pd 1958; C; 500;
59.85 × 3.41 (196 × 11.18); M; 9; 'B51' type.

P4   M₂F; H

87000: PERVOMAYSK Ru/De 1959; FC; 3300; 94.8 × 4.37 (311.02
× 14.34); M; 13. Sisters (Ru flag).

P4   M₂F; H1

87640: BEGA Rm/Rm 1972; C; 1900; 85.88 × 5.1 (281.76 × 16.73); M; 13.25. Sisters (Rm flag).

P4   M₂F; H1

87740: KRASNAL Pd/Pd 1959; C; 500/900; 66.2 × 3.68/— (217.19 × 12.07/—); M; 11.5; 'B-57' type. Similar—some may be converted to cargo/container (Pd flag).

P4   M₂F; H12

87940: 'KORSAKOV' type Ru/Hu; Passenger/cargo conversions of class; See MKMF 'KORSAKOV' type & OLENSK.

P4   M₂F; H12

87950: ZVAYGZNE Ru/De 1953; FC; 1700; 70.01 × 4.31 (229.69 × 14.14); M; 10.75.

P4   M₂F; H13

88130: YAKAN Ru/Fi 1952; C; 900; 59.47 × 4.57 (195.11 × 14.99); M; 10.

P4   M₂F; H13

88230: KHOLMSK Ru/Pd 1955; C; 600; 57.64 × 4.25 (189.11 × 13.94); M;10; 'B-53' type. 'MELITOPOL' class. Similar (Ru flag).

P4   M₂F; H13

88250: MOLDOVA Rm/Ys 1953; C; 607; 54.84 × 3.86 (179.92 × 12.66); M; 9.5.

P4   M₂F; H13

88380: ZAGLEBIE DABROWSKIE Pd/Pd 1967; B; 11000; 156.37 × 9.51 (513.02 × 31.2); M; 15.5; 'B-520' type. Sisters (Pd flag).

P4   M₂F; H13

88600: ELENA Bu/Bu 1970; Con; 1300/1800; 80.73 × 4.34/5.31 (264.86 × 14.27/17.42); M; —; Converted from general cargo; Others of this class may be similarly converted.

P4   M₂F; H13

88885: ROSITZA Bu/It 1967; Tk; 2100; 82.71 × 5.67 (271.36 × 18.6); M; 11.

P4   M₂F; H13

88920: TARAKLIYA Ru/Hu 1962; VO/WT; 1300; 74.48 × 4.66 (244.36 × 15.29); M; 10.25; Converted from general cargo. Sister (Ru flag).

P4   M₂F; H13

88985: 'VODA' class Ru/— approx 1956; Wa; 3000 Dspl; 81.5 × 4 (267.3 × 13.2); TSM; 12; Naval manned. Sisters—some do not have catwalk (Ru flag).

P4   M₂F; H13

89200: KEKHRA Ru/Hu 1966; C; 1200; 74.55 × 4.67 (244.59 × 15.32); M; 11.5; Sisters—some of the Russian vessels have a large house ahead of bridge and may be naval auxiliaries. (Ru & Hu flags).

P4   M₂F; H13

89250: SPARTAK Ru/Hu 1967; C; 1500; 77.81 × 4.73 (255.28 × 15.52); M; 12.5. Sisters (Ru flag).

Tripod

P4   M₂F; H13

89460: YURYUZAN Ru/Ru 1957; Tk; 795; 63.96 × 3.71 (209.84 × 12.17); TSM; 12.5. Sisters (Ru flag).

P4   M₂F; H13

89500: AYSBERG Ru/Ru 1960; FC; 500; 51.9 × 2.94 (170.28 × 9.65); M; 9. Sister (Ru flag).

P4   M₂F; H13

89515: ROYA Ru/Hu 1959; C; 1200; 70.19 × 3.83 (230.28 × 12.57); TSM; 9.5.

P4   M₂F; H13

89540: PETRILA Rm/Rm 1964; C; 1300; 70.54 × 4.9 (231.43 × 16.08); M; 11.5. Sisters—converted to livestock carriers, probably altered in appearance (Rm flag).

P4   M₂F; H13

89680: SEVERODVINSKIY Ru/Br 1966; D; 2000; 82.05 × 4.13 (269.19 × 13.55); TS D-E; 11.5. Sisters (Ru flag).

P4   M₂FK; H13

89980: GORLITZ DDR/Ru 1974; B; 22800; 201.38 × 11.21 (660.7 × 36.78); M; 15.5; 'Baltika' type. Sisters (DDR flag); Similar—crane aft (DDR flag); Similar (Ru flag).

P4   M₂FK; H13

90030: 'BALTIYSKIY' type Ru/Ru 1962-68; C (sea/river); 1900; 96.02 × 3.26 (315.03 × 10.7); TSM; 10; Vessel illustrated is **Baltiyskiy 32**; Some have lower funnels; After kingpost omitted on some vessels. Sisters (Ru flag): from **Baltiyskiy 1** to **Baltiyskiy 73** inclusive (*Baltiyskiy 41* was a total loss).

P4   M₂FK; H13

90150: MAGADAN Ru/Sw 1956; FC; 1800; 79.25 × 6.12 (260 × 20.08); M; 13.5. Sisters (Ru flag).

P4   M₂FK; H13

90190: YANA Ru/Ne 1974; D; —; 72 × — (236.22 × —); M;—. Sister (Ru flag).

P4   M₂KFK; H13

90420: 'VOLGONEFT' type Ru/Ru and Bu 1969/72; Tk; 3600; 135.01 × 3.5 (442.95 × 11.48); TSM; 10.5; This drawing represents the later vessels of this type. For earlier ships see 'VOLGONEFT' under M₄F; Names have the prefix 'VOLGONEFT' and a number; There are approx 27 in the whole group.

P4   M₂KMF; H13

90560: PECHORALES Ru/Ru 1963; C; 4600; 121.8 × 7.14 (399.61 × 23.43); GT; 14.25. Sister (Ru flag).

P4   M₂KMF; H13

90600: OELSA DDR/DDR 1967; C; 2500; 92.82 × 5.92 (304.53 × 19.42); M; 12.75. Sisters (DDR flag).

P4   M₂KMFM; H13

90720: INTERNATSIONAL Ru/Pd 1968; Tk; 14200; 177.27 × 9.37 (581.59 × 30.74); M; 16; 'B-72' type. Sisters (Ru flag).

P4   M₃F; H13

91224: IVAN AIVAZOVSKIY Ru/Ru 1963; FC; 6100; 130 × 7.17 (426.51 × 23.52); D-E; 16.5. Sisters (Ru, Bu, DDR & Rm flags).

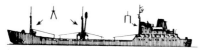

P4　M₃F; H13

91260: PAVLIN VINOGRADOV Ru/Ru 1960; C; 4600; 121.77 × 7.06 (399.51 × 23.16); GT; 14.

P4　M₃F; H13

91700: SOFIA Bu/Bu 1963; C; 2900/4400; 114.18 × 6.32/7.54 (374.61 × 20.73/24.74); M; 14. Sister (Bu flag).

P4　M₃F; H3

91770: HARMATTAN Pd/FRG 1967; FC; 900/1700; 88.68 × 4.11/5.23 (290.94 × 13.48/17.16); M; 16.5.

P4　M₃FK; H13

91910: KAMCHATSKIE GORY Ru/Sw 1964; FC; 9700; 153.5 × 7.47 (503.61 × 24.51); M; 17. Sisters (Ru flag).

P4　M₄F; H13

92030: 'VOLGONEFT' type Ru/Ru and Bu 1966-69; Tk; 3500; 132.59 × 3.58 (435 × 11.75); TSM; 10.5; This drawing represents the earlier vessels of this type. For later vessels see 'VOLGONEFT' under M₂KFK. Names have the prefix 'VOLGONEFT' and a number. Approx. 27 in the whole group.

Twin Funnels

P5   CMC₂KMF; H1

92150: VOSTOCK Ru/Ru 1971; FF; 26400; 224.57 × 10.02 (736.78 × 32.87); TST; 19.

P5   CMFM; H2

92160: EMBA Ru/Fi 1980; Cbl; 1900; 75.9 × 3 (249 × 9.84); TS D-E; approx 11. Sisters (Ru flag).

P5   CMFM; H2

92165: BIRYUSA Ru/Fi 1986; Cbl; 2600; 86.06 × 3.0 (282.35 × 9.84); TS D-E;11.8; May be spelt **BIRIUSA** or **BERYUSA**. Sister (Ru flag).

P5   KMCKMFKF; H13

92380: DALNIY VOSTOK Ru/FRG 1963; FF; 17000; 182 × 8.89 (597.11 × 29.16); M; 14; Converted from Whale Factory to Fish Cannery/Fish Factory 1980; Kingposts abaft forward superstructure are probably removed. Sister (Ru flag).

P5   KMF; H13

92435: KOSMONAUT YURIY GAGARIN Ru/Ru 1971; MTV; 32300;
231.71 × 10 (760 × 32.81); T; 17.75.

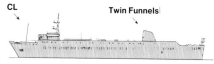

P5   KMF; H2

92437: PERIS Rm/Rm 1985; RoC; 8200; 128.4 × 6.56 (421.26 ×
21.52); TSM; 20. Sisters (Rm flag).

P5   KM₂F; H

92680: SOVIETSKIY DAGESTAN Ru/Ys 1984; P/RoC/TF; 11500;
154.46 × 4.25 (506.76 × 13.94); TSM; —; Stern ramp. Sisters (Ru
flag).

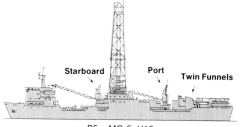

P5   MC₂F; H13

92880: VALENTIN SHASHKIN Ru/F 1981; DS; 11300; 149.41 × 7.3
(490.19 × 23.95); TS D-E; 12. Sisters (Ru flag).

P5   MCMFK; H2

93060: TRAPEZITZA Bu/Sw 1979; RoC; 8500; 166 × 7.9 (544.62 ×
25.92); TSM; 18; Twin stern ramps (slewing). Sister (Bu flag).

204

Tripod

P5 MFM; H2

93268: VSEVOLOD BERYEZKIN Ru/Ru 1975; RS; 700; 54.79 × 4.16 (179.75 × 13.65); M; 11.75. Sisters—some have modified stern without the knuckle and dish amidships is absent in some (Ru flag).

P5 MKF; H

93380: VLADIMIR ILYCH Ru/DDR 1976; Riv/P; 4900; 128.02 × — (420 × —); —;—. Sisters (Ru flag).

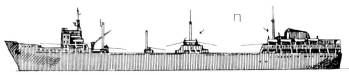

P5 MK₂M₂F; H

93630: SOVIETSKAYA ROSSIYA Ru/Ru 1961; WF; 33200; 217.51 × 10.85 (713.61 × 35.59); TSM; 16.

Twin Funnels

P5 MKMF; H1

93660: VOSTOCK Ru/Ru 1971; FF; 26400; 224.57 × 10.02 (736.78 × 32.87); TST; 19.

P5   MKMF; H1

93670: GEROITE NA SEVASTOPOL Bu/No 1978; RoC/TF; 9600; 185.45 × 7.42 (608.43 × 24.34); TSM; 19; Stern door. Sister (Bu flag); Similar (Ru flag).

P5   MKMF; H13

93680: ANDREY ZAKHAROV Ru/Ru 1960; FF; 12700; 162.16 × 7.02 (532.02 × 23.03); TSM; 12.5. Sisters—one fitted with large gantry for handling small fishing craft (Ru flag).

P5   MKMF; H1

93695: IERONIM UBOREVICH Ru/Ru 1968; FF; 13500; 162.01 × 7.02 (531.53 × 23.03); TSM; 12.75. Sisters (Ru flag).

P5   MKMKF; H13

93780: VILIS LACIS Ru/FRG 1966; FF; 16500; 167.24 × 7.49 (548.68 × 24.57); M; 14. Sisters (Ru flag).

P5   MKMKFK; H13

93800: SEVEROURALSK Ru/Ja 1966; FF; 18000; 174.33 × 7.32 (571.94 × 24.01); M; 14.5. Sisters (Ru flag).

206

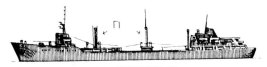

P5   MKMKMF; H1

93820: POGRANICHNIK LEONOV Ru/Pd 1972; FF; 13100; 164.01
× 8.08 (538.09 × 26.5); M; 15.25; 'B69' type. Similar (Ru flag).

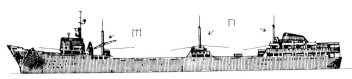

P5   MKM₂F; H1

93860: SOVIETSKAYA UKRAINA Ru/Ru 1959; WF; 32000; 217.51
× 10.85 (713.61 × 35.59); TSM; 16.

P5   MKM₂F; H1

93870: PIONERSK Ru/Pd 1963; FF; 13600; 165.46 × 8.1 (542.84 × 26.57); M; 14.25; 'B-64' type. Sisters (Ru flag); Similar—'B67' type (Pd flag).

P5   MKM₂FK; H13

93884: SEVERODONETSK Ru/Ja 1966; FF; 18000; 174.33 × 7.32 (571.95 × 24.02); M; 14.5.

P5 $M_2F; H$

93930: PUCK Pd/No 1972; RoC/Con/Pap; 2400; 118.17 × 5.98 (387.7 × 19.62); TSM; 11.75; Bow door/ramp; stern door/ramp.

P5 $M_2F; H$

94010: ASCHBERG DDR/Fi 1972; RoC; 3200; 113.52 × 6.25 (372.44 × 20.51); M; 16; Stern door/ramp. Sister (DDR flag).

P5 $M_2F; H$

94280: KOSMONAUT VLADIMIR KOMAROV Ru/Ru 1966; MTV; 13900; 155.8 × 8.5 (511 × 27.89); M; 17.5; Launched as *Genichesk*; Converted from 'Poltava' class cargo ship.

P5 $M_2F; H2$

94490: FICHTELBERG DDR/No 1975; RoC/Con; 4000; 137.55 × 7.18 (451.28 × 23.56); TSM; 18.5; Bow and stern doors.

P5 $M_2F; H2$

94550: INOWROCLAW Pd/Fi 1980; RoC/Con; 6400; 137.19 × 7.4 (450.1 × 24.28); TSM; 15; 2 stern doors/ramps.

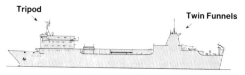

P5 $M_2F; H2$

94565: GLEICHBERG DDR/DDR 1982; RoC/Con; 4700; 138.54 × 7.23 (454.53 × 23.72); TSM; 14.5; Stern door/ramp. Sisters (DDR & Rm flags).

P5   M₃F; H13

95015: LENA Ru/— 1961; RT; 7200 Dspl; 122.1 × 6.2 (400.3 × 20.3); TSM; 17; Ru Navy. Modified 'UDA' class. Sisters (Ru flag).

P5   M₃FC; H2

95042: MODUL Ru/Ru 1981; RS; 700; 53.75 × 4.29 (176.35 × 14.07); M; 12.5. Sisters—some may have A-frame aft (Ru flag).

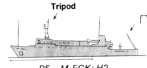

P5   M₃FCK; H2

95043: VEKTOR Ru/Ru 1980; RS; 170; 53.73 × 4.29 (176.28 × 14.07); M; 12.5.

P5   MN₂FM; H1

95250: BROCKEN DDR/Ne 1976; RoC/HL; 1200; 81.01 × 3.95 (265.78 × 12.96); TSM; 11.75; Bow door/ramp; Stern ramp.

INDEXES

Initials and abbreviations. Initials are regarded as words in their own right. For example, a name such as V KUCHER appears at the beginning of the V section. There are instances, however, where what appear to be initials appear as a word, eg BP, CP and TFL. Abbreviations of titles, such as DR for DOCTOR or ST for SAINT, are inserted under their abbreviated form.

Transliterations. Transliterated names, such as those from Russian or Bulgarian, can vary according to the source of the transliteration. A typical example is a Russian name such as YAROSLAVL, which could be spelt JAROSLAVL. Crosschecking may be necessary with these types of names.

NUMERICAL INDEX

00140
  ADMIRAL GOLOVKO (Ru)
  ADMIRAL KOLYSHKIN (Ru)
  ALEKSANDR TORTSYEV (Ru)
  IVAN SIVKO (Ru)
  KAPITAN TELOV (Ru)
  MARSHAL YAKUBOVSKIY (Ru)
  PYOTR SGIBNEV (or PETR
    SGIBNEV) (Ru)
  ALEKSEY GENERALOV (Ru)
  GENERAL RODIMTSYEV (Ru)
  KAPITAN MAKLAKOV (Ru)
  KONSTANTIN DUSHENOV (Ru)
00240
  YULIUS FUCHIK (Ru)
  TIBOR SZAMUELY (Ru)
00250
  KOSMONAUT PAVEL
    BELYAEV (Ru)
  KOSMONAUT GEORGIY
    DOBROVOLSKIY (Ru)
  KOSMONAUT VIKTOR
    PATSAYEV (Ru)
  KOSMONAUT VLADISLAV
    VOLKOV (Ru)

00280
  ANATOLIY
    ZHELEZNYAKOV (Ru)
  NIKOLAY MARKIN (Ru)
00330
  ALEKSANDROVSK (Ru)
  ATKARSK (Ru)
  BERDYANSK (Ru)
00340
  ALAPAYEVSK (Ru)
  ALMETYEVSK (Ru)
00350
  TAUYSK (Ru)
00850
  IZHEVSK (Ru)
00965
  ALEKSEY KOSYGIN (Ru)
  SHARAF RASHIDOV (Ru)
  INDIRA GANDHI (Ru)
00967
  BORIS POLEVOY (Ru)
  PAVEL ANTOKOLSKIY (Ru)
01020
  ALAPAYEVSK (Ru)
  ALMATYEVSK (Ru)

01070
  BELORETSK (Ru)
  BELITSK (Ru)
  BEREZNIKI (Ru)
  BIYSK (Ru)
01100
  PYATIDYESYATILETIYE
    KOMSOMOLA (Ru)
01380
  'KALININGRAD' type
  DONETSKIY
    KOMSOMOLETS (Ru)
  DONETSKIY KHIMIK (Ru)
  DONETSKIY METALLURG (Ru)
  DONETSKIY SHAKHTER (Ru)
  KOMSOMOLETS (Ru)
  BRYANSKIY
    MASHINOSTROITEL (Ru)
  LENINSKIYE ISKRY (Ru)
  KRASNOYARSKI
    KOMSOMOLETS (Ru)
  KOMSOMOLETS ARMENII (Ru)
  KOMSOMOLETS
    AZERBAYDZHANA (Ru)
  KOMSOMOLETS GRUZII (Ru)

  KOMSOMOLETS
    MOLDAVII (Ru)
  KOMSOMOLETS
    SPASSKA (Ru)
  KOMSOMOLETS
    USSURIYSKA (Ru)
  KOMSOMOLETS
    VLADIVOSTOKA (Ru)
  KOMSOMOLETS ROSSII (Ru)
  KOMSOMOLETS
    KAZAKHSTANA (Ru)
  KOMSOMOLETS
    ADZHARII (Ru)
  KOMSOMOLETS
    BYELORUSSII (Ru)
  KOMSOMOLETS
    TURKMENII (Ru)
  KOMSOMOLETS PRAVDA (Ru)
  MOSKOVSKIY
    KOMSOMOLETS (Ru)
  ZHDANOVSKIY
    KOMSOMOLETS (Ru)
  30-LETIYE POBEDY (or
    TRIDTSATILETIYE
    POBEDY) (Ru)

  RABOCHAYA SMENA (Ru)
  STARYY BOLSHEVIK (Ru)
  SALAJ (Rm)
  NASAUD (Rm)
01540
  OTRADNOE (Ru)
  OLA (Ru)
  OREKHOV (Ru)
  ORSHA (Ru)
  OSTROGOZHSK (Ru)
01560
  AKADEMIK SHIMANSKIY (Ru)
  FREDERIK ZHOLIO-KYURI (Ru)
  LENINSKIY PIONER (Ru)
  PARIZHSKAYA KOMMUNA (Ru)
  RAVENSTVO (Ru)
  SVOBODA (Ru)
  VALENTINA TERESHKOVA (Ru)
  YUNYY LENINETS (Ru)
  KHIMIK ZELINSKIY (Ru)
01640
  'KALININGRAD' type
  DONETSKIY
    KOMSOMOLETS (Ru)
  DONETSKIY KHIMIK (Ru)

DONETSKIY METALLURG (Ru)
DONETSKIY SHAKHTER (Ru)
KOMSOMOLETS (Ru)
BRYANSKIY
   MASHINOSTROITEL (Ru)
LENINSKIYE ISKRY (Ru)
KRASNOYARSKI
   KOMSOMOLETS (Ru)
KOMSOMOLETS ARMENII (Ru)
KOMSOMOLETS
   AZERBAYDZHANA (Ru)
KOMSOMOLETS GRUZII (Ru)
KOMSOMOLETS
   MOLDAVII (Ru)
KOMSOMOLETS
   SPASSKA (Ru)
KOMSOMOLETS
   USSURIYSKA (Ru)
KOMSOMOLETS
   VLADIVOSTOKA (Ru)
KOMSOMOLETS ROSSII (Ru)
KOMSOMOLETS
   KAZAKHSTANA (Ru)
KOMSOMOLETS
   ADZHARII (Ru)
KOMSOMOLETS
   BYELORUSSII (Ru)
KOMSOMOLETS
   TURKMENII (Ru)
KOMSOMOLETS PRAVDA (Ru)
MOSKOVSKIY
   KOMSOMOLETS (Ru)
ZHDANOVSKIY
   KOMSOMOLETS (Ru)
30-LETIYE POBEDY (or
   TRIDTSATILETIYE
   POBEDY) (Ru)
RABOCHAYA SMENA (Ru)
STARYY BOLSHEVIK (Ru)
SALAJ (Rm)
NASAUD (Rm)
01733
   'MOMA' class
KOPERNIK (Pd)
ALTAIR (Ru)
ANADYR (Ru)
ANDROMEDA (Ru)
ANTARES (Ru)

ANTARKTYDA (Ru)
ARKTIDA (Ru)
ASKOLD (Ru)
BEREZAN (Ru)
CHELEKEN (Ru)
ELTON (Ru)
KOLGUYEV (Ru)
KRILON (Ru)
LIMAN (Ru)
MARS (Ru)
MORZHOVETS (Ru)
OKEAN (Ru)
SEVER (Ru)
TAYMYR (Ru)
ZAPOLYARYE (Ru)
01736
   'SAMARA' class
AZIMUT (Ru)
DEVIATOR (Ru)
GIGROMETR (Ru)
GLUBOMER (Ru)
GORIZONT (Ru)
GRADUS (Ru)
KOLESNIKOV (Ru)
KOMPAS (Ru)
RUMB (Ru)
TROPIK (Ru)
ZENIT (Ru)
01750
ALEKSANDR PUSHKIN (Ru)
IVAN FRANKO (Ru)
TARAS SHEVCHENKO (Ru)
01935
ANTONINA NEZHDANOVA (Ru)
OLGA SADOVSKAYA (Ru)
KLAVDIYA YELANSKAYA (Ru)
OLGA ANDROVSKAYA (Ru)
01960
YUNOST (Ru)
ALUSHTA (Ru)
GURIEV (Ru)
SOLOVKI (Ru)
VASIL KOLAROV (Ru)
ADMIRAL LUNIN (Ru)
ALUPKA (Ru)
SARICH (Ru)
01980
   GEORGI DIMITROV (Bu)

VASIL KOLAROV (Bu)
02060
KAPITAN SOROKIN (Ru)
KAPITAN NIKOLAYEV (Ru)
KAPITAN DRANITSYN (Ru)
KAPITAN KLEBNIKOV (Ru)
02070
MOSKVA (Ru)
KIEV (Ru)
LENINGRAD (Ru)
MURMANSK (Ru)
VLADIVOSTOK (Ru)
02080
KAPITAN M IZMAYLOV (Ru)
KAPITAN A RADZHABOV (Ru)
KAPITAN KOSOLAPOV (Ru)
02105
VENTA (Ru)
VILYUY (Ru)
02110
INGUL (Ru)
JANA (may be spelt YANA) (Ru)
02120
BAYKAL (Ru)
GRIGORIY
   ORDZHONKIDZE (Ru)
KHABAROVSK (Ru)
MARIYA ULYANOVA (Ru)
M URITSKIY (Ru)
NIKOLAYEVSK (Ru)
PETROPAVLOVSK (Ru)
VATSLAV VOROVSKIY (Ru)
02140
BASHKIRIYA (Ru)
KUBAN (Ru)
02150
ADZHARIYA (Ru)
02160
ESTONIYA (Ru)
LATVIYA (Ru)
MIKHAIL KALININ (Ru)
FELIKS DZERZHINSKIY (Ru)
LITVA (Ru)
PRIAMURYE (Ru)
TURKMENIYA (Ru)
ARMENIYA (Ru)
02180
   STEFAN BATORY (Pd)

02230
KAPITAN SOROKIN (Ru)
KAPITAN NIKOLAYEV (Ru)
KAPITAN DRANITSYN (Ru)
KAPITAN KLEBNIKOV (Ru)
02270
MUSSON (Ru)
ERNST KRENKEL (Ru)
GEORGIY USHAKOV (Ru)
OKEAN (Ru)
PASSAT (Ru)
PRIBOY (Ru)
PRILIV (Ru)
VIKTOR BUGAYEV (Ru)
VOLNA (Ru)
02280
KATYN (Ru)
DONETS (Ru)
ZNA (or TSNA) (Ru)
ZEYA (Ru)
TAVDA (Ru)
KALAR (Ru)
02340
MARIYA YERMOLOVA (Ru)
ALLA TARASOVA (Ru)
LYUBOV ORLOVA (Ru)
MARIYA SAVINA (Ru)
OLGA ANDROVSKAYA (Ru)
02350
KOLKHIDA (Ru)
BUKOVINA (Ru)
KIRGHIZSTAN (Ru)
MOLDAVIA (Ru)
TADZHAKISTAN (Ru)
TALLINN (Ru)
TATARIYA (Ru)
UZBEKISTAN (Ru)
AFGHANISTAN (Ru)
02415
ARKTIKA (Ru)
SIBIR (Ru)
02417
SERGEY KRAVKOV (Ru)
NIKOLAY
   KOLOMEYTSYEV (Ru)
DMITRIY LAPTEV (Ru)
DMITRIY STERLIGOV (Ru)
EDUARD TOLL (Ru)

STEPAN MALYGIN (Ru)
VALERIAN ALBANOV (Ru)
VLADIMIR SUKHOTSKIY (Ru)
NIKOLAY YEVGENOV (Ru)
DMITRIY OVTSYN (Ru)
02460
AKADEMIK KRYLOV (Ru)
02520
IRKUTSK (Ru)
IZHORA (Ru)
IZMAIL (Ru)
KARAGANDA (Ru)
TULA (Ru)
SANTIAGO DE CUBA (Ru)
AKADEMIK FILATOV (Ru)
AKADEMIK IOSIF ORBELI (Ru)
AKADEMIK RYKACHEV (Ru)
AKADEMIK SHUKHOV (Ru)
AKADEMIK YURYEV (Ru)
02670
SVETLOGORSK (Ru)
AKADEMIK EVGENIY
   PATON (Ru)
ILYA KULIK (Ru)
SEREBRYANSK (Ru)
SEVAN (Ru)
SYZRAN (Ru)
SARNY (Ru)
SEROV (Ru)
SEVERODONETSK (Ru)
SLAVYANSK (Ru)
SVANETIYA (Ru)
KOMSOMOLSKAYA
   SLAVA (Ru)
SOCHI (Ru)
02690
NOVGOROD (Ru)
NOVOSIBIRSK (Ru)
NOVOKUZNETSK (Ru)
NOVOKUIBYSHEVSK (Ru)
NOVOMOSKOVSK (Ru)
NOVOTROITSK (Ru)
NOVOVYATSK (Ru)
NOVOALTAISK (Ru)
NOVOMIRGOROD (Ru)
NOVOPOLOTSK (Ru)
NOVODRUZHESK (Ru)
NOVOLVOVSK (Ru)

NOVZYBKOV (Ru)
NOVOGRUDOK (Ru)
NOVOVOLYNSK (Ru)
02724
NORILSK (Ru)
YURIY ARSHINEVSKIY (Ru)
VASILIY BURKHANOV (Ru)
IVAN DANIKIN (Ru)
NIZHNEYANSK (Ru)
MONCHEGORSK (Ru)
OKHA (Ru)
TIKSI (Ru)
IGARKA (Ru)
BRATSK (Ru)
KOLA (Ru)
ARKHANGELSK (Ru)
AMDERMA (Ru)
KANDALAKSHA (Ru)
KEMEROVO (Ru)
ANADYR (Ru)
NIKEL (Ru)
ANATOLIY
  KOLESNICHENKO (Ru)
KAPITAN MAN (Ru)
02790
KAPITAN ALEKSEYEV (Ru)
KAPITAN DZURASHEVICH (Ru)
KAPITAN KADETSKIY (Ru)
KAPITAN KUSHNARENKO (Ru)
KAPITAN
  ANISTRATYENKO (Ru)
KAPITAN GEORGIY
  BAGLAY (Ru)
KAPITAN LEONTIY
  BORISENKO (Ru)
KAPITAN LEV SOLOVYEV (Ru)
KAPITAN MODEST
  IVANOV (Ru)
KAPITAN SLIPKO (Ru)
02847
AKADEMIK N. VAVILOV (Ru)
AKADEMIK ZAVARITSKIY (Ru)
SKULPTOR TOMSKIY (Ru)
02900
PERM (Ru)
PALANGA (Ru)
PAMIR (Ru)
PARAMUSHIR (Ru)

PAROMAY (Ru)
PARGOLOVO (Ru)
PAVLOVO (Ru)
PECHENGA (Ru)
PERTOMINSK (Ru)
PETROKREPOST (Ru)
PETROVSKIY (Ru)
PETROZAVODSK (Ru)
PLESETSK (Ru)
POMORYE (Ru)
PONOY (Ru)
PROKOPYEVSK (Ru)
PREZHEVALSK (Ru)
PULKOVO (Ru)
PUSHLAKHTA (Ru)
PUSTOZERSK (Ru)
03040
KALININABAD (Ru)
KANEV (Ru)
KRASNOUFIMSK (Ru)
03060
HARRY POLLITT (Ru)
VALERIAN KUIBYSHEV (Ru)
WILLIAM FOSTER (Ru)
ANATOLIY
  LUNACHARSKIY (Ru)
ANNA ULYANOVA (Ru)
ALEKSANDR ULYANOV (Ru)
DMITRIY ULYANOV (Ru)
ILYA ULYANOV (Ru)
NIKOLAY KRYLENKO (Ru)
NIKOLAY POGODIN (Ru)
OLGA ULYANOVA (Ru)
VLADIMIR ILYCH (Ru)
BORIS ZHEMCHUZIN (Ru)
03110
NOVGOROD (Ru)
NOVOSIBIRSK (Ru)
NOVOKUZNETSK (Ru)
NOVOKUIBYSHEVSK (Ru)
NOVOMOSKOVSK (Ru)
NOVOTROITSK (Ru)
NOVOVYATSK (Ru)
NOVOALTAISK (Ru)
NOVOMIRGOROD (Ru)
NOVOPOLOTSK (Ru)
NOVODRUZHESK (Ru)
NOVOLVOVSK (Ru)

NOVOZYBKOV (Ru)
NOVOGRUDOK (Ru)
NOVOVOLYNSK (Ru)
03150
KARL MARX (DDR)
FRIEDRICH ENGELS (DDR)
03230
RADZIONKOW (Pd)
BOCHNIA (Pd)
CHELM (Pd)
GARWOLIN (Pd)
HENRYK LEMBERG (Pd)
OSTROLEKA (Pd)
WIELICZKA (Pd)
SKOCZOW (Pd)
SIEMIATYCZE (Pd)
03260
KULDIGA (Ru)
KANDAVA (Ru)
03270
OMSK (Ru)
OKHOTSK (Ru)
ORENBURG (Ru)
03400
AKADEMIK FEDOROV (Ru)
03423
KURSK (Ru)
BYELGOROD (Ru)
BELGOROD (Ru)
JAN KALBERZIN (Ru)
AKADEMIK
  CHELOMEY (Ru)
ARVID PELSHE (Ru)
AKADEMIK BOCHVAR (Ru)
CAMILO CIENFUEGOS (Ru)
03620
RADZIONKOW (Pd)
BOCHNIA (Pd)
CHELM (Pd)
GARWOLIN (Pd)
HENRYK LEMBERG (Pd)
OSTROLEKA (Pd)
SKOCZOW (Pd)
SIEMIATYCZE (Pd)
WIELICZKA (Pd)
03650
HARRY POLLITT (Ru)
VALERIAN KUIBYSHEV (Ru)

BORIS ZHEMCHUZIN (Ru)
WILLIAM FOSTER (Ru)
ANATOLIY
  LUNACHARSKIY (Ru)
ANNA ULYANOVA (Ru)
ALEKSANDR ULYANOV (Ru)
DIMITRIY ULYANOV (Ru)
ILYA ULYANOV (Ru)
NIKOLAY KRYLENKO (Ru)
NIKOLAY POGODIN (Ru)
OLGA ULYANOVA (Ru)
VLADIMIR ILYCH (Ru)
03690
WARNEMUNDE (Ru)
PALEKH (Ru)
PAVLODAR (Ru)
PAVLOGRAD (Ru)
PESTOVO (Ru)
PETRODVORETS (Ru)
POLESSK (Ru)
PRAVDINSK (Ru)
PRIMORSK (Ru)
PSKOV (Ru)
PUTIVL (Ru)
PERVOMAYSK (Ru)
SALVADOR ALLENDE (Ru)
WALTER ULBRICHT (Ru)
DEKABRIST (Ru)
NADEZHDA KRUPSKAYA (Ru)
MUHLHAUSEN THOMAS-
  MUNTZERSTADT (DDR)
NORDHAUSEN (DDR)
SANGERHAUSEN (DDR)
SONDERHAUSEN (DDR)
03770
LENINSKAYA GVARDIYA (Ru)
ALEKSANDR VINOKUROV (Ru)
ALEKSANDRA
  ARTYUKHINA (Ru)
ANDREY ANDREYEV (Ru)
FEDOR PETROV (Ru)
GLEB KRZHIZHANOVSKIY (Ru)
IOSIF DUBROVINSKIY (Ru)
IVAN BYELOSTOTSKIY (Ru)
IVAN POKROVSKIY (Ru)
IOHANNES LAURISTIN (Ru)
LEON POPOV (Ru)
LYUDMILA STAL (Ru)

MATVEY MURANOV (Ru)
MAKSIM LITVINOV (Ru)
MIKHAIL VLADIMIRSKY (Ru)
MIKHAIL OLMINSKIY (Ru)
NIKOLAY SEMASHKA (Ru)
NIKOLAY SHVERNIK (Ru)
OLGA VARENTSOVA (Ru)
OSIP PYATNITSKIY (Ru)
PANTELEYMON
  LEPESHINSKIY (Ru)
PETR KRASIKOV (Ru)
SERGEY GUSEV (Ru)
SUREN SPANDARYAN (Ru)
VERA LEBEDYEVA (Ru)
VIKTOR KURNATOVSKIY (Ru)
VASILY SHELGUNOV (Ru)
YAAN ANVELT (Ru)
PAVEL DAUGE (Ru)
SVORTSOV-STEPANOV (Ru)
YEMELYAN
  YAROSLAVSKIY (Ru)
03870
ALTENBURG (DDR)
BERNBURG (DDR)
BLANKENBURG (DDR)
BOIZENBURG (DDR)
EILENBURG (DDR)
FREYBURG (DDR)
MAGDEBURG (DDR)
MEYENBURG (DDR)
NAUMBURG (DDR)
NIENBURG (DDR)
ORANIENBURG (DDR)
QUEDLINBURG (DDR)
ROSTOCK (DDR)
NEUBRANDENBURG (DDR)
RONNEBURG (DDR)
SCHWARZBURG (DDR)
03930
KLIN (Ru)
KOMSOMOLETS ESTONII (Ru)
KOMSOMOLETS LATVII (Ru)
KOMSOMOLETS LITVY (Ru)
KOMSOMOLETS
  TADZHIKISTANA (Ru)
KOMSOMOLETS
  UZBEKISTANA (Ru)
KOMMUNARSK (Ru)

KRASNOGVARDEYSK (Ru)
KRASNOKAMSK (Ru)
KRASNODON (Ru)
KRASNOUFIMSK (Ru)
KRASNOURALSK (Ru)
KRASNOZAVODSK (Ru)
KRASNOE SELO (Ru)
03950
SOSNOGORSK (Ru)
SIDOR KOVPAK (Ru)
SOKOL (Ru)
SUZDAL (Ru)
KAPITAN PLAUSHEVSKIY (Ru)
STOLETIYE PARIZHOSKOY
KOMMUNY (Ru)
IVAN KOROBTSOV (Ru)
GENERAL VLADIMIR
ZAIMOV (Ru)
VALERIY MEZHLAUK (Ru)
VALENTIN KHUTORSKOY (Ru)
KAPITAN LUKHMANOV (Ru)
ALEKSANDR TSYURUPA (Ru)
ANDREY LAVROV (Ru)
KAPITAN SHANTSBERG (Ru)
KLIM VOROSHILOV (Ru)
KOMANDARM MATVEYEV (Ru)
PROFESSOR BUZNIK (Ru)
AKADEMIK YANGEL (Ru)
04010
LENINSKAYA GVARDIYA (Ru)
ALEKSANDR VINOKUROV (Ru)
ALEKSANDRA
ARTYUKHINA (Ru)
ANDREY ANDREYEV (Ru)
FEDOR PETROV (Ru)
GLEB KRZHIZHANOVSKIY (Ru)
IOSIF DUBROVINSKIY (Ru)
IVAN BYELOSTOTSKIY (Ru)
IVAN POKROVSKIY (Ru)
IOHANNES LAURISTIN (Ru)
LEON POPOV (Ru)
LYUDMILA STAL (Ru)
MATVEY MURANOV (Ru)
MAKSIM LITVINOV (Ru)
MIKHAIL VLADIMIRSKY (Ru)
MIKHAIL OLMINSKIY (Ru)
NIKOLAY SEMASHKO (Ru)
NIKOLAY SHVERNIK (Ru)

OLGA VARENTSOVA (Ru)
OSIP PYATNITSKIY (Ru)
PANTELEYMON
LEPESHINSKIY (Ru)
PETR KRASIKOV (Ru)
SERGEY GUSEV (Ru)
SUREN SPANDARYAN (Ru)
VERA LEBEDYEVA (Ru)
VIKTOR KURNATOVSKIY (Ru)
VASILIY SHELGUNOV (Ru)
YAAN ANVELT (Ru)
YELENA STASOVA (Ru)
PAVEL DAUGE (Ru)
SVORTSOV—STEPANOV (Ru)
YEMELYAN
YAROSLAVSKIY (Ru)
04065
'KAMENKA' class (Ru)
ASTRONOM (Ru)
BUK (DDR)
04066
'KAMENKA' class
GS. 107 (Ru)
04067
'BIYA' class (Ru)
04068
'SAMARA' class (Ru)
PAMYAT MERKURIYA (Ru)
04080
STROPTIVYY (Ru)
SPRAVEDLIVYY (Ru)
STAKHANOVETS (Ru)
SIBIRSKIY (Ru)
SUVOROVETS (Ru)
FOBOS (Ru)
DEIMOS (Ru)
04088
PLANETA (Pd)
04180
KIROVSKLES (Ru)
BAYKALLES (Ru)
KAMCHATSKLES (Ru)
KARELYALES (Ru)
KOLYMALES (Ru)
KRASNOGORSKLES (Ru)
KUNGURLES (Ru)
KOVDALES (Ru)
VOLOGDALES (Ru)

04200
'TOMBA' class (Ru)
04210
INGURI (Ru)
04215
SHOTA RUSTAVELI (Ru)
04216
FYODOR MATISEN (Ru)
PAVEL BASHMAKOV (Ru)
GEORGIY MAKSIMOV (Ru)
IVAN KIREYEV (Ru)
YAKOV SMIKNITSKIY (Ru)
04225
AKADEMIK
GAMBURTSYEV (Ru)
04226
PROFESSOR BOGOROV (Ru)
PROFESSOR SHTOKMAN (Ru)
PROFESSOR KURENTSOV (Ru)
PROFESSOR
VODYANITSKIY (Ru)
04230
WILHELM FLORIN (DDR)
EDGAR ANDRE (DDR)
ERNST SCHNELLER (DDR)
WERNER
SEELENBINDER (DDR)
04240
ADMIRAL VLADIMIRSKIY (Ru)
IVAN KRUZHENSTERN (Ru)
04270
TAYMYR (Ru)
04275
AKADEMIK SHULEYKIN (Ru)
ARNOLD VEIMER (Ru)
AKADEMIK SHOKALSKIY (Ru)
PROFESSOR KHROMOV (Ru)
PROFESSOR
MULTANOVSKIY (Ru)
PROFESSOR PAVEL
MOLCHANOV (Ru)
PROFESSOR
BAYKONOVSKIY (Ru)
04312
KATUN (Ru)
ALDOMA (Ru)
04400
HEL (Pd)

JASTARNIA-BOR (Pd)
JURATA (Pd)
KUZNICA (Pd)
WLADYSLAWOWO (Pd)
04423
ALTENBURG (DDR)
BERNBURG (DDR)
BLANKENBURG (DDR)
BOIZENBURG (DDR)
EILENBURG (DDR)
FREYBURG (DDR)
MAGDEBURG (DDR)
MEYENBURG (DDR)
NAUMBURG (DDR)
NIENBURG (DDR)
ORANIENBURG (DDR)
QUEDLINBURG (DDR)
ROSTOCK (DDR)
NEUBRANDENBURG (DDR)
RONNEBURG (DDR)
SCHWARZBURG (DDR)
04520
NATALIYA KOVSHOVA (Ru)
ANATOLIY KHALIN (Ru)
MARIYA POLIVANOVA (Ru)
OGOSTA (Bu)
04860
MIKOLAJ REJ (Pd)
FRYCZ MODRZEWSKI (Pd)
04910
DRESDEN (DDR)
HALLE (DDR)
SUHL (DDR)
KARL MARX STADT (DDR)
COTTBUS (DDR)
FRANKFURT/ODER (DDR)
ERFURT (DDR)
BERLIN-HAUPSTADT DER
DDR (DDR)
LEIPZIG (DDR)
POTSDAM (DDR)
05410
VOLCHANSK (Ru)
05620
IGNATIY SERGEYEV (Ru)
GEORGIY CHICHERIN (Ru)
GEORGIY DIMITROV (Ru)
ERNST THALMANN (Ru)

GIUSEPPE DI VITTORIO (Ru)
50 LET SOVIET
SOVIETSKOY (Ru)
UKRAINY (Ru)
HO CHI MIN (Ru)
INESSA ARMAND (Ru)
IONA YAKIR (Ru)
JEANNE LABOURBE (Ru)
KARL LIEBKNECHT (Ru)
KOMMUNIST (Ru)
KOMMUNISTICHESKOYE
ZNAMYA (Ru)
BELA KUN (Ru)
DMITRY POLUYAN (Ru)
NIKOLAY
KREMLYANSKIY (Ru)
FRIEDRICH ENGELS (Ru)
ROSA LUXEMBURG (Ru)
FRANTS BOGUSH (Ru)
TOYVO
ANTIKAYNEN (Ru)
KONIN (Pd)
06060
VELIKIYE LUKI (Ru)
VEREYA (Ru)
VELIZH (Ru)
06069
COTNARI (Rm)
MIR (Cz)
DRAGASANI (Rm)
FOCSANI (Rm)
06090
WLADYSLAW ORKAN (Pd)
LUCJAN SZENWALD (Pd)
06142
ALBA IULIA (Rm)
CURTEA DE ARGES (Rm)
06200
LEONID SOBINOV (Ru)
FEDOR SHALYAPIN (Ru)
06380
HEINZ KAPELLE (DDR)
LIESELOTTE HERRMANN (DDR)
RUDOLF BREITSCHIED (DDR)
MATHIAS THESEN (DDR)
06770
BEREZNIK (Ru)
GUS-KHRUSTALNYY (Ru)

KAPSUKAS (Ru)
KASHINO (Ru)
KARA (Ru)
KALININGRAD (Ru)
KAPITAN GASTELLO (Ru)
KEDAYNYAY (Ru)
KINGISEPP (Ru)
KOPORYE (Ru)
KRASNOBORSK (Ru)
KOSTINO (Ru)
KUZMINKI (Ru)
KUPISHKIS (Ru)
KUNTSEVO (Ru)
LYUBAN (Ru)
JOSE DIAS (Ru)
TURKU (Ru)
VORONEZH (Ru)
SOFIYA PEROVSKAYA (Ru)
TSIGLOMEN (Ru)
VELIKIYE USTYUG (Ru)
KICHIK (Ru)
KAMCHADAL (Ru)
06795
UNZHA (Ru)
ALDAN (Ru)
AYAN (or AJAN) (Ru)
EGVEKINOT (Ru)
JANA (or YANA) (Ru)
KEM (Ru)
KONDOPOGA (Ru)
KORSAKOV (Ru)
LAKHTA (Ru)
OMOLON (Ru)
PROKOPIY
   GALUSHIN (Ru)
SELENGA (Ru)
SIBIRLES (Ru)
SIBIRTSYEVO (Ru)
TERNEY (Ru)
VERKHOYANSKLES (Ru)
VYATKALES (Ru)
VZMORYE (Ru)
ANTON BUYUKLY (Ru)
YAKUTSKLES (Ru)
BORIS NIKOLAICHUK (Ru)
CHERNIGOV (Ru)
KARAGA (Ru)
KATANGLI (Ru)
KAVALEROVO (Ru)

KAZATIN (Ru)
KILIYA (Ru)
KIRENSK (Ru)
KOREIZ (Ru)
KRASNOARMEYSK (Ru)
KRASNOPOLYE (Ru)
KRASNOTURINSK (Ru)
KRYMSK (Ru)
KULUNDA (Ru)
KUSTANAY (Ru)
KUZNETSK (Ru)
LEONID SMIRNYKH (Ru)
STEPAN SAVUSHKIN (Ru)
TUSHINO (Ru)
TYMOVSK (Ru)
YEVGENIY CHAPLANOV (or
   EVGENIY CHAPLANOV) (Ru)
06825
ABKHAZIYA (Ru)
ADZHARIYA (Ru)
BASHKIRIYA (Ru)
MOLDAVIYA (Ru)
07440
MAJOR SUCHARSKI (Pd)
MARIAN BUCZEK (Pd)
07460
DZIECI POLSKIE (Pd)
GDYNSKI KOSYNIER (Pd)
ZYRARDOW (Pd)
07470
´ATLANTIK´ type (Ru)
BAROGRAF (Ru)
DIPLOT (Ru)
GEROI
   ADZHIMUSHKAYA (Ru)
KURSOGRAF (Ru)
MAKELIS BUKA (Ru)
RODONIT (Ru)
SERDOLIK (Ru)
07550
´BEREZNIK´ class (Ru)
CHAZHMA (Ru)
BLAGOVESHCHENSK (Ru)
ILYINSK (Ru)
ILICHOVO (Ru)
KAMCHADAL (Ru)
TOBOL (Ru)
YANTARNYY (Ru)
KRETINGA (Ru)

KOZYREVSK (Ru)
LOMONOSOVO (Ru)
PRAVDA (Ru)
MIRNYY (Ru)
PALANA (Ru)
VAGA (Ru)
KHARLOV (Ru)
KRASNOYARSK (Ru)
LIGOVO (Ru)
KAMCHATSKIY (Ru)
KOMSOMOLETS (Ru)
TURKU (Ru)
LYUBAN (Ru)
KINGISEPP (Ru)
KRASNOBORSK (Ru)
VELIKIY USTYUG (Ru)
TSIGLOMEN (Ru)
KUPISHKIS (Ru)
KALININGRAD (Ru)
KUZMINKI (Ru)
KOSTINO (Ru)
KARA (Ru)
GUS-KHRUSTALNYY (Ru)
KOPORYE (Ru)
KASHINO (Ru)
KIKHCHIK (Ru)
KAPITAN GASTELLO (Ru)
SOFIYA PEROVSKAYA (Ru)
JOSE DIAS (Ru)
VORONEZH (Ru)
KUNTSEVO (Ru)
KIMRY (Ru)
KEDAYNYAY (Ru)
KAPSUKAS (Ru)
TAMPERE (Ru)
SHUSENSKOYE (Ru)
07600
LENALES (Ru)
07610
LYONYA GOLIKOV (Ru)
07620
AKADEMIK KURCHATOV. (Ru)
AKADEMIK VERNADSKIY (Ru)
DMITRIY MENDELEYEV (Ru)
07860
ANTONI
   GARNUSZEWSKI (Pd)
KAPITAN LEDOCHOWSKI (Pd)
NEPTUN (Rm)

NICOLA VAPTZAROV (Bu)
07900
MINSK (Ru)
MATSESTA (Ru)
MARGELAN (Ru)
MARIINSK (Ru)
MARNEULI (Ru)
MTSENSK (Ru)
MEDYN (Ru)
MEZHDURECHENSK (Ru)
MEZHGORYE (Ru)
MICHURIN (Ru)
MILLEROVO (Ru)
MOZHAYSK (Ru)
MOLOCHANSK (Ru)
MORSHANSK (Ru)
MUKACHEVO (Ru)
MOLODOGVARDEYSK (Ru)
MOZYR (Ru)
MUROM (Ru)
MYTISHCHI (Ru)
ALEKSEY TOLSTOY (Ru)
BORIS GORBATOV (Ru)
DMITRIY FURMANOV (Ru)
IVAN GONCHAROV (Ru)
NIKOLAY NEKRASOV (Ru)
SAMUIL MARSHAK (Ru)
ANTON MAKARENKO (Ru)
BORIS LAVRENEV (Ru)
FEDOR GLADKOV (Ru)
ROMAN ROLLAN (Ru)
07947
TARKHANSK (Ru)
KASHIRSKOYE (Ru)
KULIKOVO (Ru)
SARATOVSK (Ru)
TALNIKI (Ru)
TARASOVSK (Ru)
TEREKHOVSK (Ru)
TERNOVSK (Ru)
TIMOFEYEVSK (Ru)
TITOVSK (Ru)
TOKARYEVSK (Ru)
TRUNOVSK (Ru)
TULSK (Ru)
08030
VYBORG (Ru)
VATUTINO (Ru)
VYAZMA (Ru)

VOLZHSK (Ru)
08115
AKADEMIK SERGEY
   KOROLOV (Ru)
08170
POMERANIA (Pd)
SILESIA (Pd)
08565
NAVIGATOR (Pd)
HYDROGRAF (Pd)
08778
ERNST THALMANN (DDR)
WILHELM PIECK (DDR)
08834
ARAKS (Ru)
KURA (Ru)
LYUTOGA (Ru)
PORONAY (Ru)
SAMUR (Ru)
BAZALT (Pd)
GRANIT (Pd)
ANDOGA (Ru)
ATREK (Ru)
ATMIS (Ru)
AURA (Ru)
08846
RIONI (Ru)
NERCHA (Ru)
YARENGA (Ru)
OM (Ru)
08849
´SAMARA´ class (modified) (Ru)
TURA (Ru)
VAYGACH (Ru)
09035
SB-406 (Ru)
SB-408 (Ru)
SB-921 (Ru)
SB-922 (Ru)
09080
PROFESSOR
   SHCHYOGOLEV (Ru)
PROFESSOR KUDREVICH (Ru)
PROFESSOR ANICHKOV (Ru)
PROFESSOR PAVLENKO (Ru)
PROFESSOR
   RYBALTOVSKIY (Ru)
PROFESSOR KHLYUSTIN (Ru)
PROFESSOR YUSHENKO (Ru)

PROFESSOR UKHOV (Ru)
PROFESSOR MINYAYEV (Ru)
09120
  SPRUT (Ru)
09210
  PRIAMURYE (Ru)
  ZABAYKALYE (Ru)
09360
  GRUMANT (Ru)
  GEIZER (Ru)
  GLETCHER (Ru)
  KAPITAN SKORNYAKOV (Ru)
  KURS (Ru)
  NAVIGATOR (Ru)
  SKAZOCHNIK ANDERSEN (Ru)
  PAVLOVO (Ru)
  PELENGATOR (Ru)
  PEREMYSHLJ (Ru)
  PRILUKI (Ru)
  PROKOPYEVSK (Ru)
  ZELENOBORSK (Ru)
  MAGNIT (Ru)
  BUSSOL (Ru)
  EKHOLOT (Ru)
  LOKATOR (Ru)
09380
  SKRYPLEV (Ru)
  DAVYDOV (Ru)
  SOVIETSK (Ru)
  VITUS BERING (Ru)
  ZAPOLYARNYY (Ru)
  APETIT (Ru)
  KOMPAS (Ru)
  KONDOR (Ru)
09899
  BAKERIT (Ru)
  BAVENIT (Ru)
09995
  GAMZAT TSADASA (Ru)
  IVAN KOTLYAREVSKIY (Ru)
  KONSTANTIN
    PAUSTOVSKIY (Ru)
  NOVIKOV PRIBOY (Ru)
10250
  WALTER DEHMEL (DDR)
  BERNHARD
    KELLERMANN (DDR)
  PETER KAST (DDR)

PETER NELL (DDR)
RUDOLF LEONHARD (DDR)
10260
  BURAN (Pd)
  HALNIAK (Pd)
  LEWANTER (Pd)
10280
  K. I. GALCZYNSKI (Pd)
  HENRYK JENDZHA (Pd)
  PAWEL SZWYDKOJ (Pd)
10350
  STEFAN CZARNIECKI (Pd)
  GRUNWALD (Pd)
  WESTERPLATTE (Pd)
10535
  DELTA DUNARII (Rm)
  MAREA NEAGRA (Rm)
10540
  REGULUS (Pd)
  SAGITTA (Pd)
  ANTARES (Pd)
  ARCTURUS (Pd)
  INDUS (Pd)
10570
  FRANCESCO NULLO (Pd)
  LENINO (Pd)
  ALEKSANDER ZAWADSKI (Pd)
  GWARDIA LUDOWA (Pd)
  LENINGRAD (Pd)
  PIOTR DUNIN (Pd)
  SMOLNY (Pd)
10610
  SIMFEROPOL (Ru)
  SALAVAT (Ru)
  SEMIPALATINSK (Ru)
  SLAVSK (Ru)
  SLUTSK (Ru)
  SOVIETSK (Ru)
10720
  YANIS RAYNIS (Ru)
  ALEKSANDRA
    KOLLONTAY (Ru)
  HENRI BARBUSSE (Ru)
  LARISA REYSNER (Ru)
  KARLIS ZIEDINS (Ru)
  KLARA ZETKIN (Ru)
  MARINA RASKOVA (Ru)
  OTOMAR OSHKALIN (Ru)

POLINA OSIPENKO (Ru)
YANIS LENTSMANIS (Ru)
YAKOV ALKSNIS (Ru)
ZENTA OZOLA (Ru)
10740
  NIKOLAY KOPERNIK (Ru)
  ARISTARKH
    BYELOPOLSKIY (Ru)
  FEDOR BREDIKHIN (Ru)
  MIKHAIL LOMONOSOV (Ru)
  PAVEL PARENAGO (Ru)
  PAVEL SHTERNBERG (Ru)
  VASILIY FESENKOV (Ru)
  VASILIY STRUVE (Ru)
  IVAN POLZUNOV (Ru)
  IVAN KULIBIN (Ru)
  PROFESSOR POPOV (Ru)
  ILYA METCHNIKOV (Ru)
  AKADEMIK
    ARTOBOLEVSKIY (Ru)
  AKADEMIK KHOKHLOV (Ru)
  GDYNSKI KOSYNIER (Pd)
  DZIECI POLSKIE (Pd)
  ZYRARDOW (Pd)
10760
  BURAN (Pd)
  HALNIAK (Pd)
  LEWANTER (Pd)
10780
  OKAH (Ru)
10810
  SEJWAL (Pd)
  FOKA (Pd)
  KASZALOT (Pd)
  NARWAL (Pd)
  HOMAR (Pd)
  ORKA (Pd)
  FINWAL (Pd)
  LANGUSTA (Pd)
  PLETWAL (Pd)
10880
  SLAVA SEVASTOPOLYA (Ru)
11140
  THEODOR STORM (DDR)
  THEODOR FONTANE (DDR)
11300
  KOPET-DAG (Ru)
  ALTAY (Ru)

AMBARCHIK (Ru)
ASKANIYA (Ru)
BELOMORY (Ru)
ELBRUS (Ru)
GOLFSTRIM (Ru)
KHOLMOGORY (Ru)
KIVACH (Ru)
PAMIR (Ru)
PEVEK (Ru)
PODMOSKOVYE (Ru)
POLESYE (Ru)
KARPATY (Ru)
BEREZNIKI (Ru)
NOKUYEV (Ru)
KARAKUMY (Ru)
VOLGOBALT (Ru)
ANDREY ANDREYEV (Ru)
RZHEV (Ru)
KHIBINY (Ru)
DIKSON (Ru)
PRIKARPATYE (Ru)
ZAKAVKAZYE (Ru)
KOTELNICH (Ru)
POVOLZHYE (Ru)
KARPOGORY (Ru)
PRIONEZHYE (Ru)
VERKHOYANY (Ru)
ZAVOLZHYE (Ru)
VALDAY (Ru)
11333
  BALAKHNA (Ru)
  BAYKOVSK (Ru)
  BAZHENOVSK (Ru)
  BORISOV (Ru)
  BUTOVSK (Ru)
  GENERAL KHLEBNIKOV (Ru)
  GEROI SHIRONINTSY (Ru)
  IRTYSHK (Ru)
  IVAN LYUDNIKOV (Ru)
  IVAN KUZNETSOV (Ru)
  KHOTIN (Ru)
  KOLPASHEVO (Ru)
  KONDRAT BILYUTIN (Ru)
  MARSHAL KRYLOV (Ru)
  MARSHAL NIVOKOV (Ru)
  MARSHAL VASILYEVSKIY (Ru)
  MOSKOVSKAYA
    OLIMPIADA (Ru)

PORFIRIY CHANCHIBADZE (Ru)
PYOTR SHAFRANOV (Ru)
SOKOLOVO (Ru)
VLADIMIR KURASOV (Ru)
XXVI SYEZD KPSS (Ru)
PIONER NIKOLAYEVKA (Ru)
XVII SYEZD
  PROFSOYUSOV (Ru)
GEOLOG PYOTR
  ANTROPOV (Ru)
MORSKOY GEOLOG (Ru)
AKADEMIK ALEKSANDR
  KARPINSKIY (Ru)
AKADEMIK ALEKSANDR
  SIDORENKO (Ru)
GEOLOG FERSMAN (Ru)
BAKLANOVO (Ru)
ALEKSANDR TYURIN (Ru)
ALEKSEY STAKHANOV (Ru)
BABAYEVSK (Ru)
BABYKINO (Ru)
BAGANOVO (Ru)
BAGAREVO (Ru)
BAYEVO (Ru)
KAPITAN REDKOKASHA (Ru)
MYS ZOLOTOY (Ru)
PULKOVSKIY MERIDIAN (Ru)
NOVOURALSK (Ru)
SLAVYANSKIY (Ru)
ALEKSANDR
  KSENOFONTOV (Ru)
GENERAL DEDAYEV (Ru)
GRIGORIY KOVTUN (Ru)
IVAN BURMAKOV (Ru)
KAPITAN
  SUKHONDYAYEVSKIY (Ru)
MARSHAL KOSHEVOY (Ru)
ODISHI (Ru)
VOLOPAS (Ru)
11337
  AQUILA (Pd)
  CASSJOPEJA (Pd)
  AQUARIUS (Pd)
11380
  BOROVICHI (Ru)
  KEGOSTROV (Ru)
  MORZHOVETS (Ru)
  NEVEL (Ru)

11430
CHULYMLES (Ru)
ISAKOGORKA (Ru)
IVAN CHERNYKH (Ru)
KILDIN (Ru)
KRASNAYA GORKA (Ru)
NISHNI TAGIL (Ru)
NOVAYA LADOGA (Ru)
NOVAYA ZEMLYA (Ru)
OKA (Ru)
PORKHOV (Ru)
SANGARLES (Ru)
TAYMYR (Ru)
VASYA ALEKSEYEV (Ru)
VOSKHOD (Ru)
VOSTOK 2 (Ru)
VOSTOK 5 (Ru)
VOSTOK 6 (Ru)
YAMAL (Ru)
ZOLOTITZA (Ru)
11460
BASKUNCHAK (Ru)
APSHERON (Ru)
DAURIYA (Ru)
DIKSON (Ru)
DONBASS (Ru)
SEVAN (Ru)
TAMAN (Ru)
11490
INDIGA (Ru)
JANALES (Ru)
KHATANGALES (Ru)
KOSTROMALES (Ru)
KODINO (Ru)
NEVALES (Ru)
OLYUTORKA (Ru)
DIKSON (Ru)
KOLGUYEV (Ru)
PERVOURALSK (Ru)
SALDUS (Ru)
SHEKSNALES (Ru)
ZEYALES (Ru)
KAMALES (Ru)
11575
'VISHNYA' class (Ru)
11580
PLANETA (Ru)
GRIGORIY POLUYANOV (Ru)

ILYA KATUNIN (Ru)
KILDIN (Ru)
KOLSKIY (Ru)
MIKHAIL IVCHENKO (Ru)
OLENEGORSK (Ru)
PLUTONIY (Ru)
PERLAMUTR (Ru)
POLYARNYY (Ru)
REVOLYUTSIYA (Ru)
RYBACHIY (Ru)
TRALFLOT (Ru)
VOSKHOD (Ru)
VSPOLOKH (Ru)
ZARNITSA (Ru)
BISON (Ru)
LUNJ (Ru)
MUROMSK (Ru)
PARALLAKS (Ru)
KIROVSK (Ru)
OLENTUY (Ru)
ONEKOTAN (Ru)
SIYANIE (Ru)
PROGRESS (Ru)
NIKOLAY KONONOV (Ru)
POLYARNOYE SIYANIE (Ru)
11610
SMOLNYY (Ru)
POLOTSK (Ru)
SELIGER (Ru)
KAPITAN DEMIDOV (Ru)
KRASNOPUTILOVETS (Ru)
LAZURNYY (Ru)
NOVOKUIBYSHEVSK (Ru)
PINAGORIY (Ru)
VASILIY KOSENKHOV (Ru)
VAYGACH (Ru)
SLAVGOROD (Ru)
VYBORGSKAYA STORONA (Ru)
VYMPEL (Ru)
BOLSHEVIK (Ru)
SEVERYANIN (Ru)
ANATOLIY BREDOV (Ru)
NIKYEL (Ru)
TIMOFEY KHRYUKIN (Ru)
SULOY (Ru)
ANTON LOPATIN (Ru)
TOROS (Ru)
SALYUT (Ru)

NARVSKAYA ZASTAVA (Ru)
ZODCHIY (Ru)
LENINGRAD (Ru)
ZELENETS (Ru)
YURIY KOSTIKOV (Ru)
11640
ANDROMEDA (Pd)
MERKURY (Pd)
JOWISZ (Pd)
11670
VEGA (Pd)
DENEBOLA (Pd)
PERSEUS (Pd)
GEMINI (Pd)
SIRIUS (Pd)
HARGHITA (Rm)
IEZER (Rm)
SEMENIC (Rm)
CLABUCET (Rm)
INAU (Rm)
MINDRA (Rm)
11690
PROFESSOR SIEDLECKI (Pd)
11695
CARINA (Pd)
11700
RETEZATUL (Rm)
MOLDOVEANU (Rm)
NEGOIU (Rm)
SINOE (Rm)
CARAIMAN (Rm)
CEAHLEAUL (Rm)
RAZELM (Rm)
TUCANA (Pd)
LEPUS (Pd)
LACERTA (Pd)
SATURN (Pd)
LYRA (Pd)
TAURUS (Pd)
LIBRA (Pd)
11720
TARUSA (Ru)
BYKOVO (Ru)
BYELOMORSK (Ru)
LOVOZYERO (Ru)
MYS GROTOVYY (Ru)
MYS KURILSKIY (Ru)
MYS LOPATKA (Ru)

MYS PROKOFYEVA (Ru)
MYS RATMANOVA (Ru)
MYS TAYMYR (Ru)
MYS VAYGACH (Ru)
MYS VORONINA (Ru)
NAROCH (Ru)
NEVYANSK (Ru)
BORISPOL (Ru)
DOMODYEDOVO (Ru)
KRONSHTADT (Ru)
MYS ARKTICHESKIY (Ru)
TORZHOK (Ru)
SOLOVIETSKIY (Ru)
SHEREMTYEVO (Ru)
GEROI ZAPOLYARYA (Ru)
BIRYUSINSK (Ru)
VNUKOVO (Ru)
NOVYY MIR (Ru)
ZELEZNOGORSK (Ru)
ZNAMYA POBEDY (Ru)
30-LETIYE POBEDY (Ru)
MYS BUDYONNOGO (Ru)
MYS CHELYUSKIN (Ru)
MYS FRUNZE (Ru)
MYS KRONOTSKIY (Ru)
MYS OTRADNYY (Ru)
MYS VODOPADNYY (Ru)
URGAL (Ru)
KHAROVSK (Ru)
TIKHOOKEANSKIY (Ru)
TYNDA (Ru)
MYS ILMOVYY (Ru)
MYS KUZNETSOVA (Ru)
MYS SILINA (Ru)
MYS CHASOVOY (Ru)
MYS CHAYKOVSKOGO (Ru)
MYS GROZNYY (Ru)
MYS SKALISTYY (Ru)
MURMANSELD (Ru)
VERKHOVINA (Ru)
MYS SVOBODNYY (Ru)
SOVGANSKIY
KOMSOMOLETS (Ru)
GANGUT (Ru)
TSIMLYANSK (Ru)
VYSOVSK (Ru)
VYSHOGOROD (Ru)
MYS TIKHIY (Ru)

MYS DALNIY (Ru)
NIKOLAYEVSKIY
KORABEL (Ru)
ANDREY MARKIN (Ru)
ILYA VOLYNKIN (Ru)
IYUN KORAN (Ru)
TANTAL (Ru)
XVI SYEZD
PROFSOYUZOV (Ru)
XVIII SYEZD VLKSM (Ru)
MYS BABUSHKIN (Ru)
MYS OSTROVSKOGO (Ru)
MYS YUNONY (Ru)
11790
WLOCZNIK (Pd)
POLLUX (Pd)
11800
'ATLANTIK' class
AYU-DAG (Ru)
AKHILLES (Ru)
AKHTUBA (Ru)
AKHUN (Ru)
AKMOLINSK (Ru)
AKUSTIK (Ru)
ALEKSANDROVSK (Ru)
ALEKSEY BORDUNOV (Ru)
ALMA (Ru)
ALSU (Ru)
AMDERMA (Ru)
AMGA (Ru)
ASPHERON (Ru)
ARDATOV (Ru)
ARGUN (Ru)
ARMENIYA (Ru)
ARTEK (Ru)
ARZAMAS (Ru)
ASTRONOM (Ru)
ATOLL (Ru)
AVIATOR (Ru)
AY-PETRI (Ru)
AZURIT (Ru)
BALTA (Ru)
BATUMI (Ru)
BAZALT (Ru)
BEREZEN (Ru)
BUREVESTNIK (Ru)
BYELOVO (Ru)

DARYAL (Ru)
DNEPRODZERZHINSK (Ru)
DRUZHBA SSSR-GDR (Ru)
YEYSK (or EYSK) (Ru)
FEDOR GLADKOV (Ru)
GELIOGRAF (Ru)
GEROI ADZHIMUSHKAYA (Ru)
ILMEN (Ru)
ILYICHYOVSK (Ru)
IMERITI (Ru)
IZMAIL (Ru)
KAKHETI (Ru)
KAZANTIP (Ru)
KIROVOGRAD (Ru)
KOBULETI (Ru)
KORUND (Ru)
KVADRANT (Ru)
LENINOGORSK (Ru)
LIMAN (Ru)
LVOV (Ru)
MIKHAIL BORISOV (Ru)
MEGANOM (Ru)
MELITOPOL (Ru)
METEORIT (Ru)
MIKHAIL VIDOV (Ru)
MITRIDAT (Ru)
NADEZHDA (Ru)
NIKOLAY BROVTSYEV (Ru)
NIKOLAYEV (Ru)
OKTANT (Ru)
OKTYABRSKOYE (Ru)
OREL (Ru)
ORLETS (Ru)
ORLINOYE (Ru)
PEREDOVIK (Ru)
PETR LIZYUKOV (Ru)
PISATEL (Ru)
PITSUNDA (Ru)
PLANERIST (Ru)
PLUTON (Ru)
POLEVOD (Ru)
POLTAVA (Ru)
PRAVOVYED (Ru)
PRILIV (Ru)
PROLIV (Ru)
PROMYSLOVIK (Ru)
PROPAGANDIST (Ru)
PROSVETITEL (Ru)

PUBLIKIST (Ru)
PYATIGORSK (Ru)
POET (Ru)
SADKO (Ru)
SAKARTVELO (Ru)
SALKHINO (Ru)
SAPUN GORA (Ru)
SERGEY KANDACHIK (Ru)
SHVENTOY (Ru)
SIVASH (Ru)
SKALISTYY (Ru)
SOKOLINOYE (Ru)
SOLNTSEDAR (Ru)
SOPKA GEROYEV (Ru)
SOYUZ (Ru)
MIKHAIL KORNITSKIY (Ru)
SUMY (Ru)
TAGANROG (Ru)
TAVRIDA (Ru)
TIKHORETSK (Ru)
TIMOFEY GORNOV (Ru)
TSKHALTUBO (Ru)
TULEN KABILOV (Ru)
UGOLNYY (Ru)
VASILY GOLOVKIN (Ru)
VENERA IV (Ru)
VOLKHOVSTROY (Ru)
VOLNOMER (Ru)
VZMORYE (Ru)
YUKHAN SMUUL (Ru)
YULIMISTE (Ru)
YURIY MALAKHOV (Ru)
YUTNIEKS (Ru)
YUZHNOMORSK (Ru)
ZHEMAYTIYA (Ru)
ZOLOTOY KOLOS (Ru)
AGATOVYY (Ru)
ARAGONIT (Ru)
BARIT (Ru)
BOKSIT (Ru)
DIONIS (Ru)
DOLOMIT (Ru)
IZUMRUDNYY (Ru)
KALINOVO (Ru)
KALTAN (Ru)
KARAGACH (Ru)
KAVRAY (Ru)
KHRUSTALNYY (Ru)

KREMEN (Ru)
KLIMOVO (Ru)
MAKELIS BUKA (Ru)
MRAMORNY (Ru)
PIRIT (Ru)
RODONIT (Ru)
RUBINOVYY (Ru)
SEDA (Ru)
TESEY (Ru)
ZYEMCHUSNYY (Ru)
SERDOLIK (Ru)
ALBA (Ru)
ASTEROID (Ru)
ARTEMIDA (Ru)
BAKHCHISARAY (Ru)
CHATYR-DAG (Ru)
EVRIKA (Ru)
FIOLENT (Ru)
GERAKL (Ru)
KAMENSKOYE (Ru)
KARA-DAG (Ru)
KHRONOMETR (Ru)
MILOGRADOVO (Ru)
PROFESSOR
PROFESSOR
  MESYATSYEV (Ru)
SHANTAR (Ru)
ZUND (Ru)
ZVEZDA KRIMA (Ru)
ALKA (Bu)
BEKAS (Bu)
FLAMINGO (Bu)
GLARUS (Bu)
KONDOR (Bu)
LIMOZA (Bu)
LORNA (Bu)
MELANITA (Bu)
OLUSHA (Bu)
PINGVIN (Bu)
RALIDA (Bu)
ZIKONIYA (Bu)
IALOMITA (Rm)
JIUL (Rm)
MILCOV (Rm)
MURES (Rm)
NEAJLOV (Rm)
SIRET (Rm)
SOMES (Rm)

TROTUS (Rm)
11995
  SSV 465 (Ru)
12000
  AKADEMIK KOROLYOV (Ru)
  AKADEMIK SHIRSHOV (Ru)
  PROFESSOR VIZE (Ru)
  PROFESSOR ZUBOV (Ru)
12230
  KERCH (Ru)
  ALIOT (Ru)
  ANTARES (Ru)
  ARGO (Ru)
  BOLSHEVO (Ru)
  DENEB (Ru)
  DOBROVOLSK (Ru)
  FEODOSIYA (Ru)
  GORECHJE (Ru)
  GURIYA (Ru)
  HERKULES (Ru)
  IVAN GOLUBETS (Ru)
  KALJMAR (Ru)
  KARTLI (Ru)
  KASSIOPEYA (Ru)
  KOLKHIDA (Ru)
  KRASNODAR (Ru)
  KOREIZ (Ru)
  LIVADIYA (Ru)
  MTSKHETSA (Ru)
  MIZAR (Ru)
  NIKOLSK (Ru)
  OREANDRA (Ru)
  REPINO (Ru)
  ROSLAVL (Ru)
  RUSLAN (Ru)
  RUSTAVI (Ru)
  RUZA (Ru)
  SATURN (Ru)
  STRELETS (Ru)
  TBILISI (Ru)
  VEGA (Ru)
  YALTA (Ru)
  YEVPATORIYE (Ru)
  YUZHNYY KREST (Ru)
  ZARAYSK (Ru)
  KALLISTO (Ru)
  KOMSOMOLETS (Ru)
  KOZEROG (Ru)

NAUKA (Ru)
PEGAS (Ru)
RADUGA (Ru)
SHEDAR (Ru)
BUREVESTNIK (Bu)
FENIX (Bu)
PELIKAN (Bu)
TCHAIKA (Bu)
12340
  'PUSHKIN' class
    (modified) (Ru)
  DUSHANBE (Ru)
  KHABAROVSK (Ru)
  MURMANSK (Ru)
  ZLATOUST (Ru)
  ZHIGULEVSK (Ru)
12360
  'MAYAKOVSKIY' class (Ru)
  BELINSKIY (Ru)
  GLEB USPENSKIY (Ru)
  RADISHEV (Ru)
  ZHUKOVSKIY (Ru)
12380
  'MAYAKOVSKIY' class
    (modified)
  AFANASAY NIKITIN (Ru)
  AGAT (Ru)
  ALEKSANDR MAKSUTOV (Ru)
  ALEKSEY GMYREV (Ru)
  ALEKSEY MAKHALIN (Ru)
  ALMAZ (Ru)
  AMURSK (Ru)
  ANISIMOVKA (Ru)
  ANTCHAR (Ru)
  ANTS LAYKMAA (Ru)
  ARKOVO (Ru)
  ARSENEYEV (Ru)
  ASKOLD (Ru)
  ASTRA (Ru)
  AUGUST ALLE (Ru)
  BAKAYEVO (Ru)
  BAYKAL (Ru)
  BASARGIN (Ru)
  BIKIN (Ru)
  BIRSHTONAS (Ru)
  BIRYUZA (Ru)
  BOSFOR (Ru)
  BYELKINO (Ru)

DANKO (Ru)
DIOMID (Ru)
DMITRY FURMANOV (Ru)
DRUSKININKAY (Ru)
DZINTARYURA (Ru)
EDUARD VEYDENBAUM (Ru)
ELEKRENAY (Ru)
ESTAFETA OKTYABRYA (Ru)
FEDOR KRAYNOV (Ru)
50 LET VLKSM (Ru)
15 SYEZD VLKSM (Ru)
GALIFAN BATARSHIN (Ru)
GRIGORIY SHELKOV (Ru)
GUBERTAS BORISA (Ru)
HANS LIEBERECHT (Ru)
IMANT SUDMALIS (Ru)
JAKHONT (Ru)
IOKHAN KYOLER (Ru)
IONAS BILYUNAS (Ru)
IOZAS VITAS (Ru)
ITELMAN (Ru)
IVAN DVORSKIY (Ru)
IVAN CHERNOPYATKO (Ru)
IVAN PANOV (Ru)
YAAN KOORT (Ru)
YAKOV SMUSHKEVICH (Ru)
YAN BERZIN (Ru)
JAN FABRITSIUS (Ru)
JAN RUDZUTAK (Ru)
JOHANNES RUVEN (Ru)
YUOZAS VAREYKIS (Ru)
YUOZAS
   GREYFENBERGERIS (Ru)
KAAREL LIYMAND (Ru)
KAPITAN ANDREI TARAN (Ru)
KAROLIS POZHELA (Ru)
KASKAD (Ru)
KHERMAN ARBON (Ru)
KINGAN (Ru)
KOMMUNIST (Ru)
KOMMUNIST UKRAINY (Ru)
KOMSOMOL UKRAINI (Ru)
KORALL (Ru)
KRAYEV (Ru)
KRISTALL (Ru)
KRISTIONAS DONELAYTIS (Ru)
KRISTYAN RAUD (Ru)
KUBA (Ru)

LAGUNA (Ru)
LAZURIT (Ru)
LESOGORSK (Ru)
LINARD LAYTSEN (Ru)
MALAKHIT (Ru)
MAMIN SIBIRYAK (Ru)
MARK RESHETNIKOV (Ru)
MART SAAR (Ru)
MATIS PLUDON (Ru)
MESKUPAS ADOMAS (Ru)
MIKOLOYUS
   CHYURLYONIS (Ru)
MONGOLIYA (Ru)
MRAMOR (Ru)
NADEZHDINSK (Ru)
NAKHODKA (Ru)
NIKOLAY OSTROVSKIY (Ru)
NOVAYA ERA (Ru)
OPALA (Ru)
OSKAR LUTS (Ru)
OTROG (Ru)
OZYORNYE KLYUCHI (Ru)
PAKHACHA (Ru)
PASIONARIYA (Ru)
PECHENGA (Ru)
PEREKAT (Ru)
PETR STUCHKA (Ru)
PETRODVORETS (Ru)
PIONER UKRAINY (Ru)
PIONER ZAPOLYARYA (Ru)
POSYET (Ru)
PRIAMURYE (Ru)
PRIOZERSK (Ru)
PRANAS
   EYDUKYAVICHUS (Ru)
PULKOVO (Ru)
PUTIVL (Ru)
PYOTR OVCHINNIKOV (Ru)
ROBERT EYDEMAN (Ru)
RUBIN (Ru)
RUDOLF BLAUMANIS (Ru)
SAMARGA (Ru)
SAPFIR (Ru)
SEMYON DEZHNEV (Ru)
SEROGLAZKA (Ru)
SEVERNAYA PALMIRA (Ru)
SHTURMAN YELAGIN (Ru)
SHYAULYAY (Ru)

SIBIRYAK (Ru)
SNABZHENETS PERVYY (Ru)
SOVGAVAN (Ru)
SOVIETSKIE
   PROFSOYUZY (Ru)
STANYUKOVICH (Ru)
STAR (Ru)
TADZHIKISTAN (Ru)
TAYSHET (Ru)
TAMAN (Ru)
TEODOR NETTE (Ru)
TERNEY (Ru)
TIKHVIN (Ru)
TOPAZ (Ru)
TRETYAKOVO (Ru)
TRUDOVYE RESERVY (Ru)
TURMALIN (Ru)
VALENTIN
   KOTELNIKOV (Ru)
VASILY VINEVITIN (Ru)
VITALIY BONIVUR (Ru)
VITAUTAS PUTNA (Ru)
VLADAS REKASHYUS (Ru)
VLADIMIR ATLASOV (Ru)
VOSKHOD (Ru)
YANTAR (Ru)
YARONIMAS
   UBORYAVICHUS (Ru)
YASHMA (Ru)
YUBILEY OKTYABRYA (Ru)
YUNOST (Ru)
YUOZAS GARYALIS (Ru)
YUOZAS VAREYKIS (Ru)
ZIGMAS ANGARETIS (Ru)
BAKLAN (Ru)
FREGATA (Bu)
12570
AKADEMIK KNIPOVICH (Ru)
PERSEY III (Ru)
PROFESSOR DERYUGIN (Ru)
AKADEMIK BERG (Ru)
ATLANT (Ru)
ANDRUS YOKHANI (Ru)
ARGUS (Ru)
EKVATOR (Ru)
GIZHIGA (Ru)
NEPTUN (Ru)
POSEYDON (Ru)

12585
ODISSEY (Ru)
IKHTIANDR (Ru)
12587
SSV 502 (Ru)
SSV 464 (Ru)
SSV 501 (Ru)
12590
'LESKOV' class (Ru)
DRUZHBA (Ru)
KUPRIN (Ru)
LESKOV (Ru)
MIR (Ru)
MAMIN SIBIRYAK (Ru)
SPUTNIK (Ru)
12610
JUPITER (Pd)
NEPTUN (Pd)
URAN (Pd)
12620
BERTOLT BRECHT (DDR)
ERIK WEINERT (DDR)
F. C. WEISKOPF (DDR)
JOHANNES R. BECKER (DDR)
12630
WALTER DEHMEL (DDR)
BERNHARD
   KELLERMANN (DDR)
FRIEDRICH WOLF (DDR)
PETER KAST (DDR)
PETER NELL (DDR)
RUDOLF LEONHARD (DDR)
12680
KAPITAN SMIRNOV (Ru)
VLADIMIR VASLYAYEV (Ru)
KAPITAN MEZENTSYEV (Ru)
INZHENER YERMOSHKIN (Ru)
12685
TADEUSZ KOSCIUSKO (Pd)
KAZIMIERZ PULASKI (Pd)
STEFAN STARZYNSKI (Pd)
WLADYSLAW SIKORSKI (Pd)
13010
INGURLES (Ru)
LESOZAVODSK (Ru)
SOLNECHNOGORSK (Ru)
13590
OB (Ru)

YENISEY (Ru)
13650
'SUPER ATLANTIK' type
AKHILLEON (Ru)
AUKSHAYTIKA (Ru)
APOGEY (Ru)
ARABAT (Ru)
BATILMAN (Ru)
BERKUT (Ru)
BAGRATIONOVSK (Ru)
BIOSFERA (Ru)
FOROS (Ru)
GRANIT (Ru)
GEFEST (Ru)
GARPUNER
   PROKOPYENKO (Ru)
GENERAL OSTRYAKOV (Ru)
GRIGORIY OVODOVSKIY (Ru)
IOSIF LAPUSHKIN (Ru)
YAN RAYNBERG (Ru)
IOAKIM VATSIETIS (Ru)
KURSHAYA DUGA (Ru)
KOMMUNAR (Ru)
LYUDMILA PAVLICHENKO (Ru)
LEMBIT PERN (Ru)
MAMAYEV KURGAN (Ru)
MUSTYARV (Ru)
MALAYA ZEMLYA (Ru)
MYS CHAKO (Ru)
MEZOSFERA (Ru)
MIKHAIL ORLOV (Ru)
NIKOLAY BERAZIN (Ru)
NIKIFOR PAVLOV (Ru)
NIKOLAY TSYGANOV (Ru)
ORFEY (Ru)
PATROKL (Ru)
PRESIDENT PIK (Ru)
PERIGEY (Ru)
PEYPSI (Ru)
PETROGRADSKAYA
   STORONA (Ru)
RETAVAS (Ru)
SALANTI (Ru)
SERGEY LYULIN (Ru)
SCHILUTE (Ru)
SAADYARV (Ru)
STRATOSFERA (Ru)
TRIPOSFERA (Ru)

218

TRITON (Ru)
TRUSEVIK MORYA (Ru)
TEMRYUCHANIN (Ru)
TAURAGE (Ru)
TURAYDA (Ru)
TSEMESSKAYA BUKHTA (Ru)
TAMULA (Ru)
VAGULA (Ru)
VASILIY FOMIN (Ru)
VOROSHILOVGRAD (Ru)
VASILIY REVYAKIN (Ru)
YURMALA (Ru)
YURBARKAS (Ru)
YONAVA (Ru)
ZVEZDA (Ru)
ZNAMYA KERCHIL (Ru)
ZEFIR (Ru)
BISTRITA (Rm)
CERNA (Rm)
CINDRELUL (Rm)
DORNA (Rm)
PUTNA (Rm)
TIRNAVA (Rm)
LUDWIG TUREK (DDR)
AZOV (Ru)
PROMETEY (Ru)
SUVALKIYA (Ru)
GENERAL
    CHERNYAKHOVSKIY (Ru)
13745
PRIZVANIE (Ru)
GLOBUS (Ru)
PROFESSOR KLENOVA (Ru)
PROFESSOR KOZHIN (Ru)
PROFESSOR NIKOLSKIY (Ru)
PROFESSOR VOYEVODIN (Ru)
13751
Later 'SUPER ATLANTIK'
    type
ADAYKHOKH (Ru)
AKHMETA (Ru)
BALTISKAYA KOSA (Ru)
BORIS TSINDELIS (Ru)
DARVIN (Ru)
DONISAR (Ru)
GALDOR (Ru)
ILYA KULIN (Ru)
GEYA (Ru)

GRIGORIY TERENTYEV (Ru)
GEROYEVKA (Ru)
GARPUNER ZARVA (Ru)
KALPER (Ru)
IVAN KORZUNOV (Ru)
KONSTANTIN
    ALEKSEYEV (Ru)
KULIKOVO POLYE (Ru)
NARODNYY
    OPOLCHENETS (Ru)
NIKOLAY GRIBANOV (Ru)
NOVOANGARSK (Ru)
NOVOARKHANGELSK (Ru)
NOVASBEST (Ru)
NOVOBATAYSK (Ru)
NOVOBIRYUSINSKIY (Ru)
NOVOBOBRUYSK (Ru)
NOVODRUTSK (Ru)
NOVOKACHALINSK (Ru)
NOVOKAZALINSK (Ru)
NOVOKIYEVKA (Ru)
NOVOKOTORSK (Ru)
NOVOLADOZHSKIY (Ru)
NOVOMALTINSK (Ru)
NOVONIKOLSK (Ru)
NOVOORSK (Ru)
NOVOORENBURG (Ru)
NOVOPSKOV (Ru)
NOVOSOKOLNIKI (Ru)
NOVOYELNYA (Ru)
NOVOYENISEYSK (Ru)
NOVOZLATOPOL (Ru)
SELENA (Ru)
SOKRAT (Ru)
SUGAN (Ru)
STRALSUNDSKIY
    KORABEL (Ru)
URANIYA (Ru)
VIYTNA (Ru)
VOZROZHDENIYE (Ru)
ASTAN KESAYEV (Ru)
ELVA (Ru)
BORIS ALEKSEYEV (Ru)
GROM (Ru)
FYODOR YEROZIDI (Ru)
PELAGIAL (Ru)
NEVSKAYA DUBROVSKA (Ru)
MISA (Ru)

NIKOLAY
    PUSTOVOYTENKO (Ru)
KAUGURI (Ru)
NOVOROSSIYSKIY
    RABOCHIY (Ru)
KHARKU (Ru)
TSVETKOVO (Ru)
NIKOLAY AFANASYEV (Ru)
MAKSIM KHOMYAKOV (Ru)
CHERCHESK (Ru)
ARKADIY CHERNYSHEV (Ru)
GAZGAN (Ru)
BORODINSKOYE POLYE (Ru)
GISSAR (Ru)
GNEVNYY (Ru)
INZHENER YUDINTSYEV (Ru)
LIMB (Ru)
MECHISLOVAS GEDVILAS (Ru)
MLECHNYY PUT (Ru)
PATRIOT (Ru)
RUSSOYE POLYE (Ru)
SEKSTAN (Ru)
SHAPOSHNIKOVO (Ru)
SHAKOPOVO (Ru)
SHEPETOVKA (Ru)
TELSHYAY (Ru)
VASILIY GRECHISNIKOV (Ru)
YASTREBOVO (Ru)
VOLNYY VETER (Ru)
ZVYEZDA ASOVA (Ru)
YEVGENIY POLYAKOV (Ru)
PROSTOR (Ru)
ZVYEZDACHERNOMORYA (Ru)
ZVYEZDA
    SEVASTOPOLYA (Ru)
KAPITAN PURGIN (Ru)
ALEKSEY GRACHYEV (Ru)
AZIMUT (Ru)
BAZALETI (Ru)
KRYMSKIY RABOCHIY (Ru)
KURTNA (Ru)
PETROPAVLOVSKAYA
    KREPOST (Ru)
TSEFEY (Ru)
EDUARD CLAUDIUS (DDR)
ARNOLD ZWEIG (DDR)
LUDWIG RENN (DDR)
HANS MARCHWITZA (DDR)

BRUNO APITZ (DDR)
BAHLUI (Rm)
CRISUL ALB (Rm)
DIMBOVITA (Rm)
JIJIA (Rm)
OLTET (Rm)
OZANIA (Rm)
PARING (Rm)
RODNA (Rm)
MAGURA (Rm)
NOVOCHEBOKSARSK (Ru)
NOVOUKRAINA (Ru)
NOVOLYANOVSK (Ru)
13850
MAMAIA (Rm)
RUZA (Rm)
14370
PULA (Ru)
ALEKSANDR BLOK (Ru)
ALEKSANDR GERTSEN (Ru)
ALEKSANDR GRIN (Ru)
ALEKSANDR
    SERAFIMOVICH (Ru)
ALEKSANDR VERMISHEV (Ru)
ALISHER NAVOI (Ru)
ANTON CHEKOV (Ru)
ARKADIY GAYDAR (Ru)
DEMYAN BEDNYY (Ru)
DMITRIY GULIA (Ru)
DUBROVNIK (Ru)
GAVRIL DERZHAVIN (Ru)
MAKHTUM-KULI (Ru)
MUSA DZHALIL (Ru)
NAZIM KHIKMET (Ru)
NIKOLAY DUBROLYUBOV (Ru)
NIKOLAY GOGOL (Ru)
NIKOLAY KARAMZIM (Ru)
NIKOLAY OGARYEV (Ru)
OVANES TUMANYAN (Ru)
SERGEY YESENIN (Ru)
SULEYMAN STALSKIY (Ru)
VISSARION BELINSKIY (Ru)
VLADIMIR KOROLENKO (Ru)
VLADIMIR MAYAKOVSKIY (Ru)
14450
IGNATIY SERGEYEV (Ru)
GEORGIY CHICHERIN (Ru)
GEORGIY DMITROV (Ru)

ERNST THALMANN (Ru)
GIUSEPPE DI VITTORIO (Ru)
50 LET SOVIETSKOY
    UKRAINY (Ru)
HO CHI MIN (Ru)
INESSA ARMAND (Ru)
IONA YAKIR (Ru)
JEANNE LABOURBE (Ru)
KARL LIEBKNECHT (Ru)
KOMMUNIST (Ru)
KOMMUNISTICHESKOYE-ZNAMYA (Ru)
BELA KUN (Ru)
DMITRY POLUYAN (Ru)
NIKOLAY KREMLYANSKIY (Ru)
FRIEDRICH ENGELS (Ru)
ROSA LUXEMBURG (Ru)
FRANTS BOGUSH (Ru)
TOYVO ANTIKAYNEN (Ru)
KONIN (Ru)
14480
FRANCISZEK ZUBRZYCKI (Pd)
BRONISLAW LACHOWICZ (Pd)
EUGENIUSZ
    KWIATKOWSKI (Pd)
MIECZYSLAW
    KALINOWSKI (Pd)
ROMAN PAZINSKI (Pd)
TADEUSZ OCIOSZYNSKI (Pd)
GENERAL STANISLAW
    POPLAWSKI (Pd)
14700
DIVNOGORSK (Ru)
14770
URSUS (Pd)
SWIECIE (Pd)
14800
WLADYSLAW ORKAN (Pd)
LUCJAN SZENWALD (Pd)
14905
VITYAZ (Ru)
AKADEMIK ALEXSANDR
    NESMEYANOV (Ru)
AKADEMIK ALEKSANDR
    VINOGRADOV (Ru)
14910
WLADYSLAW JAGIELLO (Pd)
WLADYSLAW LOKIETEK (Pd)
ZYGMUNT AUGUST (Pd)

219

ZYGMUNT STARY (Pd)
ZYGMUNT III WAZA (Pd)
MIESZKO 1 (Pd)
BOLESLAW CHOBRY (Pd)
BOLESLAW SMIALY (Pd)
BOLESLAW KRZYWOUSTY (Pd)
CSOKONAI (Hu)
RADNOTI (Hu)
14955
 AKADEMIK MSTISLAV
  KELDYSH (Ru)
14962
 IRBIS (Ru)
 NIKOLAYEV (Ru)
 TIGR (Ru)
 YASNIY (Ru)
 NEFTEGAZ-1 (Ru)
 NEFTEGAZ-2 (Ru)
 NEFTEGAZ-3 (Ru)
 NEFTEGAZ-5 (Ru)
 NEFTEGAZ-6 (Ru)
 NEFTEGAZ-7 (Ru)
 NEFTEGAZ-8 (Ru)
 NEFTEGAZ-9 (Ru)
 NEFTEGAZ-10 (Ru)
 NEFTEGAZ-11 (Ru)
 NEFTEGAZ-12 (Ru)
 NEFTEGAZ-13 (Ru)
 NEFTEGAZ-14 (Ru)
 NEFTEGAZ-15 (Ru)
 NEFTEGAZ-16 (Ru)
 NEFTEGAZ-17 (Ru)
 NEFTEGAZ-18 (Ru)
 NEFTEGAZ-19 (Ru)
 NEFTEGAZ-20 (Ru)
 NEFTEGAZ-21 (Ru)
 NEFTEGAZ-22 (Ru)
 NEFTEGAZ-23 (Ru)
 NEFTEGAZ-24 (Ru)
 NEFTEGAZ-25 (Ru)
 NEFTEGAZ-26 (Ru)
 NEFTEGAZ-27 (Ru)
 NEFTEGAZ-28 (Ru)
 NEFTEGAZ-29 (Ru)
 NEFTEGAZ-30 (Ru)
 NEFTEGAZ-31 (Ru)
 NEFTEGAZ-32 (Ru)
 ILGA (Ru)
 GEPARD (Ru)

14975
 YULIUS FUCHIK (Ru)
 TIBOR SZAMUELY (Ru)
14983
 NEFTEGAZ 51 (Ru)
 NEFTEGAZ 52 (Ru)
 NEFTEGAZ 53 (Ru)
14986
 AKADEMIK FERSMAN (Ru)
 AKADEMIK SHATSKIY (Ru)
 AKADEMIK SESKIY (Ru)
 AKADEMIK LAZAROV (Ru)
14988
 AKADEMIK OPARIN (Ru)
15000
 'PROFESSOR' class (Ru)
15003
 AKADEMIK M A
  LAVRENTYEV (Ru)
 AKADEMIK BORIS
  PETROV (Ru)
 AKADEMIK NIKOLAY
  STRAKHOV (Ru)
15040
 MIKOLAJ KOPERNIK (Pd)
 JAN HEWELIUSZ (Pd)
15090
 KRIVAN (Cz)
 RADHOST (Cz)
 SITNO (Cz)
 BLANIK (Cz)
15095
 AKADEMIK MSTISLAV
  KELDYSH (Ru)
15120
 ALEKSANDR
  DOVZHENKO (Ru)
 GEORGIY VASILYEV (Ru)
 SERGEY EYZENSHTEYN (Ru)
 SERGEY VASILYEV (Ru)
 VSEVOLOD PUDOVKIN (Ru)
15310
 MAJOR SUCHARSKI (Pd)
 MARIAN BUCZEK (Pd)
15340
 FRANCESCO NULLO (Pd)
 LENINO (Pd)
 ALEKSANDER ZAWADSKI (Pd)
 GWARDIA LUDOWA (Pd)

 LENINGRAD (Pd)
 PIOTR DUNIN (Pd)
 SMOLNY (Pd)
15360
 PULKOWNIK DABEK (Pd)
15410
 HEINZ KAPELLE (DDR)
 LIESELOTTEHERRMANN (DDR)
 RUDOLF BREITSCHEID (DDR)
 MATHIAS THESEN (DDR)
15420
 BUCURESTI (Rm)
 DOBROGEA (Rm)
15459
 MUDYUG (Ru)
15460
 SINEGORSK (Ru)
 BARGUZIN (Ru)
 BIRYUZA (Ru)
 BUKHTARMA (Ru)
 DALNEGORSK (Ru)
 GORNO-ALTAYSK (Ru)
 GRISHA AKOPIAN (Ru)
 GRUMANT (Ru)
 GULBENE (Ru)
 HELTERMAA (Ru)
 KAMCHATKA (Ru)
 KOKHTLA (Ru)
 KOVDOR (Ru)
 KYPU (Ru)
 MANYCH (Ru)
 MURMAN (Ru)
 NEVER (Ru)
 NIZHNEUDINSK (Ru)
 OLENEGORSK (Ru)
 PAYDE (Ru)
 PERESLAVL-
  ZALESSIK (Ru)
 SEGEZHA (Ru)
 SELEMDZHA (Ru)
 SEVORODVINSK (Ru)
 SHILKA (Ru)
 SPASSK-DALNIY (Ru)
 STEPAN KHALTURIN (Ru)
 SVIRSK (Ru)
 SYKTYVKAR (Ru)
 TUNGUSKA (Ru)
 USSURI (Ru)
 VILYANY (Ru)

 VYRU (Ru)
 ZAPOLYARNYY (Ru)
 RISTNA (Ru)
15500
 PYARNU (Ru)
 NOVOVORONEZH (Ru)
 POVOVETS (Ru)
15510
 SHURA KOBER (Ru)
 ARKADIY KAMANIN (Ru)
 BORIYA TSARIKOV (Ru)
 GALYA KOMLEVA (Ru)
 KOLYA MYGATIN (Ru)
 LARA MIKHEYENKO (Ru)
 LYONYA GOLYKOV (Ru)
 MARAT KOZEY (Ru)
 NINA KUKOVEROVA (Ru)
 PAVLIK LARISHKIN (Ru)
 PIONER (Ru)
 PIONERSKAYA PRAVDA (Ru)
 PIONERSKAYA ZORKA (Ru)
 SASHA BORODULIN (Ru)
 SASHA KONDRATYEV (Ru)
 SASHA KOTOV (Ru)
 SASHA KOVALYOV (Ru)
 TOLYA KOMAR (Ru)
 TOLYA SHUMOV (Ru)
 TONYA BONDARCHUK (Ru)
 VALYA KOTIK (Ru)
 VALERIY VOLKOV (Ru)
 VASYA KOROBKO (Ru)
 VASYA SHISHKOVSKIY (Ru)
 VITYA CHALENKO (Ru)
 VITYA KHONENKO (Ru)
 VITYA SITNITSA (Ru)
 VOLODYA
  SCHERBATSEVICH (Ru)
 YUTA
  BONDAROVSKAYA (Ru)
 ZINA PORTNOVA (Ru)
15580
 KRASZEWSKI (Pd)
15720
 WLADYSLAW JAGIELLO (Pd)
 WLADYSLAW LOKIETEK (Pd)
 ZYGMUNT AUGUST (Pd)
 ZYGMUNT STARY (Pd)
 ZYGMUNT III WAZA (Pd)
 MIESZKO 1 (Pd)

 BOLESLAW CHOBRY (Pd)
 BOLESLAW SMIALY (Pd)
 BOLESLAW KRZYWOUSTY (Pd)
 CSOKONAI (Hu)
 RADNOTI (Hu)
16000
 STRAZAK-5 (Pd)
 STRAZAK-14 (Pd)
 STRAZAK-25 (Pd)
16140
 UKRAINA (Ru)
16205
 NEVER (Ru)
 NEREIDA (Ru)
 NERITSA (Ru)
 NARVAL (Ru)
16270
 JASLO (Pd)
16810
 MAKSIM GORKIY (Ru)
16925
 ARKONA (DDR)
16960
 ODESSA (Ru)
17257
 TRANSSHELF (Ru)
17320
 ZARNITZA (Ru)
17323
 TITAN-1 (Ru)
 TITAN-2 (Ru)
17327
 STANISLAV YUDIN (Ru)
17329
 JUPITER (Bu)
 THALE (DDR)
17350
 SPRUT (Ru)
17480
 WARNEMUNDE (DDR)
17500
 DOVATOR (Ru)
 ALEKSANDR NEVSKII (Ru)
 ALIOSHA POPOVICH (Ru)
 ALTAI (Ru)
 BAGRATION (Ru)
 CHKALOV (Ru)
 DMITRIY
  POZHARSKIY (Ru)

DMITRIY DONSKOY (Ru)
DOBRYNA NIKITCH (Ru)
ERNST TELMAN (Ru)
FRIDRICH ENGELS (Ru)
G. V. PLEKHANOV (Ru)
GENERAL
    CHERNYAKOVSKIY (Ru)
GOGOL (Ru)
ILITCH (Ru)
ILYA MUROMETS (Ru)
KARL LIEBKNECHT (Ru)
KARL MARX (Ru)
KAVRAZ (Ru)
KRUPSKAYA (Ru)
KRYLOV (Ru)
MATROSOV (Ru)
MIKHAIL KUTUZOV (Ru)
N. GASTELLO (Ru)
RODINA (Ru)
RYLYEV (Ru)
TARAS SHEVCHENKO (Ru)
TIMIRYAZEV (Ru)
URAL (Ru)
VYSHINSKIY (Ru)
17560
  PETR LEBEDEV (Ru)
  SERGEY VAVILOV (Ru)
17580
  CELTIC PRIDE (Pd)
17634
  KRAB-2 (Ru)
  MARS (Ru)
17637
  KAPITAN ARON (Ru)
  OSTROMITYANIN (Ru)
  ALGORITM (Ru)
  PRAKTICHNYY (Ru)
  OZORNOY (Ru)
  USPESHNYY (Ru)
  USTOYCHIVYY (Ru)
  ALAG (Ru)
  AYDAR (Ru)
  ASNINO (Ru)
  ASTRILOVO (Ru)
  OLKHOVSKIY (Ru)
  ORLVSKIY (Ru)
  TAVROVO (Ru)
  OBRUCHEV (Ru)

OGNYEVO (Ru)
OLGINO (Ru)
OLINSK (Ru)
OLKHOVATKA (Ru)
OLSHANY (Ru)
ORON (Ru)
OTPOR (Ru)
TEPLOOZERSKIY (Ru)
TUMNIN (Ru)
CHAGODA (Ru)
CHERNIGOV (Ru)
SHAKHTERSK (Ru)
UTENA (Ru)
GAYDAMAK (Ru)
KURSHENAY (Ru)
LIKENAY (Ru)
OKLAN (Ru)
SHVENCHENELYAY (Ru)
SINITSINO (Ru)
VOLODARSK (Ru)
YARKIY (Ru)
YASNYY (Ru)
SVETLYY (Ru)
USTUPCHIVYY (Ru)
17639
  BAKLAN (Ru)
  GRYF (Ru)
17660
  GALATI (Rm)
  CONSTANTA (Rm)
17670
  ERNST HAECKEL (DDR)
17830
  FASTOV (Ru)
  FLORESHTY (Ru)
17920
  ADMIRAL SARYCHEV (Ru)
  BOSHNYAKOVO (Ru)
  NIKOLAY BOSHNYAK (Ru)
  MOREKHOD (Ru)
  KUSKOV (Ru)
17940
  'B 31' type (Ru)
17950
  ZVYEROBOY (Ru)
  LAPLANDIYA (Ru)
  SEREBRYANKA (Ru)
  BYELOKAMENKA (Ru)

ZALESOVO (Ru)
LIMENDA (Ru)
ZAGORIANA (Ru)
ZASLONOVO (Ru)
ZYKOVO (Ru)
ZVYAGIHO (Ru)
TAYBOLA (Ru)
GREMIKHA (Ru)
ZAKHAROVO (Ru)
ZVYERYEVO (Ru)
ZUBOVO (Ru)
VARSHUGA (Ru)
TIERIBERKA (Ru)
PROFESSOR SERGEY
    DOROFEYEV (Ru)
PROFESSOR NESTOR
    SMYERNOV (Ru)
TITOVKA (Ru)
ZADORIE (Ru)
ZAGORSKIY (Ru)
ZUBARYEVO (Ru)
MEZEN (Ru)
KHARLOVKA (Ru)
17980
  BODO UHSE (DDR)
  WILLI BREDEL (DDR)
17985
  GRANITZ (DDR)
  STUBNITZ (DDR)
17990
  MARTIN ANDERSEN
    NEXO (DDR)
18090
  MIKHAIL LOMONOSOV (Ru)
18270
  HAVANA (Ru)
  BORA (Ru)
  MUSSON (Ru)
  PASSAT (Ru)
  PLAYA HIRON (Ru)
18280
  KUBA (Ru)
18320
  TSIKLON (Ru)
  URAGAN (Ru)
18615
  AKADEMIK A.
    KOVALEVSKIY (Ru)

18720
  NORDSEE (DDR)
  ATLANTIK (DDR)
  BARENTSEE (DDR)
  GROSSER BELT (DDR)
  JAN MAYEN (DDR)
  KATTEGAT (DDR)
  LOFOTEN (DDR)
  MALANGEN (DDR)
  NORDMEER (DDR)
  ORKNEY (DDR)
  SILVER PIT (DDR)
  SUND (DDR)
  SVINOY (DDR)
  SKAGERRAK (DDR)
18740
  LASKARA (Pd)
  KABRYL (Pd)
  KANARYJKA (Pd)
  KANTAR (Pd)
  KNIAZIK (Pd)
  KOLEN (Pd)
  KORWIN (Pd)
  KULBAK (Pd)
  KULBIN (Pd)
  KUNATKA (Pd)
  LATERNA (Pd)
  LIKODYN (Pd)
  LIKOMUR (Pd)
  LIKOSAR (Pd)
  LIKOWAL (Pd)
  LODOWIK (Pd)
  LUTJAN (Pd)
  LUZYTANKA (Pd)
19985
  ROSTOCK (DDR)
20310
  SAKHALIN-1 (Ru)
  SAKHALIN-2 (Ru)
  SAKHALIN-3 (Ru)
  SAKHALIN-4 (Ru)
  SAKHALIN-5 (Ru)
  SAKHALIN-6 (Ru)
  SAKHALIN-7 (Ru)
  SAKHALIN-8 (Ru)
  SAKHALIN-9 (Ru)
20320
  SOVIETSKIY

  AZERBAIDZHAN (Ru)
SOVIETSKIY
  TURKMENISTAN (Ru)
SOVIETSKIY
  KAZAKHSTAN (Ru)
SOVIETSKIY UZBEKISTAN (Ru)
GAMID SULTANOV (Ru)
20353
  DMITRIY SHOSTAKOVICH (Ru)
  MIKHAIL SHOLOKHOV (Ru)
  KONSTANTIN
    CHERNENKO (Ru)
  LEV TOLSTOY (Ru)
  KONSTANTIN SIMONOV (Ru)
  MIKHAIL SUSLOV (Ru)
  GEORG OTS (Ru)
20370
  BYELORUSSIYA (Ru)
  GRUZIYA (Ru)
  AZERBAYDZHAN (Ru)
  LEONID BREZHNEV (Ru)
  KAZAKHSTAN (Ru)
20650
  AYVAZOVSKIY (Ru)
20655
  ILYCH (Ru)
20731
  AYU-DAG (Ru)
  AY-PETRI (Ru)
  PITSUNDA (Ru)
  PROFESSOR KOLESNIKOV (Ru)
20735
  DIMITAR BLAGOEV (Bu)
  GEORGI KIRKOV (Bu)
20738
  KANIN (Ru)
  KAMENSK (Ru)
  YUSHAR (Ru)
20745
  B.K. BABA ZADE (Ru)
  VOLGOGRAD (Ru)
20790
  BELINSKIY (Ru)
  BALKHASH (Ru)
  BAYKAL (Ru)
  CHERNISHEVSKIY (Ru)
  ISYK KOL (Ru)
  KOROLENKO (Ru)

KOTOVSKIY (Ru)
LADOGA (Ru)
LENINSKIY (Ru)
MAMIN SIBIRYAK (Ru)
MEKHANIK KALUSHNIKOV (Ru)
MEKHANIK KULUBIN (Ru)
ONEGA (Ru)
RADISHEV (Ru)
SERGEY TSENSKAY (Ru)
SEVAN (Ru)
20870
YERMAK (Ru)
ADMIRAL MAKAROV (Ru)
KRASIN (Ru)
20875
KAPITAN YEVDOKIMOV (Ru)
KAPITAN MOSHKIN (Ru)
KAPITAN BABICHEV (Ru)
KAPITAN CHUDINOV (Ru)
KAPITAN BORODKIN (Ru)
KAPITAN DEMIDOV (Ru)
KAPITAN MECAIK (Ru)
AVRAAMIY ZAVENYAGIN (Ru)
20880
PERKUN (Pd)
21220
ARAGVI (Ru)
INGUR (Ru)
KURA (Ru)
21240
TSIKLON (Ru)
URAGAN (Ru)
DNEPROVSKIY LIMAN (Ru)
DNESTROVSKIY LIMAN (Ru)
21260
SCHTORM (Ru)
BRIS (Ru)
BURJA (Ru)
TAYFUN (Ru)
VETER (Ru)
21450
SHKVAL (Ru)
21560
FALESHTY (Ru)
FARAB (Ru)
FIRYUZA (Ru)
21580
JANA (Ru)

INDIGIRKA (Ru)
KONDA (Ru)
KULOY (Ru)
NEMAN (Ru)
TULOMA (Ru)
UMAN (Ru)
21600
ZELENOGORSK (Ru)
BALTIYSK (Ru)
CHERNYAKHOVSK (Ru)
GVARDEYSK (Ru)
21610
AMGUEMA (Ru)
PENZHINA (Ru)
GIZHIGA (Ru)
KAPITAN
  BONDARENKO (Ru)
KAPITAN GOTSKIY (Ru)
KAPITAN KONDRATYEV (Ru)
KAPITAN MARKOV (Ru)
KAPITAN MYSHEVSKIY (Ru)
NAVARIN (Ru)
PAVEL PONOMARYEV (Ru)
VANKAREM (Ru)
VASILIY FEDOSEYEV (Ru)
MIKHAIL SOMOV (Ru)
21945
RIFT (Ru)
21947
'MIRNY' class (Ru)
BAKAN (Ru)
LOTSMAN (Ru)
VAL (Ru)
VERTIKAL (Ru)
22135
'OREL' class (Ru)
SMELYY (Ru)
STREMITELNIY (Ru)
STROGIY (Ru)
RAMBINAS (Ru)
DEKABRIST (Ru)
ISPOLNITELNYY (Ru)
22137
'OREL' class (modified) (Ru)
KAPITAN NOKHRIN (Ru)
URAGAN (Ru)
GORDYY (Ru)
RESHITELNYY (Ru)

STEREGUSHCHIY (Ru)
BESSTRASHNYY (Ru)
BESSTRASHNYY (Ru)
KRYM (Ru)
22138
JANTAR (Pd)
KORAL (Pd)
22139
'OKHTENSKIY' class (Ru)
22150
MB 18 (Ru)
MB 15 (Ru)
MB 105 (Ru)
MB 119 (Ru)
22154
BIZON (Ru)
ZUBR (Ru)
22155
GERAKL (Ru)
DIOKL (Ru)
GEKTOR (Ru)
GIGANT (Ru)
22159
'PAMIR' class (Ru)
AGATAN (Ru)
ALDAN (Ru)
SSV-480 (Ru)
PELENG (Ru)
22160
YAGUAR (Ru)
BARS (Ru)
MASHUK (Ru)
PAMIR (Ru)
22173
PURGA (Ru)
NAPORISTYY (Ru)
DMITRIY
  DUDCHENKO (Ru)
KASTITIS (Ru)
MOSHCHNYY (Ru)
VAYGACH (Ru)
AGAT (Ru)
ALMAZ (Ru)
PRIMERNYY (Ru)
SNOROVISTYY (Ru)
UTYOS (Ru)
VILNIS (Ru)
AMETIST (Ru)

KONSTANTIN
  KOROBTSOV (Ru)
MALYY TAYMYR (Ru)
SATURN (Ru)
MURMANRYBA (Ru)
NASTOROZHENNYY (Ru)
MIKULA (Ru)
PREDANNYY (Ru)
TSENTAVR (Ru)
ZEYA (Ru)
RUBIN (Ru)
SHUYA (Ru)
AVIOR (Ru)
EPRON (Ru)
UTYOS (Ru)
KALININGRADETS (Ru)
AMUR (Ru)
NEMAN (Ru)
BERZIN (Ru)
PRIMORYE (Ru)
BREST (Ru)
SAKHALIN (Ru)
CHUKOTKA (Ru)
ZABAYKALYE (Ru)
KAMCHATKA (Ru)
ZAPOLYARYE (Ru)
LADOGA (Ru)
NEPTUNIA (Pd)
POSEJDON (Pd)
PERUN (Bu)
NEOTRAZIMYY (Ru)
22175
GORDYY (Ru)
GORDIY (Ru)
GROMKIY (Ru)
GORDELIVYY (Ru)
GORYACHIY (Ru)
GREMUCHIY (Ru)
GROMOVOY (Ru)
GRYADUSHCHIY (Ru)
22178
ATLANT (Ru)
DIOMID (Ru)
KAPITAN AFANASYEV (Ru)
ATLAS (Ru)
KAPITAN V. FEDETOV (Ru)
VULKAN (Ru)
POSEYDON (Ru)

PROTEY (Ru)
TRITON (Ru)
ZEVS (Ru)
GELIOS (or HELIOS) (Ru)
GERMES (or HERMES) (Ru)
VITEAZUL (Rm)
VOINICUL (Rm)
22180
NIKOLAY ZUBOV (Ru)
ALEKSEY CHIRIKOV (Ru)
ANDREY VILKITSKIY (Ru)
BORIS DAVIDOV (Ru)
FEDOR LITKE (Ru)
SEMYON CHELYUSKIN (Ru)
SEMYON DEZHNEV (Ru)
T BELLINGSGAUSEN (Ru)
VASILIY GOLOVNIN (Ru)
GAVRIL SARITCHEV (Ru)
KHARITON LAPTEV (Ru)
22195
NEVELSKOY (Ru)
22200
KAPITAN CHECHKIN (Ru)
KAPITAN CHADAYEV (Ru)
KAPITAN PLAHIN (Ru)
KAPITAN ZARUBIN (Ru)
KAPITAN BUKAYEV (Ru)
KAPITAN KRUTOV (Ru)
22220
DOBRINYA NIKITICH (Ru)
AFANASIY NIKITIN (Ru)
BURAN (Ru)
YEROFEY KHABAROV (Ru)
FEDOR LITKE (Ru)
ILYA MUROMETS (Ru)
IVAN MOSKVITIN (Ru)
IVAN KRUZENSHTERN (Ru)
PERESVET (Ru)
PLUG (Ru)
SADKO (Ru)
SEMYON DEZHNEV (Ru)
SEMYON CHELYUSKIN (Ru)
VASILIY POYARKHOV (Ru)
VASILIY PRONCHISHCHEV (Ru)
VLADIMIR RUSANOV (Ru)
YURIY LISYANSKIY (Ru)
VYUGA (Ru)
STEPHAN JANTZEN (DDR)

22240
OTTO SCHMIDT (Ru)
GEORGIY SEDOV (Ru)
PYOTR PAKHTUSOV (Ru)
22250
KAPITAN M IZMAYLOV (Ru)
KAPITAN A RADZHABOV (Ru)
KAPITAN KOSOLAPOV (Ru)
22290
ANDREY I. KOROBITSIN (Ru)
NIKOLAY KAPLUNOV (Ru)
SHUYA (Ru)
YURYUZAN (Ru)
22325
SEVER (Ru)
22327
ALPINIST (Ru)
GUMANIST (Ru)
RUMB (Ru)
SOLVYCHEGODSK (Ru)·
SOYUZ-9 (Ru)
SOYUZ-10 (Ru)
STROYNYY (Ru)
BALASHOV (Ru)
GABIBULLA GUSEYNOV (Ru)
NEMUNELIS (Ru)
NERIS (Ru)
SADGORA (Ru)
SAMOTLOR (Ru)
SAVINTSY (Ru)
SAZHINO (Ru)
SAZONOVO (Ru)
SOLNECHNOGORSK (Ru)
SOSNOGORSK (Ru)
DALNERECHENSK (Ru)
KALAMUS (Ru)
MAKRURUS (Ru)
NAYADA (Ru)
SALAVATOVO (Ru)
SEMIYARSK (Ru)
SLAVYANOGORSK (Ru)
SLAVYANOSERBSK (Ru)
SOLIGALICH (Ru)
SOSNOVOBORSK (Ru)
STAROBELSK (Ru)
SURSK (Ru)
SVETLOVODSK (Ru)
SYKTYVKAR (Ru)

VOLGOGRADSKIY
KOMSOMOLETS (Ru)
YEVGENIY BURYKHIN (Ru)
ZHUVINTAS (Ru)
SARAPUL (Ru)
SATINO (Ru)
SAVINO (Ru)
SAYAK (Ru)
SEGOZERO (Ru)
SEMILUKI (Ru)
SEVERO-KURILSK (Ru)
SEVKAR (Ru)
SINEGORE (Ru)
SLAVUTA (Ru)
SNEZHNOYE (Ru)
SOLNTSEVO (Ru)
SOROCHINSK (Ru)
STALSK (Ru)
SUSANINO (Ru)
SVATOVO (Ru)
SVETLOGRAD (Ru)
ALEKSANDR KULIK (Ru)
ALEKSEY RENZAYEV (Ru)
IVAN POLOZKOV (Ru)
MIKHAIL LARIN (Ru)
SANGAR (Ru)
SAVRAN (Ru)
SEBEZH (Ru)
SELETS (Ru)
SERDEZH (Ru)
SERGACH (Ru)
SOGDA (Ru)
SOKOLOVKA (Ru)
STARODUBSKOYE (Ru)
STOLIN (Ru)
STUPINO (Ru)
SURAZH (Ru)
APOGON (Ru)
BATTERFISH (Ru)
FEDOR LYSENKO (Ru)
LOBAN (Ru)
NITSA (Ru)
OPORNYY (Ru)
POLYARNIK (Ru)
RUTSAVA (Ru)
SARDINELLA (Ru)
SARGUS (Ru)
SKAP (Ru)

SMOLYANINOVO (Ru)
STASIS SHEYNAUSKAS (Ru)
STREZHEVOY (Ru)
SUKHANOVO (Ru)
SUPUTINO (Ru)
SVERDLOVO (Ru)
SVETLODOLINSK (Ru)
VARENA (Ru)
SABUROVO (Ru)
SAGAYDAK (Ru)
SARGAN (Ru)
SAYANOGORSK (Ru)
SEMIGORSK (Ru)
SKADOVSK (Ru)
SKORODUM (Ru)
SOLIKAMSK (Ru)
SOLOVEVSK (Ru)
SREDNEKOLYMSKIY (Ru)
SREDNEURALSKIY (Ru)
SUKHODOL (Ru)
SVETLOMORSK (Ru)
CHESMA (Ru)
LAYMA (Ru)
SABURSK (Ru)
SADOVSK (Ru)
SKOLE (Ru)
VAKHRUCHEVSK (Ru)
VALDAYSK (Ru)
VALUYSK (Ru)
VANINSK (Ru)
VASILYEVSK (Ru)
VAZHGORSK (Ru)
YABLONOVSKIY (Ru)
KOLKA (Ru)
LAUMA (Ru)
SAFONOVO (Ru)
SALOMATINSK (Ru)
SARAN (Ru)
SARYCHEVSK (Ru)
SAZHINSK (Ru)
SKALAT (Ru)
SLANTSY (Ru)
SUROVSK (Ru)
SYCHEVO (Ru)
VEZUVSK (Ru)
YAMALSKIY (Ru)
SELENUR (Ru)
SURSKOYE (Ru)

22330
BELONA (Pd)
ALBAKORA (Pd)
BARAKUDA (Pd)
BARBATA (Pd)
BARWENA (Pd)
GRANIK (Pd)
KONGER (Pd)
RAMADA (Pd)
TARPOL (Pd)
TASERGAL (Pd)
22350
RYBAK MORSKI (Pd)
ADMIRAL ARCISZEWSKI (Pd)
22550
ROBERT KOCH (DDR)
22720
SPASSK (Ru)
CHUKOTKA (Ru)
SAKHALIN (Ru)
SIBIR (Ru)
22840
YEYSK (Ru)
DALNERECHENSK (Ru)
HOLMOGORY (Ru)
KYARDLA (Ru)
MURMASH (Ru)
NAMANGAN (Ru)
POLYARNYY (Ru)
POSYET (Ru)
RAKVERE (Ru)
REVDA (Ru)
RENI (Ru)
SHENKURSK (Ru)
SOBOLEVO (Ru)
SIGULDA (Ru)
SYRVE (Ru)
SINEGORSK (Ru)
23195
COTTBUS (DDR)
BRANDENBURG (DDR)
GERA (DDR)
23305
ARNEB (Ru)
ULAN (Ru)
LIDER (Ru)
OPTIMIST (Ru)
ZHELEZHNYY POTOK (Ru)

ALEKSANDR
TKHORZHEVSKIY (Ru)
ALEKSANDR YEVSEYEV (Ru)
DMITRIY ZHABINSKIY (Ru)
KIEVSKIY KOMSOMOLETS (Ru)
LEOPOLD NEKRASOV (Ru)
MENKAR (Ru)
MOREPLAVATEL (Ru)
PATRIOT (Ru)
PRIMORETS (Ru)
REGUL (Ru)
SEMYON VOLKOV (Ru)
SPIKA (Ru)
YELAGIN (Ru)
YUZHNAYA ZVEZDA (Ru)
ALDEBARAN (Ru)
ALGENIB (Ru)
FERGANA (Ru)
ALGAYBA (Ru)
ACHUYEVSKIY (Ru)
NAYSSAAR (Ru)
23307
EISVOGEL (DDR)
23335
TEKHUMARDI (Ru)
AVACHINSKIY (Ru)
BOSFOR VOSTOCHNYY (Ru)
KERCHENSKIY-1 (Ru)
23337
KERCHENSKIY-2 (Ru)
KOGUVA (Ru)
23390
ZVEZDA (Ru)
ZARNITSA (Ru)
YUG (Ru)
23410
RYBAK (Ru)
RYBACHKA (Ru)
BRUNO TESCH (DDR)
CARLO SCHONHAAR (DDR)
ELVIRA
EISENSCHNEIDER (DDR)
ERICH STEINFURTH (DDR)
EUGEN SCHONHAAR (DDR)
GRETE WALTER (DDR)
HANNO GUNTHER (DDR)
HEINZ KAPELLE (DDR)
HEINZ PRIESS (DDR)

223

HERBERT BAUM (DDR)
HERBERT TSCHAPE (DDR)
HERTA LINDER (DDR)
KARL WOLF (DDR)
MAGNUS POSER (DDR)
PETER GORING (DDR)
PHILIPP MULLER (DDR)
RUDI ARNT (DDR)
RUDOLF SCHWARZ (DDR)
WALTER BARTH (DDR)
WERNER KUBE (DDR)
23440
AFALA (Bu)
AKTINJA (Bu)
ALFEUS (Bu)
ARGONAUT (Bu)
FIZALIA (Bu)
KAPRELA (Bu)
OFELIA (Bu)
ROTALIA (Bu)
SAGITA (Bu)
AMAREL (Pd)
BONITO (Pd)
DELFIN (Pd)
GARNELA (Pd)
GRINWAL (Pd)
HAJDUK (Pd)
HUMBAK (Pd)
KALMAR (Pd)
MORS (Pd)
PARMA (Pd)
REKIN (Pd)
WALEN (Pd)
23474
KOLIAS (Pd)
MANTA (Pd)
MARLIN (Pd)
MUSTEL (Pd)
ORCYN (Pd)
ORLEN (Pd)
OTOL (Pd)
PROFESSOR BOGUCKI (Pd)
TAZAR (Pd)
TUNEK (Pd)
23480
'LUCHEGORSK' class (Ru)
MATEMATIK (Ru)
MYS SINYAVINA (Ru)

MYS YEGOROVA (Ru)
MYS YELAGINA (Ru)
RUSNE (Ru)
LUNOKHOD 1 (Ru)
SINYAVINO (Ru)
VIKTOR KHUDYAKOV (Ru)
MYS BELKINA (Ru)
LUCHEGORSK (Ru)
MYS BOBROVA (Ru)
MYS GAMOVA (Ru)
MYS KRYLOVA (Ru)
MYS LAZARYEVA (Ru)
MYS OBRUCHYEVA (Ru)
MYS BARANOVA (Ru)
MYS GRINA (Ru)
MYS MALTSYEVA (Ru)
MYS NADEZHDY (Ru)
MYS OREKHOVA (Ru)
MYS OSIPOVA (Ru)
MYS YERMAK (Ru)
MYS YUDINA (Ru)
RUDOLF SIRGE (Ru)
RUDOLF VAKMAN (Ru)
SAMSHIT (Ru)
SUDUVA (Ru)
TRAKAY (Ru)
TURKUL (Ru)
TYMLAT (Ru)
VOLDEMAR AZIN (Ru)
BURAN (Ru)
IVAN GREN (Ru)
KVARTS (Ru)
OTTO RYASTAS (Ru)
TIRASPOL (Ru)
VULKAN (Ru)
ALEKSANDR
  BOGOLYUBOV (Ru)
KUULUNDA (Ru)
GDOV (Ru)
XV SYEZD PROFSOYUZOV (Ru)
DZUKIYA (Ru)
DZINTERKRASTS (Ru)
VALKA (Ru)
TRUSKAVETS (Ru)
PSKOV (Ru)
ALEKSANDRIT (Ru)
TIGIL (Ru)
PETROZAVODSK (Ru)

KORCHAGINETS (Ru)
NIKOLAYEVSKIY
  KOMSOMOLETS (Ru)
PAUDZHA (Ru)
FEODOR OKK (Ru)
IOKHANNES SEMPER (Ru)
KARAGAT (Ru)
MIKHAIL BARSUKOV (Ru)
MYS SHELIKHOVA (Ru)
KAZALINSK (Ru)
PETROKREPOST (Ru)
SAMARA (Ru)
KAZATIN (Ru)
KOMSOMOL LATVII (Ru)
TOLBACHIK (Ru)
TUMAN-2 (Ru)
DAYNAVA (Ru)
DZINTARZEME (Ru)
AKVAMARIN (Ru)
GRAD (Ru)
KALAR (Ru)
KALITVA (Ru)
KANDALAKSHA (Ru)
KHAYRYUZOVO (Ru)
KIRIR (Ru)
KLYUCHEYSKOY (Ru)
KOTAYKA (Ru)
KORENGA (Ru)
KRASNOGVARDEYETS (Ru)
KUSHKA (Ru)
LABRADOR (Ru)
MALKI (Ru)
MEDIK (Ru)
METEOROLOG (Ru)
MARS-2 (Ru)
NIDA (Ru)
NIKOLAY PAPIVIN (Ru)
PASSAT-2 (Ru)
RIKHARD MIRRING (Ru)
PROGRESS (Ru)
SALEKHARD (Ru)
VOLZHANIN (Ru)
23605
'MAYAK' class (Ru)
23607
'OKEAN' class (Ru)
23608
'LENTRA' class (Ru)

23609
'LENTRA' class (modified) (Ru)
GS 43 (Ru)
GS 55 (Ru)
23640
VLADIMIR KAVRAYSKIY (Ru)
23664
VOLGOGRAD (Ru)
AKHTUBINSK (Ru)
ZARYA (Ru)
VOSKHOD (Ru)
KALARAND (Ru)
VIRURAND (Ru)
ZALIV (Ru)
KOMSOMOLETS TATARII (Ru)
YAROSLAVL (Ru)
OSTROV (Ru)
PYARNURAND (Ru)
TORMIDERAND (Ru)
23665
SB-365 (Ru)
MB-32 (Ru)
MB-35 (Ru)
MB-36 (Ru)
MB-38 (Ru)
MB-61 (Ru)
MB-62 (Ru)
MB-64 (Ru)
MB-108 (Ru)
23685
'SURA' or 'KIL' class (Ru)
23710
WAWEL (Pd)
23760
BATAYSK (Ru)
23770
ALEKSANDR IVANOVICH
  VOEYKOV (Ru)
23820
LANCUT (Pd)
23860
PLUTON (Ru)
GIDROLOG (Ru)
PEGAS (Ru)
PERSEY (Ru)
SENEZH (Ru)
STRELETS (Ru)
TAYGA (Ru)

YUG (Ru)
ZODIAC (Ru)
BRIZ (Ru)
GALS (Ru)
MANGYSHLAK (Ru)
MARSHAL GELOVANI (Ru)
NIKOLAY MATUSEVICH (Ru)
VIZIR (Ru)
STVOR (Ru)
GORIZONT (Ru)
23880
NORILSK (Ru)
23970
KAPITAN BELOUSOV (Ru)
KAPITAN MELEKHOV (Ru)
KAPITAN VORONIN (Ru)
24030
VOLGOLES (Ru)
ALATYRLES (Ru)
ALDANLES (Ru)
ANADYRLES (Ru)
ANDOMALES (Ru)
ANGARSKLES (Ru)
DVINOLES (Ru)
KAPITAN BELOSHAPKIN (Ru)
KOMILES (Ru)
PRIMORLES (Ru)
SEVERLES (Ru)
BELOMORSKLES (Ru)
ALTAYLES (Ru)
ARGUN (Ru)
AMURSKLES (Ru)
ANGARLES (Ru)
BALAKHNALES (Ru)
BUREYALES (Ru)
BRATSKLES (Ru)
BUKHARA (Ru)
BARNAUL (Ru)
BELOZERSKLES (Ru)
BAYKONUR (Ru)
BOBRUYSKLES (Ru)
BODAYBO (Ru)
DARASUN (Ru)
DZHURMA (Ru)
GRODEKOVO (Ru)
ELEKTROSTAL (Ru)
KRASKINO (Ru)
KUNGUR (Ru)

KANDALAKSHALES (Ru)
KRANSK (Ru)
KHATANGA (Ru)
KHOLMSK (Ru)
KOVDA (Ru)
MIRONYCH (Ru)
MEKHANIK RYBASHUK (Ru)
NORDVIK (Ru)
NARYAN—MAR (Ru)
NIKOLAY MIRONOV (Ru)
OREKHOVO—
  ZUYEVO (Ru)
PORONIN (Ru)
KAPITAN ABAKUMOV (Ru)
PUTYATIN (Ru)
POBYEDINO (Ru)
RUBTSOVSK (Ru)
SAKHALINLES (Ru)
SHADRINSK (Ru)
SAYANLES (Ru)
SEGEZHALES (Ru)
SALEKHARD (Ru)
SHATURA (Ru)
RAYCHIKHINSK (Ru)
SELENGALES (Ru)
SUNGARI (Ru)
TOBOLLES (Ru)
TAYGONOS (Ru)
TULOMA (Ru)
TYUMEN (Ru)
TAYGA (Ru)
TAYSHEN (Ru)
ULAN-UDE (Ru)
URALLES (Ru)
VETLUGALES (Ru)
VYCHEGDALES (Ru)
VILYUYLES (Ru)
VOSRESENSK (Ru)
VALDAYLES (Ru)
VOLGA (Ru)
VORKUTA (Ru)
ZABAYKALSK (Ru)
24145
  SSV 591 (Ru)
  SSV 590 (Ru)
24160
  JUNGE GARDE (DDR)
  JUNGE WELT (DDR)

24200
  EISBAR (DDR)
24310
  RODINA (Ru)
  TIORA (Ru)
  TROCHUS (Ru)
  UVAROVSK (Ru)
  IVAN BORZOV (Ru)
  UZGORSK (Ru)
  ZEMLYANSK (Ru)
  GORYACHEGORSK (Ru)
  YEVGENIY
    PREOBRAZENSKIY (Ru)
  TRYDAKNA (Ru)
24560
  SIENKIEWICZ (Pd)
24630
  PETAR BARON (Bu)
25550
  'KHASAN' class (Ru)
  ALCHEVSK (Ru)
  ARMAVIR (Ru)
  DNESTR (Ru)
  DONETS (Ru)
  DONETSK (Ru)
  IMANDRA (Ru)
  MOGILEV (Ru)
  PRIKUMSK (Ru)
  SLAVYANKA (Ru)
25780
  VRANCEA (Rm)
25840
  SEVERODVINSK (Ru)
  ARMAN (Ru)
  CHUKOTKO (Ru)
  IVAN FEDEROV (Ru)
  PECHENGA (Ru)
  SOVIETSKAYA SAKHALIN (Ru)
  SOVIETSKAYA LITVA (Ru)
  SVIATOGOR (Ru)
  JOHANNES VARES (Ru)
  RIGA (Ru)
26210
  BARENTSYEVO MORE (Ru)
  BELOYE MORE (Ru)
  ROSTA (Ru)
  INTSY (Ru)
  KINESHMA (Ru)

KIZHI (Ru)
KRENOMETR (Ru)
NIZHNEANGARSK (Ru)
NOVOAZOVSK (Ru)
RYBAK ZAPOLYARYA (Ru)
VADINSK (Ru)
ZHIZDRA (Ru)
KOSTOPOL (Ru)
KRASNOLESYE (Ru)
KRASNOPEREKOPSK (Ru)
KRASNOSELSK (Ru)
KRASNOSLOBODSK (Ru)
KRASNOTURANSK (Ru)
KRASNOZNAMENSK (Ru)
KALACHINSK (Ru)
KALININSK (Ru)
KANTEMIR (Ru)
KARPINSK (Ru)
KATAYSK (Ru)
KIREYEVSK (Ru)
KIROVAKAN (Ru)
KLIMOVSK (Ru)
DOKUCHAYEVSK (Ru)
DOVSK (Ru)
KLINTSY (Ru)
KRASNOKAMENSK (Ru)
KURGANINSK (Ru)
ZASTAVNA (Ru)
ZEMLYANSK (Ru)
ZNAMENSK (Ru)
KONOTOP (Ru)
KORENOVSK (Ru)
LENSK (Ru)
MEDVEZHYEGORSK (Ru)
MENEZELINSK (Ru)
ZERNOGRAD (Ru)
ZOLOCHYEV (Ru)
ARTYOMOVSK (Ru)
GEORGIYEVSK (Ru)
GREMYACHINSK (Ru)
MISHUKOV (Ru)
NAGORSK (Ru)
NOVOUZENSK (Ru)
ZELENOKUMSK (Ru)
DVURECHENSK (Ru)
GORSK (Ru)
KHVALYNSK (Ru)
KOKSHAYSK (Ru)

TSIVILSK (Ru)
XX SYEZD KOMSOMOLA
  LITVY (Ru)
ZHDANOVSK (Ru)
ACHINSK (Ru)
MAKAYEVKA (Ru)
MOZDOK (Ru)
VETLUGA (Ru)
VILNIUS (Ru)
28060
  'KOLOMNA' type
  SMELA (Ru)
  KOTLAS (Ru)
28490
  LEONID LEONIDOV (Ru)
28600
  'ATLANTIK 333' type (Ru)
  OMEGA (Ru)
  ORLYONOK (Ru)
  OSKOL (Ru)
  OBLUKOVINA (Ru)
  OBOLYANKA (Ru)
  OBSHA (Ru)
  OBVA (Ru)
  OCHAKOV (Ru)
  OCHER (Ru)
  OKHOTA (Ru)
  OSKU (Ru)
  OLANGA (Ru)
  OLAYNE (Ru)
  OLENTY (Ru)
  OM (Ru)
  OMA (Ru)
  OMNYA (Ru)
  OMULENKA (Ru)
  ONDOZERO (Ru)
  OPON (Ru)
  OPTUKHA (Ru)
  OR (Ru)
  ORCHIK (Ru)
  ORLIK (Ru)
  OSTER (Ru)
  OSUGA (Ru)
  OZHOGIMA (Ru)
  OBLUCHE (Ru)
  ODINTSOVO (Ru)
  ODOYEV (Ru)
  OGNEVKA (Ru)

OKAREM (Ru)
OKNITSA (Ru)
OKULOVKA (Ru)
OLCHAN (Ru)
OLENINO (Ru)
OLESKO (Ru)
OLEVSK (Ru)
OLGINKA (Ru)
OMUL (Ru)
OLISHEVKA (Ru)
OLKHOVKA (Ru)
OLOY (Ru)
OLSHANA (Ru)
OLYKA (Ru)
OMALO (Ru)
OMCHAK (Ru)
ONUSHKIS (Ru)
OREANDA (Ru)
OREDEZH (Ru)
ORGEYEV (Ru)
ORKHEVI (Ru)
ORLOVKA (Ru)
ORSK (Ru)
OSHA (Ru)
OSVEYSKOYE (Ru)
OYTAL (Ru)
OZARICHI (Ru)
OZERY (Ru)
OZHERELYE (Ru)
VLADIMIR KALININ (Ru)
OBOLON (Ru)
MARTIN ARENDSEE (Ru)
ORICHI (Ru)
PYOT BULKO (Ru)
OREL (Ru)
KOLOMENSKOYE (Ru)
ORDYNSKOYE (Ru)
KARACHAROVO (Ru)
OKHOTINO (Ru)
IVAN VERNIGORENKO (Ru)
OCHKAMURI (Ru)
BERNARD KOENEN (Ru)
OCHERETINO (Ru)
ALEKSANDR LAVRENOV (Ru)
OBUKHOVO (Ru)
OLOMNA (Ru)
OLGINO (Ru)
OLEMA (Ru)

28750
BOGDAN
KHMELNITSKY (Ru)
28980
IVAN BABUSHKIN (Ru)
NIKOLAY OSTROVSKIY (Ru)
VASILIY DOKUCHAEV (Ru)
YAKOV SVERDLOV (Ru)
BURGAS (Bu)
SLIVEN (Bu)
GABROVO (Bu)
31050
LENINSKIY KOMSOMOL (Ru)
FIZIK LEBEDYEV (Ru)
31150
GEROITE NA
SEVASTOPOL (Bu)
GEROITE NA ODESSA (Bu)
GEROI PLEVNY (Ru)
GEROI SHIPKI (Ru)
31180
GRUDZIADZ (Pd)
GLOGOW (Pd)
31185
MUKRAN (DDR)
WISMAR (DDR)
GREIFSWALD (DDR)
KLAYPEDA (Ru)
VILNYUS (Ru)
KAUNAS (Ru)
31770
LEWANT II (Pd)
LECHISTAN II (Pd)
31830
ARZAMAS (Ru)
31890
MALAYA VISHERA (Ru)
MALOYAROSLAVETS (Ru)
SUKHONALES (Ru)
32065
LENIN (Ru)
32080
GENERAL GAMIDOV (Ru)
32715
WILANOW (Pd)
WAWEL (Pd)
32890
RUGEN (DDR)

32915
OSETIYA (Ru)
33015
SADKO (Ru)
ANATOL (Pd)
GRZEGORS (Pd)
HEROS (Pd)
TUMAK (Pd)
ZBIGNIEW (Pd)
MARIAN (Pd)
MIECZYSLAW (Pd)
STANISLAW (Pd)
ROSOMAK (Pd)
MSCIWOJ (Pd)
MASLAW (Pd)
ROBERT (Pd)
MERKURY (Ru)
ADMIRAL MAKAROV (Ru)
SAKHALINNEFT (Ru)
CHEMPION (Ru)
OLIMPIYETS (Ru)
VOSTOK (Ru)
PODVODNIK (Ru)
GALS (Ru)
PORTOVIK (Ru)
BUREVESTNIK (Ru)
TOPAZ (Ru)
FLOTINSPEKTSIYA-02 (Ru)
SESTRORETSK (Ru)
GIDROSTROITEL (Ru)
BUG (Ru)
BELOMORSK (Ru)
KOMMUNALNIK (Ru)
TALISMAN (Ru)
ETALON (Ru)
BOREY (Ru)
MERIDIAN (Ru)
POLYARNIK (Ru)
SHAKHTYOR (Ru)
VYBORG (Ru)
OREOL (Ru)
MUROMETS (Ru)
NEPTUN (Ru)
33017
GIRULYAY (Ru)
KVEDARNA (Ru)
PAYURIS (Ru)
AUSHRA (Ru)

SORGU (Ru)
MRTR-0407 (Ru)
MRTR-0408 (Ru)
VEVIS (Ru)
VIRBALIS (Ru)
BEREZINO (Ru)
33035
'MOMA' class
(modified)
RYBACHI (Ru)
YUPITER (Ru)
SSV 472 (Ru)
SSV 509 (Ru)
SSV 512 (Ru)
SSV 514 (Ru)
JUPITER (Ru)
33065
LEOPARD (Ru)
33076
NADEZHNYY (Ru)
KAGANSK (Ru)
KAZANSK (Ru)
KAINSK (Ru)
KALINOVSK (Ru)
KALYADINSK (Ru)
KALACHEVSK (Ru)
KAMSKIY (Ru)
KAMYSHEVSK (Ru)
KARGATSK (Ru)
KALACHINSK (Ru)
KAIGA (Ru)
KALININSK (Ru)
KALUGA (Ru)
KAZHEK (Ru)
33193
MIEDWIE (Pd)
MAMRY (Pd)
MIELNO (Pd)
MORAG (Pd)
MORSKIE OKO (Pd)
SNIARDWY (Pd)
WICKO (Pd)
WIECZNO (Pd)
WIGRY (Pd)
GOPLO (Pd)
JAMNO (Pd)
JASIEN (Pd)
SEJNO (Pd)

33197
HYDROMET (Pd)
33198
DYUNY (Ru)
KURZEME (Ru)
SHUSHVE (Ru)
LESNOYE (Ru)
VZMORE (Ru)
MINIYA (Ru)
PRIMORYE (Ru)
USHAKOVO (Ru)
ARINAS (Ru)
AVIRIS (Ru)
LUKSTAS (Ru)
REKIVA (Ru)
ALAUSHAS (Ru)
KRASNOFLOTSKOYE (Ru)
METELIS (Ru)
SALOS (Ru)
DISNAY (Ru)
KHRABROVO (Ru)
MITUVA (Ru)
STREVE (Ru)
VISHTITIS (Ru)
KATRAN (Ru)
PAGRUS (Ru)
SHIRVINTA (Ru)
DANE (Ru)
KATRA (Ru)
LIKENAY (Ru)
YARA (Ru)
BIRVETA (Ru)
IZHEVSKOYE (Ru)
MATROSOVO (Ru)
NOVA (Ru)
UPITE (Ru)
33280
INOWROCLAW (Pd)
33305
RADUZHNYY (Ru)
KENGARAGS (Ru)
MANGALI (Ru)
PECHORSK (Ru)
RECHITSA (Ru)
REDUT (Ru)
MALAKHITOVYY (Ru)
KORALLOVYY (Ru)
KORUNDOVYY (Ru)

KRISTALNYY (Ru)
GRANATOVYY (Ru)
BASTION (Ru)
AZURITOVYY (Ru)
BAZALTOVYY (Ru)
APATITOVYY (Ru)
BOKSITOVYY (Ru)
AKVAMARINOVYY (Ru)
GRAFITOVVY (Ru)
MANGAZEYA (Ru)
KVARTSEVYY (Ru)
VSEVOLOD TIMONOV (Ru)
33527
SULLEYMAN BAGIROV (Ru)
33560
JAMNO (Pd)
WIGRY (Pd)
33605
AKADEMIK PETROVSKIY (Ru)
33620
YEYSKIY LIMAN (Ru)
AKHTARSKIY LIMAN (Ru)
33870
FERDINAND
FREILIGRATH (DDR)
GEORG WEERTH (DDR)
33900
BRESTSKAYA KREPOST (Ru)
33910
KOTOVSKIY (Ru)
NIKOLAY SHCHORS (Ru)
PARKHOMENKO (Ru)
SERGEY LAZO (Ru)
CHAPAYEV (Ru)
33980
POLYUS (Ru)
33990
BAYKAL (Ru)
BALKHASH (Ru)
34100
AMGUEMA (Ru)
34200
GERHART HAUPTMANN (DDR)
ERNST MORITZ ARNDT (DDR)
THEODOR KORNER (DDR)
34240
NIKOLAY BURDYENKO (Ru)
NIKOLAY PIROGOV (Ru)

SERGEY BOTKIN (Ru)
34290
  SHKVAL (Ru)
34330
  JOHN BRINCKMAN (DDR)
  FRITZ REUTER (DDR)
34360
  SANDOMIERZ (Pd)
  SANOK (Pd)
  SLUPSK (Pd)
34405
  MAGADAN (Ru)
  DIKSON (Ru)
34470
  YEYSK (Ru)
  DALNERECHENSK (Ru)
  HOLMOGORY (Ru)
  KYARDLA (Ru)
  MURMASHI (Ru)
  NAMANGAN (Ru)
  POLYARNYY (Ru)
  POSYET (Ru)
  RAKVERE (Ru)
  REVDA (Ru)
  RENI (Ru)
  SHENKURSK (Ru)
  SOBOLEVO (Ru)
  SIGULDA (Ru)
  SYRVE (Ru)
  SINEGORSK (Ru)
  ZAISAN (Ru)
34610
  TARUSA (Ru)
  BYKOVO (Ru)
  BYELOMORSK (Ru)
  LOVOZYERO (Ru)
  MYS GROTOVYY (Ru)
  MYS KURILSKIY (Ru)
  MYS LOPATKA (Ru)
  MYS PROKOFYEVA (Ru)
  MYS RATMANOVA (Ru)
  MYS TAYMYR (Ru)
  MYS VAYGACH (Ru)
  MYS VORONINA (Ru)
  NAROCH (Ru)
  NEVYANSK (Ru)
  BORISPOL (Ru)
  DOMODYEDOVO (Ru)

KRONSHTADT (Ru)
MYS ARKTICHESKIY (Ru)
TORZHOK (Ru)
SOLOVIETSKIY (Ru)
SHEREMTYEVO (Ru)
GEROI ZAPOLYARYA (Ru)
BIRYUSINSK (Ru)
VNUKOVO (Ru)
NOVYY MIR (Ru)
ZELEZNOGORSK (Ru)
ZNAMYA POBEDY (Ru)
30-LET POBEDY (Ru)
MYS BUDYONNOGO (Ru)
MYS CHELYUSKIN (Ru)
MYS FRUNZE (Ru)
MYS KRONOTSKIY (Ru)
MYS OTRADNYY (Ru)
MYS VODOPADNYY (Ru)
URGAL (Ru)
KHAROVSK (Ru)
TIKHOOKEANSKIY (Ru)
TYNDA (Ru)
MYS ILMOVYY (Ru)
MYS KUZNETSOVA (Ru)
MYS SILINA (Ru)
MYS CHASOVOY (Ru)
MYS CHAYKOVSKOGO (Ru)
MYS GROZNYY (Ru)
MYS SKALISTYY (Ru)
MURMANSELD (Ru)
VERKHOVINA (Ru)
MYS SVOBODNYY (Ru)
SOVGANSKIY
  KOMSOMOLETS (Ru)
GANGUT (Ru)
TSIMLYANSK (Ru)
VYOVSK (Ru)
VYSHOGOROD (Ru)
MYS TIKHIY (Ru)
MYS DALNIY (Ru)
NIKOLAYEVSKIY
  KORABEL (Ru)
MYS BABUSKIN (Ru)
MYS OSTROVSKOGO (Ru)
MYS YUNONY (Ru)
34710
  ZENIT (Ru)
  GORIZONT (Ru)

34872
  IVAN BOCHKOV (Ru)
  KOKAND (Ru)
  NIKOLAY VARLAMOV (Ru)
  DALMOR II (Pd)
  ALEKSANDR BORISOV (Ru)
  ALEKSANDR GRIAZNOV (Ru)
  NIKOLAY ZAKORKIN (Ru)
  IVAN ZIMAKOV (Ru)
  MIKHAIL KVASHNIKOV (Ru)
  PAVEL KAYKOV (Ru)
  KAZAN (or KASAN) (Ru)
  LEONID YELKIN (Ru)
  MIKHAIL BORONIN (Ru)
  SEMYON LAPSHENKOV (Ru)
  VIKTOR STRELTSOV (Ru)
  LEONID IVANOV (Ru)
  MIKHAIL VERBITSKIY (Ru)
  YEOFIM KRIVOSEYEV (Ru)
  KONSTANTIN
    FOMTSHENKO (Ru)
  KAPITAN ARDEYEV (Ru)
  SERGEY MAKAREVICH (Ru)
  LEONID NOVOSPASSKIY (Ru)
  PAVEL PANIN (Ru)
  DMITRIY POKROVICH (Ru)
  PAVEL STRELTSOV (Ru)
  NIKOLAY KUROPATKIN (Ru)
  SERGEY KORSHUNOVICH (Ru)
  VIKTOR MIRONOV (Ru)
  VLADIMIR BRODYUK (Ru)
34880
  SPRUT (Ru)
  ARKHIMED (Ru)
  PLUNGE (Ru)
  PRUZANIY (Ru)
  PASVALIS (Ru)
34960
  WISMAR (DDR)
  FREDERIC JOLIOT
    CURIE (DDR)
  STOLLBERG (DDR)
  WITTENBERG (DDR)
34985
  KLYKACH (Ru)
35150
  STAKHANOVETS
    KOTOV (Ru)

STAKHANOVETS
  PETRASH (Ru)
STAKHANOVETS
  YERMOLENKO (Ru)
35170
  INGUL (Ru)
  JANA (Ru)
35180
  KATUNJ (Ru)
  DONETS (Ru)
  TSNA (Ru)
35190
  INGURI (Ru)
35310
  KASPIY (Ru)
  NEVEZHIS (Ru)
  NEVKA (Ru)
  OKA (Ru)
  LENA (Ru)
  AKHTUBA (Ru)
  AMU-DARYA (Ru)
  FONTANKA (Ru)
  GORKY (Ru)
  INDIGIRKA (Ru)
  KAMA (Ru)
  KAPITAN EVSEYEV (Ru)
  KURA (Ru)
  KOLYMA (Ru)
  LENINGRADETS (Ru)
  OB (Ru)
  PSKOVITYANKA (Ru)
  RAZLIV (Ru)
  RADVILISKIS (Ru)
  ROKISHKIS (Ru)
  SUKHONA (Ru)
  SVIR (Ru)
  TAMAN (Ru)
  VYCHEGDA (Ru)
  50 LET VLKSM (Ru)
  ANADYR (Ru)
  RAND-1 (Ru)
  RAND-2 (Ru)
  RAND-3 (Ru)
  RAND-4 (Ru)
35370
  KOLKHIDA (Ru)
  BUKOVINA (Ru)
  KIRGHIZSTAN (Ru)

MOLDAVIA (Ru)
TADZHAKISTAN (Ru)
TALLIN (Ru)
TATARIYA (Ru)
UZBEKISTAN (Ru)
AFGHANISTAN (Ru)
35390
  IZUMRUD (Ru)
35480
  BOJNICE (Cz)
  LEDNICE (Cz)
36140
  DRUZHBA SSSR-DDR (Ru)
36235
  'LUZA' class (Ru)
  ALAMBAY (Ru)
  ARAGVI (Ru)
  BARGUZIN (Ru)
  DON (Ru)
  KAMA (Ru)
  SELENGA (Ru)
36250
  BUNKEROVSCHCHIK-3 (Ru)
  ARTYOM (Ru)
  MOZYR (Ru)
  PIRYATIN (Ru)
  VENTSPILS (Ru)
  VILYUYSK (Ru)
  ZOLOTOY ROG (Ru)
  KOKAND (Ru)
36300
  ZWICKAU (DDR)
36390
  PERELIK (Bu)
36460
  ZWICKAU (DDR)
36820
  TOUNDYA (Bu)
36840
  PRAGA (Ru)
  VARSHAVA (Ru)
36890
  EVENSK (Ru)
  ALUKSNE (Ru)
  APPE (Ru)
  AKTASH (Ru)
  AMURSK (Ru)
  APSHERONSK (Ru)

ARAKS (Ru)
ANAPKA (Ru)
LYUBERTSY (Ru)
SINEGORSK (Ru)
ALEKSEYEVKA (Ru)
ALEKSEYEVSK (Ru)
ANIVA (Ru)
ALAGIR (Ru)
ANAPA (Ru)
ABAGUR (Ru)
ARDATOV (Ru)
DARNITZA (Ru)
EREBUS (Ru)
IMAN (Ru)
RADIY (Ru)
ABAKAN (Ru)
TYUMENNEFT (Ru)
YUGLA (Ru)
37310
 PLISKA (Bu)
 RUSSE (Bu)
37780
 TRUD (Ru)
38530
 PLYAVINYAS (Ru)
 PREYLI (Ru)
 RIGA (Ru)
 VALMIERA (Ru)
 TALSY (Ru)
 TSESIS (Ru)
38580
 GIORDANO BRUNO (Ru)
 FYODOR
  POLETAYEV (Ru)
38610
 BALDONE (Ru)
 BALAKLAVA (Ru)
 BALVY (Ru)
38950
 DESNA (Ru)
 ALATYR (Ru)
 VOLKHOV (Ru)
39110
 CHAZHMA (Ru)
 CHUMIKAN (Ru)
 DESNA (Ru)
39120
 OLEKMA (Ru)

39130
 BOGDAN (Bu)
39290
 DRUZHBA (Ru)
 ASSORA (Ru)
 OPALA (Ru)
 PYMTA (Ru)
 KOSMONAUT TITOV (Ru)
 ALEUT (Ru)
 IRTYSH (Ru)
 KOLPAKOVO (Ru)
 KRUTOGOROVO (Ru)
 MAGO (Ru)
 KARAGA (Ru)
 STARITSA (Ru)
 ZHUPANOVO (Ru)
 AMUR (Ru)
 KAPITAN SHAULSKIY (Ru)
 OB (Ru)
 OBZHA (Ru)
 SAMARKAND (Ru)
 YENISEY (Ru)
39300
 POEL (DDR)
 HIDDENSEE (DDR)
 RIEMS (DDR)
39450
 RODINA (Ru)
 TIORA (Ru)
 UVAROVSK (Ru)
 UZGORSK (Ru)
 GORYACHEGORSK (Ru)
 TROCHUS (Ru)
 IVAN BORZOV (Ru)
 ZEMLYANSK (Ru)
 YEVGENIY
  PREOBRAZENSKIY (Ru)
 TRYDAKNA (Ru)
39660
 BAIA MARE (Rm)
 CLUJ (Rm)
 VICTORIA (Rm)
39670
 GALATI (Rm)
 SUCEAVA (Rm)
 BRAILA (Rm)
39960
 KLAIPEDA (Ru)

39970
 KERCH (Ru)
 TENDRA (Ru)
 CHKALOV (Ru)
 IVANOVO (Ru)
 CHEBOKSARY (Ru)
 ZHITOMIR (Ru)
 KOMSOMOLETS
  UKRAINY (Ru)
 MOSKALVO (Ru)
 KOMSOMOL (Ru)
 KURSK (Ru)
40580
 ANTON IVANOV (Bu)
40660
 LOKBATAN (Ru)
41310
 ORADEA (Rm)
 CRAIOVA (Rm)
 TIMISOARA (Rm)
 BRASOV (Rm)
 DEVA (Rm)
 IASI (Rm)
 SIBIU (Rm)
 BACAU (Rm)
 TIRGOVISTE (Rm)
 TIRGU MURES (Rm)
 VASLUI (Rm)
41630
 PRAHOVA (Rm)
42800
 PEVEK (Ru)
 ARTYOM (Ru)
 MOZYR (Ru)
 PIRYATIN (Ru)
 VENTSPILS (Ru)
 VILYUYSK (Ru)
 ZOLOTOY ROG (Ru)
 KOKAND (Ru)
42960
 VOLNOVAKHA (Ru)
43110
 ZWICKAU (DDR)
43300
 LAMUT (Ru)
 NIKOLAY ISAYENKO (Ru)
43520
 AMBURAN (Ru)

43540
 IMPULS (DDR)
43790
 EVENSK (Ru)
 ALUKSNE (Ru)
 APPE (Ru)
 AKTASH (Ru)
 AMURSK (Ru)
 APSHERONSK (Ru)
 ARAKS (Ru)
 ANAPKA (Ru)
 LYUBERTSY (Ru)
 SINEGORSK (Ru)
 ALEKSEYEVKA (Ru)
 ALEKSEYEVSK (Ru)
 ANIVA (Ru)
 ALAGIR (Ru)
 ANAPA (Ru)
 ABAGUR (Ru)
 ARDATOV (Ru)
 DARNITZA (Ru)
 EREBUS (Ru)
 IMAN (Ru)
 RADIY (Ru)
 ABAKAN (Ru)
 TYUMENNEFT (Ru)
 YUGLA (Ru)
44100
 BOLSHEVIK KARAYEV (Ru)
 PAMYAT 26 KOMISSAROV (Ru)
 ALMA-ATA (Ru)
 GYURGYAN (Ru)
 DZHEBRAIL (Ru)
 AY-PETRI (Ru)
 NUREK (Ru)
 SURAKHANY (Ru)
 ORDZHONIKIDZENNEFT (Ru)
 SABUNCHI (Ru)
 SHIRVANNEFT (Ru)
 BUZOVNY (Ru)
 DZHORAT (Ru)
 MARDAKYANY (Ru)
 MASHITAGI (Ru)
 KARAKUM KANAL (Ru)
 MANGYSHLAK (Ru)
 KIROVABAD (Ru)
 EMBA (Ru)
 NAKHICHEVAN (Ru)

 PORT ILYICH (Ru)
 VOLGONEFTGAROZ (Ru)
 ZHIGANSK (Ru)
44370
 ELGAVA (Ru)
44620
 LIEPAYA (Ru)
 YELNYA (Ru)
 YESSENTUKI (Ru)
44890
 RAVA RUSSKAYA (Ru)
45110
 KALININGRAD (Ru)
 SEVASTOPOL (Ru)
 SIMFEROPOL (Ru)
 ARSENYEV (Ru)
 EGERSHELD (Ru)
 CHURKIN (Ru)
 IRKUTSK (Ru)
45120
 YANTARNYY (Ru)
 BASHKIR (Ru)
 AUGUST JAKOBSON (Ru)
 NIKOLAY ZYSTSTAR (Ru)
 VOLCHANSK (Ru)
 VOLOGDA (Ru)
 KOMISSAR POLUKHIN (Ru)
 KOSMONAUT KOMAROV (Ru)
 ZABAYKALYE (Ru)
45210
 KAMENOGORSK (Ru)
 TITANIYA (Ru)
 TSELINOGRAD (Ru)
 VOLOCHAYEVSK (Ru)
 PRIVOLZHSK (Ru)
 YAROSLAVL (Ru)
 KUYBYSHEVGES (Ru)
45270
 KONSTITUTSIYA SSSR (Ru)
 RYBAK KAMCHATSKIY (Ru)
 RYBAK PRIMORIYA (Ru)
 RYBAK CHUKOTKI (Ru)
 PISHCHEVAYA
  INDUSTRIYA (Ru)
 RYBAK VLADIVOSTOKA (Ru)
45290
 PYATIDYESYATILYETIYE
  SSSR (Ru)

VASILIY CHERNYSHYEV (Ru)
YEVGENIY LEBEDYEV (Ru)
45350
POLTAVA (Ru)
BEZHITSA (Ru)
PEREKOP (Ru)
POLOTSK (Ru)
PAVLOVSK (Ru)
PRIDNEPROVSK (Ru)
BABUSHKIN (Ru)
BAKURIANI (Ru)
BERISLAV (Ru)
PARTIZANSKAYA ISKRA (Ru)
PARTIZANSKAYA SLAVA (Ru)
BRYANSKIY RABOCHIY (Ru)
BALASHIKHA (Ru)
BAYMAK (Ru)
BELGOROD
    DNESTROVSKIY (Ru)
BEREZOVKA (Ru)
OKTYABRSKAYA (Ru)
REVOLYUTSIYA (Ru)
ADY (Hu)
PETOFI (Hu)
45540
'OSKOL' class (Ru)
45590
MANYCH (Ru)
TAGIL (Ru)
45630
OLA (Ru)
OTRADNOE (Ru)
OREKHOV (Ru)
ORSHA (Ru)
OSTRAGOZHSK (Ru)
45680
IZHMALES (Ru)
IRKUTSKLES (Ru)
IGARKALES (Ru)
INKURLES (Ru)
IRBITLES (Ru)
IRSHALES (Ru)
IZHEVSKLES (Ru)
ILMENLES (Ru)
IRTYSHLES (Ru)
IZHORALES (Ru)
ISTRA (Ru)
PERMLES (Ru)

45700
'OSKOL III' type (Ru)
45715
KODOR (Ru)
OLENEGORSK (Ru)
TULCHIN (Ru)
SEDANKA (Ru)
SKRYPLEV (Ru)
ALGA (Ru)
45720
'ALLIGATOR III' class (Ru)
45730
'AMGA' class (Ru)
DAUGAVA (Ru)
VETLUGA (Ru)
45850
GOTHA (DDR)
APOLDA (DDR)
46370
LIEBENWALDE (DDR)
CUNEWALDE (DDR)
LUCKENWALDE (DDR)
SCHONWALDE (DDR)
GERINGSWALDE (DDR)
MITTENWALDE (DDR)
FURSTENWALDE (DDR)
EICHWALDE (DDR)
RUDOLF DIESEL (DDR)
BLANKENSEE (DDR)
FLEESENSEE (DDR)
MUGGELSEE (DDR)
WERBELLINSEE (DDR)
KOLPINSEE (DDR)
INSELSEE (DDR)
RHINSEE (DDR)
SCHWIELOSEE (DDR)
TRENNTSEE (DDR)
46424
KAPITAN TRUBKIN (Ru)
46547
PAHOM MAKARENKO (Ru)
46550
KAPITAN PENKOV (Ru)
PETR VASEV (Ru)
46560
VLADIMIR GAVRILOV (Ru)
PYOTR SMORODIN (Ru)
MIKHAIL STELMAKH (Ru)

46580
ADLER (Ru)
AYTODOR (or AITODOR) (Ru)
ANAPA (Ru)
46620
YASNOYE (Ru)
47070
LIEBENWALDE (DDR)
CUNEWALDE (DDR)
LUCKENWALDE (DDR)
SCHONWALDE (DDR)
GERINGSWALDE (DDR)
MITTENWALDE (DDR)
FURSTENWALDE (DDR)
EICHWALDE (DDR)
RUDOLF DIESEL (DDR)
BLANKENSEE (DDR)
FLEESENSEE (DDR)
MUGGELSEE (DDR)
WERBELLINSEE (DDR)
KOLPINSEE (DDR)
INSELSEE (DDR)
RHINSEE (DDR)
SCHWIELOSEE (DDR)
TRENNTSEE (DDR)
47150
MEGANOM (Ru)
TARKHANKUT (Ru)
47167
KAPITAN A POLKOVSKIY (Ru)
47540
RADAUTI (Rm)
CALUGARENI (Ru)
COSTINESTI (Ru)
DEJ (Ru)
FALCIU (Ru)
FELDIOARA (Ru)
FELEAC (Ru)
FILARET (Ru)
FILIOARA (Ru)
FILIPESTI (Ru)
FINTINELE (Ru)
FLORESTI (Ru)
FOISOR (Ru)
FRASIN (Ru)
FUNDENI (Ru)
GORGOVA (Ru)
GORUN (Ru)

GOSTINU (Ru)
GRUIA (Ru)
HAGIENI (Ru)
HUMULESTI (Ru)
ILFOV (Ru)
LUGOJ (Ru)
MOINESTI (Ru)
MOLDOVITA (Ru)
NICORESTI (Ru)
PLATORESTI (Ru)
VILCEA (Ru)
MIZIL (Ru)
MEHEDINTI (Ru)
FAGET (Rm)
FIERBINTI (Rm)
FILIDARA (Rm)
CALIMANESTI (Rm)
FAUREI (Rm)
FAGARAS (Rm)
BUSTENI (Rm)
TELEORMAN (Rm)
FIRIZA (Rm)
BIHOR (Rm)
OLANESTI (Rm)
FILIASI (Rm)
SATU MARE (Rm)
ODORHEI (Rm)
SIMERIA (Rm)
GORJ (Rm)
FRUNZANESTI (Rm)
FRASINET (Rm)
FELIX (Rm)
DOLJ (Rm)
CACIULATA (Rm)
FIENI (Rm)
RUPEA (Rm)
HATEG (Rm)
ORAVITA (Rm)
GOVORA (Rm)
FUNDULEA (Rm)
GIURGIU (Rm)
HIRSOVA (Rm)
HUSI (Rm)
GRIVITA (Rm)
GIURGENI (Rm)
GRADISTEA (Rm)
HOREZU (Rm)
STEFAN KARADJA (Bu)

ZAHARI STOIANOV (Bu)
47674
ROMAN KARMEN (Ru)
VASILIY MATUZENKO (Ru)
PETR TOMASEVICH (or PYOTR
    TOMASEVICH) (Ru)
47860
VASILIY AZHAYEV (Ru)
DNEPROGES (Ru)
47939
CHERNOVTSY (Ru)
47990
LENINSK (Ru)
GORLOVKA (Ru)
48150
SVILEN RUSSEV (Bu)
LILIANA DIMITROVA (Bu)
MEKHANIK P.
    KILIMENCHUK (Ru)
DIMITROVSKIY
    KOMSOMOL (Bu)
ALEXANDER DIMITROV (Bu)
GEORGI GRIGOROV (Bu)
48240
HENNIGSDORF (DDR)
CHELYABINSK (Ru)
CHERENKHOVO (Ru)
BRANDENBURG (DDR)
CALBE (DDR)
RIESA (DDR)
CHERKASSY (Ru)
48380
AVDEYEVKA (Ru)
48383
ROJEN (Bu)
MALYOVITZA (Bu)
48407
WARSZAWA II (Pd)
LUBLIN II (Pd)
SZCZECIN (Pd)
KRAKOW II (Pd)
48430
IVAN ZAGUBANSKI (Bu)
CHRISTO BOTEV (Bu)
GOTZE DELCHEV (Bu)
LUBEN KARAVELOV (Bu)
KAPITAN PETKO
    VOIVODA (Bu)

VASIL LEVSKY (Bu)
GRIGORIY PETRENKO (Ru)
NIKITA MITCHENKO (Ru)
PETR DUTOV (Ru)
IVAN PEREVERZEV (Ru)
VALERIYA BARSOVA (Ru)
ALEKSANDR OGNIVTSEV (Ru)
IVAN SHEPETKOV (Ru)
IVAN MOSKALENKO (Ru)
GEROI PANFILOVTSY (Ru)
VASILY KLOCHKOV (Ru)
NIKOLAY ANANYEV (Ru)
NIKOLAY MAKSIMOV (Ru)
PETR YEMTSOV (Ru)
YAKOV BONDARENKO (Ru)
SOVIETSKIYE
 PROFSOYUZY (Ru)
ARAM KHACHATURYAN (Ru)
BORIS BABOCHKIN (Ru)
ZALAU (Rm)
VOROSMARTY (Hu)
48480
 PREDEAL (Rm)
48650
 VASILIY KOVAL (Ru)
 PROFESSOR KOSTIUKOV (Ru)
 ALEKSANDR SAVELIEV (Ru)
 INZHENIER PARKHONTUK (Ru)
48660
 KOPALNIA GRZYBOW (Pd)
 KOPALNIA MACHOW (Pd)
48835
 KOPALNIA JASTRZEBIE (Pd)
 KOPALNIA MYSLOWICE (Pd)
 KOPALNIA SIEMIANOWICE (Pd)
 KOPALNIA SZOMBIERKI (Pd)
48845
 BERDYANSK (Ru)
 ZHADANOV (Ru)
48860
 STEPAN ARTEMENKO (Ru)
 KAPITAN MEDVEDEV (Ru)
 MEKHANIK DREN (Ru)
48878
 SVETLOMOR (Ru)
49040
 PIRIN (Bu)
 SREDNA GORA (Bu)

STARA PLANINA (Bu)
STRADJA (Bu)
49100
 YASENYEVO (Ru)
49160
 BUZLUDJA (Bu)
 MURGASH (Bu)
 LUDOGORETZ (Bu)
 OBORISHTE (Bu)
49170
 KAPITAN FOMIN (Ru)
49210
 KOPALNIA PIASECZNO (Pd)
 KOPALNIA JEZIORKO (Pd)
49240
 KISHINEV (Ru)
 ALEKSANDR POKALCHUK (Ru)
 GORKOVSKAYA
 KOMSOMOLIYA (Ru)
 NIKOLAY SHCHETININ (Ru)
 PETR GUTCHENKO (Ru)
 SHURA BURLACHENKO (Ru)
 GORNYAK (Ru)
 HELME (Ru)
 MUOSTAKH (Ru)
 SERGEY BURYACHEK (Ru)
49342
 VIKTOR TKACHYOV (Ru)
 KAPITAN BOCHEK (Ru)
 KAPITAN CHUKHCHIN (Ru)
 KAPITAN SVIRIDOV (Ru)
 KAPITAN V TSIRUL (Ru)
 KAPITAN VODENKO (Ru)
 IVAN BOGUN (Ru)
 IVAN SUSANIN (Ru)
 IVAN MAKARIN (Ru)
 PAVEL VAVILOV (Ru)
 KAPITAN KUDLAY (Ru)
 KAPITAN VAKULA (Ru)
 ANATOLIY
 LYAPIDEVSKIY (Ru)
 KAPITAN NAZAREV (Ru)
 TIM BUCK (Ru)
49470
 IVAN ZAGUBANSKI (Bu)
 CHRISTO BOTEV (Bu)
 GOTZE DELCHEV (Bu)
 LUBEN KARAVELOV (Bu)

KAPITAN PETKO
 VOIVODA (Bu)
VASIL LEVSKY (Bu)
GRIGORIY PETRENKO (Ru)
NIKITA MITCHENKO (Ru)
PETR DUTOV (Ru)
IVAN PEREVERZEV (Ru)
VALERIYA BARSOVA (Ru)
ALEKSANDR OGNIVTSEV (Ru)
IVAN SHEPETKOV (Ru)
IVAN MOSKALENKO (Ru)
GEROI PANFILOVTSY (Ru)
VASILY KLOCHKOV (Ru)
NIKOLAY ANANYEV (Ru)
NIKOLAY MAKSIMOV (Ru)
PETR YEMTSOV (Ru)
YAKOV BONDARENKO (Ru)
SOVIETSKIYE
 PROFSOYUZY (Ru)
ARAM KHACHATURYAN (Ru)
BORIS BABOCHKIN (Ru)
ZALAU (Rm)
VOROSMARTY (Hu)
49520
 ALBA (Rm)
49655
 JACEK MALCZEWSKI (Pd)
 ARTUR GROTTGER (Pd)
 BOLESLAW RUMINSKI (Pd)
 JOZEF CHELMONSKI (Pd)
49720
 OMSK (Ru)
 OKHOTSK (Ru)
 ORENBURG (Ru)
49740
 IVAN ZAGUBANSKI (Bu)
 CHRISTO BOTEV (Bu)
 GOTZE DELCHEV (Bu)
 LUBEN KARAVELOV (Bu)
 KAPITAN PETKO
 VOIVODA (Bu)
 VASIL LEVSKY (Bu)
 GRIGORIY PETRENKO (Ru)
 NIKITA MITCHENKO (Ru)
 PETR DUTOV (Ru)
 IVAN PEREVERZEV (Ru)
 VALERIYA BARSOVA (Ru)
 ALEKSANDR OGNIVTSEV (Ru)

IVAN SHEPETKOV (Ru)
IVAN MOSKALENKO (Ru)
GEROI PANFILOVTSY (Ru)
VASILY KLOCHKOV (Ru)
NIKOLAY ANANYEV (Ru)
NIKOLAY MAKSIMOV (Ru)
PETR YEMTSOV (Ru)
YAKOV BONDARENKO (Ru)
SOVIETSKIYE
 PROFSOYUZY (Ru)
ARAM KHACHATURYAN (Ru)
BORIS BABOCHKIN (Ru)
ZALAU (Rm)
VOROSMARTY (Hu)
49785
 PEYO IAVOROV (Bu)
 GEO MILEV (Bu)
 ALEKO KONSTANTINOV (Bu)
 KAPITAN TEMKIN (Ru)
 KAPITAN V.OVODOVSKIY (Ru)
49810
 ARNOLD SOMMERLING (Ru)
 IVAN RABCHINSKIY (Ru)
 OSVALD TULL (Ru)
50112
 PAVLIN VINOGRADOV (Ru)
50125
 VARNA (Bu)
 BURGAS (Bu)
50128
 HALBERSTADT (DDR)
 JOHANNGEORGENSTADT (DDR)
 JOHSTADT (DDR)
 NEUSTADT (DDR)
 ARNSTADT (DDR)
 RUDOLSTADT (DDR)
50275
 'MORSKOY 1' class (Ru)
50280
 SOVIETSKIY VOIN (Ru)
 KONSTANTIN SHESTAKOV (Ru)
 ALEKSANDR PANKRATOV (Ru)
 ARSENIY MOSKVIN (Ru)
 EVGENIY NIKONOV (Ru)
 KONSTANTIN SAVELYEV (Ru)
 ANDREY IVANOV (Ru)
 EVGENIY ONUFRIEV (Ru)
 YAKOB KUNDER (Ru)

KONSTANTIN
 KORSHUNOV (Ru)
NARVSKAYA ZASTAVA (Ru)
VYBORGSKAYA STORONA (Ru)
LENINGRADSKIY
 OPOLCHENETS (Ru)
LENINGRADSKIY
 PARTIZAN (Ru)
SOVIETSKIY
 POGRANICHNIK (Ru)
ALEKSANDR
 MIROSHNIKOV (Ru)
NIKOLAY EMELYANOV (Ru)
SOVIETSKIY MORYAK (Ru)
VYACHESLAV DENISOV (Ru)
YAKOV REZNICHENKO (Ru)
50440
 MARLOW (DDR)
 HAGENOW (DDR)
 MILTZOW (DDR)
 MIROW (DDR)
 NEUBOKOW (DDR)
 RAKOW (DDR)
 SATOW (DDR)
 SEMLOW (DDR)
 TORGELOW (DDR)
 ZUROW (DDR)
 ZUSSOW (DDR)
50460
 BOLESLAWIEC (Pd)
 CHORZOW (Pd)
 WYSZKOW (Pd)
 MLAWA (Pd)
 GNIEZNO II (Pd)
 SIERADZ (Pd)
 BYTOM (Pd)
 ZGORZELEC (Pd)
 KOSCIERZYNA (Pd)
 LOMZA (Pd)
 WIELUN (Pd)
50570
 'AMUR' class (Ru)
50670
 GRIGORIY ALEKSEYEV (Ru)
 PAVEL RYBIN (Ru)
50730
 SOVIETSKAYA YAKUTIYA (Ru)
 AFANASIY BOGATYREV (Ru)

FYODOR POPOV (Ru)
YAKUB KOLAS (Ru)
IVAN STROD (Ru)
KONSTANTIN ZASLONOV (Ru)
KOZELSK (Ru)
KHUDOZHNIK KUINDZHA (Ru)
YANKA KUPALA (Ru)
FIZULI (Ru)
VAGIF (Ru)
VASILIY YAN (Ru)
AVETIK ISAAKYAN (Ru)
BERDY KERBABAYEV (Ru)
BULUNKHAN (Ru)
KIGILYAKH (Ru)
ANDREY KIZHEVATOV (Ru)
DMITRIY KANTEMIR (Ru)
KHUDOZHNIK PLASTOV (Ru)
SERGEY GRITSEVETS (Ru)
FYODOR OKHLOPOV (Ru)
MIKAIL MUSHFIK (Ru)
KOMANDARM GAY (Ru)
ISIDOR BARAKHOV (Ru)
ILYA SELVINSKIY (Ru)
MAKSIM AMMOSOV (Ru)
NIKOLAY ZAZOLOTSKIY (Ru)
NIZAMI (Ru)
PLATON OYUNSKIY (Ru)
OGNYAN NAYDOV (Ru)
ASHUG ALEKSER (Ru)
DZHAFER DZHABARLY (Ru)
KOSTA KHETAGUROV (Ru)
50763
VASILIY SHUKSHIN (Ru)
AKADEMIK POZDYUNIN (Ru)
PROFESSOR BUBNOV (Ru)
PROFESSOR PAPKOVICH (Ru)
MAKSIM RYLSKIY (Ru)
MIKHAIL LUKONIN (Ru)
SADRIDDIN AYNI (Ru)
SERGEY SMIRNOV (Ru)
VIKTOR KHARA (Ru)
YURIY KRIMOV (Ru)
MIKHAIL ISAKOVSKIY (Ru)
TIKHON SYOMUSHKIN (Ru)
VITALIY DYAKONOV (Ru)
KHAMZA (Ru)
MUKHTAR AUEZOV (Ru)
BORIS LAVROV (Ru)

50770
BAKU (Ru)
INZHENIER BELOV (Ru)
AGDAM (Ru)
AKSTAFA (Ru)
GEOKCHAY (Ru)
MURGAB (Ru)
SHAMKHOR (Ru)
ASTARA (Ru)
KASPIY (Ru)
HIMKI (Ru)
SABIRABAD (Ru)
KUBATLY (Ru)
NAVASHINO (Ru)
SAATLY (Ru)
ZANGELAN (Ru)
KHASAVYURT (Ru)
50900
DOLMATOVO (Ru)
50908
DOBRUDJA (Bu)
50909
BODROG (Hu)
KOROS (Hu)
SAJO (Hu)
BANSKA BYSTRICA (Cz)
50910
KALININABAD (Ru)
KANEV (Ru)
KRASNOUFIMSK (Ru)
51212
ASTRAKHAN (Ru)
KORSUN
SCHEVCHENKOVSKIY (Ru)
SAMARKAND (Ru)
TRUSKAVETS (Ru)
ZHITOMIR (Ru)
ROSTOV (Ru)
VINNITSA (Ru)
KREMENCHUG (Ru)
BUDAPESHT (Ru)
BREST (Ru)
SAMARKAND (Ru)
TRUSKAVETS (Ru)
ZHITOMIR (Ru)
ROVNO (Ru)
KOSTROMA (Ru)
KERCH (Ru)

SVERDLOVSK (Ru)
ULAN-BATOR (Ru)
51260
KWIDZYN (Pd)
LEBORK (Pd)
WEJHEROWO (Pd)
51370
VAYDAGHUBSKIY (Ru)
51410
DMITRIY MEDVEDYEV (Ru)
MOSKOVSKIY FESTIVAL (Ru)
GRIGORIY NESTORENKO (Ru)
VLADIMIR KOKKINAKI (Ru)
NODAR DUMBADZE (Ru)
EVGENIY TITOV (or YEVGENIY
TITOV) (Ru)
MARSHAL GELOVANI (Ru)
GEORGIY
KHOLOSTYAKOV (Ru)
51416
CHERNOE MORE (Ru)
BALTIYSKOYE MORE (Ru)
51570
POLAR (DDR)
51672
ION SOLTYS (Ru)
NIKOLAY KUZNETSOV (Ru)
ALEKSEY DANCHENKO (Ru)
AKADEMIK
BLAGONRAVOV (Ru)
MIKOLA BAZHAN (Ru)
UNAN AVETISYAN (Ru)
RODINA (Ru)
AKADEMIK BAKULEV (Ru)
GEROI STALINGRADA (Ru)
KHARITON GREKU (Ru)
51780
BALATON (Hu)
KAPOS (Hu)
51910
GOGLAND (Ru)
51986/1
ALEKSANDR KAVERZNEV (Ru)
52000
MARLOW (DDR)
HAGENOW (DDR)
MILTZOW (DDR)
MIROW (DDR)

NEUBOKOW (DDR)
RAKOW (DDR)
SATOW (DDR)
SEMLOW (DDR)
TORGELOW (DDR)
ZUROW (DDR)
ZUSSOW (DDR)
52020
BALKHASH (Ru)
BAKHCHISARAY (Ru)
BELOMORYE (Ru)
52070
BUNA (DDR)
SCHKOPAU (DDR)
52270
URAL (Ru)
52304
VENTSPILS (Ru)
VANINO (Ru)
TAGANROG (Ru)
NAGAYEVKO (Ru)
RAZDOLNOYE (Ru)
KASHIRA (Ru)
ALEYSK (Ru)
DAUGAVA (Ru)
DALNERECHENSK (Ru)
USSURIYSK (Ru)
52440
KHAN ASPARUKH (Bu)
52466
LUBOMIR (Pd)
MURAN (Pd)
PALICA (Pd)
ROMANKA (Pd)
52605
'MUNA' class (Ru)
52612/1
JOSIP BROZ TITO (Ru)
KAPITAN NAGONYUK (Ru)
NATA VACHNADZE (Ru)
YUSUP KOBALADZE (Ru)
KAPITAN A. KACHARAVA (Ru)
KAPITAN
MAKATSARIYA (Ru)
DAVID BAKARADZE (Ru)
BOLSHEVIK KAMO (Ru)
KAPITAN YERSHOV (Ru)
MORIS BISHOP (Ru)

PANTELEYMON
PONOMARENKO (Ru)
OYAR VATSIETIS (Ru)
ZHAN GRIVA (Ru)
YULIY DANISHEVSKIY (Ru)
AKADEMIK VEKÜS (Ru)
ILYA ERENBURG (Ru)
52616
VENTSPILS (Ru)
VANINO (Ru)
TAGANROG (Ru)
RAZDOLNOYE (Ru)
KASHIRA (Ru)
ALEYSK (Ru)
DAUGAVA (Ru)
NAGAYEVO (Ru)
DALNERECHENSK (Ru)
USSURIYSK (Ru)
52745
ALI AMIROV (Ru)
52805
PRACA (Pd)
POKOJ (Pd)
52927
ORLIK (Cz)
53160
MANGYSHLAK (Ru)
GENERAL ASLANOV (Ru)
GENERAL BABAYAN (Ru)
KAFUR MAMEDOV (Ru)
NIKIFOR ROGOV (Ru)
RUKHULLA AKHUNDOV (Ru)
53190
SCHWEDT (DDR)
53535
LENSOVET (Ru)
MOSSOVET (Ru)
53537
SMOLNYY (Ru)
54630
DONUZLAV (Ru)
DERBENT (Ru)
54710
NIKOLAY NOVIKOV (Ru)
IVAN SYRYKH (Ru)
VLADIMIR MORDVINOV (Ru)
VLADIMIR TIMOFEYEV (Ru)
KAPITAN MOCHALOV (Ru)

KAPITAN BAKANOV (Ru)
KAPITAN KIRIY (Ru)
KONSTANTIN
    PETROVSKIY (Ru)
MEKHANIK GORDYENKO (Ru)
VLAS NICHKOV (Ru)
KAPITAN DUBLITSKIY (Ru)
KAPITAN MILOVZOROV (Ru)
KAPITAN SAMOYLENKO (Ru)
PETR SMIDOVICH (Ru)
VASILIY MUSINSKIY (Ru)
KAPITAN BURMAKIN (Ru)
KAPITAN GLAZACHYEV (Ru)
KAPITAN VASILYEVSKIY (Ru)
KAPITAN ZAMYATIN (Ru)
YURIY SAVINOV (Ru)
BOTSMAN MOSHKOV (Ru)
FEDOR VARAKSIN (Ru)
KAPITAN SHEVCHENKO (Ru)
KAPITAN LYUBCHENKO (Ru)
PETR STRELKOV (Ru)
54870
    MESTA (Bu)
    OSAM (Bu)
54970
    JOZEF CONRAD
        KORZENIOWSKI (Pd)
    ADAM MICKIEWICZ (Pd)
    GENERAL FR KLEEBERG (Pd)
55060
    DONUZLAV (Ru)
    DERBENT (Ru)
55100
    UELEN (Ru)
55130
    KARSKOYE MORE (Ru)
    OKHOTSKOYE MORE (Ru)
55410
    MUSALA (Bu)
    RUEN (Bu)
    VEJEN (Bu)
55780
    BANAT (Rm)
    CRISANA (Rm)
    DACIA (Rm)
    MUNTENIA (Rm)
56155
    BUSSEWITZ (DDR)

56270
    DUBNA (Ru)
    IRKUT (Ru)
    PECHENGA (Ru)
    SVENTA (Ru)
56480
    BANAT (Rm)
    CRISANA (Rm)
    DACIA (Rm)
    MUNTENIA (Rm)
56633
    PROFESOR SZAFER (Pd)
    PROFESOR
        MIERZEJEWSKI (Pd)
    PROFESOR RYLKE (Pd)
56638
    VALENTIN ZOLOTAREV (Ru)
    PYOTR ALEYINIKOV (Ru)
    RADEBEUL (DDR)
    GRIGORIY KOZINTSEV (Ru)
56639
    BORIS ANDREYEV (Ru)
    MEKHANIK BARDETSKIY (Ru)
57200
    DAGONYS (Ru)
57475
    ASKOLD (Ru)
57540
    BOLGRAD (Ru)
    BORISLAV (Ru)
57630
    LENINAKAN (Ru)
    LYUDINOVO (Ru)
    LENKORAN (Ru)
    LYUBOTIN (Ru)
57760
    IZVESTIYA (Ru)
    KNUD JESPERSEN (Ru)
58140
    KARLOVY VARY (Cz)
58510
    PYATIDYESYATILYETIYE
        SSSR (Ru)
    BERINGOV PROLIV (Ru)
    IRBENSKIY PROLIV (Ru)
    PROLIV LAPERUZA (Ru)
    PROLIV SANNIKOVO (Ru)
    KAMCHATSKIY PROLIV (Ru)

SANGARSKIY PROLIV (Ru)
PROLIV VILKITSKOGO (Ru)
XXV SYEZD KPSS (Ru)
CHYORNOE MORE (Ru)
KERCHENSKIY PROLIV (Ru)
PROLIV KRUZENSHTERNA (Ru)
PROLIV NADEZHDY (Ru)
PROLIV SHOKALSKOGO (Ru)
60 LET OKTYABRYA (Ru)
UKRAINSKIY
    KOMSOMOLETS (Ru)
PROLIV DIANY (Ru)
PROLIV LONGA (Ru)
PROLIV VIKTORIYA (Ru)
58730
    NIEWIADOW (Pd)
    LIPSK N/BIEBRZA (Pd)
58995
    SERGEY KIROV (Ru)
    MESHADI AZIZBEKOV (Ru)
    ALI BAYRAMOV (Ru)
    ALESHA DZHAPARIDZE (Ru)
59220
    FILIPP MAKHARADZE (Ru)
    NIKO NIKOLADZE (Ru)
    MIKHA TSKHAKAYA (Ru)
    OBRONCY POCZTY (Pd)
    POWSTANIEC SLASKI (Pd)
    SIEKIERKI (Pd)
    TOBRUK (Pd)
59230
    SLAPY (Cz)
    LIPNO (Cz)
    ORAVA (Cz)
59650
    KLOSTERFELDE (DDR)
    NEUHAUSEN (DDR)
    RADEBERG (DDR)
59690
    ZULAWY (Pd)
    KASZUBY II (Pd)
    WINETA (Pd)
    MAZURY (Pd)
59880
    BORIS CHILIKIN (Ru)
    DNESTR (Ru)
    GENRIK GASANOV (Ru)
    IVAN BUBNOV (Ru)

VLADIMIR KOLECHITSKY (Ru)
59890
    VELIKIY OKTYABR (Ru)
    POBYEDA OKTYABRYA (Ru)
    TSEZAR KUNIKOV (Ru)
    NIKOLAY SIPYAGIN (Ru)
    KERCH (Ru)
    EYZHENS BERGS (Ru)
    KONSTANTIN
        TSIOLKOVSKIY (Ru)
    GENERAL BAGRATION (Ru)
    ZAKHARIY PALIASHVILI (Ru)
    FRIDRIKH TSANDER (Ru)
    VASILIY KIKVIDZE (Ru)
    MARITZA (Bu)
    REZVAYA (Bu)
    VELEKA (Bu)
60360
    BELCHATOW (Pd)
    TUROSZOW (Pd)
60373
    OLEG KOSHEVOY (Ru)
    GEROY HYUSEYNOV (Ru)
    LYUBOV SHEVTSOVA (Ru)
    VIKTOR TARASOV (Ru)
    SERGEY TYULENIN (Ru)
    GEROY ASADOV (Ru)
    GEROY I. MAMEDOV (Ru)
    GENERAL SABIR
        RAKHIMOV (Ru)
    GENERAL GEYDAROV (Ru)
    GEROY OSIPOV (Ru)
    GEROY K. NAZAROVA (Ru)
    GEROY GUSEYNOV (Ru)
    PAVLIK MOROZOV (Ru)
    LIZA CHAYKINA (Ru)
    IVAN ZEMNUKHOV (Ru)
    MIRZO TURSUN-ZADE (Ru)
60484
    LEOPOLD STAFF (Pd)
60500
    GIUSEPPE VERDI (Ru)
    GALILEO GALILEI (Ru)
60620
    DAUGAVPILS (Ru)
    GRIGORIY ACHKANOV (Ru)
    SPLIT (Ru)
    GORI (Ru)

VASILIY PORIK (Ru)
GENERAL ZHDANOV (Ru)
MARSHAL BIRYUZOV (Ru)
OLEKO DUNDICH (Ru)
PETR ALEKSEYEV (Ru)
BORZHOMI (Ru)
GENERAL KARBYSHEV (Ru)
DMITRIY ZHLOBA (Ru)
NIKOLOZ
    BARATASHVILI (Ru)
ERIFAN KOVITYUKH (Ru)
MITROFAN SEDIN (Ru)
MOS SHOVGENOV (Ru)
STEPAN VOSTRETSOV (Ru)
PYATIDYESYATILYETIYE
    SOVIETSKOY GRUZII (Ru)
PAVEL DYBENKO (Ru)
REZEKNE (Ru)
RIYEKA (Ru)
GENERAL BOCHAROV (Ru)
GENERAL KRAVTSOV (Ru)
GENERAL
    SHKODUNOVICH (Ru)
NIKOLAY PODVOSKIY (Ru)
60660
    LUBNY (Ru)
    LENINO (Ru)
    LYUBLINO (Ru)
    LUKHOVITSY (Ru)
60670
    LENKORAN (Ru)
    LYUBOTIN (Ru)
60680
    INTERNATSIONAL (Ru)
    DRUZHBA NARODOV (Ru)
    ISKRA (Ru)
    LENINSKOYE ZNAMYA (Ru)
    NAKHODKA (Ru)
    PROLETARSKAYA
        POBYEDA (Ru)
    PAMYAT LENINA (Ru)
    PETR STUCHKA (Ru)
    ZAVYETY ILYICHA (Ru)
60720
    STRUMA (Bu)
60900
    GEORGIY LEONIDZE (Ru)
    GENERAL LESELIDZE (Ru)

232

60971
POLAR VII (Rm)
POLAR VIII (Rm)
POLAR IX (Rm)
POLAR X (Rm)
POLAR XI (Rm)
POLAR XII (Rm)
60978
RAZBOIENI (Rm)
LERESTI (Rm)
ROMAN (Rm)
MIRASLAU (Rm)
VALEA ALBA (Rm)
VORONET (Rm)
GROZAVESTI (Rm)
POSADA (Rm)
AVRAMESTI (Rm)
COZIA (Rm)
DRAGOMIRESTI (Rm)
61020
RIURENI (Rm)
MARASESTI (Rm)
MARASTI (Rm)
OITUZ (Rm)
CALAFAT (Rm)
61090
KOPALNIA MOSZCZENICA (Pd)
KOPALNIA KLEOFAS (Pd)
KOPALNIA MARCEL (Pd)
KOPALNIA SOSNICA (Pd)
KOPALNIA
SZCZYGLOWICE (Pd)
KOPALNIA WIREK (Pd)
GLIWICE II (Pd)
61100
RIZHSKIY ZALIV (Ru)
AMURSKIY ZALIV (Ru)
BOTNICHESKIY ZALIV (Ru)
DVINSKIY ZALIV (Ru)
FINSKIY ZALIV (Ru)
KANDALAKSHSKIY ZALIV (Ru)
NARVSKIY ZALIV (Ru)
ONEZHSKIY ZALIV (Ru)
TAGANROGSKIY ZALIV (Ru)
USSURIYSKIY ZALIV (Ru)
61270
PRIBOY (Ru)
KARL LINNEY (Ru)

KHIBINSKIE GORY (Ru)
KRYMSKIE GORY (Ru)
LENINSKIYE GORY (Ru)
URALJSKIE GORY (Ru)
61400
CRIMMITSCHAU (DDR)
FLIEGERSKOSMONAUT DER
DDR SIGMUND JAHN (DDR)
PRITZWALK (DDR)
PASEWALK (DDR)
GLACHAU (DDR)
61700
BURG (DDR)
BERGEN (DDR)
HETTSTEDT (DDR)
AKEN (DDR)
FREITAL (DDR)
KOTHEN (DDR)
KONSTANTINOVKA (Ru)
GENERAL BLAZHEVICH (Ru)
KRAMATORSK (Ru)
FASTOV (Ru)
FATEZH (Ru)
61840
YAKHROMA (Ru)
62050
FIOLENT (Ru)
62460
ZVENIGOROD (Ru)
ZAPOROZHY (Ru)
ZAKARPATYE (Ru)
ZADONSK (Ru)
ZARECHENSK (Ru)
ZLATOUST (Ru)
ZORINSK (Ru)
ZIEMIA KRAKOWSKA (Pd)
ZIEMIA LUBELSKA (Pd)
ZAGLEBIE MIEDZIOWE (Pd)
62480
IZVESTIYA (Ru)
KNUD JESPERSEN (Ru)
62495
ADYGEJA (Ru)
62570
LUBNY (Ru)
LENINO (Ru)
LYUBLINO (Ru)
LUKHOVITSY (Ru)

62580
DAUGAVPILS (Ru)
GRIGORIY ACHKANOV (Ru)
SPLIT (Ru)
GORI (Ru)
VASILIY PORIK (Ru)
GENERAL ZHDANOV (Ru)
MARSHAL BIRYUZOV (Ru)
OLEKO DUNDICH (Ru)
PETR ALEKSEYEV (Ru)
BORZHOMI (Ru)
GENERAL KARBYSHEV (Ru)
DMITRIY ZHLOBA (Ru)
NIKOLOZ BARATASHVILI (Ru)
EPIFAN KOVTYUKH (Ru)
MITROFAN SEDIN (Ru)
MOS SHOVGENOV (Ru)
STEPAN VOSTRETSOV (Ru)
PYATIDYESYATILYETIYE
SOVIETSKOY GRUZII (Ru)
PAVEL DYBENKO (Ru)
REZEKNE (Ru)
RIYEKA (Ru)
GENERAL BOCHAROV (Ru)
GENERAL KRAVTSOV (Ru)
GENERAL
SHKODUNOVICH (Ru)
NIKOLAY PODVOYSKIY (Ru)
62671
ALMAZNYY BEREG (Ru)
BALTIYSKIY ZON (Ru)
VOLSKIY ZALIV (Ru)
REUTERSHAGEN (DDR)
AMURSKIY BEREG (Ru)
BALTIYSKIY BEREG (Ru)
BEREG MECHTY (Ru)
BEREG NADEZHDY (Ru)
CHUKOTSKIY BEREG (Ru)
KAMCHATSKIY BEREG (Ru)
KAPITAN KULINICH (Ru)
KHRUSTALNYY BEREG (Ru)
PRIMORSKIY BEREG (Ru)
TAMBOV (Ru)
VOSTOCHNIY BEREG (Ru)
ZVYOZDNYY BEREG (Ru)
KOMSOMOLETS
PRIMORYA (Ru)
ZOLOTYE DYUNY (Ru)

TAYOZHNYY BEREG (Ru)
BEREG YUNOSTI (Ru)
KALININGRADSKIY
BEREG (Ru)
MOTOVSKIY ZALIV (Ru)
OLYUTORSKIY ZALIV (Ru)
ULBANSKIY ZALIV (Ru)
USSURIYSKAYA TAYGA (Ru)
BEREG VETROV (Ru)
PENZHINSKIY ZALIV (Ru)
HERMANN MATERN (DDR)
62680
KARL LIEBKNECHT (Ru)
LAZURNYY BEREG (Ru)
SOLNECHNYY BEREG (Ru)
YANTARNYY BEREG (Ru)
62701
ANTANAS SNECHKUS (Ru)
DIMANT (Ru)
ERNST THALMANN (Ru)
FRITZ HECKERT (Ru)
GRANITNYY BEREG (Ru)
IZUMRUDNYY BEREG (Ru)
MATHIAS THESEN (Ru)
OTTO GROTEWOHL (Ru)
ROSA LUXEMBURG (Ru)
SKALISTYY BEREG (Ru)
WILHELM PIEK (Ru)
ZHEMCHUYNYY BEREG (Ru)
POLAR III (Rm)
POLAR IV (Rm)
POLAR V (Rm)
POLAR VI (Rm)
LICHTENHAGEN (DDR)
62730
DUBNA (Ru)
IRKUT (Ru)
PECHENGA (Ru)
SVENTA (Ru)
63570
BORIS BUTOMA (Ru)
AKADEMIK SECHENOV (Ru)
GAMAL ABDEL NASER (Ru)
IVAN TEVOSYAN (Ru)
63640
YURMALA (Ru)
BOLDURI (Ru)
DUBULTY (Ru)

DZINTARI (Ru)
LIELUPE (Ru)
MAYORI (Ru)
63975
POBYEDA (Ru)
SOROKALETIYE POBEDY (Ru)
MARSHAL BAGRAMYAN (Ru)
MARSHAL CHUYKOV (Ru)
MARSHAL VASILYEVSKIY (Ru)
GENERAL TYULENEV (Ru)
63980
KRYM (Ru)
KUBAN (Ru)
63982
KAVKAZ (Ru)
KRIVBASS (Ru)
KUZBASS (Ru)
SOVIETSKAYA NEFT (Ru)
64568
KAPITAN E. EGOROV (Ru)
KAPITAN VALENTIN
IVANOV (Ru)
65850
FELIKS DZIERZYNSKI (Pd)
WALKA MLODYCH (Pd)
UNIWERSYTET SLASKI (Pd)
POWSTANIEC
WARSZAWSKI (Pd)
JANUSZ KUSOCINSKI (Pd)
66170
GEROI SEVASTOPOLYA (Ru)
GEROI CHERNOMORYA (Ru)
GEROI NOVOROSSIYSKA (Ru)
66380
KALININGRADNEFT (Ru)
OKHANEFT (Ru)
GALVYE (Ru)
KALININGRADSKIY-NEFTYANIK (Ru)
MYS SARYCH (Ru)
UST-KARSK (Ru)
UST-KUT (Ru)
VESYEGONSK (Ru)
VIDNOYE (Ru)
LINKUVA (Ru)
DELEGAT (Ru)
KROPOTKIN (Ru)
MYS KHRUSTALNYY (Ru)
UST-ILIMSK (Ru)

UST-KAN (Ru)
MYS KODOSH (Ru)
LUKOMORYE (Ru)
ARGUN (Ru)
GEOLOG YURIY BILIBIN (Ru)
MINUSINSK (Ru)
MYS PAVLOVSKIY (Ru)
SHUYA (Ru)
UST-IZHMA (Ru)
UST-LABINSK (Ru)
VYAZMA (Ru)
66980
JAROSLAW (Pd)
67010
ANTON GUBARYEV (Ru)
DZHEMS BANKOVICH (Ru)
GRISHA PODOBEDOV (Ru)
KHENDRIK KUYVAS (Ru)
LIDA DEMESH (Ru)
MALDIS SKREYA (Ru)
MARAT KOZLOV (Ru)
NADE RIBAKOVAYTE (Ru)
NYURA KIZHEVATOVA (Ru)
PECHORA (Ru)
PETYA KOVALYENKO (Ru)
PETYA SHITIKOV (Ru)
PINEGA (Ru)
RICHARDAS BUKAUSKAS (Ru)
TANYA KARPINSKAYA (Ru)
TURGAY (Ru)
VALYA KURAKINA (Ru)
VANYA KOVALYEV (Ru)
YASHA GORDIYENKO (Ru)
VASYA STABROVSKIY (Ru)
VASYA KURKA (Ru)
VITYA NOVITSKIY (Ru)
YUNYY PARTIZAN (Ru)
67081
FLORA (Pd)
67170
BELOPOLYE (Ru)
67350
ROSTOK (Ru)
CHITA (Ru)
KHASAN (Ru)
NOVOCHERKASSK (Ru)
RYSHKANY (Ru)
RUSHANY (Ru)

RUDNYY (Ru)
ROMNY (Ru)
RUBEZHNOYE (Ru)
RZHEV (Ru)
RAKHOV (Ru)
REUTOV (Ru)
RATNO (Ru)
RADOMYSHL (Ru)
RYAZAN (Ru)
ROSLAVL (Ru)
RYBINSK (Ru)
MAGO (Ru)
67395
'VOLGONEFT' type (Ru)
67530
ISKAR 2 (Bu)
67650
VELIKIY OKTYABR (Ru)
POBYEDA OKTYABRYA (Ru)
TSEZAR KUNIKOV (Ru)
NIKOLAY SIPYAGIN (Ru)
KERCH (Ru)
EYZHEN BERG (Ru)
KONSTANTIN
  TSIOLKOVSKIY (Ru)
GENERAL BAGRATION (Ru)
ZAKHARIY PALIASHVILI (Ru)
FRIDRIKH TSANDER (Ru)
VASILIY KIKVIDZE (Ru)
MARITZA (Bu)
REZVAYA (Bu)
VELEKA (Bu)
67670
ASHKHABAD (Ru)
TUAPSE (Ru)
LIPETSK (Ru)
67677
TATRY (Pd)
PIENINY II (Pd)
67680
KOMANDARM FEDKO (Ru)
GENERAL MERKVILADZE (Ru)
GENERAL PLIYEV (Ru)
KHERSON (Ru)
VSEVELOD KOCHETOV (Ru)
ALEKSANDR
  KORNEYCHUK (Ru)
YAN SUDRABKALN (Ru)

67690
FELIKS DZIERZYNSKI (Pd)
WALKA MLODYCH (Pd)
UNIWERSYTET SLASKI (Pd)
POWSTANIEC
  WARSZAWSKI (Pd)
JANUSZ KUSOCINSKI (Pd)
68250
MARSHAL BUDYONNYY (Ru)
MARSHAL KONYEV (Ru)
MARSHAL
  ROKOSSOVSKIY (Ru)
MARSHAL ZHUKOV (Ru)
68560
MESTA (Bu)
OSAM (Bu)
68800
MARSHAL BUDYONNYY (Ru)
MARSHAL KONYEV (Ru)
MARSHAL
  ROKOSSOVSKIY (Ru)
MARSHAL ZHUKOV (Ru)
68805
MARSHAL GRECHKO (Ru)
MARSHAL GOVOROV (Ru)
MARSHAL ZAKHAROV (Ru)
68920
ZAWRAT (Pd)
CZANTORIA (Pd)
SOKOLICA II (Pd)
69310
NIKOLAY ZHUKHOV (Ru)
NIKOLAY MOROZOV (Ru)
GRIGORIY KOVALCHUK (Ru)
KONSTANTIN ZANKOV (Ru)
VASILIY
  BYELOKONYENKO (Ru)
VITALIY KRUCHINA (Ru)
IVAN KOROTEYEV (Ru)
MIKHAIL STENKO (Ru)
NIKOLAY SHCHUKIN (Ru)
PETR STAROSTIN (Ru)
ANDRIAN GONCHAROV (Ru)
INZHENIER YAMBURENKO (Ru)
69725
ISKAR (Bu)
70020
SAMOTLOR (Ru)

URENGOY (Ru)
BEREZOVO (Ru)
GORNOPRAVDINSK (Ru)
NADYM (Ru)
NIZHNEVARTOVSK (Ru)
SAMBURG (Ru)
USINSK (Ru)
BAM (Ru)
VILYUYSK (Ru)
LENINSK-KUZNETSKIY (Ru)
KAMENSK-URALSKIY (Ru)
YENISEYSK (Ru)
IGRIM (Ru)
70165
URZHUM (Ru)
DZERZHINSK (Ru)
NOVOROSSIYSK (Ru)
STAVROPOL (Ru)
ULYANOVSK (Ru)
70540
SYN PULKU (Pd)
CEDYNIA (Pd)
MIROSLAWIEC (Pd)
NARWIK II (Pd)
POWSTANIEC
  WIELKOPOLSKI (Pd)
STUDZIANKI (Pd)
70572
MAYKOP (Ru)
APSHERON (Ru)
GROZNY (Ru)
GUDERMES (Ru)
MAKHACHKALA (Ru)
70590
MATE ZALKA (Ru)
ANTONIO GRAMSCI (Ru)
PABLO NERUDA (Ru)
DAVID SIQUEIROS (Ru)
VIKTORIO CODOVILLA (Ru)
JACQUES DUCLOS (Ru)
JOHN REED (Ru)
JOSE MARTI (Ru)
PAUL ROBESON (Ru)
KLEMENT GOTTWALD (Ru)
SUKHE BATOR (Ru)
70610
KUTAISI (Ru)
SUKHUMI (Ru)

70695
JENA (DDR)
MEISSEN (DDR)
WEIMAR (DDR)
70698
ZIEMIA CHELMINSKA (Pd)
ZIEMIA SUWALSKA (Pd)
ZIEMIA GNIEZNIENSKA (Pd)
ZIEMIA ZAMOJSKA (Pd)
ZIEMIA TARNOWSKA (Pd)
ZIEMIA ZACHODNIE (Pd)
70740
KAPITAN SHVETSOV (Ru)
DROGOBYCH (Ru)
KAPITAN IZOTOV (Ru)
INZHEHIER AGEYEV (Ru)
KAPITAN GRIBIN (Ru)
FORE MOSULISHVILI (Ru)
KAPITAN DYACHUK (Ru)
KAPITAN DOTSYENKO (Ru)
KAPITAN KOBETS (Ru)
KAPITAN NEVEZHKIN (Ru)
70760
AKTAU (Ru)
AKTYUBINSK (Ru)
AMGUN (Ru)
ADYGENI (Ru)
ANAKLIYA (Ru)
AYKHAL (Ru)
AKHALTSIKHE (Ru)
ARARAT (Ru)
AYNAZHI (Ru)
AYON (Ru)
ANTARES (Ru)
ABAVA (Ru)
ANUYU (Ru)
ASPINDZA (Ru)
RAUMA (Ru)
BIRYUZA (Ru)
OMSK (Ru)
YUGANSK (Ru)
ZHALGIRIS (Ru)
ZUGDIDI (Ru)
SURUGUTNEFT (Ru)
ILIM (Ru)
NEFTEGORSK (Ru)
DEBRECEN (Ru)
NEFTEKAMSK (Ru)

RUMBALA (Ru)
SAKHALINNEFT (Ru)
SIBIRNEFT (Ru)
70800
AUSKEKLIS (Ru)
AUTSE (Ru)
70810
PRUT (Ru)
ALTAY (Ru)
KOLA (Ru)
TARKHANKUT (Ru)
YELNYA (Ru)
YEGORLIK (Ru)
IZHORA (Ru)
70955
TERRAL (Pd)
TORNADO (Pd)
SOLANO (Pd)
ZONDA (Pd)
71040
PIONER MOSKVY (Ru)
PIONER ARKHANGELSKA (Ru)
PIONER SAKHALINA (Ru)
PIONER YUZHNO
SAKHALINSKA (Ru)
PIONER CHUKOTKI (Ru)
PIONER KHOLMSKA (Ru)
PIONER ONEGI (Ru)
PIONER ESTONII (Ru)
PIONER KAMCHATKI (Ru)
PIONER ROSSI (Ru)
PIONER BURYATII (Ru)
PIONER LITVY (Ru)
PIONER SEVERODVINSKA (Ru)
PIONER SLAVYANKI (Ru)
PIONER AYKUTII (Ru)
PIONER BELORUSSII (Ru)
PIONER KARELII (Ru)
PIONER KAZAKHSTANA (Ru)
PIONER KIRGIZII (Ru)
PIONER KOLY (Ru)
PIONER MOLDAVII (Ru)
PIONER UZBEKISTANA (Ru)
HEIDENAU (DDR)
RABENAU (DDR)
71310
OSTROV RUSSKIY (Ru)
OSTROV ATLASOVA (Ru)

OSTROV BERINGA (Ru)
OSTROV KARAKINSKIY (Ru)
OSTROV KOTLIN (Ru)
OSTROV LISYANSKOGO (Ru)
OSTROV LITKE (Ru)
OSTROV MEDNYY (Ru)
OSTROV SHMIDTA (Ru)
OSTROV SHOKALSKOGO (Ru)
OSTROV SIBIRYAKOVA (Ru)
OSTROV USHAKOVA (Ru)
71360
ROSTOK (Ru)
CHITA (Ru)
KHASAN (Ru)
MAGO (Ru)
NOVOCHERKASSK (Ru)
RYSHKANY (Ru)
RUSHANY (Ru)
RUDNYY (Ru)
ROMNY (Ru)
RUBEZHNOYE (Ru)
RZHEV (Ru)
RAKHOV (Ru)
REUTOV (Ru)
RATNO (Ru)
RADOMYSHL (Ru)
RYAZAN (Ru)
ROSLAVL (Ru)
RYBINSK (Ru)
71433
ALEKSANDR
TSULUKIDZE (Ru)
GRIGORIY NIKOLAYEV (Ru)
71530
MAGNITOGORSK (Ru)
KOMSOMOLSK (Ru)
ANATOLIY VASILYEV (Ru)
SMOLENSK (Ru)
71670
LENINSKIY LUCH (Ru)
KRASNYY LUCH (Ru)
SOLNECHNYY LUCH (Ru)
YARKIY LUCH (Ru)
SVETLYY LUCH (Ru)
71680
PRIGNITZ (DDR)
FLAMING (DDR)
EICHSFELD (DDR)

71810
JOZEF CONRAD
KORZENIOWSKI (Pd)
ADAM MICKIEWICZ (Pd)
GENERAL KLEEBERG (Pd)
71820
50 LET SSSR (Ru)
BERINGOV PROLIV (Ru)
IRBENSKIY PROLIV (Ru)
PROLIV LAPERUZA (Ru)
PROLIV SANNIKOVO (Ru)
PROLIV VILKITSKOGO (Ru)
XXV SYEZD KPSS (Ru)
CHYORNOE MORE (Ru)
KERCHENSKIY PROLIV (Ru)
PROLIV KRUZENSHTERNA (Ru)
PROLIV NADEZHDY (Ru)
PROLIV SHOKALSKOGO (Ru)
60 LET OKTYABRYA (Ru)
UKRAINSKIY
KOMSOMOLETS (Ru)
PROLIV DIANY (Ru)
PROLIV LONGA (Ru)
PROLIV VIKTORIYA (Ru)
KAMCHATSKIY PROLIV (Ru)
SANGARSKIY PROLIV (Ru)
71900
ARTERN (DDR)
COSWIG (DDR)
72115
MAJOR HUBAL (Pd)
RODLO (Pd)
MACIEJ RATAJ (Pd)
POWSTANIEC
LISTOPADOWY (Pd)
BRONISLAW CZECH (Pd)
POWSTANIEC
STYCZNIOWY (Pd)
BATALION CZWARTAKOW (Pd)
ARMIA LUDOWA (Pd)
IGNACY DASZYNSKI (Pd)
WLADYSLAW GOMULKA (Pd)
72116
PETROSENI (Rm)
73290
ZOYA
KOSMODEMYANSKAYA (Ru)
ALEKSANDR MATROSOV (Ru)

ION SOLTYS (Ru)
IZGUTTY AYTYKOV (Ru)
PARFENTIY GRECHANYY (Ru)
UNAN AVETISYAN (Ru)
BULGARIA (Bu)
RODINA (Bu)
73374
OSSOLINEUM (Pd)
MANIFEST PKWN (Pd)
73550
TARNOBRZEG (Pd)
PROFESSOR K
BOHDANOWICZ (Pd)
SIARKOPOL (Pd)
ZAGLEBIE SIARKOWE (Pd)
73650
SYRENKA (Pd)
WROZKA (Pd)
73997
SIBIRSKIY 2101 (Ru)
SIBIRSKIY 2102 (Ru)
SIBIRSKIY 2108 (Ru)
SIBIRSKIY 2109 (Ru)
SIBIRSKIY 2123 (Ru)
SIBIRSKIY 2124 (Ru)
SIBIRSKIY 2125 (Ru)
SIBIRSKIY 2126 (Ru)
SIBIRSKIY 2127 (Ru)
SIBIRSKIY 2128 (Ru)
74000
SIO (Hu)
74140
NALECZOW (Pd)
POLCZYN ZDROJ (Pd)
74515
ZIEMIA KIELECKA (Pd)
ZIEMIA KOSZALINSKA (Pd)
74540
FILIPP MAKHARADZE (Ru)
NIKO NIKOLADZE (Ru)
MIKHA TSKHAKAYA (Ru)
OBRONCY POCZTY (Pd)
POWSTANIEC SLASKI (Pd)
SIEKIERKI (Pd)
TOBRUK (Pd)
74655
KOPALNIA GOTTWALD (Pd)
KOPALNIA MIECHOWICE (Pd)

KOPALNIA SIERSZA (Pd)
74660
ZIEMIA BYDGOSKA (Pd)
ZIEMIA MAZOWIECKA (Pd)
74820
THALE (DDR)
75170
BUNA (DDR)
SCHKOPAU (DDR)
75312
KAPITAN VOOLENS (Ru)
MEKHANIK KRULL (Ru)
YURIY KLEMENTYEV (Ru)
75320
BOLTENHAGEN (DDR)
DIERHAGEN (DDR)
NIENHAGEN (DDR)
TRINWILLERSHAGEN (DDR)
FRITSIS GAYLIS (Ru)
V KUCHER (Ru)
75327
HAJNOWKA (Pd)
BARLINEK (Pd)
RUCIANE (Pd)
75330
FRITSIS ROSIN (Ru)
GLEB SEDIN (Ru)
WARIN (DDR)
BANSIN (DDR)
TESSIN (DDR)
KROPELIN (DDR)
RECHLIN (DDR)
75350
'BALTIYSKIY' class (Ru)
KILIYA (Ru)
VLAS CHUBAR (Ru)
GOROKHOVETS (Ru)
75360
'LADOGA' class (Ru)
LADOGA 1 (Ru)
LADOGA 2 (Ru)
LADOGA 3 (Ru)
LADOGA 4 (Ru)
LADOGA 5 (Ru)
LADOGA 6 (Ru)
LADOGA 7 (Ru)
LADOGA 8 (Ru)
LADOGA 9 (Ru)

75380
  BALTIYSKIY 101 (Ru)
  BALTIYSKIY 102 (Ru)
  BALTIYSKIY 103 (Ru)
  VASILIY MALOV (Ru)
  BALTIYSKIY 105 (Ru)
  BALTIYSKIY 106 (Ru)
  BALTIYSKIY 107 (Ru)
  BALTIYSKIY 108 (Ru)
  BALTIYSKIY 109 (Ru)
  BALTIYSKIY 110 (Ru)
  BALTIYSKIY 111 (Ru)
75392
  PAVEL YABLOCHKOV (Ru)
  ALEKSANDR POPOV (Ru)
  IVAN KULIBIN (Ru)
  IVAN POLZUNOV (Ru)
  VASILIY KALASHNIKOV (Ru)
75400
  SAYMENSKIY KANAL (Ru)
  LADOGA 11 (Ru)
  LADOGA 12 (Ru)
  LADOGA 13 (Ru)
  LADOGA 14 (Ru)
  LADOGA 15 (Ru)
  LADOGA 16 (Ru)
  LADOGA 17 (Ru)
  LADOGA 18 (Ru)
  LADOGA 19 (Ru)
  LADOGA 20 (Ru)
75412
  MIELEC (Pd)
  WARKA (Pd)
  MALBORK II (Pd)
  GOLENIOW (Pd)
75640
  KESSULAID (Ru)
  MANILAID (Ru)
  SUURLAID (Ru)
  HEINLAID (Ru)
  VIIRELAID (Ru)
75730
  ZAGLEBIE DABROWSKIE (Pd)
  DOLNY SLASK (Pd)
  PODHALE (Pd)
  KUJARWY (Pd)
75770
  TARNOW (Pd)

KEDZIERZYN (Pd)
NOWY SACZ (Pd)
EUGENIE COTTON (Pd)
75790
  VERILA (Bu)
  VESLETS (Bu)
  VIDEN (Bu)
76220
  STAROGARD GDANSKI (Pd)
76310
  ALTAIR (Ru)
  ARKTUR (Ru)
76580
  ABRAM ARKHIPOV (Ru)
  VLADIMIR FAVORSKIY (Ru)
  MITROFAN GREKOV (Ru)
  VASILIY POLENOV (Ru)
  NIKOLAY YAROSHENKO (Ru)
  NIKOLAY KASATKIN (Ru)
  KONSTANTIN YUON (Ru)
  IGOR GRABAR (Ru)
  IVAN SHADR (Ru)
  MIKHAIL CHEREMNYKH (Ru)
  VERA MUKHINA (Ru)
  YEKATERINA BELASHOVA (Ru)
76665
  SNIEZKA (Pd)
76715
  TURINSK (Ru)
  GAUYA (Ru)
76865
  SREDETZ (Bu)
76890
  ALIOT (Ru)
  POLLUKS (Ru)
  PROTSION (Ru)
76900
  STAROGARD GDANSKI (Pd)
76945
  DNEPR (Ru)
  DON (Ru)
  DONETS (Ru)
  DUNAY (Ru)
  SAMUR (Ru)
  SULAK (Ru)
  YERUSLAN (Ru)
  ARAKS (Ru)
  BUG (Ru)

BUZAN (Ru)
DNESTR (Ru)
INGUL (Ru)
TAGIL (Ru)
TEREK (Ru)
URAL (Ru)
YENISEY (Ru)
ANGARA (Ru)
INGULETS (Ru)
ISHIM (Ru)
PRUT (Ru)
76984
  HUTA LENINA (Pd)
  HUTA KATOWICE (Pd)
77060
  ALEKSANDR FADEYEV (Ru)
  ALEKSANDR PROKOFYEV (Ru)
  ALEKSANDR
    TVARDOVSKIY (Ru)
  MIKHAIL PRISHVIN (Ru)
  MIKHAIL SVETLOV (Ru)
77080
  KHUDOZHNIK
    FEDOROVSKIY (Ru)
  BUMBESTI (Rm)
  LIVEZINI (Rm)
  LOTRU (Rm)
  MOTRU (Rm)
  SALVA (Rm)
  VIDRARU (Rm)
  VISEU (Rm)
  KHUDOZHNIK A
    GERASIMOV (Ru)
  KHUDOZHNIK
    GABASHVILI (Ru)
  KHUDOZHNIK KASIYAN (Ru)
  KHUDOZHNIK
    KUSTODIYEV (Ru)
  KHUDOZHNIK TOIDZE (Ru)
  KHUDOZHNIK VLADIMIR
    SEROV (Ru)
  SOVIETSKIY KHUDOZHNIK (Ru)
  CHIPKA (or SHIPKA) (Bu)
  RILA (Bu)
  RODOPI (Bu)
  VITOCHA (Bu)
  MILIN KAMAK (Bu)
  SLAVIANKA (Bu)

OKOLTCHITZA (Bu)
KAPITAN GEORGI
  GEORGIEV (Bu)
VIHREN (Bu)
KAMENITZA (Bu)
77105
  MAXHUTTE (DDR)
  STASSFURT (DDR)
77127
  GENERAL BERLING (Pd)
  GENERAL DABROWSKI (Bu)
  GENERAL
    GROT-ROWECKI (Bu)
  YORDAN LUTIBRODSKI (Bu)
77340
  KHUDOZHNIK SARYAN (Ru)
  KHUDOZHNIK IOGANSON (Ru)
  KHUDOZHNIK PAKHOMOV (Ru)
  KHUDOZHNIK PROROKOV (Ru)
  KHUDOZHNIK REPIN (Ru)
  KHUDOZHNIK ROMAS (Ru)
  KHUDOZHNIK ZHUKOV (Ru)
  NADEZHDA OBUKHOVA (Ru)
  NIKOLAY GOLOVANOV (Ru)
  MAKSIM MIKHAYLOV (Ru)
77398
  WOLGAST (DDR)
  BARTH (DDR)
77560
  BEIUS (Rm)
  BICAZ (Rm)
  BIRLAD (Rm)
  BOCSA (Rm)
  BORSEC (Rm)
  BOTOSANI (Rm)
  BREADZA (Rm)
  BUHUSI (Rm)
  CALLATIS (Rm)
  TOMIS (Rm)
  BLAJ (Rm)
  BUZIAS (Rm)
  BAIA DE ARAMA (Rm)
  BAIA DE CRIS (Rm)
  BANEASA (Rm)
  BARAGANUL (Rm)
  BISTRET (Rm)
  BOBILNA (Rm)
  BORZESTI (Rm)

BRANESTI (Rm)
BUJORENI (Rm)
BAILESTI (Rm)
BALS (Rm)
BORSA (Rm)
BRATULESTI (Rm)
BALOTA (Rm)
BACESTI (Rm)
BAIA DE ARIES (Rm)
BAIA DE FIER (Rm)
BARAOLT (Rm)
BASARABI (Rm)
BECHET (Rm)
BORCEA (Rm)
77980
  LYULIN (Bu)
  PLANA (Bu)
  BELASITZA (Bu)
  HEMUS (Bu)
  OGRAJDAN (Bu)
  OSOGOVO (Bu)
78010
  KAPITAN PANFILOV (Ru)
  KAPITAN KHROMTSOV (Ru)
  KAPITAN DUBININ (Ru)
  KAPITAN IZHMYAKOV (Ru)
  KAPITAN
    MESHCHRYAKOV (Ru)
  KAPITAN REUTOV (Ru)
  KAPITAN GUDIN (Ru)
  KAPITAN STULOV (Ru)
  KAPITAN VAVILOV (Ru)
  IVAN NESTEROV (Ru)
  YUSTAS PALECKIS (Ru)
78041
  SIBIRSKIY 2113 (Ru)
  SIBIRSKIY 2114 (Ru)
  SIBIRSKIY 2116 (Ru)
  SIBIRSKIY 2117 (Ru)
  SIBIRSKIY 2118 (Ru)
  SIBIRSKIY 2119 (Ru)
  SIBIRSKIY 2130 (Ru)
  SIBIRSKIY 2131 (Ru)
  SIBIRSKIY 2132 (Ru)
  SIBIRSKIY 2133 (Ru)
78060
  IVAN SKURIDIN (Ru)
  GAVRILL KIRDISHCHEV (Ru)

YURIY SMIRNOV (Ru)
NIKOLAY VILKOV (Ru)
IVAN DERBENEV (Ru)
ZNAMYA OKTYABRYA (Ru)
KATYA ZELENKO (Ru)
ALEKSANDR OSIPOV (Ru)
TIMUR FRUNZE (Ru)
BORIS BUVIN (Ru)
VIKTOR TALALIKHIN (Ru)
VERA KHORUZHKAYA (Ru)
MARJAN (Ru)
YURIY AVOT (Ru)
NIKOLAY PRZHEVALSKIY (Ru)
SHESTIDESYATILETIYE
   SSSR (Ru)
DEVYATNADTSATYY SYEZD
   VLKSM (Ru)
DONETSK (Ru)
KUZMA GNIDASH (Ru)
NIKOLAY YANSON (Ru)
ALEKSANDR
   STAROSTENKO (Ru)
78140
ZIEMIA BYDGOSKA (Pd)
ZIEMIA MAZOWIECKA (Pd)
78290
HUTA ZGODA (Pd)
HUTA ZYGMUNT (Pd)
BUDOWLANY (Pd)
ROLNIK (Pd)
KOPALNIA SOSNOWIEC (Pd)
KOPALNIA WALBRZYCH (Pd)
KOPALNIA ZOFIOWKA (Pd)
78300
KOPALNIA PIASECZNO (Pd)
KOPALNIA JEZIORKO (Pd)
78355
CHKALOVSK (Ru)
CHUSOVOY (Ru)
78520
SOVFRACHT (Ru)
SOVINFLOT (Ru)
78540
ZARECHENSK (Ru)
ZVENIGOROD (Ru)
ZAPOROZHYE (Ru)
ZAKARPATYE (Ru)
ZADONSK (Ru)

ZLATOUST (Ru)
ZORINSK (Ru)
ZIEMIA KRAKOWSKA (Pd)
ZIEMIA LUBELSKA (Pd)
ZAGLEBIE MIEDZIOWE (Pd)
78580
BUCEGI (Rm)
RESITA (Rm)
HUNEDOARA (Rm)
LUPENI (Rm)
CARPATI (Rm)
DUNAREA (Rm)
MARAMURES (Rm)
OLTUL (Rm)
78680
UNIWERSYTET
   JAGIELLONSKI (Pd)
78730
GORLITZ (DDR)
GRODITZ (DDR)
NIKOLAY VOZNESENSKIY (Ru)
COLDITZ (DDR)
PREMNITZ (DDR)
78841
PIONIERUL (Rm)
TIRGU BUJOR (Rm)
TIRGU LAPUS (Rm)
TIRGU FRUMOS (Rm)
TIRGU NEAMT (Rm)
TIRGU OCNA (Rm)
TIRGU SECUIESC (Rm)
TIRGU TROTUS (Rm)
78850
MUSALA (Bu)
RUEN (Bu)
VEJEN (Bu)
78891
VLADIMIR LENORSKIY (Ru)
ARSHINTSEVO (Ru)
AZOVSTAL (Ru)
MAKAR MAZAY (Ru)
NIKITOVKA (Ru)
STEPAN MARKYELOV (Ru)
YENAKIYEVO (Ru)
78980
GENERAL SWIERCZEWSKI (Pd)
GENERAL BEM (Pd)
GENERAL JASINSKI (Pd)

GENERAL MADALINSKI (Pd)
GENERAL PRADZYNSKI (Pd)
JORDANKA NIKOLOVA (Bu)
PETIMATA OT RMS (Bu)
ADALBERT ANTONOV (Bu)
MEKHANIK P
   KILIMENCHUK (Ru)
79110
UNIWERSYTET
   WARSZAWSKI (Pd)
UNIWERSYTET
   WROCLAWSKI (Pd)
79230
GEORGIY LEONIDZE (Ru)
GENERAL LESELIDZE (Ru)
BRATISLAVA (Cz)
PRAHA (Cz)
TRINEC (Cz)
79315
VOGTLAND (DDR)
HAVELLAND (DDR)
79340
'VOLGO-BALT' type (Ru)
'SORMOVSKIY' type
SORMOVSKIY 3003 (Ru)
SORMOVSKIY 3004 (Ru)
SORMOVSKIY 3005 (Ru)
SORMOVSKIY 3006 (Ru)
SORMOVSKIY 3007 (Ru)
SORMOVSKIY 43 (Ru)
SORMOVSKIY 44 (Ru)
SORMOVSKIY 45 (Ru)
SORMOVSKIY 46 (Ru)
SORMOVSKIY 48 (Ru)
SORMOVSKIY 119 (Ru)
SORMOVSKIY 121 (Ru)
SORMOVSKIY 122 (Ru)
AFANASIY
   MATYUSHENKO (Ru)
ANDREY UPITS (Ru)
AVIAKONSTRUKTOR
   POLIKARPOV (Ru)
IVAN SERGIYENKO (Ru)
MARTYN LATSIS (Ru)
NIKOLAY KRIVORUCHKO (Ru)
NIKOLAY KUZNETSOV (Ru)
SEMYON RUDNYEV (Ru)
TOYVO VYAKHYA (Ru)

VASILIY BOZHENKO (Ru)
YELENA LITVINOVA (Ru)
SOVIETSKAYA RODINA (Ru)
ZNAMYA OKTYABRYA (Ru)
DRUZHBA NARADOV (Ru)
XI PYATILETKA (Ru)
65 LET SOVIETSKOY
   VLASTI (Ru)
LENINSKIY KOMSOMOL (Ru)
SORMOVSKIY 3051 (Ru)
SORMOVSKIY 3052 (Ru)
SORMOVSKIY 3053 (Ru)
SORMOVSKIY 3054 (Ru)
XVII SYEZD
   PROFSOYUZOV (Ru)
SORMOVSKIY 3055 (Ru)
SORMOVSKIY 3056 (Ru)
SORMOVSKIY 3057 (Ru)
SORMOVSKIY 3058 (Ru)
KAVARNA (Bu)
POMORIE (Bu)
SOZOPOL (Bu)
SORMOVSKIY 2 (Ru)
ALEKSANDR PASHKOV (Ru)
SORMOVSKIY 5 (Ru)
SORMOVSKIY 6 (Ru)
SORMOVSKIY 7 (Ru)
SORMOVSKIY 9 (Ru)
NIKOLAY LEBEDYEV (Ru)
SORMOVSKIY 12 (Ru)
SAVVA LOSHKIN (Ru)
SORMOVSKIY 14 (Ru)
SORMOVSKIY 17 (Ru)
SORMOVSKIY 18 (Ru)
SORMOVSKIY 19 (Ru)
SORMOVSKIY 22 (Ru)
SORMOVSKIY 27 (Ru)
SORMOVSKIY 28 (Ru)
SORMOVSKIY 29 (Ru)
SORMOVSKIY 30 (Ru)
SORMOVSKIY 31 (Ru)
SORMOVSKIY 33 (Ru)
SORMOVSKIY 34 (Ru)
SORMOVSKIY 40 (Ru)
SORMOVSKIY 41 (Ru)
SORMOVSKIY 118 (Ru)
SORMOVSKIY 3001 (Ru)
SORMOVSKIY 3002 (Ru)

SORMOVSKIY 42 (Ru)
SORMOVSKIY 109 (Ru)
SORMOVSKIY 110 (Ru)
SORMOVSKIY 112 (Ru)
SORMOVSKIY 117 (Ru)
50 LET SOVIETSKOY
   VLASTI (Ru)
BUREVESTNIK
   REVOLYUTSKIY (Ru)
ALEKSANDR VERMISHEV (Ru)
LENINSKAYA SMENA (Ru)
VELIKIY POCHIN (Ru)
VOZNESENSK (Ru)
ALEKSANDR TSYURUPA (Ru)
DMITRY MANUILSKIY (Ru)
SHUSHENSKOYE (Ru)
STANISLAV KOSIOR (Ru)
ALEKSANDR PROKOFYEV (Ru)
PARIZHSKAYA KOMMUNA (Ru)
GEROY MEKHTI (Ru)
ANATOLIY VANEYEV (Ru)
PYOTR BOGDANOV (Ru)
STRANA SOVIETOV (Ru)
50 LET S. S. S. R. (Ru)
NIKOLAY BAUMAN (Ru)
PYOTR ZAPOROZHETS (Ru)
IVAN KOLYSHKIN (Ru)
POET SABIR (Ru)
ALEKSANDR PASHKOV (Ru)
DESYATAYA PYATILETKA (Ru)
POET VIDADI (Ru)
DZHAMBUL DZHABAYEV (Ru)
GRIGORIY PETROVSKIY (Ru)
50 LET VLKSM (Ru)
VISHNEVOGORSK (Ru)
GORKY LENINSKIYE (Ru)
PYOTR ZALOMOV (Ru)
XVI SYEZD VLKSM (Ru)
DEVYATAYA PYATILETKA (Ru)
NIZHEGORODSKIY
   KOMSOMOLETS (Ru)
750—LETIYE GORODA
   GORKOGO (Ru)
XXIV SYEZD KPSS (Ru)
50 LET PIONERII (Ru)
KEMINE (Ru)
SOVIETSKIY SEVER (Ru)
VLADIMIR ZATONSKIY (Ru)

NASIMI (Ru)
PETR LIDOV (Ru)
XVII SYEZD VLKSM (Ru)
9 MAYA 1945 GODA (Ru)
SEMYON MOROZOV (Ru)
VITALIY PRIMAKOV (Ru)
ALEKSEY VIKHORYEV (Ru)
FEDOR PODTELKOV (Ru)
PROFESSOR I.I.
  KRAKOVSKIY (Ru)
ALIYA MOLDAGULOV (Ru)
XVIII SYEZD VLKSM (Ru)
GAZLI (Ru)
IVAN LESOVIKOV (Ru)
IVAN KUDRIYA (Ru)
LENINGRADSKIY
  KOMSOMOLETS (Ru)
MARSHAL VOROBYEV (Ru)
MIKHAIL KRIVOSHLIKOV (Ru)
MUKHTAR ASHRAFI (Ru)
PAVEL GRABOVSKIY (Ru)
PAVEL MOCHALOV (Ru)
PROFESSOR KERICHYEV (Ru)
60 LET VELIKOGO
  OKTYABR (Ru)
60 LET VLKSM (Ru)
TAVRIYA (Ru)
UZEIR GADZHIBEKOV (Ru)
YURIY KOTSYUBINSKY (Ru)
VERA VOLOSHINA (Ru)
79450
  'NEFTERUDOVOZ' type (Ru)
79500
  'BALTIYSKIY' type (Ru)
79550
  PIONER NAKHODKI (Ru)
  SESTRORETSK (Ru)
  PIONER ODESSY (Ru)
  PIONER VLADIVOSTOKA (Ru)
  PIONER PRIMORYA (Ru)
  PIONER VYBORGA (Ru)
79640
  BELMEKEN (Bu)
  GENERAL VLADIMIR
    ZAIMOV (Bu)
  BALKAN (Bu)
  ZIEMIA BIALOSTOCKA (Pd)
  ZIEMIA OLSZTYNSKA (Pd)

ZIEMIA OPOLSKI (Pd)
79730
  ESPENHAIN (DDR)
  SENFTENBERG (DDR)
  TRATTENDORF (DDR)
79870
  SUWALKI (Pd)
  KUTNO II (Pd)
  PIOTRKOW TRYBUNALSKI (Pd)
  WADOWICE (Pd)
  CIECHANOW (Pd)
  STARACHOWICE (Pd)
  PRZEMYSL (Pd)
79930
  ABRAM ARKHIPOV (Ru)
  VLADIMIR FAVORSKIY (Ru)
  MITROFAN GREKOV (Ru)
  VASILIY POLENOV (Ru)
  NIKOLAY YAROSHENKO (Ru)
  NIKOLAY KASATKIN (Ru)
  KONSTANTIN YUON (Ru)
  IGOR GRABAR (Ru)
  IVAN SHADR (Ru)
  MIKHAIL CHEREMNYKH (Ru)
  VERA MUKHINA (Ru)
  YEKATERINA BELASHOVA (Ru)
79945
  SEREBRYANKA (Ru)
79985
  COLDITZ (DDR)
79990
  KAPITAN PANFILOV (Ru)
  KAPITAN KHROMTSOV (Ru)
  KAPITAN DUBININ (Ru)
  KAPITAN IZHMYAKOV (Ru)
  KAPITAN
    MESHCHRYAKOV (Ru)
  KAPITAN REUTOV (Ru)
  KAPITAN GUDIN (Ru)
  KAPITAN STULOV (Ru)
  KAPITAN VAVILOV (Ru)
  IVAN NESTEROV (Ru)
  YUSTAS PALECKIS (Ru)
80000
  KHUDOZHNIK
    FEDOROVSKIY (Ru)
  KHUDOZHNIK A
    GERASIMOV (Ru)

KHUDOZHNIK
  GABASHVILI (Ru)
KHUDOZHNIK KASIYAN (Ru)
KHUDOZHNIK
  KUSTODIYEV (Ru)
KHUDOZHNIK TOIDZE (Ru)
KHUDOZHNIK VLADIMIR
  SEROV (Ru)
SOVIETSKIY KHUDOZHNIK (Ru)
CHIPKA (or SHIPKA) (Bu)
RILA (Bu)
RODOPI (Bu)
VITOCHA (Bu)
MILIN KAMAK (Bu)
SLAVIANKA (Bu)
OKOLTCHITZA (Bu)
KAPITAN GEORGI
  GEORGIEV (Bu)
VIHREN (Bu)
KAMENITZA (Bu)
BUMBESTI (Rm)
LIVEZINI (Rm)
LOTRU (Rm)
MOTRU (Rm)
SALVA (Rm)
VIDRARU (Rm)
VISEU (Rm)
80010
  BORIS LIVANOV (Ru)
  VIKTOR KINGISEPP (Ru)
  VASILIY SOLOVYEV
    SEDOY (Ru)
  LEONID SOBOLYEV (Ru)
  SERGO ZARIADZE (Ru)
  SKULPTOR MATVEYEV (Ru)
  KHUDOZHNIK KRAYNEV (Ru)
  GRIGORIY ALEKSANDROV (Ru)
80020
  HUTA ZGODA (Pd)
  HUTA ZYGMUNT (Pd)
  BUDOWLANY (Pd)
  ROLNIK (Pd)
  KOPALNIA SOSNOWIEC (Pd)
  KOPALNIA WALBRZYCH (Pd)
  KOPALNIA ZOFIOWKA (Pd)
80052
  SIMON BOLIVAR (Ru)
  PYER PUYYAD (Ru)

GENERAL GORBATOV (Ru)
KAPITAN ARTYUKH (Ru)
STOYKO PEEV (Ru)
KRASNOGVARDEYETS (Ru)
ROSTOV NA DONU (Ru)
STANKO STAIKOV (Bu)
YURIY LEVITAN (Ru)
80060
  KAPITAN TOMSON (Ru)
  KAPITAN YAKOVLEV (Ru)
80071
  BAZIAS 1 (Rm)
  BAZIAS 2 (Rm)
  BAZIAS 3 (Rm)
  BAZIAS 4 (Rm)
  BAZIAS 5 (Rm)
  BAZIAS 6 (Rm)
  BAZIAS 7 (Rm)
  BAZIAS 8 (Rm)
80090
  INZHENIER MACHULSKIY (Ru)
  INZHENIER BASHKIROV (Ru)
  INZHENIER SUKHORUKOV (Ru)
  INZHENIER KREYLIS (Ru)
  MEKHANIK KONOVALOV (Ru)
  INZHENIER
    NECHIPORENKO (Ru)
  MEKHANIK FEDOROV (Ru)
  MEKHANIK YEVGRAFOV (Ru)
  MEKHANIK GERASIMOV (Ru)
80100
  KAPITAN KANEVSKIY (Ru)
  KAPITAN GAVRILOV (Ru)
  KAPITAN KOZLOVSKIY (Ru)
  KAPITAN V. USHAKOV (Ru)
  KAPITAN V. TRUSH (Ru)
  NIKOLAY TIKHONOV (Ru)
  TIKHON KISELYEV (Ru)
  GEROI MONKADIY (Ru)
  PROFESSOR TOVSTYKH (Ru)
  BOLSHEVIK M TOMAS (Ru)
80109
  RUHLAND (DDR)
  RUEBELAND (DDR)
  SOHLAND (DDR)
80130
  ZARECHENSK (Ru)
  ZVENIGOROD (Ru)

ZAPOROZHYE (Ru)
ZAKARPATYE (Ru)
ZADONSK (Ru)
ZLATOUST (Ru)
ZORINSK (Ru)
ZIEMIA KRAKOWSKA (Pd)
ZIEMIA LUBELSKA (Pd)
ZAGLEBIE MIEDZIOWE (Pd)
80171
  DMITRIY DONSKOY (Ru)
  DMITRIY POZHARSKIY (Ru)
  ALEKSANDR NEVSKIY (Ru)
  ALEKSANDR SUVOROV (Ru)
  MIKHAIL KUTUZOV (Ru)
  ADMIRAL USHAKOV (Ru)
  KUZMA MININ (Ru)
  PETR VELIKIY (Ru)
  STEPAN RAZIN (Ru)
  YEMELYAN PUGACHEV (Ru)
80200
  MAGNITOGORSK (Ru)
  KOMSOMOLSK (Ru)
  ANATOLIY VASILYEV (Ru)
  SMOLENSK (Ru)
80205
  POZNAN (Pd)
  KATOWICE II (Pd)
  GDANSK II (Pd)
  WROCLAW (Pd)
80250
  AKADEMIK ARTSIMOVICH (Ru)
  AKADEMIK GUBER (Ru)
  AKADEMIK KUPREVICH (Ru)
  AKADEMIK
    MILLIONSCHIKOV (Ru)
  AKADEMIK STECHKIN (Ru)
  AKADEMIK TUPOLEV (Ru)
80260
  SKULPTOR KONENKOV (Ru)
  SKULPTOR VUCHETICH (Ru)
  SKULPTOR GOLUBKINA (Ru)
  SKULPTOR ZALKALNS (Ru)
  NIKOLAY CHERKASOV (Ru)
  AGOSTINHO NETO (Ru)
  PETR MASHEROV (Ru)
  GEORGIY PYASETSKIY (Ru)
  AKADEMIK GORBUNOV (Ru)
  YURIY MAKSAYEV (Ru)

80750
LEONID TELIGA (Pd)
80890
ADAM ASNYK (Pd)
80900
PETKO R. SLAVEJNOV (Bu)
IVAN VAZOV (Bu)
80920
LENKORAN (Ru)
LYUBOTIN (Ru)
81000
NOVY BUG (Ru)
NOVY DONBASS (Ru)
NOVAYA KAKHOVKA (Ru)
NOVORZHEV (Ru)
NOVOSHAKHTINSK (Ru)
81195
TATARSTAN (Ru)
TURKMENISTAN (Ru)
UZBEKISTAN (Ru)
KOMSOMOLIYA
KALININGRADA (Ru)
KOMSOMOLSKAYA
SMENA (Ru)
81305
CARANSEBES (Rm)
SIGHISOARA (Rm)
81350
ZULAWY (Pd)
KASZUBY II (Pd)
WINETA (Pd)
MAZURY (Pd)
81400
ALIOT (Ru)
POLLUKS (Ru)
PROTSION (Ru)
81450
LEONID TELIGA (Pd)
81490
PRIBOY (Ru)
KARL LINNEY (Ru)
KHIBINSKIE GORY (Ru)
KRYMSKIE GORY (Ru)
LENINSKIYE GORY (Ru)
URALSKIE GORY (Ru)
81555
SLATINA (Rm)
SLOBOZIA (Rm)

81640
ZAKOPANE (Pd)
ZAMOSC (Pd)
ZAMBRZE (Pd)
ZAMBROW (Pd)
ZAWICHOST (Pd)
ZAWIERCIE (Pd)
81860
CIECHOCINEK (Pd)
82110
BRAD (Rm)
SMIRDAN (Rm)
COVASNA (Rm)
DRAGANESTI (Rm)
SALONTA (Rm)
SASCUT (Rm)
SEIMINI (Rm)
SOLCA (Rm)
STEFANESTI (Rm)
SUCIDAVA (Rm)
TELEGA (Rm)
ZARNESTI (Rm)
ZIMNICEA (Rm)
AZUGA (Rm)
TIRGU JIU (Rm)
CODLEA (Rm)
SULINA (Rm)
TIRNAVENI (Rm)
RIMNICU VILCEA (Rm)
PLOPENI (Rm)
FALTICENI (Rm)
SACELE (Rm)
DUMBRAVENI (Rm)
CALARASI (Rm)
GHEORGHIENI (Rm)
SADU (Rm)
SADOVA (Rm)
SNAGOV (Rm)
TOPOLOVENI (Rm)
SOVEJA (Rm)
SOVATA (Rm)
SEGARCEA (Rm)
SAVINESTI (Rm)
SAVENI (Rm)
SUCEVITA (Rm)
SOUSA (Rm)
SALISTE (Rm)
SABARENI (Rm)

SCAIENI (Rm)
SLANIC (Rm)
SEBES (Rm)
LOVECH (Bu)
82220
URICANI (Rm)
ANINA (Rm)
CUGIR (Rm)
ROVINARI (Rm)
VULCAN (Rm)
MUSCEL (Rm)
CIMPULUNG (Rm)
AGNITA (Rm)
CALAN (Rm)
82260
PLOCK (Pd)
KOLOBRZEG II (Pd)
OSWIECIM (Pd)
CHRZANOW (Pd)
RYBNIK (Pd)
JELCZ II (Pd)
82460
OSTROV RUSSKIY (Ru)
OSTROV ATLASOVA (Ru)
OSTROV BERINGA (Ru)
OSTROV KARAKINSKIY (Ru)
OSTROV KOTLIN (Ru)
OSTROV LISYANSKOGO (Ru)
OSTROV LITKE (Ru)
OSTROV MEDNYY (Ru)
OSTROV SHMIDTA (Ru)
OSTROV SHOKALSKOGO (Ru)
OSTROV SIBIRYAKOVA (Ru)
OSTROV USHAKOVA (Ru)
82651
KOMSOMOLETS
PRIMORYA (Ru)
BALTIYSKIY ZON (Ru)
VOLSKIY ZALIV (Ru)
REUTERSHAGEN (DDR)
ZOLOTYE DYUNY (Ru)
TAYOZHNYY BEREG (Ru)
KALININGRADSKIY
BEREG (Ru)
MOTOVSKIY ZALIV (Ru)
OLYUTORSKIY ZALIV (Ru)
ULBANSKIY ZALIV (Ru)
USSURIYSKAYA TAYGA (Ru)

BEREG VETROV (Ru)
PENZHINSKIY ZALIV (Ru)
HERMANN MATERN (DDR)
83430
DUBNO (Ru)
DUBOSSARY (Ru)
DIMITROVO (Ru)
DAGESTAN (Ru)
DASHAVA (Ru)
DNEPRODZERZHINSK (Ru)
DONSKOY (Ru)
DEDOVSK (Ru)
83600
NORDSTERN (DDR)
MALCHIN (DDR)
83680
CHEREPOVETS (Ru)
SOSNOVETS (Ru)
SARATA (Ru)
SOSNOVKA (Ru)
SUVOROVO (Ru)
SERNOVODSK (Ru)
SNEZHNOGORSK (Ru)
SUDAK (Ru)
SLAUTNOYE (Ru)
SOFIYSK (Ru)
SURGUT (Ru)
NAZARCEA (Rm)
PALAS (Rm)
POIANA (Rm)
NOVACI (Rm)
83720
BATAK (Bu)
83930
BELLATRIX (DDR)
84150
BALKHASH (Ru)
BAKHCHISARAY (Ru)
BELOMORYE (Ru)
84210
KITEN (Bu)
PAPIA (Bu)
84330
ZVAYGZNE (Ru)
REFRIGERATOR No 5 (Ru)
REFRIGERATOR No 13 (Ru)
GORNOZAVODSK (Ru)
PROVORNY (Ru)

TRUDOLYUBIVYY (Ru)
84360
KHASAN (Ru)
KHANKA (Ru)
ELTON (Ru)
MIKHAYLO LOMONOSOV (Ru)
84460
IRTISH (Ru)
KARTALY (Ru)
84510
PALEKH (Ru)
84710
BOTEVGRAD (Bu)
84810
LENINAKAN (Ru)
LYUDINOVO (Ru)
NOVOROSSISKIY
PARTIZAN (Ru)
LENKORAN (Ru)
LYUBOTIN (Ru)
84930
CONDOR (DDR)
FLAMINGO (DDR)
PINGUIN (DDR)
84940
OELSA (DDR)
EISENBERG (DDR)
HELLERAU (DDR)
THEMAR (DDR)
ZEULENRODA (DDR)
85170
BOTEVGRAD (Bu)
85185
BREZA (Bu)
85320
DALNEVOSTOCHNY (Ru)
VOLZHSK (Ru)
ANDREY EVDANOV (Ru)
SOVIETSKAYA LATVIYA (Ru)
SOVIETSKAYA RODINA (Ru)
VITALIY BONIVUR (Ru)
BUREVESTNIK (Ru)
DMITRY CHASOVITIN (Ru)
KAZIS GEDRIS (Ru)
RUDNYY (Ru)
ALTAIR (Ru)
MIKHAIL YANKO (Ru)
NEVELSKIY (Ru)

OKTYABRSK (Ru)
SEREBRYANSK (Ru)
SVETLYY (Ru)
IRBIT (Ru)
ISHIM (Ru)
ISKONA (Ru)
PRANAS ZIBERTAS (Ru)
SALNA (Ru)
SARMA (Ru)
PARSLA (Ru)
SAYANI (Ru)
SUKHINICHI (Ru)
GUTSUL (Ru)
MONGOL (Ru)
NANAYETS (Ru)
PFUSUNG (Ru)
AUGUST KORK (Ru)
BOYEVOY (Ru)
LEDUS (Ru)
KOSMONAUT (Ru)
MOLODYOZNYY (Ru)
MOREKHOD (Ru)
VETERAN (Ru)
DON (Ru)
KREUTSWALD (Ru)
NAMANGAN (Ru)
VIKTORAS
   YATSENYAVICHUS (Ru)
BREITLING (DDR)
85610
BIRA (Ru)
BUREYA (Ru)
85895
KONDA (Ru)
ROSSOSH (Ru)
SOYANA (Ru)
YAKHROMA (Ru)
85970
KRIPTON (Ru)
UKHTA (Ru)
GROZNYY (Ru)
ABAKAN (Ru)
AKADEMIK MAMEDALIEV (Ru)
EKIMCHAN (Ru)
LASPI (Ru)
EVENSK (Ru)
TEMRYUK (Ru)
KEKUR (Ru)

NIVA (Ru)
NEFTEGORSK (Ru)
NERCHINSK (Ru)
SOVIETSKIY
   POGRANICHNIK (Ru)
IMANT SUDMALIS (Ru)
NIKOPOL (Ru)
NOGINSK (Ru)
SEVAN (Ru)
FIORD (Ru)
NOVIK (Ru)
KHRUSTALNYY (Ru)
SAMTREDIA (Ru)
SILVET (Ru)
BERDSK (Ru)
SOLNECHNYY (Ru)
STEPANOKERT (Ru)
BALADZHARY (Ru)
BELOYARSK (Ru)
BORISOGLEBSK (Ru)
KARAKUMNEFT (Ru)
KARELI (Ru)
NARYMNEFT (Ru)
BEREZOVNEFT (Ru)
ICHA (Ru)
ELTIGEN (Ru)
KUMBYSH (Ru)
NADEZHDA
   KURCHYENKO (Ru)
KERCHENSKIY
   KOMMUNIST (Ru)
CHAYA (Bu)
VACHA (Bu)
86070
'KORSAKOV' type (Ru)
OKHA (Ru)
NALCHIK (Ru)
TIKHORETSK (Ru)
TRUSKAVETS (Ru)
VILSANDI (Ru)
KAGUL (Ru)
KREMENETS (Ru)
NARYN (Ru)
ZAYARSK (Ru)
JAN KREUKS (Ru)
KANIN (Ru)
TAKELI (Ru)
BELBECK (Ru)

86110
   BUDAPEST (Hu)
   HUNGARIA (Hu)
86170
   OLENSK (Ru)
   TSELINOGRAD (Ru)
   IVAN BOGUN (Ru)
   SCHOLLAR (Ru)
   ALEKSANDR OBUKHOV (Ru)
   BUZAU (Rm)
   ARAD (Rm)
   PITESTI (Rm)
   ROMAN (Rm)
86220
   ANANYEV (Ru)
   KOTOVSK (Ru)
   PILTUN (Ru)
   TARTU (Ru)
   TERMEZ (Ru)
   VILKOVO (Ru)
   BELTSY (Ru)
   KONOSHA (Ru)
   SERGEY KIROV (Ru)
   TAMSALU (Ru)
   PALDISKI (Ru)
   PINEGA (Ru)
   GLUKHOV (Ru)
   KIHELKONA (Ru)
   VILYANDY (Ru)
   ENGURE (Ru)
86420
   EISENHUTTENSTADT (DDR)
86470
   KEGUMS (Ru)
   KRASLAVA (Ru)
86540
   OZERNOYE (Ru)
   DIVNOGORSK (Ru)
86824
   KAPITAN ZBIGNIEW
      SZYMANSKI (Pd)
87000
   PERVOMAYSK (Ru)
   NEVA (Ru)
   YULYUS YANONIS (Ru)
87640
   BEGA (Rm)
   MEDIAS (Rm)

   TIMIS (Rm)
   DROBETA 1850 (Rm)
87740
   KRASNAL (Pd)
   GOPLANA (Pd)
   CHOCHLIK (Pd)
   NIMFA (Pd)
   RUSALKA (Pd)
   SWIETLIK (Pd)
87940
   'KORSAKOV' type (Ru)
87950
   ZVAYGZNE (Ru)
88130
   YAKAN (Ru)
88230
   KHOLMSK (Ru)
   MELITOPOL (Ru)
   VORMSI (Ru)
88250
   MOLDOVA (Rm)
88380
   ZAGLEBIE DABROWSKIE (Pd)
   DOLNY SLASK (Pd)
   PODHALE (Pd)
   KUJAWY (Pd)
88600
   ELENA (Bu)
88885
   ROSITZA (Bu)
88920
   TARAKLIYA (Ru)
   SEVERNYY DONETS (Ru)
88985
   'VODA' class (Ru)
   ABAKAN (Ru)
   SURA (Ru)
89200
   KEKHRA (Ru)
   KUNDA (Ru)
   OTEPYA (Ru)
   ARTSIZ (Ru)
   KUYVASTU (Ru)
   MASSANDRA (Ru)
   TIRASPOL (Ru)
   VYANDRA (Ru)
   KALMIUS (Ru)
   SOLOMBALA (Ru)

VIRTSU (Ru)
BEREZINA (Ru)
OSMUSSAAR (Ru)
TAKHUNAAR (Ru)
KARL KRUSHTEYN (Ru)
DEBRECEN (Hu)
HEVIZ (Hu)
89250
SPARTAK (Ru)
IVAN BOLOTNIKOV (Ru)
KONDRATIY BULAVIN (Ru)
NIKOLAY BAUMAN (Ru)
PETR KAKHOVSKIY (Ru)
SALAVAT YULAYEV (Ru)
AEGNA (Ru)
ANGYALFOLD (Ru)
AUGUST KULBERG (Ru)
ANABAR (Ru)
MOKHNI (Ru)
ARAKS (Ru)
KABONA (Ru)
VITIM (Ru)
SEMYON ROSHAL (Ru)
TERIBERKA (Ru)
AMBLA (Ru)
RAPLA (Ru)
89460
YURYUZAN (Ru)
SULA (Ru)
BAYMAK (Ru)
BUGURUSLAN (Ru)
ALEKSANDR LEYNER (Ru)
VYRU (Ru)
KANDAGACH (Ru)
METAN (Ru)
89500
AYSBERG (Ru)
KAPITAN KARTASHOV (Ru)
89515
ROYA (Ru)
89540
PETRILA (Rm)
PIATRA NEAMT (Rm)
VATRA DORNEI (Rm)
89680
SEVERODVINSKIY (Ru)
ARABATSKIY (Ru)
ONEGSKIY (Ru)

240

89980
  GORLITZ (DDR)
  GRODITZ (DDR)
  NIKOLAY VOZNESENSKIY (Ru)
  COLDITZ (DDR)
  PREMNITZ (DDR)
90030
  'BALTIYSKIY' type (Ru)
90150
  MAGADAN (Ru)
  ZELENOGRAD (Ru)
90190
  YANA (Ru)
  URENGOI (Ru)
90420
  'VOLGONEFT' type (Ru)
90560
  PECHORALES (Ru)
  JOHANN MAHMASTAL (Ru)
90600
  OELSA (DDR)
  EISENBERG (DDR)
  HELLERAU (DDR)
  THEMAR (DDR)
  ZEULENRODA (DDR)
90720
  INTERNATSIONAL (Ru)
  DRUZHBA NARODOV (Ru)
  ISKRA (Ru)
  LENINSKOE ZNAMYA (Ru)
  NAKHODKA (Ru)
  PROLETARSKAYA
    POBEDA (Ru)
  PAMYAT LENINA (Ru)
  PYOTR STUCHKA (Ru)
  ZAVYETY ILYICHA (Ru)
91224
  IVAN AIVAZOVSKIY (Ru)
  ALEKSEY VENETSIANOV (Ru)
  VIKTOR VASTNETSOV (Ru)
  ALEKSANDR IVANOV (Ru)
  VASILIY PEROV (Ru)
  ILYA REPIN (Ru)
  VASILIY POLENOV (Ru)
  MOLODAYA GVARDIYA (Ru)
  IMENI 61 KOMMUNARA (Ru)
  PIONER MURMANA (Ru)
  HANS POGELMANN (Ru)

SEVERNYY VETER (Ru)
DEMYAN KOROTCHENKO (Ru)
MARSHAL
  ROKOSSOVSKIY (Ru)
GORETS (Ru)
ALMAZNYY (Ru)
SIBIR (Ru)
KONSTANTIN
  OLSHANSKIY (Ru)
ARKHIP KUINDZHI (Ru)
VIKTOR LYAGIN (Ru)
IVAN SHISHKIN (Ru)
VASILIY SURIKOV (Ru)
ZOLOTOY ROG (Ru)
KHUDOZHNIK S.
  GERASIMOV (Ru)
PIONER VOLKOV (Ru)
KAZIS PREYKSHAS (Ru)
ULAN-UDE (Ru)
POLYARNYE ZORI (Ru)
KHUDOZHNIK DEYNEKA (Ru)
KHUDOZHNIK VRUBEL (Ru)
GRANITNYY (Ru)
VASILY
  VERESCHCHAGIN (Ru)
IVAN KRAMSKOY (Ru)
VALENTIN SEROV (Ru)
KOSMONAUT GAGARIN (Ru)
OBUKHOVSKAYA
  OBORONA (Ru)
MARSHAL MALINOVSKIY (Ru)
POLYARNYY KRUG (Ru)
SLANCHEV BRIAG (Bu)
ZLATNI PIASATZI (Bu)
LAZUREN BRIAG (Bu)
ALBENA (Bu)
KITEN (Bu)
EVERSHAGEN (DDR)
LUTTENKLEIN (DDR)
POLAR 1 (Rm)
POLAR II (Rm)
91260
  PAVLIN VINOGRADOV (Ru)
91700
  SOFIA (Bu)
  VELIKO TIRNOVO (Bu)
91770
  HARMATTAN (Pd)

91910
  KAMCHATSKIE GORY (Ru)
  SAYANSKIE GORY (Ru)
  SAKHALINSKIE GORY (Ru)
92030
  'VOLGONEFT' type (Ru)
92150
  VOSTOCK (Ru)
92160
  EMBA (Ru)
  NEPRYADVA (Ru)
  SETUN (Ru)
92165
  BIRYUSA (Ru)
  KEMJ (Ru)
92380
  DALNIY VOSTOK (Ru)
  VLADIVOSTOK (Ru)
92435
  KOSMONAUT YURIY
    GAGARIN (Ru)
92437
  PERIS (Rm)
  PALTINIS (Rm)
  PASCANI (Rm)
  PAULIS (Rm)
92680
  SOVIETSKIY DAGESTAN (Ru)
  SOVIETSKIY
    TADZHIKISTAN (Ru)
  SOVIETSKAYA ARMENIYA (Ru)
  SOVIETSKAYA GRUZIYA (Ru)
  SOVIETSKAYA
    KALMYKIYA (Ru)
  SOVIETSKAYA KIRGIZIYA (Ru)
  SOVIETSKAYA
    BYELORUSSIYA (Ru)
  SOVIETSKIY
    NAKHICHEVAN (Ru)
92880
  VALENTIN SHASHKIN (Ru)
  VIKTOR MURAVLENKO (Ru)
  MIKHAIL MIRCHINK (Ru)
93060
  TRAPEZITZA (Bu)
  TZAREVETZ (Bu)
93268
  VSEVOLOD BERYEZKIN (Ru)

VALERIAN URYVAYEV (Ru)
YAKOV GAKKEL (Ru)
DALNIYE ZELYENTSY (Ru)
ISKATEL (Ru)
ISSLEDOVATEL (Ru)
LEV TITOV (Ru)
MORSKOY GEOFIZIK (Ru)
RUDOLF SAMOYLOVICH (Ru)
VULKANLOG (Ru)
VYACHESLAV FROLOV (Ru)
93380
  VLADIMIR ILYCH (Ru)
  MARIYA ULYANOVA (Ru)
  SOVIETSKAYA ROSSIYA (Ru)
  60 LET OKTYABRYA (Ru)
  ALEKSANDR ULYANOV (Ru)
  YEVGENIY VUCHETICH (Ru)
93630
  SOVIETSKAYA ROSSIYA (Ru)
93660
  VOSTOCK (Ru)
93670
  GEROITE NA
    SEVASTOPOL (Bu)
  GEROITE NA ODESSA (Bu)
  GEROI PLEVNY (Bu)
  GEROI SHIPKI (Bu)
93680
  ANDREY ZAKHAROV (Ru)
  PAVEL CHEBOTNYAGIN (Ru)
  YEVGENIY NIKISHIN (Ru)
  KONSTANTIN SUKHANOV (Ru)
  VASILIY BLUKHER (Ru)
  MIKHAIL TUKACHEVSKIY (Ru)
  PAVEL POSTYSHEV (Ru)
  SEGEY LAZO (Ru)
  VASILIY PUTINTSEV (Ru)
93695
  IERONIM UBOREVICH (Ru)
  KORABLESTEROITYEL
    KLOPOTOV (Ru)
  KRONID KORENOV (Ru)
93780
  VILIS LACIS (Ru)
  BOYEVAYA SLAVA (Ru)
  RYBATSKAYA SLAVA (Ru)
  TRUDOVAYA SLAVA (Ru)
  BALTISKAYA SLAVA (Ru)

CHERNOMORSKAYA
  SLAVA (Ru)
KRONSHTADTSKAYA
  SLAVA (Ru)
LENINGRADSKAYA
  SLAVA (Ru)
93800
  SEVEROURALSK (Ru)
  SHALVA NADIBAIDZE (Ru)
  SLAVYANSK (Ru)
  SPASSK (Ru)
  SUKHONA (Ru)
  SULAK (Ru)
  SUZDAL (Ru)
93820
  POGRANICHNIK LEONOV (Ru)
  FELIKS KON (Ru)
  NAKHICHEVAN (Ru)
  ROBERT EYKHE (Ru)
  YULIAN MARKHLEVSKIY (Ru)
  KALININGRADSKIY
    KOMSOMOLETS (Ru)
  SEVERNYY POLYUS (Ru)
  SOVIETSKIY
    ZAPOLYARYE (Ru)
  TOMSK (Ru)
  LENINSKAYA ISKRA (Ru)
  MARSHAL MERETSKOV (Ru)
  NOVAYA KAKHOVKA (Ru)
  NOVAYA LADOGA (Ru)
  ARKTIKA (Ru)
  OROCHON (Ru)
  PALANGA (Ru)
  SOVIETSKOYE PRIMORYE (Ru)
  AVACHA (Ru)
  RYBAK BALTIKA (Ru)
  ANTARKTIKA (Ru)
  LENINSKIY PUT (Ru)
  SOVIETSKAYA SIBIR (Ru)
  YUZHNO-SAKHALINSK (Ru)
  PRIBALTIKA (Ru)
  RIZHSKOYE VZMORYE (Ru)
  50 LET OKTYABRYA (Ru)
  VINTSAS MITSKYAVICHUS-
    KAPSUKAS (Ru)
  SOVIETSKAYA BURYATYA (Ru)
  ALEKSANDROVSK
    SAKHALINSKIY (Ru)

241

KOMSOMOLETS
    MAGADANA (Ru)
KOMSOMOLSK NA
    AMURE (Ru)
MARSHAL SOKOLOVSKIY (Ru)
RYBAK LATVII (Ru)
PROFESSOR BARANOV (Ru)
93860
    SOVIETSKAYA UKRAINA (Ru)
93870
    PIONERSK (Ru)
    DAURIYA (Ru)
    MATOCHKIN SHAR (Ru)

RYBNYY MURMAN (Ru)
FRYDERYK CHOPIN (Ru)
POLYARNAYA ZVEZDA (Ru)
SEVRYBA (Ru)
ALEKSEY KHLOBYSTOV (Ru)
ALEKSEY POZDNYAKOV (Ru)
GRIGORIY LYSENKO (Ru)
NIKOLAY DANILOV (Ru)
SERGEY VASILISIN (Ru)
STANISLAV
    MONYUSHKO (Ru)
VIKTOR KINGISEPP (Ru)
POMORZE (Pd)

GRYF POMORSKY (Pd)
93884
    SEVERODONETSK (Ru)
93930
    PUCK (Pd)
94010
    ASCHBERG (DDR)
    BEERBERG (DDR)
94280
    KOSMONAUT VLADIMIR
        KOMAROV (Ru)
94490
    FICHTELBERG (DDR)

94550
    INOWROCLAW (Pd)
94565
    GLEICHBERG (DDR)
    AUERSBERG (DDR)
    KAHLEBERG (DDR)
    TUTOVA (Rm)
    TUZLA (Rm)
95015
    LENA (Ru)
    DUNAY (Ru)
    SHEKSNA (Ru)
    TEREK (Ru)

95042
    MODUL (Ru)
    GEOFIZIK (Ru)
    PROFESSOR FEDYINSKIY (Ru)
    ELM (Ru)
    CHAYVO (Ru)
95043
    VEKTOR (Ru)
95250
    BROCKEN (DDR)

ALPHABETICAL INDEX

9 MAYA 1945 GODA (Ru)	79340	65 LET SOVIETSKOY		ADMIRAL MAKAROV (Ru)	33015
15 SYEZD VLKSM (Ru)	12380	VLASTI (Ru)	79340	ADMIRAL SARYCHEV (Ru)	17920
30-LET POBEDY (Ru)	34610	750—LETIYE GORODA		ADMIRAL USHAKOV (Ru)	80171
30-LETIYE POBEDY (or		GORKOGO (Ru)	79340	ADMIRAL	
TRIDTSATILETIYE				VLADIMIRSKIY (Ru)	04240
POBEDY) (Ru)	01380	ABAGUR (Ru)	36890	ADY (Hu)	45350
30-LETIYE POBEDY (or		ABAGUR (Ru)	43790	ADYGEJA (Ru)	62495
TRIDTSATILETIYE		ABAKAN (Ru)	36890	ADYGENI (Ru)	70760
POBEDY) (Ru)	01640	ABAKAN (Ru)	43790	ADZHARIYA (Ru)	02150
30-LETIYE POBEDY (Ru)	11720	ABAKAN (Ru)	85970	ADZHARIYA (Ru)	06825
50 LET OKTYABRYA (Ru)	93820	ABAKAN (Ru)	88985	AEGNA (Ru)	89250
50 LET PIONERII (Ru)	79340	ABAVA (Ru)	70760	AFALA (Bu)	23440
50 LET SOVIET		ABKHAZIYA (Ru)	06825	AFANASAY NIKITIN (Ru)	12380
SOVIETSKOY (Ru)	05620	ABRAM ARKHIPOV (Ru)	76580	AFANASIY	
50 LET SOVIETSKOY		ABRAM ARKHIPOV (Ru)	79930	BOGATYREV (Ru)	50730
UKRAINY (Ru)	14450	ACHINSK (Ru)	26210	AFANASIY	
50 LET SOVIETSKOY		ACHUYEVSKIY (Ru)	23305	MATYUSHENKO (Ru)	79340
VLASTI (Ru)	79340	ADALBERT ANTONOV (Bu)	78980	AFANASIY NIKITIN (Ru)	22220
50 LET SSSR (Ru)	71820	ADAM ASNYK (Pd)	80890	AFGHANISTAN (Ru)	02350
50 LET S. S. R. (Ru)	79340	ADAM MICKIEWICZ (Ru)	54970	AFGHANISTAN (Ru)	35370
50 LET VLKSM (Ru)	12380	ADAM MICKIEWICZ (Pd)	71810	AGAT (Ru)	12380
50 LET VLKSM (Ru)	35310	ADAYKHOKH (Ru)	13751	AGAT (Ru)	22173
50 LET VLKSM (Ru)	79340	ADLER (Ru)	46580	AGATAN (Ru)	22159
60 LET OKTYABRYA (Ru)	58510	ADMIRAL		AGATOVYY (Ru)	11800
60 LET OKTYABRYA (Ru)	71820	ARCISZEWSKI (Pd)	22350	AGDAM (Ru)	50770
60 LET OKTYABRYA (Ru)	93380	ADMIRAL GOLOVKO (Ru)	00140	AGNITA (Rm)	82220
60 LET VELIKOGO		ADMIRAL KOLYSHKIN (Ru)	00140	AGOSTINHO NETO (Ru)	80260
OKTYABR (Ru)	79340	ADMIRAL LUNIN (Ru)	01960	AKADEMIK A.	
60 LET VLKSM (Ru)	79340	ADMIRAL MAKAROV (Ru)	20870	KOVALEVSKIY (Ru)	18615

AKADEMIK ALEKSANDR		AKADEMIK	
KARPINSKIY (Ru)	11333	GORBUNOV (Ru)	80260
AKADEMIK ALEKSANDR		AKADEMIK GUBER (Ru)	80250
SIDORENKO (Ru)	11333	AKADEMIK IOSIF	
AKADEMIK ALEKSANDR		ORBELI (Ru)	02520
VINOGRADOV (Ru)	14905	AKADEMIK	
AKADEMIK ALEXSANDR		KHOKHLOV (Ru)	10740
NESMEYANOV (Ru)	14905	AKADEMIK	
AKADEMIK		KNIPOVICH (Ru)	12570
ARTOBOLEVSKIY (Ru)	10740	AKADEMIK	
AKADEMIK		KOROLYOV (Ru)	12000
ARTSIMOVICH (Ru)	80250	AKADEMIK KRYLOV (Ru)	02460
AKADEMIK BAKULEV (Ru)	51672	AKADEMIK	
AKADEMIK BERG (Ru)	12570	KUPREVICH (Ru)	80250
AKADEMIK		AKADEMIK	
BLAGONRAVOV (Ru)	51672	KURCHATOV (Ru)	07620
AKADEMIK		AKADEMIK LAZAROV (Ru)	14986
BOCHVAR (Ru)	03423	AKADEMIK M A	
AKADEMIK BORIS		LAVRENTYEV (Ru)	15003
PETROV (Ru)	15003	AKADEMIK	
AKADEMIK		MAMEDALIEV (Ru)	85970
CHELOMEY (Ru)	03423	AKADEMIK	
AKADEMIK EVGENIY		MILLIONSCHIKOV (Ru)	80250
PATON (Ru)	02670	AKADEMIK MSTISLAV	
AKADEMIK FEDOROV (Ru)	03400	KELDYSH (Ru)	14955
AKADEMIK FERSMAN (Ru)	14986	AKADEMIK MSTISLAV	
AKADEMIK FILATOV (Ru)	02520	KELDYSH (Ru)	15095
AKADEMIK		AKADEMIK N.	
GAMBURTSYEV (Ru)	04225	VAVILOV (Ru)	02847

242

AKADEMIK NIKOLAY
  STRAKHOV (Ru) 15003
AKADEMIK OPARIN (Ru) 14988
AKADEMIK
  PETROVSKIY (Ru) 33605
AKADEMIK
  POZDYUNIN (Ru) 50763
AKADEMIK
  RYKACHEV (Ru) 02520
AKADEMIK
  SECHENOV (Ru) 63570
AKADEMIK SERGEY
  KOROLOV (Ru) 08115
AKADEMIK SESKIY (Ru) 14986
AKADEMIK SHATSKIY (Ru) 14986
AKADEMIK
  SHIMANSKIY (Ru) 01560
AKADEMIK
  SHIRSHOV (Ru) 12000
AKADEMIK
  SHOKALSKIY (Ru) 04275
AKADEMIK SHUKHOV (Ru) 02520
AKADEMIK
  SHULEYKIN (Ru) 04275
AKADEMIK STECHKIN (Ru) 80250
AKADEMIK TUPOLEV (Ru) 80250
AKADEMIK VEKUS (Ru) 52612/1
AKADEMIK
  VERNADSKIY (Ru) 07620
AKADEMIK YANGEL (Ru) 03950
AKADEMIK YURYEV (Ru) 02520
AKADEMIK
  ZAVARITSKIY (Ru) 02847
AKEN (DDR) 61700
AKHALTSIKHE (Ru) 70760
AKHILLEON (Ru) 13650
AKHILLES (Ru) 11800
AKHMETA (Ru) 13751
AKHTARSKIY LIMAN (Ru) 33620
AKHTUBA (Ru) 11800
AKHTUBA (Ru) 35310
AKHTUBINSK (Ru) 23664
AKHUN (Ru) 11800
AKMOLINSK (Ru) 11800
AKSTAFA (Ru) 50770
AKTASH (Ru) 36890
AKTASH (Ru) 43790
AKTAU (Ru) 70760

AKTINJA (Bu) 23440
AKTYUBINSK (Ru) 70760
AKUSTIK (Ru) 11800
AKVAMARIN (Ru) 23480
AKVAMARINOVYY (Ru) 33305
ALAG (Ru) 17637
ALAGIR (Ru) 36890
ALAGIR (Ru) 43790
ALAMBAY (Ru) 36235
ALAPAYEVSK (Ru) 00340
ALAPAYEVSK (Ru) 01020
ALATYR (Ru) 38950
ALATYRLES (Ru) 24030
ALAUSHAS (Ru) 33198
ALBA IULIA (Rm) 06142
ALBA (Rm) 49520
ALBA (Ru) 11800
ALBAKORA (Pd) 22330
ALBENA (Bu) 91224
ALCHEVSK (Ru) 25550
ALDAN (Ru) 06795
ALDAN (Ru) 22159
ALDANLES (Ru) 24030
ALDEBARAN (Ru) 23305
ALDOMA (Ru) 04312
ALEKO
  KONSTANTINOV (Bu) 49785
ALEKSANDER
  ZAWADSKI (Pd) 10570
ALEKSANDER
  ZAWADSKI (Pd) 15340
ALEKSANDR BLOK (Ru) 14370
ALEKSANDR
  BOGOLYUBOV (Ru) 23480
ALEKSANDR
  BORISOV (Ru) 34872
ALEKSANDR
  DOVZHENKO (Ru) 15120
ALEKSANDR
  FADEYEV (Ru) 77060
ALEKSANDR
  GERTSEN (Ru) 14370
ALEKSANDR
  GRIAZNOV (Ru) 34872
ALEKSANDR GRIN (Ru) 14370
ALEKSANDR IVANOV (Ru) 91224
ALEKSANDR IVANOVICH
  VOEYKOV (Ru) 23770

ALEKSANDR
  KAVERZNEV (Ru) 51986/1
ALEKSANDR
  KORNEYCHUK (Ru) 67680
ALEKSANDR
  KSENOFONTOV (Ru) 11333
ALEKSANDR KULIK (Ru) 22327
ALEKSANDR
  LAVRENOV (Ru) 28600
ALEKSANDR LEYNER (Ru) 89460
ALEKSANDR
  MAKSUTOV (Ru) 12380
ALEKSANDR
  MATROSOV (Ru) 73290
ALEKSANDR
  MIROSHNIKOV (Ru) 50280
ALEKSANDR NEVSKII (Ru) 17500
ALEKSANDR NEVSKIY (Ru) 80171
ALEKSANDR
  OBUKHOV (Ru) 86170
ALEKSANDR
  OGNIVTSEV (Ru) 48430
ALEKSANDR
  OGNIVTSEV (Ru) 49470
ALEKSANDR
  OGNIVTSEV (Ru) 49740
ALEKSANDR OSIPOV (Ru) 78060
ALEKSANDR
  PANKRATOV (Ru) 50280
ALEKSANDR
  PASHKOV (Ru) 79340
ALEKSANDR
  PASHKOV (Ru) 79340
ALEKSANDR
  POKALCHUK (Ru) 49240
ALEKSANDR POPOV (Ru) 75392
ALEKSANDR
  PROKOFYEV (Ru) 77060
ALEKSANDR
  PROKOFYEV (Ru) 79340
ALEKSANDR
  PUSHKIN (Ru) 01750
ALEKSANDR
  SAVELIEV (Ru) 48650
ALEKSANDR
  SERAFIMOVICH (Ru) 14370
ALEKSANDR
  STAROSTENKO (Ru) 78060

ALEKSANDR
  SUVOROV (Ru) 80171
ALEKSANDR
  TKHORZHEVSKIY (Ru) 23305
ALEKSANDR
  TORTSYEV (Ru) 00140
ALEKSANDR
  TSULUKIDZE (Ru) 71433
ALEKSANDR
  TSYURUPA (Ru) 03950
ALEKSANDR
  TSYURUPA (Ru) 79340
ALEKSANDR
  TVARDOVSKIY (Ru) 77060
ALEKSANDR TYURIN (Ru) 11333
ALEKSANDR
  ULYANOV (Ru) 03060
ALEKSANDR
  ULYANOV (Ru) 03650
ALEKSANDR
  ULYANOV (Ru) 93380
ALEKSANDR
  VERMISHEV (Ru) 14370
ALEKSANDR
  VERMISHEV (Ru) 79340
ALEKSANDR
  VINOKUROV (Ru) 03770
ALEKSANDR
  VINOKUROV (Ru) 04010
ALEKSANDR
  YEVSEYEV (Ru) 23305
ALEKSANDRA
  ARTYUKHINA (Ru) 03770
ALEKSANDRA
  ARTYUKHINA (Ru) 04010
ALEKSANDRA
  KOLLONTAY (Ru) 10720
ALEKSANDRIT (Ru) 23480
ALEKSANDROVSK (Ru) 00330
ALEKSANDROVSK (Ru) 11800
ALEKSANDROVSK
  SAKHALINSKIY (Ru) 93820
ALEKSEY BORDUNOV (Ru) 11800
ALEKSEY CHIRIKOV (Ru) 22180
ALEKSEY
  DANCHENKO (Ru) 51672
ALEKSEY
  GENERALOV (Ru) 00140

ALEKSEY GMYREV (Ru) 12380
ALEKSEY GRACHYEV (Ru) 13751
ALEKSEY
  KHLOBYSTOV (Ru) 93870
ALEKSEY KOSYGIN (Ru) 00965
ALEKSEY MAKHALIN (Ru) 12380
ALEKSEY
  POZDNYAKOV (Ru) 93870
ALEKSEY RENZAYEV (Ru) 22327
ALEKSEY
  STAKHANOV (Ru) 11333
ALEKSEY TOLSTOY (Ru) 07900
ALEKSEY
  VENETSIANOV (Ru) 91224
ALEKSEY VIKHORYEV (Ru) 79340
ALEKSEYEVKA (Ru) 36890
ALEKSEYEVSK (Ru) 43790
ALEKSEYEVSK (Ru) 36890
ALEKSEYEVSK (Ru) 43790
ALESHA
  DZHAPARIDZE (Ru) 58995
ALEUT (Ru) 39290
ALEXANDER
  DIMITROV (Bu) 48150
ALEYSK (Ru) 52304
ALEYSK (Ru) 52616
ALFEUS (Bu) 23440
ALGA (Ru) 45715
ALGAYBA (Ru) 23305
ALGENIB (Ru) 23305
ALGORITM (Ru) 17637
ALI AMIROV (Ru) 52745
ALI BAYRAMOV (Ru) 58995
ALIOSHA POPOVICH (Ru) 17500
ALIOT (Ru) 12230
ALIOT (Ru) 76890
ALIOT (Ru) 81400
ALISHER NAVOI (Ru) 14370
ALIYA MOLDAGULOV (Ru) 79340
ALKA (Bu) 11800
ALKA (Ru) 11800
ALLA TARASOVA (Ru) 02340
'ALLIGATOR III' class (Ru) 45720
ALMA (Ru) 11800
ALMA-ATA (Ru) 44100
ALMATYEVSK (Ru) 01020
ALMAZ (Ru) 12380
ALMAZ (Ru) 22173

Name	No.	Name	No.	Name	No.	Name	No.	Name	No.
ALMAZNYY BEREG (Ru)	62671	ANAPA (Ru)	43790	ANIVA (Ru)	43790	ARAM KHACHATURYAN (Ru)	48430	ARTEK (Ru)	11800
ALMAZNYY (Ru)	91224	ANAPA (Ru)	46580	ANNA ULYANOVA (Ru)	03060	ARAM KHACHATURYAN (Ru)	49470	ARTEMIDA (Ru)	11800
ALMETYEVSK (Ru)	00340	ANAPKA (Ru)	36890	ANNA ULYANOVA (Ru)	03650	ARAM KHACHATURYAN (Ru)	49740	ARTERN (DDR)	71900
ALPINIST (Ru)	22327	ANAPKA (Ru)	43790	ANTANAS SNECHKUS (Ru)	62701	ARARAT (Ru)	70760	ARTSIZ (Ru)	89200
ALSU (Ru)	11800	ANATOL (Pd)	33015	ANTARES (Pd)	10540	ARCTURUS (Pd)	10540	ARTUR GROTTGER (Pd)	49655
ALTAI (Ru)	17500	ANATOLIY BREDOV (Ru)	11610	ANTARES (Ru)	01733	ARDATOV (Ru)	11800	ARTYOM (Ru)	36250
ALTAIR (Ru)	01733	ANATOLIY KHALIN (Ru)	04520	ANTARES (Ru)	12230	ARDATOV (Ru)	36890	ARTYOM (Ru)	42800
ALTAIR (Ru)	76310	ANATOLIY KOLESNICHENKO (Ru)	02724	ANTARES (Ru)	70760	ARDATOV (Ru)	43790	ARTYOMOVSK (Ru)	26210
ALTAIR (Ru)	85320	ANATOLIY LUNACHARSKIY (Ru)	03060	ANTARKTIKA (Ru)	93820	ARGO (Ru)	12230	ARVID PELSHE (Ru)	03423
ALTAY (Ru)	11300	ANATOLIY LUNACHARSKIY (Ru)	03650	ANTARKTYDA (Ru)	01733	ARGONAUT (Bu)	23440	ARZAMAS (Ru)	11800
ALTAY (Ru)	70810	ANATOLIY LYAPIDEVSKIY (Ru)	49342	ANTCHAR (Ru)	12380	ARGUN (Ru)	11800	ARZAMAS (Ru)	31830
ALTAYLES (Ru)	24030	ANATOLIY VANEYEV (Ru)	79340	ANTON BUYUKLY (Ru)	06795	ARGUN (Ru)	24030	ASCHBERG (DDR)	94010
ALTENBURG (DDR)	03870	ANATOLIY VASILYEV (Ru)	71530	ANTON CHEKOV (Ru)	14370	ARGUN (Ru)	66380	ASHKHABAD (Ru)	67670
ALTENBURG (DDR)	04423	ANATOLIY VASILYEV (Ru)	80200	ANTON GUBARYEV (Ru)	67010	ARGUS (Ru)	12570	ASHUG ALEKSER (Ru)	50730
ALUKSNE (Ru)	36890	ANATOLIY ZHELEZNYAKOV (Ru)	00280	ANTON IVANOV (Ru)	40580	ARINAS (Ru)	33198	ASKANIYA (Ru)	11300
ALUKSNE (Ru)	43790	ANDOGA (Ru)	08834	ANTON LOPATIN (Ru)	11610	ARISTARKH BYELOPOLSKIY (Ru)	10740	ASKOLD (Ru)	01733
ALUPKA (Ru)	01960	ANDOMALES (Ru)	24030	ANTON MAKARENKO (Ru)	07900	ARKADIY CHERNYSHEV (Ru)	13751	ASKOLD (Ru)	12380
ALUSHTA (Ru)	01960	ANDREY ANDREYEV (Ru)	03770	ANTONI GARNUSZEWSKI (Pd)	07860	ARKADIY GAYDAR (Ru)	14370	ASKOLD (Ru)	57475
AMAREL (Pd)	23440	ANDREY ANDREYEV (Ru)	04010	ANTONINA NEZHDANOVA (Ru)	01935	ARKADIY KAMANIN (Ru)	15510	ASNINO (Ru)	17637
AMBARCHIK (Ru)	11300	ANDREY ANDREYEV (Ru)	11300	ANTONIO GRAMSCI (Ru)	70590	ARKHANGELSK (Ru)	02724	ASPHERON (Ru)	11800
AMBLA (Ru)	89250	ANDREY EVDANOV (Ru)	85320	ANTS LAYKMAA (Ru)	12380	ARKHIMED (Ru)	34880	ASPINDZA (Ru)	70760
AMBURAN (Ru)	43520	ANDREY I. KOROBITSIN (Ru)	22290	ANUYU (Ru)	70760	ARKHIP KUINDZHI (Ru)	91224	ASSORA (Ru)	39290
AMDERMA (Ru)	02724	ANDREY IVANOV (Ru)	50280	APATITOVYY (Ru)	33305	ARKONA (DDR)	16925	ASTAN KESAYEV (Ru)	13751
AMDERMA (Ru)	11800	ANDREY KIZHEVATOV (Ru)	50730	APETIT (Ru)	09380	ARKOVO (Ru)	12380	ASTARA (Ru)	50770
AMETIST (Ru)	22173	ANDREY LAVROV (Ru)	03950	APOGEY (Ru)	13650	ARKTIDA (Ru)	01733	ASTEROID (Ru)	11800
AMGA (Ru)	11800	ANDREY MARKIN (Ru)	11720	APOGON (Ru)	22327	ARKTIKA (Ru)	02415	ASTRA (Ru)	12380
'AMGA' class (Ru)	45730	ANDREY UPITS (Ru)	79340	APOLDA (DDR)	45850	ARKTIKA (Ru)	93820	ASTRAKHAN (Ru)	51212
AMGUEMA (Ru)	21610	ANDREY VILKITSKIY (Ru)	22180	APPE (Ru)	36890	ARKTUR (Ru)	76310	ASTRILOVO (Ru)	17637
AMGUEMA (Ru)	34100	ANDREY ZAKHAROV (Ru)	93680	APPE (Ru)	43790	ARMAN (Ru)	25840	ASTRONOM (Ru)	04065
AMGUN (Ru)	70760	ANDRIAN GONCHAROV (Ru)	69310	APSHERON (Ru)	11460	ARMAVIR (Ru)	25550	ASTRONOM (Ru)	11800
AMU-DARYA (Ru)	35310	ANDROMEDA (Pd)	11640	APSHERON (Ru)	70572	ARMENIYA (Ru)	02160	ATKARSK (Ru)	00330
AMUR (Ru)	22173	ANDROMEDA (Ru)	01733	APSHERONSK (Ru)	36890	ARMENIYA (Ru)	11800	ATLANT (Ru)	12570
AMUR (Ru)	39290	ANDRUS YOKHANI (Ru)	12570	APSHERONSK (Ru)	43790	ARMIA LUDOWA (Pd)	72115	ATLANT (Ru)	22178
'AMUR' class (Ru)	50570	ANGARA (Ru)	76945	AQUARIUS (Pd)	11337	ARNEB (Ru)	23305	'ATLANTIK 333' type (Ru)	28600
AMURSK (Ru)	12380	ANGARLES (Ru)	24030	AQUILA (Pd)	11337	ARNOLD SOMMERLING (Ru)	49810	ATLANTIK (DDR)	18720
AMURSK (Ru)	36890	ANGARSKLES (Ru)	24030	ARABAT (Ru)	13650	ARNOLD VEIMER (Ru)	04275	'ATLANTIK' type (Ru)	07470
AMURSK (Ru)	43790	ANGYALFOLD (Ru)	89250	ARABATSKIY (Ru)	89680	ARNOLD ZWEIG (DDR)	13751	'ATLANTIK' class (Ru)	11800
AMURSKIY BEREG (Ru)	62671	ANINA (Rm)	82220	ARAD (Rm)	86170	ARNSTADT (DDR)	50128	ATLAS (Ru)	22178
AMURSKIY ZALIV (Ru)	61100	ANISIMOVKA (Ru)	12380	ARAGONIT (Ru)	11800	ARSENEYEV (Ru)	12380	ATMIS (Ru)	08834
AMURSKLES (Ru)	24030	ANIVA (Ru)	36890	ARAGVI (Ru)	21220	ARSENIY MOSKVIN (Ru)	50280	ATOLL (Ru)	11800
ANABAR (Ru)	89250			ARAGVI (Ru)	36235	ARSENYEV (Ru)	45110	ATREK (Ru)	08834
ANADYR (Ru)	01733			ARAKS (Ru)	08834	ARSHINTSEVO (Ru)	78891	AUERSBERG (DDR)	94565
ANADYR (Ru)	02724			ARAKS (Ru)	36890			AUGUST ALLE (Ru)	12380
ANADYR (Ru)	35310			ARAKS (Ru)	43790			AUGUST JAKOBSON (Ru)	45120
ANADYRLES (Ru)	24030			ARAKS (Ru)	76945			AUGUST KORK (Ru)	85320
ANAKLIYA (Ru)	70760			ARAKS (Ru)	89250			AUGUST KULBERG (Ru)	89250
ANANYEV (Ru)	86220							AUKSHAYTIKA (Ru)	13650
ANAPA (Ru)	36890							AURA (Ru)	08834
								AUSHRA (Ru)	33017

Name	No.	Name	No.	Name	No.	Name	No.	Name	No.
AUSKEKLIS (Ru)	70800	BAHLUI (Rm)	13751	BALTIYSKIY ZON (Ru)	62671	BAYKALLES (Ru)	04180	BERDSK (Ru)	85970
AUTSE (Ru)	70800	BAIA DE ARAMA (Rm)	77560	BALTIYSKIY ZON (Ru)	82651	BAYKONUR (Ru)	24030	BERDY KERBABAYEV (Ru)	50730
AVACHA (Ru)	93820	BAIA DE ARIES (Rm)	77560	'BALTIYSKIY' type (Ru)	75350	BAYKOVSK (Ru)	11333	BERDYANSK (Ru)	00330
AVACHINSKIY (Ru)	23335	BAIA DE CRIS (Rm)	77560	'BALTIYSKIY' type (Ru)	79500	BAYMAK (Ru)	45350	BERDYANSK (Ru)	48845
AVDEYEVKA (Ru)	48380	BAIA DE FIER (Rm)	77560	'BALTIYSKIY' type (Ru)	90030	BAYMAK (Ru)	89460	BEREG MECHTY (Ru)	62671
AVETIK ISAAKYAN (Ru)	50730	BAIA MARE (Rm)	39660	BALTIYSKOYE MORE (Ru)	51416	BAZALETI (Ru)	13751	BEREG NADEZHDY (Ru)	62671
AVIAKONSTRUKTOR		BAILESTI (Rm)	77560	BALVY (Ru)	38610	BAZALT (Pd)	08834	BEREG VETROV (Ru)	62671
POLIKARPOV (Ru)	79340	BAKAN (Ru)	21947	BAM (Ru)	70020	BAZALT (Ru)	11800	BEREG VETROV (Ru)	82651
AVIATOR (Ru)	11800	BAKAYEVO (Ru)	12380	BANAT (Rm)	55780	BAZALTOVYY (Ru)	33305	BEREG YUNOSTI (Ru)	62671
AVIOR (Ru)	22173	BAKERIT (Ru)	09899	BANAT (Rm)	56480	BAZHENOVSK (Ru)	11333	BEREZAN (Ru)	01733
AVIRIS (Ru)	33198	BAKHCHISARAY (Ru)	11800	BANEASA (Rm)	77560	BAZIAS 1 (Rm)	80071	BEREZEN (Ru)	11800
AVRAAMIY		BAKHCHISARAY (Ru)	52020	BANSIN (DDR)	75330	BAZIAS 2 (Rm)	80071	BEREZINA (Ru)	89200
ZAVENYAGIN (Ru)	20875	BAKHCHISARAY (Ru)	84150	BANSKA BYSTRICA (Cz)	50909	BAZIAS 3 (Rm)	80071	BEREZINO (Ru)	33017
AVRAMESTI (Rm)	60978	BAKLAN (Bu)	12380	BARAGANUL (Rm)	77560	BAZIAS 4 (Rm)	80071	BEREZNIK (Ru)	06770
AY-PETRI (Ru)	11800	BAKLAN (Ru)	17639	BARAKUDA (Pd)	22330	BAZIAS 5 (Rm)	80071	'BEREZNIK' class (Ru)	07550
AY-PETRI (Ru)	20731	BAKLANOVO (Ru)	11333	BARAOLT (Rm)	77560	BAZIAS 6 (Rm)	80071	BEREZNIKI (Ru)	01070
AY-PETRI (Ru)	44100	BAKU (Ru)	50770	BARBATA (Pd)	22330	BAZIAS 7 (Rm)	80071	BEREZNIKI (Ru)	11300
AYAN (or AJAN) (Ru)	06795	BAKURIANI (Ru)	45350	BARENTSEE (DDR)	18720	BAZIAS 8 (Rm)	80071	BEREZOVKA (Ru)	45350
AYDAR (Ru)	17637	BALADZHARY (Ru)	85970	BARENTSYEVO MORE (Ru)	26210	BECHET (Rm)	77560	BEREZOVNEFT (Ru)	85970
AYKHAL (Ru)	70760	BALAKHNA (Ru)	11333	BARGUZIN (Ru)	15460	BEERBERG (DDR)	94010	BEREZOVO (Ru)	70020
AYNAZHI (Ru)	70760	BALAKHNALES (Ru)	24030	BARGUZIN (Ru)	36235	BEGA (Rm)	87640	BERGEN (DDR)	61700
AYON (Ru)	70760	BALAKLAVA (Ru)	38610	BARIT (Ru)	11800	BEIUS (Rm)	77560	BERINGOV PROLIV (Ru)	58510
AYSBERG (Ru)	89500	BALASHIKHA (Ru)	45350	BARLINEK (Pd)	75327	BEKAS (Bu)	11800	BERINGOV PROLIV (Ru)	71820
AYTODOR (or		BALASHOV (Ru)	22327	BARNAUL (Ru)	24030	BELA KUN (Ru)	05620	BERISLAV (Ru)	45350
AITODOR) (Ru)	46580	BALATON (Hu)	51780	BAROGRAF (Ru)	07470	BELA KUN (Ru)	14450	BERKUT (Ru)	13650
AYU-DAG (Ru)	11800	BALDONE (Ru)	38610	BARS (Ru)	22160	BELASITZA (Bu)	77980	BERLIN-HAUPTSTADT DER	
AYU-DAG (Ru)	20731	BALKAN (Bu)	79640	BARTH (DDR)	77398	BELBECK (Ru)	86070	DDR (DDR)	04910
AYVAZOVSKIY (Ru)	20650	BALKHASH (Ru)	20790	BARWENA (Pd)	22330	BELCHATOW (Pd)	60360	BERNARD KOENEN (Ru)	28600
AZERBAYDZHAN (Ru)	20370	BALKHASH (Ru)	33990	BASARABI (Rm)	77560	BELGOROD		BERNBURG (DDR)	03870
AZIMUT (Ru)	01736	BALKHASH (Ru)	52020	BASARGIN (Ru)	12380	DNESTROVSKIY (Ru)	45350	BERNBURG (DDR)	04423
AZIMUT (Ru)	13751	BALKHASH (Ru)	84150	BASHKIR (Ru)	45120	BELGOROD (Ru)	03423	BERNHARD	
AZOV (Ru)	13650	BALOTA (Rm)	77560	BASHKIRIYA (Ru)	02140	BELINSKIY (Ru)	12360	KELLERMANN (DDR)	10250
AZOVSTAL (Ru)	78891	BALS (Rm)	77560	BASHKIRIYA (Ru)	06825	BELINSKIY (Ru)	20790	BERNHARD	
AZUGA (Rm)	82110	BALTA (Ru)	11800	BASKUNCHAK (Ru)	11460	BELITSK (Ru)	01070	KELLERMANN (DDR)	12630
AZURIT (Ru)	11800	BALTISKAYA KOSA (Ru)	13751	BASTION (Ru)	33305	BELLATRIX (DDR)	83930	BERTOLT BRECHT (DDR)	12620
AZURITOVYY (Ru)	33305	BALTISKAYA SLAVA (Ru)	93780	BATAK (Bu)	83720	BELMEKEN (Bu)	79640	BERZIN (Ru)	22173
		BALTIYSK (Ru)	21600	BATALION		BELOMORSK (Ru)	33015	BESSTRASHNYY (Ru)	22137
'B 31' type (Ru)	17940	BALTIYSKIY 101 (Ru)	75380	CZWARTAKOW (Pd)	72115	BELOMORSKLES (Ru)	24030	BESSTRASHNYY (Ru)	22137
B.K. BABA ZADE (Ru)	20745	BALTIYSKIY 102 (Ru)	75380	BATAYSK (Ru)	23760	BELOMORY (Ru)	11300	BEZHITSA (Ru)	45350
BABAYEVSK (Ru)	11333	BALTIYSKIY 103 (Ru)	75380	BATILMAN (Ru)	13650	BELOMORYE (Ru)	52020	BICAZ (Rm)	77560
BABUSHKIN (Ru)	45350	BALTIYSKIY 105 (Ru)	75380	BATTERFISH (Ru)	22327	BELOMORYE (Ru)	84150	BIHOR (Rm)	47540
BABYKINO (Ru)	11333	BALTIYSKIY 106 (Ru)	75380	BATUMI (Ru)	11800	BELONA (Pd)	22330	BIKIN (Ru)	12380
BACAU (Rm)	41310	BALTIYSKIY 107 (Ru)	75380	BAVENIT (Ru)	09899	BELOPOLYE (Ru)	67170	BIOSFERA (Ru)	13650
BACESTI (Rm)	77560	BALTIYSKIY 108 (Ru)	75380	BAYEVO (Ru)	11333	BELORETSK (Ru)	01070	BIRA (Ru)	85610
BAGANOVO (Ru)	11333	BALTIYSKIY 109 (Ru)	75380	BAYKAL (Ru)	02120	BELOYARSK (Ru)	85970	BIRLAD (Rm)	77560
BAGAREVO (Ru)	11333	BALTIYSKIY 110 (Ru)	75380	BAYKAL (Ru)	12380	BELOYE MORE (Ru)	26210	BIRSHTONAS (Ru)	12380
BAGRATION (Ru)	17500	BALTIYSKIY 111 (Ru)	75380	BAYKAL (Ru)	20790	BELOZERSKLES (Ru)	24030	BIRVETA (Ru)	33198
BAGRATIONOVSK (Ru)	13650	BALTIYSKIY BEREG (Ru)	62671	BAYKAL (Ru)	33990	BELTSY (Ru)	86220	BIRYUSA (Ru)	92165

BIRYUSINSK (Ru)	11720	BOLSHEVIK	
BIRYUSINSK (Ru)	34610	KARAYEV (Ru)	44100
BIRYUZA (Ru)	12380	BOLSHEVIK M	
BIRYUZA (Ru)	15460	TOMAS (Ru)	80100
BIRYUZA (Ru)	70760	BOLSHEVIK (Ru)	11610
BISON (Ru)	11580	BOLSHEVO (Ru)	12230
BISTRET (Rm)	77560	BONITO (Pd)	23440
BISTRITA (Rm)	13650	BORA (Ru)	18270
'BIYA' class (Ru)	04067	BORCEA (Rm)	77560
BIYSK (Ru)	01070	BOREY (Ru)	33015
BIZON (Ru)	22154	BORIS ALEKSEYEV (Ru)	13751
BLAGOVESHCHENSK (Ru)	07550	BORIS ANDREYEV (Ru)	56639
BLAJ (Rm)	77560	BORIS BABOCHKIN (Ru)	48430
BLANIK (Cz)	15090	BORIS BABOCHKIN (Ru)	49470
BLANKENBURG (DDR)	03870	BORIS BABOCHKIN (Ru)	49740
BLANKENBURG (DDR)	04423	BORIS BUTOMA (Ru)	63570
BLANKENSEE (DDR)	46370	BORIS BUVIN (Ru)	78060
BLANKENSEE (DDR)	47070	BORIS CHILIKIN (Ru)	59880
BOBILNA (Rm)	77560	BORIS DAVIDOV (Ru)	22180
BOBRUYSKLES (Ru)	24030	BORIS GORBATOV (Ru)	07900
BOCHNIA (Pd)	03230	BORIS LAVRENEV (Ru)	07900
BOCHNIA (Pd)	03620	BORIS LAVROV (Ru)	50763
BOCSA (Rm)	77560	BORIS LIVANOV (Ru)	80010
BODAYBO (Ru)	24030	BORIS NIKOLAICHUK (Ru)	06795
BODO UHSE (DDR)	17980	BORIS POLEVOY (Ru)	00967
BODROG (Hu)	50909	BORIS TSINDELIS (Ru)	13751
BOGDAN (Bu)	39130	BORIS ZHEMCHUZIN (Ru)	03060
BOGDAN		BORIS ZHEMCHUZIN (Ru)	03650
KHMELNITSKY (Ru)	28750	BORISLAV (Ru)	57540
BOIZENBURG (DDR)	03870	BORISOGLEBSK (Ru)	85970
BOIZENBURG (DDR)	04423	BORISOV (Ru)	11333
BOJNICE (Cz)	35480	BORISPOL (Ru)	11720
BOKSIT (Ru)	11800	BORISPOL (Ru)	34610
BOKSITOVYY (Ru)	33305	BORIYA TSARIKOV (Ru)	15510
BOLDURI (Ru)	63640	BORODINSKOYE	
BOLESLAW CHOBRY (Pd)	14910	POLYE (Ru)	13751
BOLESLAW CHOBRY (Pd)	15720	BOROVICHI (Ru)	11380
BOLESLAW		BORSA (Rm)	77560
KRZYWOUSTY (Pd)	14910	BORSEC (Rm)	77560
BOLESLAW		BORZESTI (Rm)	77560
KRZYWOUSTY (Pd)	15720	BORZHOMI (Ru)	60620
BOLESLAW		BORZHOMI (Ru)	62580
RUMINSKI (Pd)	49655	BOSFOR (Ru)	12380
BOLESLAW SMIALY (Pd)	14910	BOSFOR	
BOLESLAW SMIALY (Pd)	15720	VOSTOCHNYY (Ru)	23335
BOLESLAWIEC (Pd)	50460	BOSHNYAKOVO (Ru)	17920
BOLGRAD (Ru)	57540	BOTEVGRAD (Bu)	84710
BOLSHEVIK KAMO (Ru)	52612/1		

BOTEVGRAD (Bu)	85170	BUJORENI (Rm)	77560
BOTNICHESKIY		BUK (DDR)	04065
ZALIV (Ru)	61100	BUKHARA (Ru)	24030
BOTOSANI (Rm)	77560	BUKHTARMA (Ru)	15460
BOTSMAN MOSHKOV (Ru)	54710	BUKOVINA (Ru)	02350
BOYEVAYA SLAVA (Ru)	93780	BUKOVINA (Ru)	35370
BOYEVOY (Ru)	85320	BULGARIA (Bu)	73290
BRAD (Rm)	82110	BULUNKHAN (Ru)	50730
BRAILA (Rm)	39670	BUMBESTI (Rm)	77080
BRANDENBURG (DDR)	23195	BUMBESTI (Rm)	80000
BRANDENBURG (DDR)	48240	BUNA (DDR)	52070
BRANESTI (Rm)	77560	BUNA (DDR)	75170
BRASOV (Rm)	41310	BUNKEROVSCHCHIK-3 (Ru)	36250
BRATISLAVA (Cz)	79230	BURAN (Pd)	10260
BRATSK (Ru)	02724	BURAN (Pd)	10760
BRATSKLES (Ru)	24030	BURAN (Ru)	22220
BRATULESTI (Rm)	77560	BURAN (Ru)	23480
BREADZA (Rm)	77560	BUREVESTNIK (Bu)	12230
BREITLING (DDR)	85320	BUREVESTNIK	
BREST (Ru)	22173	REVOLYUTSKIY (Ru)	79340
BREST (Ru)	51212	BUREVESTNIK (Ru)	11800
BRESTSKAYA		BUREVESTNIK (Ru)	33015
KREPOST (Ru)	33900	BUREVESTNIK (Ru)	85320
BREZA (Bu)	85185	BUREYA (Ru)	85610
BRIS (Ru)	21260	BUREYALES (Ru)	24030
BRIZ (Ru)	23860	BURG (DDR)	61700
BROCKEN (DDR)	95250	BURGAS (Bu)	28980
BRONISLAW CZECH (Pd)	72115	BURGAS (Bu)	50125
BRONISLAW		BURJA (Ru)	21260
LACHOWICZ (Pd)	14480	BUSSEWITZ (DDR)	56155
BRUNO APITZ (DDR)	13751	BUSSOL (Ru)	09360
BRUNO TESCH (DDR)	23410	BUSTENI (Rm)	47540
BRYANSKIY		BUTOVSK (Ru)	11333
MASHINOSTROITEL (Ru)	01380	BUZAN (Ru)	76945
BRYANSKIY		BUZAU (Rm)	86170
MASHINOSTROITEL (Ru)	01640	BUZIAS (Rm)	77560
BRYANSKIY		BUZLUDJA (Bu)	49160
RABOCHIY (Ru)	45350	BUZOVNY (Ru)	44100
BUCEGI (Rm)	78580	BYELGOROD (Ru)	03423
BUCURESTI (Rm)	15420	BYELKINO (Ru)	12380
BUDAPESHT (Ru)	51212	BYELOKAMENKA (Ru)	17950
BUDAPEST (Hu)	86110	BYELOMORSK (Ru)	11720
BUDOWLANY (Pd)	78290	BYELOMORSK (Ru)	34610
BUDOWLANY (Pd)	80020	BYELORUSSIYA (Ru)	20370
BUG (Ru)	33015	BYELOVO (Ru)	11800
BUG (Ru)	76945	BYKOVO (Ru)	11720
BUGURUSLAN (Ru)	89460	BYKOVO (Ru)	34610
BUHUSI (Rm)	77560	BYTOM (Pd)	50460

CACIULATA (Rm)		47540
CALAFAT (Rm)		61020
CALAN (Rm)		82220
CALARASI (Rm)		82110
CALBE (DDR)		48240
CALIMANESTI (Rm)		47540
CALLATIS (Rm)		77560
CALUGARENI (Ru)		47540
CAMILO CIENFUEGOS (Ru)	03423
CARAIMAN (Rm)		11700
CARANSEBES (Rm)		81305
CARINA (Pd)		11695
CARLO		
SCHONHAAR (DDR)		23410
CARPATI (Rm)		78580
CASSJOPEJA (Pd)		11337
CEAHLEAUL (Rm)		11700
CEDYNIA (Pd)		70540
CELTIC PRIDE (Pd)		17580
CERNA (Rm)		13650
CHAGODA (Ru)		17637
CHAPAYEV (Ru)		33910
CHATYR-DAG (Ru)		11800
CHAYA (Bu)		85970
CHAYVO (Ru)		95042
CHAZHMA (Ru)		07550
CHAZHMA (Ru)		39110
CHEBOKSARY (Ru)		39970
CHELEKEN (Ru)		01733
CHELM (Pd)		03230
CHELM (Pd)		03620
CHELYABINSK (Ru)		48240
CHEMPION (Ru)		33015
CHERCHESK (Ru)		13751
CHERENKHOVO (Ru)		48240
CHEREPOVETS (Ru)		83680
CHERKASSY (Ru)		48240
CHERNIGOV (Ru)		06795
CHERNIGOV (Ru)		17637
CHERNISHEVSKIY (Ru)		20790
CHERNOE MORE (Ru)		51416
CHERNOMORSKAYA		
SLAVA (Ru)		93780
CHERNOVTSY (Ru)		47939
CHERNYAKHOVSK (Ru)		21600
CHESMA (Ru)		22327
CHIPKA (or SHIPKA) (Bu)		80000
CHIPKA (or SHIPKA) (Bu)		77080

Name	No.
CHITA (Ru)	67350
CHITA (Ru)	71360
CHKALOV (Ru)	17500
CHKALOV (Ru)	39970
CHKALOVSK (Ru)	78355
CHOCHLIK (Pd)	87740
CHORZOW (Pd)	50460
CHRISTO BOTEV (Bu)	48430
CHRISTO BOTEV (Bu)	49470
CHRISTO BOTEV (Bu)	49740
CHRZANOW (Pd)	82260
CHUKOTKA (Ru)	22173
CHUKOTKA (Ru)	22720
CHUKOTKO (Ru)	25840
CHUKOTSKIY BEREG (Ru)	62671
CHULYMLES (Ru)	11430
CHUMIKAN (Ru)	39110
CHURKIN (Ru)	45110
CHUSOVOY (Ru)	78355
CHYORNOE MORE (Ru)	58510
CHYORNOE MORE (Ru)	71820
CIECHANOW (Pd)	79870
CIECHOCINEK (Pd)	81860
CIMPULUNG (Rm)	82220
CINDRELUL (Rm)	13650
CLABUCET (Rm)	11670
CLUJ (Rm)	39660
CODLEA (Rm)	82110
COLDITZ (DDR)	78730
COLDITZ (DDR)	79985
COLDITZ (DDR)	89980
CONDOR (DDR)	84930
CONSTANTA (Rm)	17660
COSTINESTI (Rm)	47540
COSWIG (DDR)	71900
COTNARI (Ru)	06069
COTTBUS (DDR)	04910
COTTBUS (DDR)	23195
COVASNA (Rm)	82110
COZIA (Rm)	60978
CRAIOVA (Rm)	41310
CRIMMITSCHAU (DDR)	61400
CRISANA (Rm)	55780
CRISANA (Rm)	56480
CRISUL ALB (Rm)	13751
CSOKONAI (Hu)	14910
CSOKONAI (Hu)	15720
CUGIR (Rm)	82220
CUNEWALDE (DDR)	46370
CUNEWALDE (DDR)	47070
CURTEA DE ARGES (Rm)	06142
CZANTORIA (Pd)	68920
DACIA (Rm)	55780
DACIA (Rm)	56480
DAGESTAN (Ru)	83430
DAGONYS (Ru)	57200
DALMOR II (Pd)	34872
DALNEGORSK (Ru)	15460
DALNERECHENSK (Ru)	22327
DALNERECHENSK (Ru)	22840
DALNERECHENSK (Ru)	34470
DALNERECHENSK (Ru)	52304
DALNERECHENSK (Ru)	52616
DALNEVOSTOCHNY (Ru)	85320
DALNIY VOSTOK (Ru)	92380
DALNIYE ZELYENTSY (Ru)	93268
DANE (Ru)	33198
DANKO (Ru)	12380
DARASUN (Ru)	24030
DARNITZA (Ru)	36890
DARNITZA (Ru)	43790
DARVIN (Ru)	13751
DARYAL (Ru)	11800
DASHAVA (Ru)	83430
DAUGAVA (Ru)	45730
DAUGAVA (Ru)	52304
DAUGAVA (Ru)	52616
DAUGAVPILS (Ru)	60620
DAUGAVPILS (Ru)	62580
DAURIYA (Ru)	11460
DAURIYA (Ru)	93870
DAVID	
BAKARADZE (Ru)	52612/1
DAVID SIQUEIROS (Ru)	70590
DAVYDOV (Ru)	09380
DAYNAVA (Ru)	23480
DEBRECEN (Ru)	89200
DEBRECEN (Ru)	70760
DEDOVSK (Ru)	83430
DEIMOS (Ru)	04080
DEJ (Ru)	47540
DEKABRIST (Ru)	03690
DEKABRIST (Ru)	22135
DELEGAT (Ru)	66380
DELFIN (Pd)	23440
DELTA DUNARII (Rm)	10535
DEMYAN BEDNYY (Ru)	14370
DEMYAN	
KOROTCHENKO (Ru)	91224
DENEB (Ru)	12230
DENEBOLA (Pd)	11670
DERBENT (Ru)	54630
DERBENT (Ru)	55060
DESNA (Ru)	38950
DESNA (Ru)	39110
DESYATAYA	
PYATILETKA (Ru)	79340
DEVA (Rm)	41310
DEVIATOR (Ru)	01736
DEVYATAYA	
PYATILETKA (Ru)	79340
DEVYATNADTSATYY SYEZD	
VLKSM (Ru)	78060
DIERHAGEN (DDR)	75320
DIKSON (Ru)	11300
DIKSON (Ru)	11460
DIKSON (Ru)	11490
DIKSON (Ru)	34405
DIMANT (Ru)	62701
DIMBOVITA (Rm)	13751
DIMITAR BLAGOEV (Bu)	20735
DIMITRIY ULYANOV (Ru)	03650
DIMITROVO (Ru)	83430
DIMITROVSKIY	
KOMSOMOL (Bu)	48150
DIOKL (Ru)	22155
DIOMID (Ru)	12380
DIOMID (Ru)	22178
DIONIS (Ru)	11800
DIPLOT (Ru)	07470
DISNAY (Ru)	33198
DIVNOGORSK (Ru)	14700
DIVNOGORSK (Ru)	86540
DMITRIY DONSKOY (Ru)	17500
DMITRIY DONSKOY (Ru)	80171
DMITRIY	
DUDCHENKO (Ru)	22173
DMITRIY FURMANOV (Ru)	07900
DMITRIY GULIA (Ru)	14370
DMITRIY KANTEMIR (Ru)	50730
DMITRIY LAPTEV (Ru)	02417
DMITRIY	
MEDVEDYEV (Ru)	51410
DMITRIY	
MENDELEYEV (Ru)	07620
DMITRIY OVTSYN (Ru)	02417
DMITRIY POKROVICH (Ru)	34872
DMITRIY	
POZHARSKIY (Ru)	17500
DMITRIY	
POZHARSKIY (Ru)	80171
DMITRIY	
SHOSTAKOVICH (Ru)	20353
DMITRIY STERLIGOV (Ru)	02417
DMITRIY ULYANOV (Ru)	03060
DMITRIY ZHABINSKIY (Ru)	23305
DMITRIY ZHLOBA (Ru)	60620
DMITRIY ZHLOBA (Ru)	62580
DMITRY CHASOVITIN (Ru)	85320
DMITRY FURMANOV (Ru)	12380
DMITRY MANUILSKIY (Ru)	79340
DMITRY POLUYAN (Ru)	05620
DMITRY POLUYAN (Ru)	14450
DNEPR (Ru)	76945
DNEPRODZERZHINSK (Ru)	11800
DNEPRODZERZHINSK (Ru)	83430
DNEPROGES (Ru)	47860
DNEPROVSKIY LIMAN (Ru)	21240
DNESTR (Ru)	25550
DNESTR (Ru)	59880
DNESTR (Ru)	76945
DNESTROVSKIY	
LIMAN (Ru)	21240
DOBRINYA NIKITICH (Ru)	22220
DOBROGEA (Rm)	15420
DOBROVOLSK (Ru)	12230
DOBRUDJA (Bu)	50908
DOBRYNA NIKITCH (Ru)	17500
DOKUCHAYEVSK (Ru)	26210
DOLJ (Rm)	47540
DOLMATOVO (Ru)	50900
DOLNY SLASK (Pd)	75730
DOLNY SLASK (Pd)	88380
DOLOMIT (Ru)	11800
DOMODYEDOVO (Ru)	11720
DOMODYEDOVO (Ru)	34610
DON (Ru)	36235
DON (Ru)	76945
DON (Ru)	85320
DONBASS (Ru)	11460
DONETS (Ru)	02280
DONETS (Ru)	25550
DONETS (Ru)	35180
DONETS (Ru)	76945
DONETSK (Ru)	25550
DONETSK (Ru)	78060
DONETSKIY KHIMIK (Ru)	01380
DONETSKIY KHIMIK (Ru)	01640
DONETSKIY	
KOMSOMOLETS (Ru)	01380
DONETSKIY	
KOMSOMOLETS (Ru)	01640
DONETSKIY	
METALLURG (Ru)	01380
DONETSKIY	
METALLURG (Ru)	01640
DONETSKIY	
SHAKHTER (Ru)	01380
DONETSKIY	
SHAKHTER (Ru)	01640
DONISAR (Ru)	13751
DONSKOY (Ru)	83430
DONUZLAV (Ru)	54630
DONUZLAV (Ru)	55060
DORNA (Rm)	13650
DOVATOR (Ru)	17500
DOVSK (Ru)	26210
DRAGANESTI (Rm)	82110
DRAGASANI (Rm)	06069
DRAGOMIRESTI (Rm)	60978
DRESDEN (DDR)	04910
DROBETA 1850 (Rm)	87640
DROGOBYCH (Ru)	70740
DRUSKININKAY (Ru)	12380
DRUZHBA NARODOV (Ru)	60680
DRUZHBA NARODOV (Ru)	79340
DRUZHBA NARODOV (Ru)	90720
DRUZHBA (Ru)	12590
DRUZHBA (Ru)	39290
DRUZHBA SSSR-DDR (Ru)	36140
DRUZHBA SSSR-GDR (Ru)	11800
DUBNA (Ru)	56270
DUBNA (Ru)	62730
DUBNO (Ru)	83430
DUBOSSARY (Ru)	83430
DUBROVNIK (Ru)	14370
DUBULTY (Ru)	63640
DUMBRAVENI (Rm)	82110
DUNAREA (Rm)	78580

DUNAY (Ru)	76945
DUNAY (Ru)	95015
DUSHANBE (Ru)	12340
DVINOLES (Ru)	24030
DVINSKIY ZALIV (Ru)	61100
DVURECHENSK (Ru)	26210
DYUNY (Ru)	33198
DZERZHINSK (Ru)	70165
DZHAFER DZHABARLY (Ru)	50730
DZHAMBUL DZHABAYEV (Ru)	79340
DZHEBRAIL (Ru)	44100
DZHEMS BANKOVICH (Ru)	67010
DZHORAT (Ru)	44100
DZHURMA (Ru)	24030
DZIECI POLSKIE (Pd)	07460
DZIECI POLSKIE (Pd)	10740
DZINTARI (Ru)	63640
DZINTARYURA (Ru)	12380
DZINTARZEME (Ru)	23480
DZINTERKRASTS (Ru)	23480
DZUKIYA (Ru)	23480
EDGAR ANDRE (DDR)	04230
EDUARD CLAUDIUS (DDR)	13751
EDUARD TOLL (Ru)	02417
EDUARD VEYDENBAUM (Ru)	12380
EGERSHELD (Ru)	45110
EGVEKINOT (Ru)	06795
EICHSFELD (DDR)	71680
EICHWALDE (DDR)	46370
EICHWALDE (DDR)	47070
EILENBURG (DDR)	03870
EILENBURG (DDR)	04423
EISBAR (DDR)	24200
EISENBERG (DDR)	84940
EISENBERG (DDR)	90600
EISENHUTTENSTADT (DDR)	86420
EISVOGEL (DDR)	23307
EKHOLOT (Ru)	09360
EKIMCHAN (Ru)	85970
EKVATOR (Ru)	12570
ELBRUS (Ru)	11300
ELEKRENAY (Ru)	12380
ELEKTROSTAL (Ru)	24030
ELENA (Bu)	88600
ELGAVA (Ru)	44370
ELM (Ru)	95042
ELTIGEN (Ru)	85970
ELTON (Ru)	01733
ELTON (Ru)	84360
ELVA (Ru)	13751
ELVIRA EISENSCHNEIDER (DDR)	23410
EMBA (Ru)	44100
EMBA (Ru)	92160
ENGURE (Ru)	86220
EPIFAN KOVTYUKH (Ru)	62580
EPRON (Ru)	22173
EREBUS (Ru)	36890
EREBUS (Ru)	43790
ERFURT (DDR)	04910
ERICH STEINFURTH (DDR)	23410
ERIFAN KOVITYUKH (Ru)	60620
ERIK WEINERT (DDR)	12620
ERNST HAECKEL (DDR)	17670
ERNST KRENKEL (Ru)	02270
ERNST MORITZ ARNDT (DDR)	34200
ERNST SCHNELLER (DDR)	04230
ERNST TELMAN (Ru)	17500
ERNST THALMANN (DDR)	08778
ERNST THALMANN (Ru)	05620
ERNST THALMANN (Ru)	14450
ERNST THALMANN (Ru)	62701
ESPENHAIN (DDR)	79730
ESTAFETA OKTYABRYA (Ru)	12380
ESTONIYA (Ru)	02160
ETALON (Ru)	33015
EUGEN SCHONHAAR (DDR)	23410
EUGENIE COTTON (Pd)	75770
EUGENIUSZ KWIATKOWSKI (Pd)	14480
EVENSK (Ru)	36890
EVENSK (Ru)	43790
EVENSK (Ru)	85970
EVERSHAGEN (DDR)	91224
EVGENIY NIKONOV (Ru)	50280
EVGENIY ONUFRIEV (Ru)	50280
EVGENIY TITOV (or YEVGENIY TITOV) (Ru)	51410
EVRIKA (Ru)	11800
EYZHEN BERG (Ru)	67650
EYZHENS BERGS (Ru)	59890
F. C. WEISKOPF (DDR)	12620
FAGARAS (Rm)	47540
FAGET (Rm)	47540
FALCIU (Ru)	47540
FALESHTY (Ru)	21560
FALTICENI (Rm)	82110
FARAB (Ru)	21560
FASTOV (Ru)	17830
FASTOV (Ru)	61700
FATEZH (Ru)	61700
FAUREI (Rm)	47540
FEDOR BREDIKHIN (Ru)	10740
FEDOR GLADKOV (Ru)	07900
FEDOR GLADKOV (Ru)	11800
FEDOR KRAYNOV (Ru)	12380
FEDOR LITKE (Ru)	22180
FEDOR LITKE (Ru)	22220
FEDOR LYSENKO (Ru)	22327
FEDOR PETROV (Ru)	03770
FEDOR PETROV (Ru)	04010
FEDOR PODTELKOV (Ru)	79340
FEDOR SHALYAPIN (Ru)	06200
FEDOR VARAKSIN (Ru)	54710
FELDIOARA (Ru)	47540
FELEAC (Ru)	47540
FELIKS DZERZHINSKIY (Ru)	02160
FELIKS DZIERZYNSKI (Pd)	65850
FELIKS DZIERZYNSKI (Pd)	67690
FELIKS KON (Ru)	93820
FELIX (Rm)	47540
FENIX (Bu)	12230
FEODOR OKK (Ru)	23480
FEODOSIYA (Ru)	12230
FERDINAND FREILIGRATH (DDR)	33870
FERGANA (Ru)	23305
FICHTELBERG (DDR)	94490
FIENI (Rm)	47540
FIERBINTI (Rm)	47540
FILARET (Ru)	47540
FILIASI (Rm)	47540
FILIDARA (Rm)	47540
FILIOARA (Ru)	47540
FILIPESTI (Ru)	47540
FILIPP MAKHARADZE (Ru)	59220
FILIPP MAKHARADZE (Ru)	74540
'FINIK' class	04088
FINSKIY ZALIV (Ru)	61100
FINTINELE (Ru)	47540
FINWAL (Pd)	10810
FIOLENT (Ru)	11800
FIOLENT (Ru)	62050
FIORD (Ru)	85970
FIRIZA (Rm)	47540
FIRYUZA (Ru)	21560
FIZALIA (Bu)	23440
FIZIK LEBEDYEV (Ru)	31050
FIZULI (Ru)	50730
FLAMING (DDR)	71680
FLAMINGO (Bu)	11800
FLAMINGO (DDR)	84930
FLEESENSEE (DDR)	46370
FLEESENSEE (DDR)	47070
FLIEGERSKOSMONAUT DER DDR SIGMUND JAHN (DDR)	61400
FLORA (Pd)	67081
FLORESHTY (Ru)	17830
FLORESTI (Ru)	47540
FLOTINSPEKTSIYA-02 (Ru)	33015
FOBOS (Ru)	04080
FOCSANI (Rm)	06069
FOISOR (Ru)	47540
FOKA (Pd)	10810
FONTANKA (Ru)	35310
FORE MOSULISHVILI (Ru)	70740
FOROS (Ru)	13650
FRANCESCO NULLO (Pd)	10570
FRANCESCO NULLO (Pd)	15340
FRANCISZEK ZUBRZYCKI (Pd)	14480
FRANKFURT/ODER (DDR)	04910
FRANTS BOGUSH (Ru)	05620
FRANTS BOGUSH (Ru)	14450
FRASIN (Ru)	47540
FRASINET (Rm)	47540
FREDERIC JOLIOT CURIE (DDR)	34960
FREDERIK ZHOLIO-KYURI (Ru)	01560
FREGATA (Bu)	12380
FREITAL (DDR)	61700
FREYBURG (DDR)	03870
FREYBURG (DDR)	04423
FRIDRICH ENGELS (Ru)	17500
FRIDRIKH TSANDER (Ru)	59890
FRIDRIKH TSANDER (Ru)	67650
FRIEDRICH ENGELS (DDR)	03150
FRIEDRICH ENGELS (Ru)	05620
FRIEDRICH ENGELS (Ru)	14450
FRIEDRICH WOLF (DDR)	12630
FRITSIS GAYLIS (Ru)	75320
FRITSIS ROSIN (Ru)	75330
FRITZ HECKERT (Ru)	62701
FRITZ REUTER (DDR)	34330
FRUNZANESTI (Rm)	47540
FRYCZ MODRZEWSKI (Pd)	04860
FRYDERYK CHOPIN (Ru)	93870
FUNDENI (Ru)	47540
FUNDULEA (Rm)	47540
FURSTENWALDE (DDR)	46370
FURSTENWALDE (DDR)	47070
FYODOR MATISEN (Ru)	04216
FYODOR OKHLOPOV (Ru)	50730
FYODOR POLETAYEV (Ru)	38580
FYODOR POPOV (Ru)	50730
FYODOR YEROZIDI (Ru)	13751
G. V. PLEKHANOV (Ru)	17500
GABIBULLA GUSEYNOV (Ru)	22327
GABROVO (Bu)	28980
GALATI (Rm)	17660
GALATI (Rm)	39670
GALDOR (Ru)	13751
GALIFAN BATARSHIN (Ru)	12380
GALILEO GALILEI (Ru)	60500
GALS (Ru)	23860
GALS (Ru)	33015
GALVYE (Ru)	66380
GALYA KOMLEVA (Ru)	15510
GAMAL ABDEL NASER (Ru)	63570
GAMID SULTANOV (Ru)	20320
GAMZAT TSADASA (Ru)	09995
GANGUT (Ru)	11720
GANGUT (Ru)	34610
GARNELA (Pd)	23440
GARPUNER PROKOPYENKO (Ru)	13650
GARPUNER ZARVA (Ru)	13751
GARWOLIN (Pd)	03230

GARWOLIN (Pd) 03620
GAUYA (Ru) 76715
GAVRIL DERZHAVIN (Ru) 14370
GAVRIL SARITCHEV (Ru) 22180
GAVRILL
  KIRDISHCHEV (Ru) 78060
GAYDAMAK (Ru) 17637
GAZGAN (Ru) 13751
GAZLI (Ru) 79340
GDANSK II (Pd) 80205
GDOV (Ru) 23480
GDYNSKI KOSYNIER (Pd) 07460
GDYNSKI KOSYNIER (Pd) 10740
GEFEST (Ru) 13650
GEIZER (Ru) 09360
GEKTOR (Ru) 22155
GELIOGRAF (Ru) 11800
GELIOS (or HELIOS) (Ru) 22178
GEMINI (Pd) 11670
GENERAL ASLANOV (Ru) 53160
GENERAL BABAYAN (Ru) 53160
GENERAL
  BAGRATION (Ru) 59890
GENERAL
  BAGRATION (Ru) 67650
GENERAL BEM (Pd) 78980
GENERAL BERLING (Ru) 77127
GENERAL
  BLAZHEVICH (Ru) 61700
GENERAL
  BOCHAROV (Ru) 60620
GENERAL
  BOCHAROV (Ru) 62580
GENERAL
  CHERNYAKHOVSKIY (Ru)13650
GENERAL
  CHERNYAKOVSKIY (Ru) 17500
GENERAL
  DABROWSKI (Bu) 77127
GENERAL DEDAYEV (Ru) 11333
GENERAL FR
  KLEEBERG (Ru) 54970
GENERAL GAMIDOV (Ru) 32080
GENERAL GEYDAROV (Ru) 60373
GENERAL GORBATOV (Ru) 80052
GENERAL
  GROT-ROWECKI (Bu) 77127
GENERAL JASINSKI (Pd) 78980

GENERAL
  KARBYSHEV (Ru) 60620
GENERAL
  KARBYSHEV (Ru) 62580
GENERAL
  KHLEBNIKOV (Ru) 11333
GENERAL KLEEBERG (Pd) 71810
GENERAL KRAVTSOV (Ru) 60620
GENERAL KRAVTSOV (Ru) 62580
GENERAL LESELIDZE (Ru) 60900
GENERAL LESELIDZE (Ru) 79230
GENERAL
  MADALINSKI (Pd) 78980
GENERAL
  MERKVILADZE (Ru) 67680
GENERAL
  OSTRYAKOV (Ru) 13650
GENERAL PLIYEV (Ru) 67680
GENERAL
  PRADZYNSKI (Pd) 78980
GENERAL
  RODIMTSYEV (Ru) 00140
GENERAL SABIR
  RAKHIMOV (Ru) 60373
GENERAL
  SHKODUNOVICH (Ru) 60620
GENERAL
  SHKODUNOVICH (Ru) 62580
GENERAL STANISLAW
  POPLAWSKI (Pd) 14480
GENERAL
  SWIERCZEWSKI (Pd) 78980
GENERAL TYULENEV (Ru) 63975
GENERAL VLADIMIR
  ZAIMOV (Ru) 79640
GENERAL VLADIMIR
  ZAIMOV (Ru) 03950
GENERAL ZHDANOV (Ru) 60620
GENERAL ZHDANOV (Ru) 62580
GENRIK GASANOV (Ru) 59880
GEO MILEV (Bu) 49785
GEOFIZIK (Ru) 95042
GEOKCHAY (Ru) 50770
GEOLOG FERSMAN (Ru) 11333
GEOLOG PYOTR
  ANTROPOV (Ru) 11333
GEOLOG YURIY
  BILIBIN (Ru) 66380

GEORG OTS (Ru) 20353
GEORG WEERTH (DDR) 33870
GEORGI DIMITROV (Bu) 01980
GEORGI GRIGOROV (Bu) 48150
GEORGI KIRKOV (Bu) 20735
GEORGIY CHICHERIN (Ru) 05620
GEORGIY CHICHERIN (Ru) 14450
GEORGIY DIMITROV (Ru) 05620
GEORGIY DMITROV (Ru) 14450
GEORGIY
  KHOLOSTYAKOV (Ru) 51410
GEORGIY LEONIDZE (Ru) 60900
GEORGIY LEONIDZE (Ru) 79230
GEORGIY MAKSIMOV (Ru) 04216
GEORGIY
  PYASETSKIY (Ru) 80260
GEORGIY SEDOV (Ru) 22240
GEORGIY USHAKOV (Ru) 02270
GEORGIY VASILYEV (Ru) 15120
GEORGIYEVSK (Ru) 26210
GEPARD (Ru) 14962
GERA (DDR) 23195
GERAKL (Ru) 11800
GERAKL (Ru) 22155
GERHART
  HAUPTMANN (DDR) 34200
GERINGSWALDE (DDR) 46370
GERINGSWALDE (DDR) 47070
GERMES or HERMES (Ru) 22178
GEROI
  ADZHIMUSHKAYA (Ru) 07470
GEROI
  ADZHIMUSHKAYA (Ru) 11800
GEROI
  CHERNOMORYA (Ru) 66170
GEROI MONKADIY (Ru) 80100
GEROI
  NOVOROSSIYSKA (Ru) 66170
GEROI PANFILOVTSY (Ru) 48430
GEROI PANFILOVTSY (Ru) 49470
GEROI PANFILOVTSY (Ru) 49740
GEROI PLEVNY (Ru) 31150
GEROI PLEVNY (Ru) 93670
GEROI
  SEVASTOPOLYA (Ru) 66170
GEROI SHIPKI (Ru) 31150
GEROI SHIPKI (Ru) 93670
GEROI SHIRONINTSY (Ru) 11333

GEROI STALINGRADA (Ru) 51672
GEROI ZAPOLYARYA (Ru) 11720
GEROI ZAPOLYARYA (Ru) 34610
GEROITE NA ODESSA (Bu) 31150
GEROITE NA ODESSA (Bu) 93670
GEROITE NA
  SEVASTOPOL (Bu) 31150
GEROITE NA
  SEVASTOPOL (Bu) 93670
GEROY ASADOV (Ru) 60373
GEROY GUSEYNOV (Ru) 60373
GEROY HYUSEYNOV (Ru) 60373
GEROY I. MAMEDOV (Ru) 60373
GEROY K.
  NAZAROVA (Ru) 60373
GEROY MEKHTI (Ru) 79340
GEROY OSIPOV (Ru) 60373
GEROYEVKA (Ru) 13751
GEYA (Ru) 13751
GHEORGHIENI (Rm) 82110
GIDROLOG (Ru) 23860
GIDROSTROITEL (Ru) 33015
GIGANT (Ru) 22155
GIGROMETR (Ru) 01736
GIORDANO BRUNO (Ru) 38580
GIRULYAY (Ru) 33017
GISSAR (Ru) 13751
GIURGENI (Rm) 47540
GIURGIU (Rm) 47540
GIUSEPPE DI
  VITTORIO (Ru) 05620
GIUSEPPE DI
  VITTORIO (Ru) 14450
GIUSEPPE VERDI (Ru) 60500
GIZHIGA (Ru) 12570
GIZHIGA (Ru) 21610
GLACHAU (DDR) 61400
GLARUS (Bu) 11800
GLEB
  KRZHIZHANOVSKIY (Ru) 03770
GLEB
  KRZHIZHANOVSKIY (Ru) 04010
GLEB SEDIN (Ru) 75330
GLEB USPENSKIY (Ru) 12360
GLEICHBERG (DDR) 94565
GLETCHER (Ru) 09360
GLIWICE II (Pd) 61090
GLOBUS (Ru) 13745

GLOGOW (Pd) 31180
GLUBOMER (Ru) 01736
GLUKHOV (Ru) 86220
GNEVNYY (Ru) 13751
GNIEZNO II (Pd) 50460
GOGLAND (Ru) 51910
GOGOL (Ru) 17500
GOLENIOW (Pd) 75412
GOLFSTRIM (Ru) 11300
GOPLANA (Pd) 87740
GOPLO (Pd) 33193
GORDELIVYY (Ru) 22175
GORDIY (Ru) 22175
GORDYY (Ru) 22137
GORDYY (Ru) 22175
GORECHJE (Ru) 12230
GORETS (Ru) 91224
GORGOVA (Ru) 47540
GORI (Ru) 60620
GORI (Ru) 62580
GORIZONT (Ru) 01736
GORIZONT (Ru) 23860
GORIZONT (Ru) 34710
GORJ (Rm) 47540
GORKOVSKAYA
  KOMSOMOLIYA (Ru) 49240
GORKY LENINSKIYE (Ru) 79340
GORKY (Ru) 35310
GORLITZ (DDR) 78730
GORLITZ (DDR) 89980
GORLOVKA (Ru) 47990
GORNO-ALTAYSK (Ru) 15460
GORNOPRAVDINSK (Ru) 70020
GORNOZAVODSK (Ru) 84330
GORNYAK (Ru) 49240
GOROKHOVETS (Ru) 75350
GORSK (Ru) 26210
GORUN (Ru) 47540
GORYACHEGORSK (Ru) 24310
GORYACHEGORSK (Ru) 39450
GORYACHIY (Ru) 22175
GOSTINU (Ru) 47540
GOTHA (DDR) 45850
GOTZE DELCHEV (Bu) 48430
GOTZE DELCHEV (Bu) 49470
GOTZE DELCHEV (Bu) 49740
GOVORA (Rm) 47540
GRAD (Ru) 23480

GRADISTEA (Rm) 47540
GRADUS (Ru) 01736
GRAFITOVVY (Ru) 33305
GRANATOVYY (Ru) 33305
GRANIK (Pd) 22330
GRANIT (Pd) 08834
GRANIT (Ru) 13650
GRANITNYY BEREG (Ru) 62701
GRANITNYY (Ru) 91224
GRANITZ (DDR) 17985
GREIFSWALD (DDR) 31185
GREMIKHA (Ru) 17950
GREMUCHIY (Ru) 22175
GREMYACHINSK (Ru) 26210
GRETE WALTER (DDR) 23410
GRIGORIY
  ACHKANOV (Ru) 60620
GRIGORIY
  ACHKANOV (Ru) 62580
GRIGORIY
  ALEKSANDROV (Ru) 80010
GRIGORIY
  ALEKSEYEV (Ru) 50670
GRIGORIY
  KOVALCHUK (Ru) 69310
GRIGORIY KOVTUN (Ru) 11333
GRIGORIY
  KOZINTSEV (Ru) 56638
GRIGORIY LYSENKO (Ru) 93870
GRIGORIY
  NESTORENKO (Ru) 51410
GRIGORIY
  NIKOLAYEV (Ru) 71433
GRIGORIY
  ORDZHONKIDZE (Ru) 02120
GRIGORIY
  OVODOVSKIY (Ru) 13650
GRIGORIY PETRENKO (Ru) 48430
GRIGORIY PETRENKO (Ru) 49470
GRIGORIY PETRENKO (Ru) 49740
GRIGORIY
  PETROVSKIY (Ru) 79340
GRIGORIY
  POLUYANOV (Ru) 11580
GRIGORIY SHELKOV (Ru) 12380
GRIGORIY
  TERENTYEV (Ru) 13751
GRINWAL (Pd) 23440

GRISHA AKOPIAN (Ru) 15460
GRISHA PODOBEDOV (Ru) 67010
GRIVITA (Rm) 47540
GRODEKOVO (Ru) 24030
GRODITZ (DDR) 78730
GRODITZ (DDR) 89980
GROM (Ru) 13751
GROMKIY (Ru) 22175
GROMOVOY (Ru) 22175
GROSSER BELT (DDR) 18720
GROZAVESTI (Rm) 60978
GROZNY (Ru) 70572
GROZNYY (Ru) 85970
GRUDZIADZ (Pd) 31180
GRUIA (Ru) 47540
GRUMANT (Ru) 09360
GRUMANT (Ru) 15460
GRUNWALD (Pd) 10350
GRUZIYA (Ru) 20370
GRYADUSHCHIY (Ru) 22175
GRYF POMORSKY (Pd) 93870
GRYF (Ru) 17639
GRZEGORS (Pd) 33015
GS 43 (Ru) 23609
GS 55 (Ru) 23609
GS. 107 (Ru) 04066
GUBERTAS BORISA (Ru) 12380
GUDERMES (Ru) 70572
GULBENE (Ru) 15460
GUMANIST (Ru) 22327
GURIEV (Ru) 01960
GURIYA (Ru) 12230
GUS-KHRUSTALNYY (Ru) 06770
GUS-KHRUSTALNYY (Ru) 07550
GUTSUL (Ru) 85320
GVARDEYSK (Ru) 21600
GWARDIA LUDOWA (Pd) 10570
GWARDIA LUDOWA (Pd) 15340
GYURGYAN (Ru) 44100

HAGENOW (DDR) 50440
HAGENOW (DDR) 52000
HAGIENI (Ru) 47540
HAJDUK (Pd) 23440
HAJNOWKA (Pd) 75327
HALBERSTADT (DDR) 50128
HALLE (DDR) 04910
HALNIAK (Pd) 10260

HALNIAK (Pd) 10760
HANNO GUNTHER (DDR) 23410
HANS LIEBERECHT (Ru) 12380
HANS MARCHWITZA (DDR) 13751
HANS POGELMANN (Ru) 91224
HARGHITA (Rm) 11670
HARMATTAN (Pd) 91770
HARRY POLLITT (Ru) 03060
HARRY POLLITT (Ru) 03650
HATEG (Rm) 47540
HAVANA (Ru) 18270
HAVELLAND (DDR) 79315
HEIDENAU (DDR) 71040
HEINLAID (Ru) 75640
HEINZ KAPELLE (DDR) 06380
HEINZ KAPELLE (DDR) 15410
HEINZ KAPELLE (DDR) 23410
HEINZ PRIESS (DDR) 23410
HEL (Pd) 04400
HELLERAU (DDR) 84940
HELLERAU (DDR) 90600
HELME (Ru) 49240
HELTERMAA (Ru) 15460
HEMUS (Bu) 77980
HENNIGSDORF (DDR) 48240
HENRI BARBUSSE (Ru) 10720
HENRYK JENDZHA (Pd) 10280
HENRYK LEMBERG (Pd) 03230
HENRYK LEMBERG (Pd) 03620
HERBERT BAUM (DDR) 23410
HERBERT TSCHAPE (DDR) 23410
HERKULES (Ru) 12230
HERMANN MATERN (DDR) 62671
HERMANN MATERN (DDR) 82651
HEROS (Pd) 33015
HERTA LINDER (DDR) 23410
HETTSTEDT (DDR) 61700
HEVIZ (Hu) 89200
HIDDENSEE (DDR) 39300
HIMKI (Ru) 50770
HIRSOVA (Rm) 47540
HO CHI MIN (Ru) 05620
HO CHI MIN (Ru) 14450
HOLMOGORY (Ru) 22840
HOLMOGORY (Ru) 34470
HOMAR (Pd) 10810
HOREZU (Rm) 47540
HUMBAK (Pd) 23440

HUMULESTI (Ru) 47540
HUNEDOARA (Rm) 78580
HUNGARIA (Hu) 86110
HUSI (Rm) 47540
HUTA KATOWICE (Pd) 76984
HUTA LENINA (Pd) 76984
HUTA ZGODA (Pd) 78290
HUTA ZGODA (Pd) 80020
HUTA ZYGMUNT (Pd) 78290
HUTA ZYGMUNT (Pd) 80020
HYDROGRAF (Pd) 08565
HYDROMET (Pd) 33197

IALOMITA (Rm) 11800
IASI (Rm) 41310
ICHA (Ru) 85970
IERONIM UBOREVICH (Ru) 93695
IEZER (Rm) 11670
IGARKA (Ru) 02724
IGARKALES (Ru) 45680
IGNACY DASZYNSKI (Pd) 72115
IGNATIY SERGEYEV (Ru) 05620
IGNATIY SERGEYEV (Ru) 14450
IGOR GRABAR (Ru) 76580
IGOR GRABAR (Ru) 79930
IGRIM (Ru) 70020
IKHTIANDR (Ru) 12585
ILFOV (Ru) 47540
ILGA (Ru) 14962
ILICHOVO (Ru) 07550
ILIM (Ru) 70760
ILITCH (Ru) 17500
ILMEN (Ru) 11800
ILMENLES (Ru) 45680
ILYA ERENBURG (Ru) 52612/1
ILYA KATUNIN (Ru) 11580
ILYA KULIK (Ru) 02670
ILYA KULIN (Ru) 13751
ILYA METCHNIKOV (Ru) 10740
ILYA MUROMETS (Ru) 17500
ILYA MUROMETS (Ru) 22220
ILYA REPIN (Ru) 91224
ILYA SELVINSKIY (Ru) 50730
ILYA ULYANOV (Ru) 03060
ILYA ULYANOV (Ru) 03650
ILYA VOLYNKIN (Ru) 11720
ILYCH (Ru) 20655
ILYICHYOVSK (Ru) 11800

ILYINSK (Ru) 07550
IMAN (Ru) 36890
IMAN (Ru) 43790
IMANDRA (Ru) 25550
IMANT SUDMALIS (Ru) 12380
IMANT SUDMALIS (Ru) 85970
IMENI 61
  KOMMUNARA (Ru) 91224
IMERITI (Ru) 11800
IMPULS (DDR) 43540
INAU (Rm) 11670
INDIGA (Ru) 11490
INDIGIRKA (Ru) 21580
INDIGIRKA (Ru) 35310
INDIRA GANDHI (Ru) 00965
INDUS (Pd) 10540
INESSA ARMAND (Ru) 05620
INESSA ARMAND (Ru) 14450
INGUL (Ru) 02110
INGUL (Ru) 35170
INGUL (Ru) 76945
INGULETS (Ru) 76945
INGUR (Ru) 21220
INGURI (Ru) 04210
INGURI (Ru) 35190
INGULES (Ru) 13010
INKURLES (Ru) 45680
INOWROCLAW (Pd) 33280
INOWROCLAW (Pd) 94550
INSELSEE (DDR) 46370
INSELSEE (DDR) 47070
INTERNATSIONAL (Ru) 60680
INTERNATSIONAL (Ru) 90720
INTSY (Ru) 26210
INZHEHIER AGEYEV (Ru) 70740
INZHENER
  YERMOSHKIN (Ru) 12680
INZHENER
  YUDINTSYEV (Ru) 13751
INZHENIER
  BASHKIROV (Ru) 80090
INZHENIER BELOV (Ru) 50770
INZHENIER
  KREYLIS (Ru) 80090
INZHENIER
  MACHULSKIY (Ru) 80090
INZHENIER
  NECHIPORENKO (Ru) 80090

Name	No.
INZHENIER PARKHONTUK (Ru)	48650
INZHENIER SUKHORUKOV (Ru)	80090
INZHENIER YAMBURENKO (Ru)	69310
IOAKIM VATSIETIS (Ru)	13650
IOHANNES LAURISTIN (Ru)	03770
IOHANNES LAURISTIN (Ru)	04010
IOKHAN KYOLER (Ru)	12380
IOKHANNES SEMPER (Ru)	23480
ION SOLTYS (Ru)	51672
ION SOLTYS (Ru)	73290
IONA YAKIR (Ru)	05620
IONA YAKIR (Ru)	14450
IONAS BILYUNAS (Ru)	12380
IOSIF DUBROVINSKIY (Ru)	03770
IOSIF DUBROVINSKIY (Ru)	04010
IOSIF LAPUSHKIN (Ru)	13650
IOZAS VITAS (Ru)	12380
IRBENSKIY PROLIV (Ru)	58510
IRBENSKIY PROLIV (Ru)	71820
IRBIS (Ru)	14962
IRBIT (Ru)	85320
IRBITLES (Ru)	45680
IRKUT (Ru)	56270
IRKUT (Ru)	62730
IRKUTSK (Ru)	02520
IRKUTSK (Ru)	45110
IRKUTSKLES (Ru)	45680
IRSHALES (Ru)	45680
IRTISH (Ru)	84460
IRTYSH (Ru)	39290
IRTYSHK (Ru)	11333
IRTYSHLES (Ru)	45680
ISAKOGORKA (Ru)	11430
ISHIM (Ru)	76945
ISHIM (Ru)	85320
ISIDOR BARAKHOV (Ru)	50730
ISKAR 2 (Bu)	67530
ISKAR (Bu)	69725
ISKATEL (Ru)	93268
ISKONA (Ru)	85320
ISKRA (Ru)	60680
ISKRA (Ru)	90720
ISPOLNITELNYY (Ru)	22135
ISSLEDOVATEL (Ru)	93268
ISTRA (Ru)	45680
ISYK KOL (Ru)	20790
ITELMAN (Ru)	12380
IVAN AIVAZOVSKIY (Ru)	91224
IVAN BABUSHKIN (Ru)	28980
IVAN BOCHKOV (Ru)	34872
IVAN BOGUN (Ru)	49342
IVAN BOGUN (Ru)	86170
IVAN BOLOTNIKOV (Ru)	89250
IVAN BORZOV (Ru)	24310
IVAN BORZOV (Ru)	39450
IVAN BUBNOV (Ru)	59880
IVAN BURMAKOV (Ru)	11333
IVAN BYELOSTOTSKIY (Ru)	03770
IVAN BYELOSTOTSKIY (Ru)	04010
IVAN CHERNOPYATKO (Ru)	12380
IVAN CHERNYKH (Ru)	11430
IVAN DANIKIN (Ru)	02724
IVAN DERBENEV (Ru)	78060
IVAN DVORSKIY (Ru)	12380
IVAN FEDEROV (Ru)	25840
IVAN FRANKO (Ru)	01750
IVAN GOLUBETS (Ru)	12230
IVAN GONCHAROV (Ru)	07900
IVAN GREN (Ru)	23480
IVAN KIREYEV (Ru)	04216
IVAN KOLYSHKIN (Ru)	79340
IVAN KOROBTSOV (Ru)	03950
IVAN KOROTEYEV (Ru)	69310
IVAN KORZUNOV (Ru)	13751
IVAN KOTLYAREVSKIY (Ru)	09995
IVAN KRAMSKOY (Ru)	91224
IVAN KRUZENSHTERN (Ru)	22220
IVAN KRUZHENSTERN (Ru)	04240
IVAN KUDRIYA (Ru)	79340
IVAN KULIBIN (Ru)	10740
IVAN KULIBIN (Ru)	75392
IVAN KUZNETSOV (Ru)	11333
IVAN LESOVIKOV (Ru)	79340
IVAN LYUDNIKOV (Ru)	11333
IVAN MAKARIN (Ru)	49342
IVAN MOSKALENKO (Ru)	48430
IVAN MOSKALENKO (Ru)	49470
IVAN MOSKALENKO (Ru)	49740
IVAN MOSKVITIN (Ru)	22220
IVAN NESTEROV (Ru)	78010
IVAN NESTEROV (Ru)	79990
IVAN PANOV (Ru)	12380
IVAN PEREVERZEV (Ru)	48430
IVAN PEREVERZEV (Ru)	49470
IVAN PEREVERZEV (Ru)	49740
IVAN POKROVSKIY (Ru)	03770
IVAN POKROVSKIY (Ru)	04010
IVAN POLOZKOV (Ru)	22327
IVAN POLZUNOV (Ru)	10740
IVAN POLZUNOV (Ru)	75392
IVAN RABCHINSKIY (Ru)	49810
IVAN SERGIYENKO (Ru)	79340
IVAN SHADR (Ru)	76580
IVAN SHADR (Ru)	79930
IVAN SHEPETKOV (Ru)	48430
IVAN SHEPETKOV (Ru)	49470
IVAN SHEPETKOV (Ru)	49740
IVAN SHISHKIN (Ru)	91224
IVAN SIVKO (Ru)	00140
IVAN SKURIDIN (Ru)	78060
IVAN STROD (Ru)	50730
IVAN SUSANIN (Ru)	49342
IVAN SYRYKH (Ru)	54710
IVAN TEVOSYAN (Ru)	63570
IVAN VAZOV (Bu)	80900
IVAN VERNIGORENKO (Ru)	28600
IVAN ZAGUBANSKI (Bu)	48430
IVAN ZAGUBANSKI (Bu)	49470
IVAN ZAGUBANSKI (Bu)	49740
IVAN ZEMNUKHOV (Ru)	60373
IVAN ZIMAKOV (Ru)	34872
IVANOVO (Ru)	39970
IYUN KORAN (Ru)	11720
IZGUTTY AYTYKOV (Ru)	73290
IZHEVSK (Ru)	00850
IZHEVSKLES (Ru)	45680
IZHEVSKOYE (Ru)	33198
IZHMALES (Ru)	45680
IZHORA (Ru)	02520
IZHORA (Ru)	70810
IZHORALES (Ru)	45680
IZMAIL (Ru)	02520
IZMAIL (Ru)	11800
IZUMRUD (Ru)	35390
IZUMRUDNYY BEREG (Ru)	62701
IZUMRUDNYY (Ru)	11800
IZVESTIYA (Ru)	57760
IZVESTIYA (Ru)	62480
JACEK MALCZEWSKI (Pd)	49655
JACQUES DUCLOS (Ru)	70590
JAKHONT (Ru)	12380
JAMNO (Pd)	33193
JAMNO (Pd)	33560
JAN FABRITSIUS (Ru)	12380
JAN HEWELIUSZ (Pd)	15040
JAN KALBERZIN (Ru)	03423
JAN KREUKS (Ru)	86070
JAN MAYEN (DDR)	18720
JAN RUDZUTAK (Ru)	12380
JANA (or YANA) (Ru)	02110
JANA (or YANA) (Ru)	06795
JANA (Ru)	21580
JANA (Ru)	35170
JANALES (Ru)	11490
JANTAR (Pd)	22138
JANUSZ KUSOCINSKI (Pd)	65850
JANUSZ KUSOCINSKI (Pd)	67690
JAROSLAW (Pd)	66980
JASIEN (Pd)	33193
JASLO (Pd)	16270
JASTARNIA-BOR (Pd)	04400
JEANNE LABOURBE (Ru)	05620
JEANNE LABOURBE (Ru)	14450
JELCZ II (Pd)	82260
JENA (DDR)	70695
JIJIA (Rm)	13751
JIUL (Rm)	11800
JOHANN MAHMASTAL (Ru)	90560
JOHANNES R. BECKER (DDR)	12620
JOHANNES RUVEN (Ru)	12380
JOHANNES VARES (Ru)	25840
JOHANNGEORGENSTADT (DDR)	50128
JOHN BRINCKMAN (DDR)	34330
JOHN REED (Ru)	70590
JOHSTADT (DDR)	50128
JORDANKA NIKOLOVA (Bu)	78980
JOSE DIAS (Ru)	06770
JOSE DIAS (Ru)	07550
JOSE MARTI (Ru)	70590
JOSIP BROZ TITO (Ru)	52612/1
JOWISZ (Pd)	11640
JOZEF CHELMONSKI (Pd)	49655
JOZEF CONRAD KORZENIOWSKI (Pd)	54970
JOZEF CONRAD KORZENIOWSKI (Pd)	71810
JUNGE GARDE (DDR)	24160
JUNGE WELT (DDR)	24160
JUPITER (Bu)	17329
JUPITER (Pd)	12610
JUPITER (Ru)	33035
JURATA (Pd)	04400
K. I. GALCZYNSKI (Pd)	10280
KAAREL LIYMAND (Ru)	12380
KABONA (Ru)	89250
KABRYL (Pd)	18740
KAFUR MAMEDOV (Ru)	53160
KAGANSK (Ru)	33076
KAGUL (Ru)	86070
KAHLEBERG (DDR)	94565
KAIGA (Ru)	33076
KAINSK (Ru)	33076
KAKHETI (Ru)	11800
KALACHEVSK (Ru)	33076
KALACHINSK (Ru)	26210
KALACHINSK (Ru)	33076
KALAMUS (Ru)	22327
KALAR (Ru)	02280
KALAR (Ru)	23480
KALARAND (Ru)	23664
KALININABAD (Ru)	03040
KALININABAD (Ru)	50910
KALININGRAD (Ru)	06770
KALININGRAD (Ru)	07550
KALININGRAD (Ru)	45110
'KALININGRAD' type (Ru)	01380
'KALININGRAD' type (Ru)	01640
KALININGRADETS (Ru)	22173
KALININGRADNEFT (Ru)	66380
KALININGRADSKIY BEREG (Ru)	62671
KALININGRADSKIY BEREG (Ru)	82651
KALININGRADSKIY KOMSOMOLETS (Ru)	93820
KALININGRADSKIY-NEFTYANIK (Ru)	66380

KALININSK (Ru) 26210
KALININSK (Ru) 33076
KALINOVO (Ru) 11800
KALINOVSK (Ru) 33076
KALITVA (Ru) 23480
KALJMAR (Ru) 12230
KALLISTO (Ru) 12230
KALMAR (Pd) 23440
KALMIUS (Ru) 89200
KALPER (Ru) 13751
KALTAN (Ru) 11800
KALUGA (Ru) 33076
KALYADINSK (Ru) 33076
KAMA (Ru) 35310
KAMA (Ru) 36235
KAMALES (Ru) 11490
KAMCHADAL (Ru) 06770
KAMCHADAL (Ru) 07550
KAMCHATKA (Ru) 15460
KAMCHATKA (Ru) 22173
KAMCHATSKIE GORY (Ru) 91910
KAMCHATSKIY
  BEREG (Ru) 62671
KAMCHATSKIY
  PROLIV (Ru) 58510
KAMCHATSKIY
  PROLIV (Ru) 71820
KAMCHATSKIY (Ru) 07550
KAMCHATSKLES (Ru) 04180
KAMENITZA (Bu) 77080
KAMENITZA (Bu) 80000
`KAMENKA` class (Ru) 04065
`KAMENKA` class (Ru) 04066
KAMENOGORSK (Ru) 45210
KAMENSK (Ru) 20738
KAMENSK-URALSKIY (Ru) 70020
KAMENSKOYE (Ru) 11800
KAMSKIY (Ru) 33076
KAMYSHEVSK (Ru) 33076
KANARYJKA (Pd) 18740
KANDAGACH (Ru) 89460
KANDALAKSHA (Ru) 02724
KANDALAKSHA (Ru) 23480
KANDALAKSHALES (Ru) 24030
KANDALAKSHSKIY
  ZALIV (Ru) 61100
KANDAVA (Ru) 03260
KANEV (Ru) 03040

KANEV (Ru) 50910
KANIN (Ru) 20738
KANIN (Ru) 86070
KANTAR (Pd) 18740
KANTEMIR (Ru) 26210
KAPITAN A
  POLKOVSKIY (Ru) 47167
KAPITAN A
  RADZHABOV (Ru) 02080
KAPITAN A
  RADZHABOV (Ru) 22250
KAPITAN A.
  KACHARAVA (Ru) 52612/1
KAPITAN ABAKUMOV (Ru) 24030
KAPITAN AFANASYEV (Ru) 22178
KAPITAN ALEKSEYEV (Ru) 02790
KAPITAN ANDREI
  TARAN (Ru) 12380
KAPITAN
  ANISTRATYENKO (Ru) 02790
KAPITAN ARDEYEV (Ru) 34872
KAPITAN ARON (Ru) 17637
KAPITAN ARTYUKH (Ru) 80052
KAPITAN BABICHEV (Ru) 20875
KAPITAN BAKANOV (Ru) 54710
KAPITAN
  BELOSHAPKIN (Ru) 24030
KAPITAN BELOUSOV (Ru) 23970
KAPITAN BOCHEK (Ru) 49342
KAPITAN
  BONDARENKO (Ru) 21610
KAPITAN BORODKIN (Ru) 20875
KAPITAN BUKAYEV (Ru) 22200
KAPITAN BURMAKIN (Ru) 54710
KAPITAN CHADAYEV (Ru) 22200
KAPITAN CHECHKIN (Ru) 22200
KAPITAN CHUDINOV (Ru) 20875
KAPITAN CHUKHCHIN (Ru) 49342
KAPITAN DEMIDOV (Ru) 11610
KAPITAN DEMIDOV (Ru) 20875
KAPITAN
  DOTSYENKO (Ru) 70740
KAPITAN DRANITSYN (Ru) 02060
KAPITAN DRANITSYN (Ru) 02230
KAPITAN DUBININ (Ru) 78010
KAPITAN DUBININ (Ru) 79990
KAPITAN DUBLITSKIY (Ru) 54710
KAPITAN DYACHUK (Ru) 70740

KAPITAN
  DZURASHEVICH (Ru) 02790
KAPITAN E. EGOROV (Ru) 64568
KAPITAN EVSEYEV (Ru) 35310
KAPITAN FOMIN (Ru) 49170
KAPITAN GASTELLO (Ru) 06770
KAPITAN GASTELLO (Ru) 07550
KAPITAN GAVRILOV (Ru) 80100
KAPITAN GEORGI
  GEORGIEV (Bu) 77080
KAPITAN GEORGI
  GEORGIEV (Bu) 80000
KAPITAN GEORGIY
  BAGLAY (Ru) 02790
KAPITAN
  GLAZACHYEV (Ru) 54710
KAPITAN GOTSKIY (Ru) 21610
KAPITAN GRIBIN (Ru) 70740
KAPITAN GUDIN (Ru) 78010
KAPITAN GUDIN (Ru) 79990
KAPITAN IZHMYAKOV (Ru) 78010
KAPITAN IZHMYAKOV (Ru) 79990
KAPITAN IZOTOV (Ru) 70740
KAPITAN KADETSKIY (Ru) 02790
KAPITAN KANEVSKIY (Ru) 80100
KAPITAN
  KARTASHOV (Ru) 89500
KAPITAN
  KHROMTSOV (Ru) 78010
KAPITAN
  KHROMTSOV (Ru) 79990
KAPITAN KIRIY (Ru) 54710
KAPITAN KLEBNIKOV (Ru) 02060
KAPITAN KLEBNIKOV (Ru) 02230
KAPITAN KOBETS (Ru) 70740
KAPITAN
  KONDRATYEV (Ru) 21610
KAPITAN
  KOSOLAPOV (Ru) 02080
KAPITAN
  KOSOLAPOV (Ru) 22250
KAPITAN
  KOZLOVSKIY (Ru) 80100
KAPITAN KRUTOV (Ru) 22200
KAPITAN KUDLAY (Ru) 49342
KAPITAN KULINICH (Ru) 62671
KAPITAN
  KUSHNARENKO (Ru) 02790

KAPITAN
  LEDOCHOWSKI (Pd) 07860
KAPITAN LEONTIY
  BORISENKO (Ru) 02790
KAPITAN LEV
  SOLOVYEV (Ru) 02790
KAPITAN
  LUKHMANOV (Ru) 03950
KAPITAN
  LYUBCHENKO (Ru) 54710
KAPITAN M
  IZMAYLOV (Ru) 02080
KAPITAN M
  IZMAYLOV (Ru) 22250
KAPITAN
  MAKATSARIYA (Ru) 52612/1
KAPITAN MAKLAKOV (Ru) 00140
KAPITAN MAN (Ru) 02724
KAPITAN MARKOV (Ru) 21610
KAPITAN MECAIK (Ru) 20875
KAPITAN MEDVEDEV (Ru) 48860
KAPITAN MELEKHOV (Ru) 23970
KAPITAN
  MESHCHRYAKOV (Ru) 78010
KAPITAN
  MESHCHRYAKOV (Ru) 79990
KAPITAN
  MEZENTSYEV (Ru) 12680
KAPITAN
  MILOVZOROV (Ru) 54710
KAPITAN MOCHALOV (Ru) 54710
KAPITAN MODEST
  IVANOV (Ru) 02790
KAPITAN MOSHKIN (Ru) 20875
KAPITAN
  MYSHEVSKIY (Ru) 21610
KAPITAN
  NAGONYUK (Ru) 52612/1
KAPITAN NAZAREV (Ru) 49342
KAPITAN NEVEZHKIN (Ru) 70740
KAPITAN NIKOLAYEV (Ru) 02060
KAPITAN NIKOLAYEV (Ru) 02230
KAPITAN NOKHRIN (Ru) 22137
KAPITAN PANFILOV (Ru) 78010
KAPITAN PANFILOV (Ru) 79990
KAPITAN PENKOV (Ru) 46550
KAPITAN PETKO
  VOIVODA (Bu) 48430

KAPITAN PETKO
  VOIVODA (Bu) 49470
KAPITAN PETKO
  VOIVODA (Bu) 49740
KAPITAN PLAHIN (Ru) 22200
KAPITAN
  PLAUSHEVSKIY (Ru) 03950
KAPITAN PURGIN (Ru) 13751
KAPITAN
  REDKOKASHA (Ru) 11333
KAPITAN REUTOV (Ru) 78010
KAPITAN REUTOV (Ru) 79990
KAPITAN
  SAMOYLENKO (Ru) 54710
KAPITAN
  SHANTSBERG (Ru) 03950
KAPITAN SHAULSKIY (Ru) 39290
KAPITAN
  SHEVCHENKO (Ru) 54710
KAPITAN SHVETSOV (Ru) 70740
KAPITAN
  SKORNYAKOV (Ru) 09360
KAPITAN SLIPKO (Ru) 02790
KAPITAN SMIRNOV (Ru) 12680
KAPITAN SOROKIN (Ru) 02060
KAPITAN SOROKIN (Ru) 02230
KAPITAN STULOV (Ru) 78010
KAPITAN STULOV (Ru) 79990
KAPITAN SUKHONDYAYEVSKIY (Ru) 11333
KAPITAN SVIRIDOV (Ru) 49342
KAPITAN TELOV (Ru) 00140
KAPITAN TEMKIN (Ru) 49785
KAPITAN TOMSON (Ru) 80060
KAPITAN TRUBKIN (Ru) 46424
KAPITAN V TSIRUL (Ru) 49342
KAPITAN V. FEDETOV (Ru) 22178
KAPITAN V. TRUSH (Ru) 80100
KAPITAN V.
  USHAKOV (Ru) 80100
KAPITAN
  V.OVODOVSKIY (Ru) 49785
KAPITAN VAKULA (Ru) 49342
KAPITAN VALENTIN
  IVANOV (Ru) 64568
KAPITAN
  VASILYEVSKIY (Ru) 54710
KAPITAN VAVILOV (Ru) 78010

KAPITAN VAVILOV (Ru)	79990	KARSKOYE MORE (Ru)	55130	KEGUMS (Ru)	86470	KHIMIK ZELINSKIY (Ru)	01560	KHUDOZHNIK S.	

KAPITAN VAVILOV (Ru) 79990
KAPITAN VODENKO (Ru) 49342
KAPITAN VOOLENS (Ru) 75312
KAPITAN VORONIN (Ru) 23970
KAPITAN YAKOVLEV (Ru) 80060
KAPITAN YERSHOV (Ru) 52612/1
KAPITAN
  YEVDOKIMOV (Ru) 20875
KAPITAN ZAMYATIN (Ru) 54710
KAPITAN ZARUBIN (Ru) 22200
KAPITAN ZBIGNIEW
  SZYMANSKI (Pd) 86824
KAPOS (Hu) 51780
KAPRELA (Bu) 23440
KAPSUKAS (Ru) 06770
KAPSUKAS (Ru) 07550
KARA (Ru) 06770
KARA (Ru) 07550
KARA-DAG (Ru) 11800
KARACHAROVO (Ru) 28600
KARAGA (Ru) 06795
KARAGA (Ru) 39290
KARAGACH (Ru) 11800
KARAGANDA (Ru) 02520
KARAGAT (Ru) 23480
KARAKUM KANAL (Ru) 44100
KARAKUMNEFT (Ru) 85970
KARAKUMY (Ru) 11300
KARELI (Ru) 85970
KARELYALES (Ru) 04180
KARGATSK (Ru) 33076
KARL KRUSHTEYN (Ru) 89200
KARL LIEBKNECHT (Ru) 05620
KARL LIEBKNECHT (Ru) 14450
KARL LIEBKNECHT (Ru) 17500
KARL LIEBKNECHT (Ru) 62680
KARL LINNEY (Ru) 61270
KARL LINNEY (Ru) 81490
KARL MARX (DDR) 03150
KARL MARX (Ru) 17500
KARL MARX STADT (DDR) 04910
KARL WOLF (DDR) 23410
KARLIS ZIEDINS (Ru) 10720
KARLOVY VARY (Cz) 58140
KAROLIS POZHELA (Ru) 12380
KARPATY (Ru) 11300
KARPINSK (Ru) 26210
KARPOGORY (Ru) 11300

KARSKOYE MORE (Ru) 55130
KARTALY (Ru) 84460
KARTLI (Ru) 12230
KASHINO (Ru) 06770
KASHINO (Ru) 07550
KASHIRA (Ru) 52304
KASHIRA (Ru) 52616
KASHIRSKOYE (Ru) 07947
KASKAD (Ru) 12380
KASPIY (Ru) 35310
KASPIY (Ru) 50770
KASSIOPEYA (Ru) 12230
KASTITIS (Ru) 22173
KASZALOT (Pd) 10810
KASZUBY II (Pd) 59690
KASZUBY II (Pd) 81350
KATANGLI (Ru) 06795
KATAYSK (Ru) 26210
KATOWICE II (Pd) 80205
KATRA (Ru) 33198
KATRAN (Ru) 33198
KATTEGAT (DDR) 18720
KATUN (Ru) 04312
KATUNJ (Ru) 35180
KATYA ZELENKO (Ru) 78060
KATYN (Ru) 02280
KAUGURI (Ru) 13751
KAUNAS (Ru) 31185
KAVALEROVO (Ru) 06795
KAVARNA (Bu) 79340
KAVKAZ (Ru) 63982
KAVRAY (Ru) 11800
KAVRAZ (Ru) 17500
KAZAKHSTAN (Ru) 20370
KAZALINSK (Ru) 23480
KAZAN (or KASAN) (Ru) 34872
KAZANSK (Ru) 33076
KAZANTIP (Ru) 11800
KAZATIN (Ru) 06795
KAZATIN (Ru) 23480
KAZHEK (Ru) 33076
KAZIMIERZ PULASKI (Pd) 12685
KAZIS GEDRIS (Ru) 85320
KAZIS PREYKSHAS (Ru) 91224
KEDAYNYAY (Ru) 06770
KEDAYNYAY (Ru) 07550
KEDZIERZYN (Pd) 75770
KEGOSTROV (Ru) 11380

KEGUMS (Ru) 86470
KEKHRA (Ru) 89200
KEKUR (Ru) 85970
KEM (Ru) 06795
KEMEROVO (Ru) 02724
KEMINE (Ru) 79340
KEMJ (Ru) 92165
KENGARAGS (Ru) 33305
KERCH (Ru) 12230
KERCH (Ru) 39970
KERCH (Ru) 51212
KERCH (Ru) 59890
KERCH (Ru) 67650
KERCHENSKIY
  KOMMUNIST (Ru) 85970
KERCHENSKIY
  PROLIV (Ru) 58510
KERCHENSKIY
  PROLIV (Ru) 71820
KERCHENSKIY-1 (Ru) 23335
KERCHENSKIY-2 (Ru) 23337
KESSULAID (Ru) 75640
KHABAROVSK (Ru) 02120
KHABAROVSK (Ru) 12340
KHAMZA (Ru) 50763
KHAN ASPARUKH (Bu) 52440
KHANKA (Ru) 84360
KHARITON GREKU (Ru) 51672
KHARITON LAPTEV (Ru) 22180
KHARKU (Ru) 13751
KHARLOV (Ru) 07550
KHARLOVKA (Ru) 17950
KHAROVSK (Ru) 11720
KHAROVSK (Ru) 34610
KHASAN (Ru) 67350
KHASAN (Ru) 71360
KHASAN (Ru) 84360
'KHASAN' class (Ru) 25550
KHASAVYURT (Ru) 50770
KHATANGA (Ru) 24030
KHATANGALES (Ru) 11490
KHAYRYUZOVO (Ru) 23480
KHENDRIK KUYVAS (Ru) 67010
KHERMAN ARBON (Ru) 12380
KHERSON (Ru) 67680
KHIBINSKIE GORY (Ru) 61270
KHIBINSKIE GORY (Ru) 81490
KHIBINY (Ru) 11300

KHIMIK ZELINSKIY (Ru) 01560
KHOLMOGORY (Ru) 11300
KHOLMSK (Ru) 24030
KHOLMSK (Ru) 88230
KHOTIN (Ru) 11333
KHRABROVO (Ru) 33198
KHRONOMETR (Ru) 11800
KHRUSTALNYY
  BEREG (Ru) 62671
KHRUSTALNYY (Ru) 11800
KHRUSTALNYY (Ru) 85970
KHUDOZHNIK A
  GERASIMOV (Ru) 77080
KHUDOZHNIK A
  GERASIMOV (Ru) 80000
KHUDOZHNIK
  DEYNEKA (Ru) 91224
KHUDOZHNIK
  FEDOROVSKIY (Ru) 77080
KHUDOZHNIK
  FEDOROVSKIY (Ru) 80000
KHUDOZHNIK
  GABASHVILI (Ru) 77080
KHUDOZHNIK
  GABASHVILI (Ru) 80000
KHUDOZHNIK
  IOGANSON (Ru) 77340
KHUDOZHNIK
  KASIYAN (Ru) 77080
KHUDOZHNIK
  KASIYAN (Ru) 80000
KHUDOZHNIK
  KRAYNEV (Ru) 80010
KHUDOZHNIK
  KUINDZHA (Ru) 50730
KHUDOZHNIK
  KUSTODIYEV (Ru) 77080
KHUDOZHNIK
  KUSTODIYEV (Ru) 80000
KHUDOZHNIK
  PAKHOMOV (Ru) 77340
KHUDOZHNIK
  PLASTOV (Ru) 50730
KHUDOZHNIK
  PROROKOV (Ru) 77340
KHUDOZHNIK REPIN (Ru) 77340
KHUDOZHNIK
  ROMAS (Ru) 77340

KHUDOZHNIK S.
  GERASIMOV (Ru) 91224
KHUDOZHNIK
  SARYAN (Ru) 77340
KHUDOZHNIK TOIDZE (Ru) 77080
KHUDOZHNIK TOIDZE (Ru) 80000
KHUDOZHNIK VLADIMIR
  SEROV (Ru) 77080
KHUDOZHNIK VLADIMIR
  SEROV (Ru) 80000
KHUDOZHNIK
  VRUBEL (Ru) 91224
KHUDOZHNIK
  ZHUKOV (Ru) 77340
KHVALYNSK (Ru) 26210
KIEV (Ru) 02070
KIEVSKIY
  KOMSOMOLETS (Ru) 23305
KIGILYAKH (Ru) 50730
KIHELKONA (Ru) 86220
KIKCHIK (Ru) 06770
KIKCHIK (Ru) 07550
'KIL' class (Ru) 23685
KILDIN (Ru) 11430
KILDIN (Ru) 11580
KILIYA (Ru) 06795
KILIYA (Ru) 75350
KIMRY (Ru) 07550
KINESHMA (Ru) 26210
KINGAN (Ru) 12380
KINGISEPP (Ru) 06770
KINGISEPP (Ru) 07550
KIRENSK (Ru) 06795
KIREYEVSK (Ru) 26210
KIRGHIZSTAN (Ru) 02350
KIRGHIZSTAN (Ru) 35370
KIRIR (Ru) 23480
KIROVABAD (Ru) 44100
KIROVAKAN (Ru) 26210
KIROVOGRAD (Ru) 11800
KIROVSK (Ru) 11580
KIROVSKLES (Ru) 04180
KISHINEV (Ru) 49240
KITEN (Bu) 84210
KITEN (Bu) 91224
KIVACH (Ru) 11300
KIZHI (Ru) 26210
KLAIPEDA (Ru) 39960

KLARA ZETKIN (Ru) 10720
KLAVDIYA
  YELANSKAYA (Ru) 01935
KLAYPEDA (Ru) 31185
KLEMENT GOTTWALD (Ru) 70590
KLIM VOROSHILOV (Ru) 03950
KLIMOVO (Ru) 11800
KLIMOVSK (Ru) 26210
KLIN (Ru) 03930
KLINTSY (Ru) 26210
KLOSTERFELDE (DDR) 59650
KLYKACH (Ru) 34985
KLYUCHEYSKOY (Ru) 23480
KNIAZIK (Pd) 18740
KNUD JESPERSEN (Ru) 57760
KNUD JESPERSEN (Ru) 62480
KOBULETI (Ru) 11800
KODINO (Ru) 11490
KODOR (Ru) 45715
KOGUVA (Ru) 23337
KOKAND (Ru) 34872
KOKAND (Ru) 36250
KOKAND (Ru) 42800
KOKHTLA (Ru) 15460
KOKSHAYSK (Ru) 26210
KOLA (Ru) 02724
KOLA (Ru) 70810
KOLEN (Pd) 18740
KOLESNIKOV (Ru) 01736
KOLGUYEV (Ru) 01733
KOLGUYEV (Ru) 11490
KOLIAS (Pd) 23474
KOLKA (Ru) 22327
KOLKHIDA (Ru) 02350
KOLKHIDA (Ru) 12230
KOLKHIDA (Ru) 35370
KOLOBRZEG II (Pd) 82260
KOLOMENSKOYE (Ru) 28600
'KOLOMNA' type (—) 28060
KOLPAKOVO (Ru) 39290
KOLPASHEVO (Ru) 11333
KOLPINSEE (DDR) 46370
KOLPINSEE (DDR) 47070
KOLSKIY (Ru) 11580
KOLYA MYGATIN (Ru) 15510
KOLYMA (Ru) 35310
KOLYMALES (Ru) 04180
KOMANDARM FEDKO (Ru) 67680

KOMANDARM GAY (Ru) 50730
KOMANDARM
  MATVEYEV (Ru) 03950
KOMILES (Ru) 24030
KOMISSAR
  POLUKHIN (Ru) 45120
KOMMUNALNIK (Ru) 33015
KOMMUNAR (Ru) 13650
KOMMUNARSK (Ru) 03930
KOMMUNIST (Ru) 05620
KOMMUNIST (Ru) 12380
KOMMUNIST (Ru) 14450
KOMMUNIST UKRAINY (Ru) 12380
KOMMUNISTICHESKOYE
  ZNAMYA (Ru) 05620
KOMMUNISTICHESKOYE-
  ZNAMYA (Ru) 14450
KOMPAS (Ru) 01736
KOMPAS (Ru) 09380
KOMSOMOL LATVII (Ru) 23480
KOMSOMOL (Ru) 39970
KOMSOMOL UKRAINI (Ru) 12380
KOMSOMOLETS
  ADZHARII (Ru) 01380
KOMSOMOLETS
  ADZHARII (Ru) 01640
KOMSOMOLETS
  ARMENII (Ru) 01380
KOMSOMOLETS
  ARMENII (Ru) 01640
KOMSOMOLETS
  AZERBAYDZHANA (Ru) 01380
KOMSOMOLETS
  AZERBAYDZHANA (Ru) 01640
KOMSOMOLETS
  BYELORUSSII (Ru) 01380
KOMSOMOLETS
  BYELORUSSII (Ru) 01640
KOMSOMOLETS
  ESTONII (Ru) 03930
KOMSOMOLETS
  GRUZII (Ru) 01380
KOMSOMOLETS
  GRUZII (Ru) 01640
KOMSOMOLETS
  KAZAKHSTANA (Ru) 01380
KOMSOMOLETS
  KAZAKHSTANA (Ru) 01640

KOMSOMOLETS
  LATVII (Ru) 03930
KOMSOMOLETS
  LITVY (Ru) 03930
KOMSOMOLETS
  MAGADANA (Ru) 93820
KOMSOMOLETS
  MOLDAVII (Ru) 01380
KOMSOMOLETS
  MOLDAVII (Ru) 01640
KOMSOMOLETS
  PRAVDA (Ru) 01380
KOMSOMOLETS
  PRAVDA (Ru) 01640
KOMSOMOLETS
  PRIMORYA (Ru) 62671
KOMSOMOLETS
  PRIMORYA (Ru) 82651
KOMSOMOLETS
  ROSSII (Ru) 01380
KOMSOMOLETS
  ROSSII (Ru) 01640
KOMSOMOLETS (Ru) 01380
KOMSOMOLETS (Ru) 01640
KOMSOMOLETS (Ru) 07550
KOMSOMOLETS (Ru) 12230
KOMSOMOLETS
  SPASSKA (Ru) 01380
KOMSOMOLETS
  SPASSKA (Ru) 01640
KOMSOMOLETS
  TADZHIKISTANA (Ru) 03930
KOMSOMOLETS
  TATARII (Ru) 23664
KOMSOMOLETS
  TURKMENII (Ru) 01380
KOMSOMOLETS
  TURKMENII (Ru) 01640
KOMSOMOLETS
  UKRAINY (Ru) 39970
KOMSOMOLETS
  USSURIYSKA (Ru) 01380
KOMSOMOLETS
  USSURIYSKA (Ru) 01640
KOMSOMOLETS
  UZBEKISTANA (Ru) 03930
KOMSOMOLETS
  VLADIVOSTOKA (Ru) 01380

KOMSOMOLETS
  VLADIVOSTOKA (Ru) 01640
KOMSOMOLIYA
  KALININGRADA (Ru) 81195
KOMSOMOLSK NA
  AMURE (Ru) 93820
KOMSOMOLSK (Ru) 71530
KOMSOMOLSK (Ru) 80200
KOMSOMOLSKAYA
  SLAVA (Ru) 02670
KOMSOMOLSKAYA
  SMENA (Ru) 81195
KONDA (Ru) 21580
KONDA (Ru) 85895
KONDOPOGA (Ru) 06795
KONDOR (Bu) 11800
KONDOR (Ru) 09380
KONDRAT BILYUTIN (Ru) 11333
KONDRATIY BULAVIN (Ru) 89250
KONGER (Ru) 22330
KONIN (Pd) 05620
KONIN (Pd) 14450
KONOSHA (Ru) 86220
KONOTOP (Ru) 26210
KONSTANTIN
  ALEKSEYEV (Ru) 13751
KONSTANTIN
  CHERNENKO (Ru) 20353
KONSTANTIN
  DUSHENOV (Ru) 00140
KONSTANTIN
  FOMTSHENKO (Ru) 34872
KONSTANTIN
  KOROBTSOV (Ru) 22173
KONSTANTIN
  KORSHUNOV (Ru) 50280
KONSTANTIN
  OLSHANSKIY (Ru) 91224
KONSTANTIN
  PAUSTOVSKIY (Ru) 09995
KONSTANTIN
  PETROVSKIY (Ru) 54710
KONSTANTIN
  SAVELYEV (Ru) 50280
KONSTANTIN
  SHESTAKOV (Ru) 50280
KONSTANTIN
  SIMONOV (Ru) 20353

KONSTANTIN
  SUKHANOV (Ru) 93680
KONSTANTIN
  TSIOLKOVSKIY (Ru) 59890
KONSTANTIN
  TSIOLKOVSKIY (Ru) 67650
KONSTANTIN YUON (Ru) 76580
KONSTANTIN YUON (Ru) 79930
KONSTANTIN
  ZANKOV (Ru) 69310
KONSTANTIN
  ZASLONOV (Ru) 50730
KONSTANTINOVKA (Ru) 61700
KONSTITUTSIYA
  SSSR (Ru) 45270
KOPALNIA
  GOTTWALD (Pd) 74655
KOPALNIA GRZYBOW (Pd) 48660
KOPALNIA
  JASTRZEBIE (Pd) 48835
KOPALNIA JEZIORKO (Pd) 49210
KOPALNIA JEZIORKO (Pd) 78300
KOPALNIA KLEOFAS (Pd) 61090
KOPALNIA MACHOW (Pd) 48660
KOPALNIA MARCEL (Pd) 61090
KOPALNIA
  MIECHOWICE (Pd) 74655
KOPALNIA
  MOSZCZENICA (Pd) 61090
KOPALNIA
  MYSLOWICE (Pd) 48835
KOPALNIA
  PIASECZNO (Pd) 49210
KOPALNIA
  PIASECZNO (Pd) 78300
KOPALNIA
  SIEMIANOWICE (Pd) 48835
KOPALNIA SIERSZA (Pd) 74655
KOPALNIA
  SOSNICA (Pd) 61090
KOPALNIA
  SOSNOWIEC (Pd) 78290
KOPALNIA
  SOSNOWIEC (Pd) 80020
KOPALNIA
  SZCZYGLOWICE (Pd) 61090
KOPALNIA
  SZOMBIERKI (Pd) 48835

Name	No.
KOPALNIA WALBRZYCH (Pd)	78290
KOPALNIA WALBRZYCH (Pd)	80020
KOPALNIA WIREK (Pd)	61090
KOPALNIA ZOFIOWKA (Pd)	78290
KOPALNIA ZOFIOWKA (Pd)	80020
KOPERNIK (Pd)	01733
KOPET-DAG (Ru)	11300
KOPORYE (Ru)	06770
KOPORYE (Ru)	07550
KORABLESTEROITYEL KLOPOTOV (Ru)	93695
KORAL (Pd)	22138
KORALL (Ru)	12380
KORALLOVYY (Ru)	33305
KORCHAGINETS (Ru)	23480
KOREIZ (Ru)	06795
KOREIZ (Ru)	12230
KORENGA (Ru)	23480
KORENOVSK (Ru)	26210
KOROLENKO (Ru)	20790
KOROS (Hu)	50909
KORSAKOV (Ru)	06795
'KORSAKOV' type (Ru)	86070
'KORSAKOV' type (Ru)	87940
KORSUN SCHEVCHENKOVSKIY (Ru)	51212
KORUND (Ru)	11800
KORUNDOVYY (Ru)	33305
KORWIN (Pd)	18740
KOSCIERZYNA (Pd)	50460
KOSMONAUT (Ru)	85320
KOSMONAUT GAGARIN (Ru)	91224
KOSMONAUT GEORGIY DOBROVOLSKIY (Ru)	00250
KOSMONAUT KOMAROV (Ru)	45120
KOSMONAUT PAVEL BELYAEV (Ru)	00250
KOSMONAUT TITOV (Ru)	39290
KOSMONAUT VIKTOR PATSAYEV (Ru)	00250
KOSMONAUT VLADIMIR KOMAROV (Ru)	94280
KOSMONAUT VLADISLAV VOLKOV (Ru)	00250
KOSMONAUT YURIY GAGARIN (Ru)	92435
KOSTA KHETAGUROV (Ru)	50730
KOSTINO (Ru)	06770
KOSTINO (Ru)	07550
KOSTOPOL (Ru)	26210
KOSTROMA (Ru)	51212
KOSTROMALES (Ru)	11490
KOTAYKA (Ru)	23480
KOTELNICH (Ru)	11300
KOTHEN (DDR)	61700
KOTLAS (Ru)	28060
KOTOVSK (Ru)	86220
KOTOVSKIY (Ru)	20790
KOTOVSKIY (Ru)	33910
KOVDA (Ru)	24030
KOVDALES (Ru)	04180
KOVDOR (Ru)	15460
KOZELSK (Ru)	50730
KOZEROG (Ru)	12230
KOZYREVSK (Ru)	07550
KRAB-2 (Ru)	17634
KRAKOW II (Pd)	48407
KRAMATORSK (Ru)	61700
KRANSK (Ru)	24030
KRASIN (Ru)	20870
KRASKINO (Ru)	24030
KRASLAVA (Ru)	86470
KRASNAL (Pd)	87740
KRASNAYA GORKA (Ru)	11430
KRASNOARMEYSK (Ru)	06795
KRASNOBORSK (Ru)	06770
KRASNOBORSK (Ru)	07550
KRASNODAR (Ru)	12230
KRASNODON (Ru)	03930
KRASNOE SELO (Ru)	03930
KRASNOFLOTSKOYE (Ru)	33198
KRASNOGORSKLES (Ru)	04180
KRASNOGVARDEYETS (Ru)	23480
KRASNOGVARDEYETS (Ru)	80052
KRASNOGVARDEYSK (Ru)	03930
KRASNOKAMENSK (Ru)	26210
KRASNOKAMSK (Ru)	03930
KRASNOLESYE (Ru)	26210
KRASNOPEREKOPSK (Ru)	26210
KRASNOPOLYE (Ru)	06795
KRASNOPUTILOVETS (Ru)	11610
KRASNOSELSK (Ru)	26210
KRASNOSLOBODSK (Ru)	26210
KRASNOTURANSK (Ru)	26210
KRASNOTURINSK (Ru)	06795
KRASNOUFIMSK (Ru)	03040
KRASNOUFIMSK (Ru)	03930
KRASNOURALSK (Ru)	03930
KRASNOYARSK (Ru)	07550
KRASNOYARSKI KOMSOMOLETS (Ru)	01380
KRASNOYARSKI KOMSOMOLETS (Ru)	01640
KRASNOZAVODSK (Ru)	03930
KRASNOZNAMENSK (Ru)	26210
KRASNYY LUCH (Ru)	71670
KRASZEWSKI (Pd)	15580
KRAYEV (Ru)	12380
KREMEN (Ru)	11800
KREMENCHUG (Ru)	51212
KREMENETS (Ru)	86070
KRENOMETR (Ru)	26210
KRETINGA (Ru)	07550
KREUTSWALD (Ru)	85320
KRILON (Ru)	01733
KRIPTON (Ru)	85970
KRISTALL (Ru)	12380
KRISTALNYY (Ru)	33305
KRISTIONAS DONELAYTIS (Ru)	12380
KRISTYAN RAUD (Ru)	12380
KRIVAN (Cz)	15090
KRIVBASS (Ru)	63982
KRONID KORENOV (Ru)	93695
KRONSHTADT (Ru)	11720
KRONSHTADT (Ru)	34610
KRONSHTADTSKAYA SLAVA (Ru)	93780
KROPELIN (DDR)	75330
KROPOTKIN (Ru)	66380
KRUPSKAYA (Ru)	17500
KRUTOGOROVO (Ru)	39290
KRYLOV (Ru)	17500
KRYM (Ru)	22137
KRYM (Ru)	63980
KRYMSK (Ru)	06795
KRYMSKIE GORY (Ru)	61270
KRYMSKIE GORY (Ru)	81490
KRYMSKIY RABOCHIY (Ru)	13751
KUBA (Ru)	12380
KUBA (Ru)	18280
KUBAN (Ru)	02140
KUBAN (Ru)	63980
KUBATLY (Ru)	50770
KUJARWY (Pd)	75730
KUJAWY (Pd)	88380
KULBAK (Pd)	18740
KULBIN (Ru)	18740
KULDIGA (Ru)	03260
KULIKOVO POLYE (Ru)	13751
KULIKOVO (Ru)	07947
KULOY (Ru)	21580
KULUNDA (Ru)	06795
KUMBYSH (Ru)	85970
KUNATKA (Pd)	18740
KUNDA (Ru)	89200
KUNGUR (Ru)	24030
KUNGURLES (Ru)	04180
KUNTSEVO (Ru)	06770
KUNTSEVO (Ru)	07550
KUPISHKIS (Ru)	06770
KUPISHKIS (Ru)	07550
KUPRIN (Ru)	12590
KURA (Ru)	08834
KURA (Ru)	21220
KURA (Ru)	35310
KURGANINSK (Ru)	26210
KURS (Ru)	09360
KURSHAYA DUGA (Ru)	13650
KURSHENAY (Ru)	17637
KURSK (Ru)	03423
KURSK (Ru)	39970
KURSOGRAF (Ru)	07470
KURTNA (Ru)	13751
KURZEME (Ru)	33198
KUSHKA (Ru)	23480
KUSKOV (Ru)	17920
KUSTANAY (Ru)	06795
KUTAISI (Ru)	70610
KUTNO II (Pd)	79870
KUULUNDA (Ru)	23480
KUYBYSHEVGES (Ru)	45210
KUYVASTU (Ru)	89200
KUZBASS (Ru)	63982
KUZMA GNIDASH (Ru)	78060
KUZMA MININ (Ru)	80171
KUZMINKI (Ru)	06770
KUZMINKI (Ru)	07550
KUZNETSK (Ru)	06795
KUZNICA (Pd)	04400
KVADRANT (Ru)	11800
KVARTS (Ru)	23480
KVARTSEVYY (Ru)	33305
KVEDARNA (Ru)	33017
KWIDZYN (Pd)	51260
KYARDLA (Ru)	22840
KYARDLA (Ru)	34470
KYPU (Ru)	15460
LABRADOR (Ru)	23480
LACERTA (Pd)	11700
LADOGA 'class' (Ru)	75360
LADOGA (Ru)	20790
LADOGA (Ru)	22173
LADOGA 1 (Ru)	75360
LADOGA 2 (Ru)	75360
LADOGA 3 (Ru)	75360
LADOGA 4 (Ru)	75360
LADOGA 5 (Ru)	75360
LADOGA 6 (Ru)	75360
LADOGA 7 (Ru)	75360
LADOGA 8 (Ru)	75360
LADOGA 9 (Ru)	75360
LADOGA 11 (Ru)	75400
LADOGA 12 (Ru)	75400
LADOGA 13 (Ru)	75400
LADOGA 14 (Ru)	75400
LADOGA 15 (Ru)	75400
LADOGA 16 (Ru)	75400
LADOGA 17 (Ru)	75400
LADOGA 18 (Ru)	75400
LADOGA 19 (Ru)	75400
LADOGA 20 (Ru)	75400
LAGUNA (Ru)	12380
LAKHTA (Ru)	06795
LAMUT (Ru)	43300
LANCUT (Pd)	23820
LANGUSTA (Pd)	10810
LAPLANDIYA (Ru)	17950
LARA MIKHEYENKO (Ru)	15510
LARISA REYSNER (Ru)	10720
LASKARA (Pd)	18740

LASPI (Ru)	85970	LENINSKIY	
LATERNA (Pd)	18740	KOMSOMOL (Ru)	31050
LATVIYA (Ru)	02160	LENINSKIY	
LAUMA (Ru)	22327	KOMSOMOL (Ru)	79340
LAYMA (Ru)	22327	LENINSKIY LUCH (Ru)	71670
LAZUREN BRIAG (Bu)	91224	LENINSKIY PIONER (Ru)	01560
LAZURIT (Ru)	12380	LENINSKIY PUT (Ru)	93820
LAZURNYY BEREG (Ru)	62680	LENINSKIY (Ru)	20790
LAZURNYY (Ru)	11610	LENINSKIYE GORY (Ru)	61270
LEBORK (Pd)	51260	LENINSKIYE GORY (Ru)	81490
LECHISTAN II (Pd)	31770	LENINSKIYE ISKRY (Ru)	01380
LEDNICE (Cz)	35480	LENINSKIYE ISKRY (Ru)	01640
LEDUS (Ru)	85320	LENINSKOE ZNAMYA (Ru)	90720
LEIPZIG (DDR)	04910	LENINSKOYE	
LEMBIT PERN (Ru)	13650	ZNAMYA (Ru)	60680
LENA (Ru)	35310	LENKORAN (Ru)	57630
LENA (Ru)	95015	LENKORAN (Ru)	60670
LENALES (Ru)	07600	LENKORAN (Ru)	80920
LENIN (Ru)	32065	LENKORAN (Ru)	84810
LENINAKAN (Ru)	57630	LENSK (Ru)	26210
LENINAKAN (Ru)	84810	LENSOVET (Ru)	53535
LENINGRAD (Pd)	10570	'LENTRA' class	
LENINGRAD (Pd)	15340	(modified) (Ru)	23609
LENINGRAD (Ru)	02070	'LENTRA' class (Ru)	23608
LENINGRAD (Ru)	11610	LEON POPOV (Ru)	03770
LENINGRADETS (Ru)	35310	LEON POPOV (Ru)	04010
LENINGRADSKAYA		LEONID BREZHNEV (Ru)	20370
SLAVA (Ru)	93780	LEONID IVANOV (Ru)	34872
LENINGRADSKIY		LEONID LEONIDOV (Ru)	28490
KOMSOMOLETS (Ru)	79340	LEONID	
LENINGRADSKIY		NOVOSPASSKIY (Ru)	34872
OPOLCHENETS (Ru)	50280	LEONID SMIRNYKH (Ru)	06795
LENINGRADSKIY		LEONID SOBINOV (Ru)	06200
PARTIZAN (Ru)	50280	LEONID SOBOLYEV (Ru)	80010
LENINO (Pd)	10570	LEONID TELIGA (Pd)	80750
LENINO (Pd)	15340	LEONID TELIGA (Pd)	81450
LENINO (Ru)	60660	LEONID YELKIN (Ru)	34872
LENINO (Ru)	62570	LEOPARD (Ru)	33065
LENINOGORSK (Ru)	11800	LEOPOLD NEKRASOV (Ru)	23305
LENINSK (Ru)	47990	LEOPOLD STAFF (Pd)	60484
LENINSK-		LEPUS (Pd)	11700
KUZNETSKIY (Ru)	70020	LERESTI (Rm)	60978
LENINSKAYA		LESKOV (Ru)	12590
GVARDIYA (Ru)	03770	'LESKOV' class (Ru)	12590
LENINSKAYA		LESNOYE (Ru)	33198
GVARDIYA (Ru)	04010	LESOGORSK (Ru)	12380
LENINSKAYA ISKRA (Ru)	93820	LESOZAVODSK (Ru)	13010
LENINSKAYA SMENA (Ru)	79340	LEV TITOV (Ru)	93268

LEV TOLSTOY (Ru)	20353	LOTRU (Rm)	80000
LEWANT II (Pd)	31770	LOTSMAN (Ru)	21947
LEWANTER (Pd)	10260	LOVECH (Bu)	82110
LEWANTER (Pd)	10760	LOVOZYERO (Ru)	11720
LIBRA (Pd)	11700	LOVOZYERO (Ru)	34610
LICHTENHAGEN (DDR)	62701	LUBEN KARAVELOV (Bu)	48430
LIDA DEMESH (Ru)	67010	LUBEN KARAVELOV (Bu)	49470
LIDER (Ru)	23305	LUBEN KARAVELOV (Bu)	49740
LIEBENWALDE (DDR)	46370	LUBLIN II (Pd)	48407
LIEBENWALDE (DDR)	47070	LUBNY (Ru)	60660
LIELUPE (Ru)	63640	LUBNY (Ru)	62570
LIEPAYA (Ru)	44620	LUBOMIR (Pd)	52466
LIESELOTTE		LUCHEGORSK (Ru)	23480
HERRMANN (DDR)	06380	'LUCHEGORSK' class (Ru)	23480
LIESELOTTE		LUCJAN SZENWALD (Pd)	06090
HERRMANN (DDR)	15410	LUCJAN SZENWALD (Pd)	14800
LIGOVO (Ru)	07550	LUCKENWALDE (DDR)	46370
LIKENAY (Ru)	17637	LUCKENWALDE (DDR)	47070
LIKENAY (Ru)	33198	LUDOGORETZ (Bu)	49160
LIKODYN (Ru)	18740	LUDWIG RENN (DDR)	13751
LIKOMUR (Pd)	18740	LUDWIG TUREK (DDR)	13650
LIKOSAR (Pd)	18740	LUGOJ (Ru)	47540
LIKOWAL (Pd)	18740	LUKHOVITSY (Ru)	60660
LILIANA DIMITROVA (Bu)	48150	LUKHOVITSY (Ru)	62570
LIMAN (Ru)	01733	LUKOMORYE (Ru)	66380
LIMAN (Ru)	11800	LUKSTAS (Ru)	33198
LIMB (Ru)	13751	LUNJ (Ru)	11580
LIMENDA (Ru)	17950	LUNOKHOD 1 (Ru)	23480
LIMOZA (Ru)	11800	LUPENI (Rm)	78580
LINARD LAYTSEN (Ru)	12380	LUTJAN (Pd)	18740
LINKUVA (Ru)	66380	LUTTENKLEIN (DDR)	91224
LIPETSK (Ru)	67670	'LUZA' class (Ru)	36235
LIPNO (Cz)	59230	LUZYTANKA (Pd)	18740
LIPSK N/BIEBRZA (Pd)	58730	LVOV (Ru)	11800
LITVA (Ru)	02160	LYONYA GOLIKOV (Ru)	07610
LIVADIYA (Ru)	12230	LYONYA GOLYKOV (Ru)	15510
LIVEZINI (Rm)	77080	LYRA (Pd)	11700
LIVEZINI (Rm)	80000	LYUBAN (Ru)	06770
LIZA CHAYKINA (Ru)	60373	LYUBAN (Ru)	07550
LOBAN (Ru)	22327	LYUBERTSY (Ru)	36890
LODOWIK (Pd)	18740	LYUBERTSY (Ru)	43790
LOFOTEN (DDR)	18720	LYUBLINO (Ru)	60660
LOKATOR (Ru)	09360	LYUBLINO (Ru)	62570
LOKBATAN (Ru)	40660	LYUBOTIN (Ru)	57630
LOMONOSOVO (Ru)	07550	LYUBOTIN (Ru)	60670
LOMZA (Pd)	50460	LYUBOTIN (Ru)	80920
LORNA (Bu)	11800	LYUBOTIN (Ru)	84810
LOTRU (Rm)	77080	LYUBOV ORLOVA (Ru)	02340

LYUBOV SHEVTSOVA (Ru)	60373		
LYUDINOVO (Ru)	57630		
LYUDINOVO (Ru)	84810		
LYUDMILA			
PAVLICHENKO (Ru)	13650		
LYUDMILA STAL (Ru)	03770		
LYUDMILA STAL (Ru)	04010		
LYULIN (Ru)	77980		
LYUTOGA (Ru)	08834		
M URITSKIY (Ru)	02120		
MACIEJ RATAJ (Pd)	72115		
MAGADAN (Ru)	34405		
MAGADAN (Ru)	90150		
MAGDEBURG (DDR)	03870		
MAGDEBURG (DDR)	04423		
MAGNIT (Ru)	09360		
MAGNITOGORSK (Ru)	71530		
MAGNITOGORSK (Ru)	80200		
MAGNUS POSER (DDR)	23410		
MAGO (Ru)	39290		
MAGO (Ru)	67350		
MAGO (Ru)	71360		
MAGURA (Rm)	13751		
MAJOR HUBAL (Pd)	72115		
MAJOR SUCHARSKI (Pd)	07440		
MAJOR SUCHARSKI (Pd)	15310		
MAKAR MAZAY (Ru)	78891		
MAKAYEVKA (Ru)	26210		
MAKELIS BUKA (Ru)	07470		
MAKELIS BUKA (Ru)	11800		
MAKHACHKALA (Ru)	70572		
MAKHTUM-KULI (Ru)	14370		
MAKRURUS (Ru)	22327		
MAKSIM AMMOSOV (Ru)	50730		
MAKSIM GORKIY (Ru)	16810		
MAKSIM			
KHOMYAKOV (Ru)	13751		
MAKSIM LITVINOV (Ru)	03770		
MAKSIM LITVINOV (Ru)	04010		
MAKSIM MIKHAYLOV (Ru)	77340		
MAKSIM RYLSKIY (Ru)	50763		
MALAKHIT (Ru)	12380		
MALAKHITOVYY (Ru)	33305		
MALANGEN (DDR)	18720		
MALAYA VISHERA (Ru)	31890		
MALAYA ZEMLYA (Ru)	13650		
MALBORK II (Pd)	75412		

256

Name	No.
MALCHIN (DDR)	83600
MALDIS SKREYA (Ru)	67010
MALKI (Ru)	23480
MALOYAROSLAVETS (Ru)	31890
MALYOVITZA (Bu)	48383
MALYY TAYMYR (Ru)	22173
MAMAIA (Rm)	13850
MAMAYEV KURGAN (Ru)	13650
MAMIN SIBIRYAK (Ru)	12380
MAMIN SIBIRYAK (Ru)	12590
MAMIN SIBIRYAK (Ru)	20790
MAMRY (Pd)	33193
MANGALI (Ru)	33305
MANGAZEYA (Ru)	33305
MANGYSHLAK (Ru)	23860
MANGYSHLAK (Ru)	44100
MANGYSHLAK (Ru)	53160
MANIFEST PKWN (Pd)	73374
MANILAID (Ru)	75640
MANTA (Pd)	23474
MANYCH (Ru)	15460
MANYCH (Ru)	45590
MARAMURES (Rm)	78580
MARASESTI (Rm)	61020
MARASTI (Rm)	61020
MARAT KOZEY (Ru)	15510
MARAT KOZLOV (Ru)	67010
MARDAKYANY (Ru)	44100
MAREA NEAGRA (Rm)	10535
MARGELAN (Ru)	07900
MARIAN BUCZEK (Pd)	07440
MARIAN BUCZEK (Pd)	15310
MARIAN (Pd)	33015
MARIINSK (Ru)	07900
MARINA RASKOVA (Ru)	10720
MARITZA (Bu)	59890
MARITZA (Bu)	67650
MARIYA POLIVANOVA (Ru)	04520
MARIYA SAVINA (Ru)	02340
MARIYA ULYANOVA (Ru)	02120
MARIYA ULYANOVA (Ru)	93380
MARIYA YERMOLOVA (Ru)	02340
MARJAN (Ru)	78060
MARK RESHETNIKOV (Ru)	12380
MARLIN (Pd)	23474
MARLOW (DDR)	50440
MARLOW (DDR)	52000
MARNEULI (Ru)	07900
MARS (Ru)	01733
MARS (Ru)	17634
MARS-2 (Ru)	23480
MARSHAL BAGRAMYAN (Ru)	63975
MARSHAL BIRYUZOV (Ru)	60620
MARSHAL BIRYUZOV (Ru)	62580
MARSHAL BUDYONNYY (Ru)	68250
MARSHAL BUDYONNYY (Ru)	68800
MARSHAL CHUYKOV (Ru)	63975
MARSHAL GELOVANI (Ru)	23860
MARSHAL GELOVANI (Ru)	51410
MARSHAL GOVOROV (Ru)	68805
MARSHAL GRECHKO (Ru)	68805
MARSHAL KONYEV (Ru)	68250
MARSHAL KONYEV (Ru)	68800
MARSHAL KOSHEVOY (Ru)	11333
MARSHAL KRYLOV (Ru)	11333
MARSHAL MALINOVSKIY (Ru)	91224
MARSHAL MERETSKOV (Ru)	93820
MARSHAL NIVOKOV (Ru)	11333
MARSHAL ROKOSSOVSKIY (Ru)	68250
MARSHAL ROKOSSOVSKIY (Ru)	68800
MARSHAL ROKOSSOVSKIY (Ru)	91224
MARSHAL SOKOLOVSKIY (Ru)	93820
MARSHAL VASILYEVSKIY (Ru)	11333
MARSHAL VASILYEVSKIY (Ru)	63975
MARSHAL VOROBYEV (Ru)	79340
MARSHAL YAKUBOVSKIY (Ru)	00140
MARSHAL ZAKHAROV (Ru)	68685
MARSHAL ZHUKOV (Ru)	68250
MARSHAL ZHUKOV (Ru)	68800
MART SAAR (Ru)	12380
MARTIN ANDERSEN NEXO (DDR)	17990
MARTIN ARENDSEE (Ru)	28600
MARTYN LATSIS (Ru)	79340
MASHITAGI (Ru)	44100
MASHUK (Ru)	22160
MASLAW (Pd)	33015
MASSANDRA (Ru)	89200
MATE ZALKA (Ru)	70590
MATEMATIK (Ru)	23480
MATHIAS THESEN (DDR)	06380
MATHIAS THESEN (DDR)	15410
MATHIAS THESEN (Ru)	62701
MATIS PLUDON (Ru)	12380
MATOCHKIN SHAR (Ru)	93870
MATROSOV (Ru)	17500
MATROSOVO (Ru)	33198
MATSESTA (Ru)	07900
MATVEY MURANOV (Ru)	03770
MATVEY MURANOV (Ru)	04010
MAXHUTTE (DDR)	77105
'MAYAK' class (Ru)	23605
'MAYAKOVSKIY' class (Ru)	12360
'MAYAKOVSKIY' class (modified) (Ru)	12380
MAYKOP (Ru)	70572
MAYORI (Ru)	63640
MAZURY (Pd)	59690
MAZURY (Pd)	81350
MB 15 (Ru)	22150
MB 18 (Ru)	22150
MB-32 (Ru)	23665
MB-35 (Ru)	23665
MB-36 (Ru)	23665
MB-38 (Ru)	23665
MB-61 (Ru)	23665
MB-62 (Ru)	23665
MB-64 (Ru)	23665
MB 105 (Ru)	22150
MB-108 (Ru)	23665
MB 119 (Ru)	22150
MECHISLOVAS GEDVILAS (Ru)	13751
MEDIAS (Rm)	87640
MEDIK (Ru)	23480
MEDVEZHYEGORSK (Ru)	26210
MEDYN (Ru)	07900
MEGANOM (Ru)	11800
MEGANOM (Ru)	47150
MEHEDINTI (Ru)	47540
MEISSEN (DDR)	70695
MEKHANIK BARDETSKIY (Ru)	56639
MEKHANIK DREN (Ru)	48860
MEKHANIK FEDOROV (Ru)	80090
MEKHANIK GERASIMOV (Ru)	80090
MEKHANIK GORDYENKO (Ru)	54710
MEKHANIK KALUSHNIKOV (Ru)	20790
MEKHANIK KONOVALOV (Ru)	80090
MEKHANIK KRULL (Ru)	75312
MEKHANIK KULUBIN (Ru)	20790
MEKHANIK P KILIMENCHUK (Ru)	48150
MEKHANIK P KILIMENCHUK (Ru)	78980
MEKHANIK RYBASHUK (Ru)	24030
MEKHANIK YEVGRAFOV (Ru)	80090
MELANITA (Bu)	11800
MELITOPOL (Ru)	11800
MELITOPOL (Ru)	88230
MENEZELINSK (Ru)	26210
MENKAR (Ru)	23305
MERIDIAN (Ru)	33015
MERKURY (Bu)	33015
MERKURY (Pd)	11640
MESHADI AZIZBEKOV (Ru)	58995
MESKUPAS ADOMAS (Ru)	12380
MESTA (Bu)	54870
MESTA (Bu)	68560
METAN (Ru)	89460
METELIS (Ru)	33198
METEORIT (Ru)	11800
METEOROLOG (Ru)	23480
MEYENBURG (DDR)	03870
MEYENBURG (DDR)	04423
MEZEN (Ru)	17950
MEZHDURECHENSK (Ru)	07900
MEZHGORYE (Ru)	07900
MEZOSFERA (Ru)	13650
MICHURIN (Ru)	07900
MIECZYSLAW KALINOWSKI (Pd)	14480
MIECZYSLAW (Pd)	33015
MIEDWIE (Pd)	33193
MIELEC (Pd)	75412
MIELNO (Pd)	33193
MIESZKO 1 (Pd)	14910
MIESZKO 1 (Pd)	15720
MIKAIL MUSHFIK (Ru)	50730
MIKHA TSKHAKAYA (Ru)	59220
MIKHA TSKHAKAYA (Ru)	74540
MIKHAIL BARSUKOV (Ru)	23480
MIKHAIL BORISOV (Ru)	11800
MIKHAIL BORONIN (Ru)	34872
MIKHAIL CHEREMNYKH (Ru)	76580
MIKHAIL CHEREMNYKH (Ru)	79930
MIKHAIL ISAKOVSKIY (Ru)	50763
MIKHAIL IVCHENKO (Ru)	11580
MIKHAIL KALININ (Ru)	02160
MIKHAIL KORNITSKIY (Ru)	11800
MIKHAIL KRIVOSHLIKOV (Ru)	79340
MIKHAIL KUTUZOV (Ru)	17500
MIKHAIL KUTUZOV (Ru)	80171
MIKHAIL KVASHNIKOV (Ru)	34872
MIKHAIL LARIN (Ru)	22327
MIKHAIL LOMONOSOV (Ru)	10740
MIKHAIL LOMONOSOV (Ru)	18090
MIKHAIL LUKONIN (Ru)	50763
MIKHAIL MIRCHINK (Ru)	92880
MIKHAIL OLMINSKIY (Ru)	03770
MIKHAIL OLMINSKIY (Ru)	04010
MIKHAIL ORLOV (Ru)	13650
MIKHAIL PRISHVIN (Ru)	77060
MIKHAIL SHOLOKHOV (Ru)	20353
MIKHAIL SOMOV (Ru)	21610
MIKHAIL STELMAKH (Ru)	46560
MIKHAIL STENKO (Ru)	69310
MIKHAIL SUSLOV (Ru)	20353
MIKHAIL SVETLOV (Ru)	77060

Name	Code
MIKHAIL TUKACHEVSKIY (Ru)	93680
MIKHAIL VERBITSKIY (Ru)	34872
MIKHAIL VIDOV (Ru)	11800
MIKHAIL VLADIMIRSKY (Ru)	03770
MIKHAIL VLADIMIRSKY (Ru)	04010
MIKHAIL YANKO (Ru)	85320
MIKHAYLO LOMONOSOV (Ru)	84360
MIKOLA BAZHAN (Ru)	51672
MIKOLAJ KOPERNIK (Pd)	15040
MIKOLAJ REJ (Pd)	04860
MIKOLOYUS CHYURLYONIS (Ru)	12380
MIKULA (Ru)	22173
MILCOV (Rm)	11800
MILIN KAMAK (Bu)	77080
MILIN KAMAK (Bu)	80000
MILLEROVO (Ru)	07900
MILOGRADOVO (Ru)	11800
MILTZOW (DDR)	50440
MILTZOW (DDR)	52000
MINDRA (Rm)	11670
MINIYA (Ru)	33198
MINSK (Ru)	07900
MINUSINSK (Ru)	66380
MIR (Cz)	06069
MIR (Ru)	12590
MIRASLAU (Rm)	60978
'MIRNY' class (Ru)	21947
MIRNYY (Ru)	07550
MIRONYCH (Ru)	24030
MIROSLAWIEC (Pd)	70540
MIROW (DDR)	50440
MIROW (DDR)	52000
MIRZO TURSUN-ZADE (Ru)	60373
MISA (Ru)	13751
MISHUKOV (Ru)	26210
MITRIDAT (Ru)	11800
MITROFAN GREKOV (Ru)	76580
MITROFAN GREKOV (Ru)	79930
MITROFAN SEDIN (Ru)	60620
MITROFAN SEDIN (Ru)	62580
MITTENWALDE (DDR)	46370
MITTENWALDE (DDR)	47070
MITUVA (Ru)	33198
MIZAR (Ru)	12230
MIZIL (Ru)	47540
MLAWA (Pd)	50460
MLECHNYY PUT (Ru)	13751
MODUL (Ru)	95042
MOGILEV (Ru)	25550
MOINESTI (Ru)	47540
MOKHNI (Ru)	89250
MOLDAVIA (Ru)	02350
MOLDAVIA (Ru)	35370
MOLDAVIYA (Ru)	06825
MOLDOVA (Rm)	88250
MOLDOVEANU (Rm)	11700
MOLDOVITA (Ru)	47540
MOLOCHANSK (Ru)	07900
MOLODAYA GVARDIYA (Ru)	91224
MOLODOGVARDEYSK (Ru)	07900
MOLODYOZNYY (Ru)	85320
'MOMA' class (modified) (Ru)	33035
'MOMA' class (Ru)	01733
MONCHEGORSK (Ru)	02724
MONGOL (Ru)	85320
MONGOLIYA (Ru)	12380
MORAG (Pd)	33193
MOREKHOD (Ru)	17920
MOREKHOD (Ru)	85320
MOREPLAVATEL (Ru)	23305
MORIS BISHOP (Ru)	52612/1
MORS (Pd)	23440
MORSHANSK (Ru)	07900
MORSKIE OKO (Pd)	33193
MORSKOY GEOFIZIK (Ru)	93268
MORSKOY GEOLOG (Ru)	11333
'MORSKOY 1' class (Ru)	50275
MORZHOVETS (Ru)	01733
MORZHOVETS (Ru)	11380
MOS SHOVGENOV (Ru)	60620
MOS SHOVGENOV (Ru)	62580
MOSHCHNYY (Ru)	22173
MOSKALVO (Ru)	39970
MOSKOVSKAYA OLIMPIADA (Ru)	11333
MOSKOVSKIY FESTIVAL (Ru)	51410
MOSKOVSKIY KOMSOMOLETS (Ru)	01380
MOSKOVSKIY KOMSOMOLETS (Ru)	01640
MOSKVA (Ru)	02070
MOSSOVET (Ru)	53535
MOTOVSKIY ZALIV (Ru)	62671
MOTOVSKIY ZALIV (Ru)	82651
MOTRU (Rm)	77080
MOTRU (Rm)	80000
MOZDOK (Ru)	26210
MOZHAYSK (Ru)	07900
MOZYR (Ru)	07900
MOZYR (Ru)	36250
MOZYR (Ru)	42800
MRAMOR (Ru)	12380
MRAMORNY (Ru)	11800
MRTR-0407 (Ru)	33017
MRTR-0408 (Ru)	33017
MSCIWOJ (Pd)	33015
MTSENSK (Ru)	07900
MTSKHETSA (Ru)	12230
MUDYUG (Ru)	15459
MUGGELSEE (DDR)	46370
MUGGELSEE (DDR)	47070
MUHLHAUSEN THOMAS-MUNTZERSTADT (DDR)	03690
MUKACHEVO (Ru)	07900
MUKHTAR ASHRAFI (Ru)	79340
MUKHTAR AUEZOV (Ru)	50763
MUKRAN (DDR)	31185
'MUNA' class (Ru)	52605
MUNTENIA (Rm)	55780
MUNTENIA (Rm)	56480
MUOSTAKH (Ru)	49240
MURAN (Pd)	52466
MURES (Rm)	11800
MURGAB (Ru)	50770
MURGASH (Bu)	49160
MURMAN (Ru)	15460
MURMANRYBA (Ru)	22173
MURMANSELD (Ru)	11720
MURMANSELD (Ru)	34610
MURMANSK (Ru)	02070
MURMANSK (Ru)	12340
MURMASH (Ru)	22840
MURMASHI (Ru)	34470
MUROM (Ru)	07900
MUROMETS (Ru)	33015
MUROMSK (Ru)	11580
MUSA DZHALIL (Ru)	14370
MUSALA (Bu)	55410
MUSALA (Bu)	78850
MUSCEL (Rm)	82220
MUSSON (Ru)	02270
MUSSON (Ru)	18270
MUSTEL (Pd)	23474
MUSTYARV (Ru)	13650
MYS ARKTICHESKIY (Ru)	11720
MYS ARKTICHESKIY (Ru)	34610
MYS BABUSHKIN (Ru)	11720
MYS BABUSKIN (Ru)	34610
MYS BARANOVA (Ru)	23480
MYS BELKINA (Ru)	23480
MYS BOBROVA (Ru)	23480
MYS BUDYONNOGO (Ru)	11720
MYS BUDYONNOGO (Ru)	34610
MYS CHAKO (Ru)	13650
MYS CHASOVOY (Ru)	11720
MYS CHASOVOY (Ru)	34610
MYS CHAYKOVSKOGO (Ru)	11720
MYS CHAYKOVSKOGO (Ru)	34610
MYS CHELYUSKIN (Ru)	11720
MYS CHELYUSKIN (Ru)	34610
MYS DALNIY (Ru)	11720
MYS DALNIY (Ru)	34610
MYS FRUNZE (Ru)	11720
MYS FRUNZE (Ru)	34610
MYS GAMOVA (Ru)	23480
MYS GRINA (Ru)	23480
MYS GROTOVYY (Ru)	11720
MYS GROTOVYY (Ru)	34610
MYS GROZNYY (Ru)	11720
MYS GROZNYY (Ru)	34610
MYS ILMOVYY (Ru)	11720
MYS ILMOVYY (Ru)	34610
MYS KHRUSTALNYY (Ru)	66380
MYS KODOSH (Ru)	66380
MYS KRONOTSKIY (Ru)	11720
MYS KRONOTSKIY (Ru)	34610
MYS KRYLOVA (Ru)	23480
MYS KURILSKIY (Ru)	11720
MYS KURILSKIY (Ru)	34610
MYS KUZNETSOVA (Ru)	11720
MYS KUZNETSOVA (Ru)	34610
MYS LAZARYEVA (Ru)	23480
MYS LOPATKA (Ru)	11720
MYS LOPATKA (Ru)	34610
MYS MALTSYEVA (Ru)	23480
MYS NADEZHDY (Ru)	23480
MYS OBRUCHYEVA (Ru)	23480
MYS OREKHOVA (Ru)	23480
MYS OSIPOVA (Ru)	23480
MYS OSTROVSKOGO (Ru)	11720
MYS OSTROVSKOGO (Ru)	34610
MYS OTRADNYY (Ru)	11720
MYS OTRADNYY (Ru)	34610
MYS PAVLOVSKIY (Ru)	66380
MYS PROKOFYEVA (Ru)	11720
MYS PROKOFYEVA (Ru)	34610
MYS RATMANOVA (Ru)	11720
MYS RATMANOVA (Ru)	34610
MYS SARYCH (Ru)	66380
MYS SHELIKHOVA (Ru)	23480
MYS SILINA (Ru)	11720
MYS SILINA (Ru)	34610
MYS SINYAVINA (Ru)	23480
MYS SKALISTYY (Ru)	11720
MYS SKALISTYY (Ru)	34610
MYS SVOBODNYY (Ru)	11720
MYS SVOBODNYY (Ru)	34610
MYS TAYMYR (Ru)	11720
MYS TAYMYR (Ru)	34610
MYS TIKHIY (Ru)	11720
MYS TIKHIY (Ru)	34610
MYS VAYGACH (Ru)	11720
MYS VAYGACH (Ru)	34610
MYS VODOPADNYY (Ru)	11720
MYS VODOPADNYY (Ru)	34610
MYS VORONINA (Ru)	11720
MYS VORONINA (Ru)	34610
MYS YEGOROVA (Ru)	23480
MYS YELAGINA (Ru)	23480
MYS YERMAK (Ru)	23480
MYS YUDINA (Ru)	23480
MYS YUNONY (Ru)	11720
MYS YUNONY (Ru)	34610
MYS ZOLOTOY (Ru)	11333
MYTISHCHI (Ru)	07900
N. GASTELLO (Ru)	17500
NADE RIBAKOVAYTE (Ru)	67010
NADEZHDA KRUPSKAYA (Ru)	03690

NADEZHDA
  KURCHYENKO (Ru) 85970
NADEZHDA
  OBUKHOVA (Ru) 77340
NADEZHDA (Ru) 11800
NADEZHDINSK (Ru) 12380
NADEZHNYY (Ru) 33076
NADYM (Ru) 70020
NAGAYEVKO (Ru) 52304
NAGAYEVO (Ru) 52616
NAGORSK (Ru) 26210
NAKHICHEVAN (Ru) 44100
NAKHICHEVAN (Ru) 93820
NAKHODKA (Ru) 12380
NAKHODKA (Ru) 60680
NAKHODKA (Ru) 90720
NALCHIK (Ru) 86070
NALECZOW (Pd) 74140
NAMANGAN (Ru) 22840
NAMANGAN (Ru) 34470
NAMANGAN (Ru) 85320
NANAYETS (Ru) 85320
NAPORISTYY (Ru) 22173
NAROCH (Ru) 11720
NAROCH (Ru) 34610
NARODNYY
  OPOLCHENETS (Ru) 13751
NARVAL (Ru) 16205
NARVSKAYA
  ZASTAVA (Ru) 11610
NARVSKAYA
  ZASTAVA (Ru) 50280
NARVSKIY ZALIV (Ru) 61100
NARWAL (Pd) 10810
NARWIK II (Pd) 70540
NARYAN—MAR (Ru) 24030
NARYMNEFT (Ru) 85970
NARYN (Ru) 86070
NASAUD (Rm) 01380
NASAUD (Rm) 01640
NASIMI (Ru) 79340
NASTOROZHENNYY (Ru) 22173
NATA VACHNADZE (Ru) 52612/1
NATALIYA
  KOVSHOVA (Ru) 04520
NAUKA (Ru) 12230
NAUMBURG (DDR) 03870
NAUMBURG (DDR) 04423

NAVARIN (Ru) 21610
NAVASHINO (Ru) 50770
NAVIGATOR (Pd) 08565
NAVIGATOR (Ru) 09360
NAYADA (Ru) 11800
NAYSSAAR (Ru) 23305
NAZARCEA (Rm) 83680
NAZIM KHIKMET (Ru) 14370
NEAJLOV (Rm) 11800
NEFTEGAZ-1 (Ru) 14962
NEFTEGAZ-2 (Ru) 14962
NEFTEGAZ-3 (Ru) 14962
NEFTEGAZ-5 (Ru) 14962
NEFTEGAZ-6 (Ru) 14962
NEFTEGAZ-7 (Ru) 14962
NEFTEGAZ-8 (Ru) 14962
NEFTEGAZ-9 (Ru) 14962
NEFTEGAZ-10 (Ru) 14962
NEFTEGAZ-11 (Ru) 14962
NEFTEGAZ-12 (Ru) 14962
NEFTEGAZ-13 (Ru) 14962
NEFTEGAZ-14 (Ru) 14962
NEFTEGAZ-15 (Ru) 14962
NEFTEGAZ-16 (Ru) 14962
NEFTEGAZ-17 (Ru) 14962
NEFTEGAZ-18 (Ru) 14962
NEFTEGAZ-19 (Ru) 14962
NEFTEGAZ-20 (Ru) 14962
NEFTEGAZ-21 (Ru) 14962
NEFTEGAZ-22 (Ru) 14962
NEFTEGAZ-23 (Ru) 14962
NEFTEGAZ-24 (Ru) 14962
NEFTEGAZ-25 (Ru) 14962
NEFTEGAZ-26 (Ru) 14962
NEFTEGAZ-27 (Ru) 14962
NEFTEGAZ-28 (Ru) 14962
NEFTEGAZ-29 (Ru) 14962
NEFTEGAZ-30 (Ru) 14962
NEFTEGAZ-31 (Ru) 14962
NEFTEGAZ-32 (Ru) 14962
NEFTEGAZ-51 (Ru) 14983
NEFTEGAZ-52 (Ru) 14983
NEFTEGAZ-53 (Ru) 14983
NEFTEGORSK (Ru) 70760
NEFTEGORSK (Ru) 85970
NEFTEKAMSK (Ru) 70760
'NEFTERUDOVOZ'
  type (Ru) 79450

NEGOIU (Rm) 11700
NEMAN (Ru) 21580
NEMAN (Ru) 22173
NEMUNELIS (Ru) 22327
NEOTRAZIMYY (Ru) 22173
NEPRYADVA (Ru) 92160
NEPTUN (Pd) 12610
NEPTUN (Rm) 07860
NEPTUN (Ru) 12570
NEPTUN (Ru) 33015
NEPTUNIA (Pd) 22173
NERCHA (Ru) 08846
NERCHINSK (Ru) 85970
NEREIDA (Ru) 16205
NERIS (Ru) 22327
NERITSA (Ru) 16205
NEUBOKOW (DDR) 50440
NEUBOKOW (DDR) 52000
NEUBRANDENBURG (DDR) 03870
NEUBRANDENBURG (DDR) 04423
NEUHAUSEN (DDR) 59650
NEUSTADT (DDR) 50128
NEVA (Ru) 87000
NEVALES (Ru) 11490
NEVEL (Ru) 11380
NEVELSKIY (Ru) 85320
NEVELSKOY (Ru) 22195
NEVER (Ru) 15460
NEVER (Ru) 16205
NEVEZHIS (Ru) 35310
NEVKA (Ru) 35310
NEVSKAYA
  DUBROVSKA (Ru) 13751
NEVYANSK (Ru) 11720
NEVYANSK (Ru) 34610
NICOLA VAPTZAROV (Bu) 07860
NICORESTI (Ru) 47540
NIDA (Ru) 23480
NIENBURG (DDR) 03870
NIENBURG (DDR) 04423
NIENHAGEN (DDR) 75320
NIEWIADOW (Pd) 58730
NIKEL (Ru) 02724
NIKIFOR PAVLOV (Ru) 13650
NIKIFOR ROGOV (Ru) 53160
NIKITA MITCHENKO (Ru) 48430
NIKITA MITCHENKO (Ru) 49470
NIKITA MITCHENKO (Ru) 49740

NIKITOVKA (Ru) 78891
NIKO NIKOLADZE (Ru) 59220
NIKO NIKOLADZE (Ru) 74540
NIKOLAY AFANASYEV (Ru) 13751
NIKOLAY ANANYEV (Ru) 48430
NIKOLAY ANANYEV (Ru) 49470
NIKOLAY ANANYEV (Ru) 49740
NIKOLAY BAUMAN (Ru) 79340
NIKOLAY BAUMAN (Ru) 89250
NIKOLAY BERAZIN (Ru) 13650
NIKOLAY BOSHNYAK (Ru) 17920
NIKOLAY BROVTSYEV (Ru) 11800
NIKOLAY
  BURDYENKO (Ru) 34240
NIKOLAY
  CHERKASOV (Ru) 80260
NIKOLAY DANILOV (Ru) 93870
NIKOLAY
  DUBROLYUBOV (Ru) 14370
NIKOLAY
  EMELYANOV (Ru) 50280
NIKOLAY GOGOL (Ru) 14370
NIKOLAY
  GOLOVANOV (Ru) 77340
NIKOLAY GRIBANOV (Ru) 13751
NIKOLAY ISAYENKO (Ru) 43300
NIKOLAY KAPLUNOV (Ru) 22290
NIKOLAY KARAMZIM (Ru) 14370
NIKOLAY KASATKIN (Ru) 76580
NIKOLAY KASATKIN (Ru) 79930
NIKOLAY
  KOLOMEYTSYEV (Ru) 02417
NIKOLAY KONONOV (Ru) 11580
NIKOLAY KOPERNIK (Ru) 10740
NIKOLAY
  KREMLYANSKIY (Ru) 05620
NIKOLAY
  KREMLYANSKIY (Ru) 14450
NIKOLAY
  KRIVORUCHKO (Ru) 79340
NIKOLAY KRYLENKO (Ru) 03060
NIKOLAY KRYLENKO (Ru) 03650
NIKOLAY
  KUROPATKIN (Ru) 34872
NIKOLAY
  KUZNETSOV (Ru) 51672
NIKOLAY
  KUZNETSOV (Ru) 79340

NIKOLAY LEBEDYEV (Ru) 79340
NIKOLAY MAKSIMOV (Ru) 48430
NIKOLAY MAKSIMOV (Ru) 49470
NIKOLAY MAKSIMOV (Ru) 49740
NIKOLAY MARKIN (Ru) 00280
NIKOLAY
  MATUSEVICH (Ru) 23860
NIKOLAY MIRONOV (Ru) 24030
NIKOLAY MOROZOV (Ru) 69310
NIKOLAY NEKRASOV (Ru) 07900
NIKOLAY NOVIKOV (Ru) 54710
NIKOLAY OGARYEV (Ru) 14370
NIKOLAY
  OSTROVSKIY (Ru) 12380
NIKOLAY
  OSTROVSKIY (Ru) 28980
NIKOLAY PAPIVIN (Ru) 23480
NIKOLAY PIROGOV (Ru) 34240
NIKOLAY PODVOSKIY (Ru) 60620
NIKOLAY
  PODVOYSKIY (Ru) 62580
NIKOLAY POGODIN (Ru) 03060
NIKOLAY POGODIN (Ru) 03650
NIKOLAY
  PRZHEVALSKIY (Ru) 78060
NIKOLAY
  PUSTOVOYTENKO (Ru) 13751
NIKOLAY SEMASHKA (Ru) 03770
NIKOLAY SEMASHKO (Ru) 04010
NIKOLAY
  SHCHETININ (Ru) 49240
NIKOLAY SHCHORS (Ru) 33910
NIKOLAY SHCHUKIN (Ru) 69310
NIKOLAY SHVERNIK (Ru) 03770
NIKOLAY SHVERNIK (Ru) 04010
NIKOLAY SIPYAGIN (Ru) 59890
NIKOLAY SIPYAGIN (Ru) 67650
NIKOLAY TIKHONOV (Ru) 80100
NIKOLAY TSYGANOV (Ru) 13650
NIKOLAY VARLAMOV (Ru) 34872
NIKOLAY VILKOV (Ru) 78060
NIKOLAY
  VOZNESENSKIY (Ru) 78730
NIKOLAY
  VOZNESENSKIY (Ru) 89980
NIKOLAY YANSON (Ru) 78060
NIKOLAY
  YAROSHENKO (Ru) 76580

Name	No.	Name	No.	Name	No.	Name	No.	Name	No.
NIKOLAY YAROSHENKO (Ru)	79930	NOVACI (Rm)	83680	NOVOORSK (Ru)	13751	OBRUCHEV (Ru)	17637	OKTYABRSKAYA (Ru)	45350
NIKOLAY YEVGENOV (Ru)	02417	NOVASBEST (Ru)	13751	NOVOPOLOTSK (Ru)	02690	OBSHA (Ru)	28600	OKTYABRSKOYE (Ru)	11800
NIKOLAY ZAKORKIN (Ru)	34872	NOVAYA ERA (Ru)	12380	NOVOPOLOTSK (Ru)	03110	OBUKHOVO (Ru)	28600	OKULOVKA (Ru)	28600
NIKOLAY ZAZOLOTSKIY (Ru)	50730	NOVAYA KAKHOVKA (Ru)	81000	NOVOPSKOV (Ru)	13751	OBUKHOVSKAYA OBORONA (Ru)	91224	OLA (Ru)	01540
NIKOLAY ZHUKHOV (Ru)	69310	NOVAYA KAKHOVKA (Ru)	93820	NOVOROSSISKIY PARTIZAN (Ru)	84810	OBVA (Ru)	28600	OLA (Ru)	45630
NIKOLAY ZUBOV (Ru)	22180	NOVAYA LADOGA (Ru)	11430	NOVOROSSIYSK (Ru)	70165	OBZHA (Ru)	39290	OLANESTI (Rm)	47540
NIKOLAY ZYSTSTAR (Ru)	45120	NOVAYA LADOGA (Ru)	93820	NOVOROSSIYSKIY RABOCHIY (Ru)	13751	OCHAKOV (Ru)	28600	OLANGA (Ru)	28600
NIKOLAYEV (Ru)	11800	NOVAYA ZEMLYA (Ru)	11430	NOVORZHEV (Ru)	81000	OCHER (Ru)	28600	OLAYNE (Ru)	28600
NIKOLAYEV (Ru)	14962	NOVGOROD (Ru)	02690	NOVOSHAKHTINSK (Ru)	81000	OCHERETINO (Ru)	28600	OLCHAN (Ru)	28600
NIKOLAYEVSK (Ru)	02120	NOVGOROD (Ru)	03110	NOVOSIBIRSK (Ru)	02690	OCHKAMURI (Ru)	28600	OLEG KOSHEVOY (Ru)	60373
NIKOLAYEVSKIY KOMSOMOLETS (Ru)	23480	NOVIK (Ru)	85970	NOVOSIBIRSK (Ru)	03110	ODESSA (Ru)	16960	OLEKMA (Ru)	39120
NIKOLAYEVSKIY KORABEL (Ru)	11720	NOVIKOV PRIBOY (Ru)	09995	NOVOSOKOLNIKI (Ru)	13751	ODINTSOVO (Ru)	28600	OLEKO DUNDICH (Ru)	60620
NIKOLAYEVSKIY KORABEL (Ru)	34610	NOVOALTAISK (Ru)	02690	NOVOTROITSK (Ru)	02690	ODISHI (Ru)	11333	OLEKO DUNDICH (Ru)	62580
NIKOLOZ BARATASHVILI (Ru)	60620	NOVOALTAISK (Ru)	03110	NOVOTROITSK (Ru)	03110	ODISSEY (Ru)	12585	OLEMA (Ru)	28600
NIKOLOZ BARATASHVILI (Ru)	62580	NOVOANGARSK (Ru)	13751	NOVOUKRAINA (Ru)	13751	ODORHEI (Rm)	47540	OLENEGORSK (Ru)	11580
NIKOLSK (Ru)	12230	NOVOARKHANGELSK (Ru)	13751	NOVOURALSK (Ru)	11333	ODOYEV (Ru)	28600	OLENEGORSK (Ru)	15460
NIKOPOL (Ru)	85970	NOVOAZOVSK (Ru)	26210	NOVOUZENSK (Ru)	26210	OELSA (DDR)	84940	OLENEGORSK (Ru)	45715
NIKYEL (Ru)	11610	NOVOBATAYSK (Ru)	13751	NOVOVOLYNSK (Ru)	02690	OELSA (DDR)	90600	OLENINO (Ru)	28600
NIMFA (Pd)	87740	NOVOBIRYUSINSKIY (Ru)	13751	NOVOVOLYNSK (Ru)	03110	OFELIA (Bu)	23440	OLENSK (Ru)	86170
NINA KUKOVEROVA (Ru)	15510	NOVOBOBRUYSK (Ru)	13751	NOVOVORONEZH (Ru)	15500	OGNEVKA (Ru)	28600	OLENTUY (Ru)	11580
NISHNI TAGIL (Ru)	11430	NOVOCHEBOKSARSK (Ru)	13751	NOVOVYATSK (Ru)	02690	OGNYAN NAYDOV (Ru)	50730	OLENTY (Ru)	28600
NITSA (Ru)	22327	NOVOCHERKASSK (Ru)	67350	NOVOVYATSK (Ru)	03110	OGNYEVO (Ru)	17637	OLESKO (Ru)	28600
NIVA (Ru)	85970	NOVOCHERKASSK (Ru)	71360	NOVOYELNYA (Ru)	13751	OGOSTA (Bu)	04520	OLEVSK (Ru)	28600
NIZAMI (Ru)	50730	NOVODRUTSK (Ru)	13751	NOVOYENISEYSK (Ru)	13751	OGRAJDAN (Bu)	77980	OLGA ANDROVSKAYA (Ru)	01935
NIZHEGORODSKIY KOMSOMOLETS (Ru)	79340	NOVODRUZHESK (Ru)	02690	NOVOZLATOPOL (Ru)	13751	OITUZ (Rm)	61020	OLGA ANDROVSKAYA (Ru)	02340
NIZHNEANGARSK (Ru)	26210	NOVODRUZHESK (Ru)	03110	NOVOZYBKOV (Ru)	03110	OKA (Ru)	11430	OLGA SADOVSKAYA (Ru)	01935
NIZHNEUDINSK (Ru)	15460	NOVOGRUDOK (Ru)	02690	NOVY BUG (Ru)	81000	OKA (Ru)	35310	OLGA ULYANOVA (Ru)	03060
NIZHNEVARTOVSK (Ru)	70020	NOVOGRUDOK (Ru)	03110	NOVY DONBASS (Ru)	81000	OKAH (Ru)	10780	OLGA ULYANOVA (Ru)	03650
NIZHNEYANSK (Ru)	02724	NOVOKACHALINSK (Ru)	13751	NOVYY MIR (Ru)	11720	OKAREM (Ru)	28600	OLGA VARENTSOVA (Ru)	03770
NODAR DUMBADZE (Ru)	51410	NOVOKAZALINSK (Ru)	13751	NOVYY MIR (Ru)	34610	OKEAN (Ru)	01733	OLGA VARENTSOVA (Ru)	04010
NOGINSK (Ru)	85970	NOVOKIYEVKA (Ru)	13751	NOVZYBKOV (Ru)	02690	OKEAN (Ru)	02270	OLGINKA (Ru)	28600
NOKUYEV (Ru)	11300	NOVOKOTORSK (Ru)	13751	NOWY SACZ (Pd)	75770	'OKEAN' class (Ru)	23607	OLGINO (Ru)	17637
NORDHAUSEN (DDR)	03690	NOVOKUIBYSHEVSK (Ru)	02690	NUREK (Ru)	44100	OKHA (Ru)	02724	OLGINO (Ru)	28600
NORDMEER (DDR)	18720	NOVOKUIBYSHEVSK (Ru)	03110	NYURA KIZHEVATOVA (Ru)	67010	OKHA (Ru)	86070	OLIMPIYETS (Ru)	33015
NORDSEE (DDR)	18720	NOVOKUIBYSHEVSK (Ru)	11610			OKHANEFT (Ru)	66380	OLINSK (Ru)	17637
NORDSTERN (DDR)	83600	NOVOKUZNETSK (Ru)	02690	OB (Ru)	13590	OKHOTA (Ru)	28600	OLISHEVKA (Ru)	28600
NORDVIK (Ru)	24030	NOVOKUZNETSK (Ru)	03110	OB (Ru)	35310	OKHOTINO (Ru)	28600	OLKHOVATKA (Ru)	17637
NORILSK (Ru)	02724	NOVOLADOZHSKIY (Ru)	13751	OB (Ru)	39290	OKHOTSK (Ru)	03270	OLKHOVKA (Ru)	28600
NORILSK (Ru)	23880	NOVOLVOVSK (Ru)	02690	OBLUCHE (Ru)	28600	OKHOTSK (Ru)	49720	OLKHOVSKIY (Ru)	17637
NOVA (Ru)	33198	NOVOLVOVSK (Ru)	03110	OBLUKOVINA (Ru)	28600	OKHOTSKOYE MORE (Ru)	55130	OLOMNA (Ru)	28600
		NOVOLYANOVSK (Ru)	13751	OBOLON (Ru)	28600	'OKHTENSKIY' class (Ru)	22139	OLOY (Ru)	28600
		NOVOMALTINSK (Ru)	13751	OBOLYANKA (Ru)	28600	OKLAN (Ru)	17637	OLSHANA (Ru)	28600
		NOVOMIRGOROD (Ru)	02690	OBORISHTE (Bu)	49160	OKNITSA (Ru)	28600	OLSHANY (Ru)	17637
		NOVOMIRGOROD (Ru)	03110	OBRONCY POCZTY (Pd)	59220	OKOLTCHITZA (Bu)	77080	OLTET (Rm)	13751
		NOVOMOSKOVSK (Ru)	02690	OBRONCY POCZTY (Pd)	74540	OKOLTCHITZA (Bu)	80000	OLTUL (Rm)	78580
		NOVOMOSKOVSK (Ru)	03110			OKTANT (Ru)	11800	OLUSHA (Bu)	11800
		NOVONIKOLSK (Ru)	13751			OKTYABRSK (Ru)	85320		
		NOVOORENBURG (Ru)	13751						

260

Name	Ref
OLYKA (Ru)	28600
OLYUTORKA (Ru)	11490
OLYUTORSKIY ZALIV (Ru)	62671
OLYUTORSKIY ZALIV (Ru)	82651
OM (Ru)	08846
OM (Ru)	28600
OMA (Ru)	28600
OMALO (Ru)	28600
OMCHAK (Ru)	28600
OMEGA (Ru)	28600
OMNYA (Ru)	28600
OMOLON (Ru)	06795
OMSK (Ru)	03270
OMSK (Ru)	49720
OMSK (Ru)	70760
OMUL (Ru)	28600
OMULENKA (Ru)	28600
ONDOZERO (Ru)	28600
ONEGA (Ru)	20790
ONEGSKIY (Ru)	89680
ONEKOTAN (Ru)	11580
ONEZHSKIY ZALIV (Ru)	61100
ONUSHKIS (Ru)	28600
OPALA (Ru)	12380
OPALA (Ru)	39290
OPON (Ru)	28600
OPORNYY (Ru)	22327
OPTIMIST (Ru)	23305
OPTUKHA (Ru)	28600
OR (Ru)	28600
ORADEA (Rm)	41310
ORANIENBURG (DDR)	03870
ORANIENBURG (DDR)	04423
ORAVA (Cz)	59230
ORAVITA (Rm)	47540
ORCHIK (Ru)	28600
ORCYN (Pd)	23474
ORDYNSKOYE (Ru)	28600
ORDZHONIKIDZENNEFT (Ru)	44100
OREANDA (Ru)	28600
OREANDRA (Ru)	12230
OREDEZH (Ru)	28600
OREKHOV (Ru)	01540
OREKHOV (Ru)	45630
OREKHOVO—ZUYEVO (Ru)	24030
OREL (Ru)	11800
OREL (Ru)	28600
'OREL' class (Ru)	22135
'OREL' class (modified) (Ru)	22137
'OREL' class (Ru)	22135
ORENBURG (Ru)	03270
ORENBURG (Ru)	49720
OREOL (Ru)	33015
ORFEY (Ru)	13650
ORGEYEV (Ru)	28600
ORICHI (Ru)	28600
ORKA (Pd)	10810
ORKHEVI (Ru)	28600
ORKNEY (DDR)	18720
ORLEN (Pd)	23474
ORLETS (Ru)	11800
ORLIK (Cz)	52927
ORLIK (Ru)	28600
ORLINOYE (Ru)	11800
ORLOVKA (Ru)	28600
ORLVSKIY (Ru)	17637
ORLYONOK (Ru)	28600
OROCHON (Ru)	93820
ORON (Ru)	17637
ORSHA (Ru)	01540
ORSHA (Ru)	45630
ORSK (Ru)	28600
OSAM (Bu)	54870
OSAM (Bu)	68560
OSETIYA (Ru)	32915
OSHA (Ru)	28600
OSIP PYATNITSKIY (Ru)	03770
OSIP PYATNITSKIY (Ru)	04010
OSKAR LUTS (Ru)	12380
'OSKOL III' type (Ru)	45700
OSKOL (Ru)	28600
'OSKOL' class (Ru)	45540
OSKU (Ru)	28600
OSMUSSAAR (Ru)	89200
OSOGOVO (Bu)	77980
OSSOLINEUM (Pd)	73374
OSTER (Ru)	28600
OSTRAGOZHSK (Ru)	45630
OSTROGOZHSK (Ru)	01540
OSTROLEKA (Pd)	03230
OSTROLEKA (Pd)	03620
OSTROMITYANIN (Ru)	17637
OSTROV ATLASOVA (Ru)	71310
OSTROV ATLASOVA (Ru)	82460
OSTROV BERINGA (Ru)	71310
OSTROV BERINGA (Ru)	82460
OSTROV KARAKINSKIY (Ru)	71310
OSTROV KARAKINSKIY (Ru)	82460
OSTROV KOTLIN (Ru)	71310
OSTROV KOTLIN (Ru)	82460
OSTROV LISYANSKOGO (Ru)	71310
OSTROV LISYANSKOGO (Ru)	82460
OSTROV LITKE (Ru)	71310
OSTROV LITKE (Ru)	82460
OSTROV MEDNYY (Ru)	71310
OSTROV MEDNYY (Ru)	82460
OSTROV RUSSKIY (Ru)	71310
OSTROV RUSSKIY (Ru)	82460
OSTROV (Ru)	23664
OSTROV SHMIDTA (Ru)	71310
OSTROV SHMIDTA (Ru)	82460
OSTROV SHOKALSKOGO (Ru)	71310
OSTROV SHOKALSKOGO (Ru)	82460
OSTROV SIBIRYAKOVA (Ru)	71310
OSTROV SIBIRYAKOVA (Ru)	82460
OSTROV USHAKOVA (Ru)	71310
OSTROV USHAKOVA (Ru)	82460
OSUGA (Ru)	28600
OSVALD TULL (Ru)	49810
OSVEYSKOYE (Ru)	28600
OSWIECIM (Pd)	82260
OTEPYA (Ru)	89200
OTOL (Pd)	23474
OTOMAR OSHKALIN (Ru)	10720
OTPOR (Ru)	17637
OTRADNOE (Ru)	01540
OTRADNOE (Ru)	45630
OTROG (Ru)	12380
OTTO GROTEWOHL (Ru)	62701
OTTO RYASTAS (Ru)	23480
OTTO SCHMIDT (Ru)	22240
OVANES TUMANYAN (Ru)	14370
OYAR VATSIETIS (Ru)	52612/1
OYTAL (Ru)	28600
OZANIA (Rm)	13751
OZARICHI (Ru)	28600
OZERNOYE (Ru)	86540
OZERY (Ru)	28600
OZHERELYE (Ru)	28600
OZHOGIMA (Ru)	28600
OZORNOY (Ru)	17637
OZYORNYE KLYUCHI (Ru)	12380
PABLO NERUDA (Ru)	70590
PAGRUS (Ru)	33198
PAHOM PAKHARENKO (Ru)	46547
PAKHACHA (Ru)	12380
PALANA (Ru)	07550
PALANGA (Ru)	02900
PALANGA (Ru)	93820
PALAS (Rm)	83680
PALDISKI (Ru)	86220
PALEKH (Ru)	03690
PALEKH (Ru)	84510
PALICA (Pd)	52466
PALTINIS (Rm)	92437
PAMIR (Ru)	02900
PAMIR (Ru)	11300
PAMIR (Ru)	22160
'PAMIR' class (Ru)	22159
PAMYAT 26 KOMISSAROV (Ru)	44100
PAMYAT LENINA (Ru)	60680
PAMYAT LENINA (Ru)	90720
PAMYAT MERKURIYA (Ru)	04068
PANTELEYMON LEPESHINSKIY (Ru)	03770
PANTELEYMON LEPESHINSKIY (Ru)	04010
PANTELEYMON PONOMARENKO (Ru)	52612/1
PAPIA (Bu)	84210
PARALLAKS (Ru)	11580
PARAMUSHIR (Ru)	02900
PARFENTIY GRECHANYY (Ru)	73290
PARGOLOVO (Ru)	02900
PARING (Rm)	13751
PARIZHSKAYA KOMMUNA (Ru)	01560
PARIZHSKAYA KOMMUNA (Ru)	79340
PARKHOMENKO (Ru)	33910
PARMA (Pd)	23440
PAROMAY (Ru)	02900
PARSLA (Ru)	85320
PARTIZANSKAYA ISKRA (Ru)	45350
PARTIZANSKAYA SLAVA (Ru)	45350
PASCANI (Rm)	92437
PASEWALK (DDR)	61400
PASIONARIYA (Ru)	12380
PASSAT (Ru)	02270
PASSAT (Ru)	18270
PASSAT-2 (Ru)	23480
PASVALIS (Ru)	34880
PATRIOT (Ru)	13751
PATRIOT (Ru)	23305
PATROKL (Ru)	13650
PAUDZHA (Ru)	23480
PAUL ROBESON (Ru)	70590
PAULIS (Rm)	92437
PAVEL ANTOKOLSKIY (Ru)	00967
PAVEL BASHMAKOV (Ru)	04216
PAVEL CHEBOTNYAGIN (Ru)	93680
PAVEL DAUGE (Ru)	03770
PAVEL DAUGE (Ru)	04010
PAVEL DYBENKO (Ru)	60620
PAVEL DYBENKO (Ru)	62580
PAVEL GRABOVSKIY (Ru)	79340
PAVEL KAYKOV (Ru)	34872
PAVEL MOCHALOV (Ru)	79340
PAVEL PANIN (Ru)	34872
PAVEL PARENAGO (Ru)	10740
PAVEL PONOMARYEV (Ru)	21610
PAVEL POSTYSHEV (Ru)	93680
PAVEL RYBIN (Ru)	50670
PAVEL SHTERNBERG (Ru)	10740
PAVEL STRELTSOV (Ru)	34872
PAVEL VAVILOV (Ru)	49342
PAVEL YABLOCHKOV (Ru)	75392
PAVLIK LARISHKIN (Ru)	15510
PAVLIK MOROZOV (Ru)	60373
PAVLIN VINOGRADOV (Ru)	50112
PAVLIN VINOGRADOV (Ru)	91260
PAVLODAR (Ru)	03690
PAVLOGRAD (Ru)	03690
PAVLOVO (Ru)	02900
PAVLOVO (Ru)	09360

Name	No.
PAVLOVSK (Ru)	45350
PAWEL SZWYDKOJ (Pd)	10280
PAYDE (Ru)	15460
PAYURIS (Ru)	33017
PECHENGA (Ru)	02900
PECHENGA (Ru)	12380
PECHENGA (Ru)	25840
PECHENGA (Ru)	56270
PECHENGA (Ru)	62730
PECHORA (Ru)	67010
PECHORALES (Ru)	90560
PECHORSK (Ru)	33305
PEGAS (Ru)	12230
PEGAS (Ru)	23860
PELAGIAL (Ru)	13751
PELENG (Ru)	22159
PELENGATOR (Ru)	09360
PELIKAN (Bu)	12230
PENZHINA (Ru)	21610
PENZHINSKIY ZALIV (Ru)	62671
PENZHINSKIY ZALIV (Ru)	82651
PEREDOVIK (Ru)	11800
PEREKAT (Ru)	12380
PEREKOP (Ru)	45350
PERELIK (Bu)	36390
PEREMYSHLJ (Ru)	09360
PERESLAVL-ZALESSIK (Ru)	15460
PERESVET (Ru)	22220
PERIGEY (Ru)	13650
PERIS (Rm)	92437
PERKUN (Pd)	20880
PERLAMUTR (Ru)	11580
PERM (Ru)	02900
PERMLES (Ru)	45680
PERSEUS (Pd)	11670
PERSEY III (Ru)	12570
PERSEY (Ru)	23860
PERTOMINSK (Ru)	02900
PERUN (Bu)	22173
PERVOMAYSK (Ru)	03690
PERVOMAYSK (Ru)	87000
PERVOURALSK (Ru)	11490
PESTOVO (Ru)	03690
PETAR BARON (Bu)	24630
PETER GORING (DDR)	23410
PETER KAST (DDR)	10250
PETER KAST (DDR)	12630
PETER NELL (DDR)	10250
PETER NELL (DDR)	12630
PETIMATA OT RMS (Bu)	78980
PETKO R. SLAVEJNOV (Bu)	80900
PETOFI (Hu)	45350
PETR ALEKSEYEV (Ru)	60620
PETR ALEKSEYEV (Ru)	62580
PETR DUTOV (Ru)	48430
PETR DUTOV (Ru)	49470
PETR DUTOV (Ru)	49740
PETR GUTCHENKO (Ru)	49240
PETR KAKHOVSKIY (Ru)	89250
PETR KRASIKOV (Ru)	03770
PETR KRASIKOV (Ru)	04010
PETR LEBEDEV (Ru)	17560
PETR LIDOV (Ru)	79340
PETR LIZYUKOV (Ru)	11800
PETR MASHEROV (Ru)	80260
PETR SMIDOVICH (Ru)	54710
PETR STAROSTIN (Ru)	69310
PETR STRELKOV (Ru)	54710
PETR STUCHKA (Ru)	12380
PETR STUCHKA (Ru)	60680
PETR TOMASEVICH (or PYOTR TOMASEVICH) (Ru)	47674
PETR VASEV (Ru)	46550
PETR VELIKIY (Ru)	80171
PETR YEMTSOV (Ru)	48430
PETR YEMTSOV (Ru)	49470
PETR YEMTSOV (Ru)	49740
PETRILA (Rm)	89540
PETRODVORETS (Ru)	03690
PETRODVORETS (Ru)	12380
PETROGRADSKAYA STORONA (Ru)	13650
PETROKREPOST (Ru)	02900
PETROKREPOST (Ru)	23480
PETROPAVLOVSK (Ru)	02120
PETROPAVLOVSKAYA KREPOST (Ru)	13751
PETROSENI (Rm)	72116
PETROVSKIY (Ru)	02900
PETROZAVODSK (Ru)	02900
PETROZAVODSK (Ru)	23480
PETYA KOVALYENKO (Ru)	67010
PETYA SHITIKOV (Ru)	67010
PEVEK (Ru)	11300
PEVEK (Ru)	42800
PEYO IAVOROV (Bu)	49785
PEYPSI (Ru)	13650
PFUSUNG (Ru)	85320
PHILIPP MULLER (DDR)	23410
PIATRA NEAMT (Rm)	89540
PIENINY II (Pd)	67677
PILTUN (Ru)	86220
PINAGORIY (Ru)	11610
PINEGA (Ru)	67010
PINEGA (Ru)	86220
PINGVIN (DDR)	84930
PINGVIN (Bu)	11800
PIONER (Ru)	15510
PIONER ARKHANGELSKA (Ru)	71040
PIONER AYKUTII (Ru)	71040
PIONER BELORUSSII (Ru)	71040
PIONER BURYATII (Ru)	71040
PIONER CHUKOTKI (Ru)	71040
PIONER ESTONII (Ru)	71040
PIONER KAMCHATKI (Ru)	71040
PIONER KARELII (Ru)	71040
PIONER KAZAKHSTANA (Ru)	71040
PIONER KHOLMSKA (Ru)	71040
PIONER KIRGIZII (Ru)	71040
PIONER KOLY (Ru)	71040
PIONER LITVY (Ru)	71040
PIONER MOLDAVII (Ru)	71040
PIONER MOSKVY (Ru)	71040
PIONER MURMANA (Ru)	91224
PIONER NAKHODKI (Ru)	79550
PIONER NIKOLAYEVKA (Ru)	11333
PIONER ODESSY (Ru)	79550
PIONER ONEGI (Ru)	71040
PIONER PRIMORYA (Ru)	79550
PIONER ROSSI (Ru)	71040
PIONER SAKHALINA (Ru)	71040
PIONER SEVERODVINSKA (Ru)	71040
PIONER SLAVYANKI (Ru)	71040
PIONER UKRAINY (Ru)	12380
PIONER UZBEKISTANA (Ru)	71040
PIONER VLADIVOSTOKA (Ru)	79550
PIONER VOLKOV (Ru)	91224
PIONER VYBORGA (Ru)	79550
PIONER YUZHNO SAKHALINSKA (Ru)	71040
PIONER ZAPOLYARYA (Ru)	12380
PIONERSK (Ru)	93870
PIONERSKAYA PRAVDA (Ru)	15510
PIONERSKAYA ZORKA (Ru)	15510
PIONIERUL (Rm)	78841
PIOTR DUNIN (Pd)	10570
PIOTR DUNIN (Pd)	15340
PIOTRKOW TRYBUNALSKI (Pd)	79870
PIRIN (Ru)	49040
PIRIT (Ru)	11800
PIRYATIN (Ru)	36250
PIRYATIN (Ru)	42800
PISATEL (Ru)	11800
PISHCHEVAYA INDUSTRIYA (Ru)	45270
PITESTI (Rm)	86170
PITSUNDA (Ru)	11800
PITSUNDA (Ru)	20731
PLANA (Bu)	77980
PLANERIST (Ru)	11800
PLANETA (Pd)	04088
PLANETA (Ru)	11580
PLATON OYUNSKIY (Ru)	50730
PLATORESTI (Ru)	47540
PLAYA HIRON (Ru)	18270
PLESETSK (Ru)	02900
PLETWAL (Pd)	10810
PLISKA (Bu)	37310
PLOCK (Pd)	82260
PLOPENI (Rm)	82110
PLUG (Ru)	22220
PLUNGE (Ru)	34880
PLUTON (Ru)	11800
PLUTON (Ru)	23860
PLUTONIY (Ru)	11580
PLYAVINYAS (Ru)	38530
POBYEDA (Ru)	63975
POBYEDA OKTYABRYA (Ru)	59890
POBYEDA OKTYABRYA (Ru)	67650
POBYEDINO (Ru)	24030
PODHALE (Pd)	75730
PODHALE (Pd)	88380
PODMOSKOVYE (Ru)	11300
PODVODNIK (Ru)	33015
POEL (DDR)	39300
POET (Ru)	11800
POET SABIR (Ru)	79340
POET VIDADI (Ru)	79340
POGRANICHNIK LEONOV (Ru)	93820
POIANA (Rm)	83680
POKOJ (Pd)	52805
POLAR (DDR)	51570
POLAR 1 (Rm)	91224
POLAR II (Rm)	91224
POLAR III (Rm)	62701
POLAR IV (Rm)	62701
POLAR V (Rm)	62701
POLAR VI (Rm)	62701
POLAR VII (Rm)	60971
POLAR VIII (Rm)	60971
POLAR IX (Rm)	60971
POLAR X (Rm)	60971
POLAR XI (Rm)	60971
POLAR XII (Rm)	60971
POLCZYN ZDROJ (Pd)	74140
POLESSK (Ru)	03690
POLESYE (Ru)	11300
POLEVOD (Ru)	11800
POLINA OSIPENKO (Ru)	10720
POLLUKS (Ru)	76890
POLLUKS (Ru)	81400
POLLUX (Pd)	11790
POLOTSK (Ru)	11610
POLOTSK (Ru)	45350
POLTAVA (Ru)	11800
POLTAVA (Ru)	45350
POLYARNAYA ZVEZDA (Ru)	93870
POLYARNIK (Ru)	22327
POLYARNIK (Ru)	33015
POLYARNOYE SIYANIE (Ru)	11580
POLYARNYE ZORI (Ru)	91224
POLYARNYY KRUG (Ru)	91224
POLYARNYY (Ru)	11580
POLYARNYY (Ru)	22840

POLYARNYY (Ru) 34470
POLYUS (Ru) 33980
POMERANIA (Pd) 08170
POMORIE (Bu) 79340
POMORYE (Ru) 02900
POMORZE (Pd) 93870
PONOY (Ru) 02900
PORFIRIY
  CHANCHIBADZE (Rd) 11333
PORKHOV (Ru) 11430
PORONAY (Ru) 08834
PORONIN (Ru) 24030
PORT ILYICH (Ru) 44100
PORTOVIK (Ru) 33015
POSADA (Rm) 60978
POSEJDON (Pd) 22173
POSEYDON (Ru) 12570
POSEYDON (Ru) 22178
POSYET (Ru) 12380
POSYET (Ru) 22840
POSYET (Ru) 34470
POTSDAM (DDR) 04910
POVOLZHYE (Ru) 11300
POVONETS (Ru) 15500
POWSTANIEC
  LISTOPADOWY (Pd) 72115
POWSTANIEC SLASKI (Pd) 59220
POWSTANIEC SLASKI (Pd) 74540
POWSTANIEC
  STYCZNIOWY (Pd) 72115
POWSTANIEC
  WARSZAWSKI (Pd) 65580
POWSTANIEC
  WARSZAWSKI (Pd) 67690
POWSTANIEC
  WIELKOPOLSKI (Pd) 70540
POZNAN (Pd) 80205
PRACA (Pd) 52805
PRAGA (Ru) 36840
PRAHA (Cz) 79230
PRAHOVA (Rm) 41630
PRAKTICHNYY (Ru) 17637
PRANAS
  EYDUKYAVICHUS (Ru) 12380
PRANAS ZIBERTAS (Ru) 85320
PRAVDA (Ru) 07550
PRAVDINSK (Ru) 03690
PRAVOVYED (Ru) 11800

PREDANNYY (Ru) 22173
PREDEAL (Rm) 48480
PREMNITZ (DDR) 78730
PREMNITZ (DDR) 89980
PRESIDENT PIK (Ru) 13650
PREYLI (Ru) 38530
PREZHEVALSK (Ru) 02900
PRIAMURYE (Ru) 02160
PRIAMURYE (Ru) 09210
PRIAMURYE (Ru) 12380
PRIBALTIKA (Ru) 93820
PRIBOY (Ru) 02270
PRIBOY (Ru) 61270
PRIBOY (Ru) 81490
PRIDNEPROVSK (Ru) 45350
PRIGNITZ (DDR) 71680
PRIKARPATYE (Ru) 11300
PRIKUMSK (Ru) 25550
PRILIV (Ru) 02270
PRILIV (Ru) 11800
PRILUKI (Ru) 09360
PRIMERNYY (Ru) 22173
PRIMORETS (Ru) 23305
PRIMORLES (Ru) 24030
PRIMORSK (Ru) 03690
PRIMORSKIY BEREG (Ru) 62671
PRIMORYE (Ru) 22173
PRIMORYE (Ru) 33198
PRIONEZHYE (Ru) 11300
PRIOZERSK (Ru) 12380
PRITZWALK (DDR) 61400
PRIVOLZHSK (Ru) 45210
PRIZVANIE (Ru) 13745
PROFESOR
  MIERZEJEWSKI (Pd) 56633
PROFESOR RYLKE (Pd) 56633
PROFESOR SZAFER (Pd) 56633
PROFESSOR (Ru) 11800
PROFESSOR
  ANICHKOV (Ru) 09080
PROFESSOR
  BARANOV (Ru) 93820
PROFESSOR
  BAYKONOVSKIY (Ru) 04275
PROFESSOR
  BOGOROV (Ru) 04226
PROFESSOR
  BOGUCKI (Pd) 23474

PROFESSOR BUBNOV (Ru) 50763
PROFESSOR BUZNIK (Ru) 03950
'PROFESSOR' class (Ru) 15000
PROFESSOR
  DERYUGIN (Ru) 12570
PROFESSOR
  FEDYINSKIY (Ru) 95042
PROFESSOR I.I.
  KRAKOVSKIY (Ru) 79340
PROFESSOR K
  BOHDANOWICZ (Pd) 73550
PROFESSOR
  KERICHYEV (Ru) 79340
PROFESSOR
  KHLYUSTIN (Ru) 09080
PROFESSOR
  KHROMOV (Ru) 04275
PROFESSOR
  KLENOVA (Ru) 13745
PROFESSOR
  KOLESNIKOV (Ru) 20731
PROFESSOR
  KOSTIUKOV (Ru) 48650
PROFESSOR
  KOZHIN (Ru) 13745
PROFESSOR
  KUDREVICH (Ru) 09080
PROFESSOR
  KURENTSOV (Ru) 04226
PROFESSOR
  MESYATSYEV (Ru) 11800
PROFESSOR
  MINYAYEV (Ru) 09080
PROFESSOR
  MULTANOVSKIY (Ru) 04275
PROFESSOR NESTOR
  SMYERNOV (Ru) 17950
PROFESSOR
  NIKOLSKIY (Ru) 13745
PROFESSOR
  PAPKOVICH (Ru) 50763
PROFESSOR PAVEL
  MOLCHANOV (Ru) 04275
PROFESSOR
  PAVLENKO (Ru) 09080
PROFESSOR POPOV (Ru) 10740
PROFESSOR
  RYBALTOVSKIY (Ru) 09080

PROFESSOR SERGEY
  DOROFEYEV (Ru) 17950
PROFESSOR
  SHCHYOGOLEV (Ru) 09080
PROFESSOR
  SHTOKMAN (Ru) 04226
PROFESSOR
  SIEDLECKI (Pd) 11690
PROFESSOR
  TOVSTYKH (Ru) 80100
PROFESSOR UKHOV (Ru) 09080
PROFESSOR VIZE (Ru) 12000
PROFESSOR
  VODYANITSKIY (Ru) 04226
PROFESSOR
  VOYEVODIN (Ru) 13745
PROFESSOR
  YUSHENKO (Ru) 09080
PROFESSOR ZUBOV (Ru) 12000
PROGRESS (Ru) 11580
PROGRESS (Ru) 23480
PROKOPIY GALUSHIN (Ru) 06795
PROKOPYEVSK (Ru) 02900
PROKOPYEVSK (Ru) 09360
PROLETARSKAYA
  POBEDA (Ru) 90720
PROLETARSKAYA
  POBYEDA (Ru) 60680
PROLIV DIANY (Ru) 58510
PROLIV DIANY (Ru) 71820
PROLIV
  KRUZENSHTERNA (Ru) 58510
PROLIV
  KRUZENSHTERNA (Ru) 71820
PROLIV LAPERUZA (Ru) 58510
PROLIV LAPERUZA (Ru) 71820
PROLIV LONGA (Ru) 58510
PROLIV LONGA (Ru) 71820
PROLIV NADEZHDY (Ru) 58510
PROLIV NADEZHDY (Ru) 71820
PROLIV (Ru) 11800
PROLIV SANNIKOVO (Ru) 58510
PROLIV SANNIKOVO (Ru) 71820
PROLIV
  SHOKALSKOGO (Ru) 58510
PROLIV
  SHOKALSKOGO (Ru) 71820
PROLIV VIKTORIYA (Ru) 58510

PROLIV VIKTORIYA (Ru) 71820
PROLIV VILKITSKOGO (Ru) 58510
PROLIV VILKITSKOGO (Ru) 71820
PROMETEY (Ru) 13650
PROMYSLOVIK (Ru) 11800
PROPAGANDIST (Ru) 11800
PROSTOR (Ru) 13751
PROSVETITEL (Ru) 11800
PROTEY (Ru) 22178
PROTSION (Ru) 76890
PROTSION (Ru) 81400
PROVORNY (Ru) 84330
PRUT (Ru) 70810
PRUT (Ru) 76945
PRUZANIY (Ru) 34880
PRZEMYSL (Pd) 79870
PSKOV (Ru) 03690
PSKOV (Ru) 23480
PSKOVITYANKA (Ru) 35310
PUBLIKIST (Ru) 11800
PUCK (Pd) 93930
PULA (Ru) 14370
PULKOVO (Ru) 02900
PULKOVO (Ru) 12380
PULKOVSKIY
  MERIDIAN (Ru) 11333
PULKOWNIK DABEK (Pd) 15360
PURGA (Ru) 22173
'PUSHKIN' class
  (modified) (Ru) 12340
PUSHLAKHTA (Ru) 02900
PUSTOZERSK (Ru) 02900
PUTIVL (Ru) 03690
PUTIVL (Ru) 12380
PUTNA (Rm) 13650
PUTYATIN (Ru) 24030
PYARNU (Ru) 15500
PYARNURAND (Ru) 23664
PYATIDYESYATILETIYE
  KOMSOMOLA (Ru) 01100
PYATIDYESYATILYETIYE
  SOVIETSKOY
  GRUZII (Ru) 60620
PYATIDYESYATILYETIYE
  SOVIETSKOY
  GRUZII (Ru) 62580
PYATIDYESYATILYETIYE
  SSSR (Ru) 45290

PYATIDYESYATILYETIYE SSSR (Ru)	58510
PYATIGORSK (Ru)	11800
PYER PUYYAD (Ru)	80052
PYMTA (Ru)	39290
PYOT BULKO (Ru)	28600
PYOTR ALEYINIKOV (Ru)	56638
PYOTR BOGDANOV (Ru)	79340
PYOTR OVCHINNIKOV (Ru)	12380
PYOTR PAKHTUSOV (Ru)	22240
PYOTR SGIBNEV (or PETR SGIBNEV) (Ru)	00140
PYOTR SHAFRANOV (Ru)	11333
PYOTR SMORODIN (Ru)	46560
PYOTR STUCHKA (Ru)	90720
PYOTR ZALOMOV (Ru)	79340
PYOTR ZAPOROZHETS (Ru)	79340
QUEDLINBURG (DDR)	03870
QUEDLINBURG (DDR)	04423
RABENAU (DDR)	71040
RABOCHAYA SMENA (Ru)	01380
RABOCHAYA SMENA (Ru)	01640
RADAUTI (Rm)	47540
RADEBERG (DDR)	59650
RADEBEUL (DDR)	56638
RADHOST (Cz)	15090
RADISHEV (Ru)	12360
RADISHEV (Ru)	20790
RADIY (Ru)	36890
RADIY (Ru)	43790
RADNOTI (Hu)	14910
RADNOTI (Hu)	15720
RADOMYSHL (Ru)	67350
RADOMYSHL (Ru)	71360
RADUGA (Ru)	12230
RADUZHNYY (Ru)	33305
RADVILISKIS (Ru)	35310
RADZIONKOW (Pd)	03230
RADZIONKOW (Pd)	03620
RAKHOV (Ru)	67350
RAKHOV (Ru)	71360
RAKOW (DDR)	50440
RAKOW (DDR)	52000
RAKVERE (Ru)	22840
RAKVERE (Ru)	34470
RALIDA (Bu)	11800
RAMADA (Pd)	22330
RAMBINAS (Ru)	22135
RAND-1 (Ru)	35310
RAND-2 (Ru)	35310
RAND-3 (Ru)	35310
RAND-4 (Ru)	35310
RAPLA (Ru)	89250
RATNO (Ru)	67350
RATNO (Ru)	71360
RAUMA (Ru)	70760
RAVA RUSSKAYA (Ru)	44890
RAVENSTVO (Ru)	01560
RAYCHIKHINSK (Ru)	24030
RAZBOIENI (Rm)	60978
RAZDOLNOYE (Ru)	52304
RAZDOLNOYE (Ru)	52616
RAZELM (Rm)	11700
RAZLIV (Ru)	35310
RECHITSA (Ru)	33305
RECHLIN (DDR)	75330
REDUT (Ru)	33305
REFRIGERATOR No 5 (Ru)	84330
REFRIGERATOR No 13 (Ru)	84330
REGUL (Ru)	23305
REGULUS (Pd)	10540
REKIN (Pd)	23440
REKIVA (Ru)	33198
RENI (Ru)	22840
RENI (Ru)	34470
REPINO (Ru)	12230
RESHITELNYY (Ru)	22137
RESITA (Rm)	78580
RETAVAS (Ru)	13650
RETEZATUL (Rm)	11700
REUTERSHAGEN (DDR)	62671
REUTERSHAGEN (DDR)	82651
REUTOV (Ru)	67350
REUTOV (Ru)	71360
REVDA (Ru)	22840
REVDA (Ru)	34470
REVOLYUTSIYA (Ru)	11580
REVOLYUTSIYA (Ru)	45350
REZEKNE (Ru)	60620
REZEKNE (Ru)	62580
REZVAYA (Bu)	59890
REZVAYA (Bu)	67650
RHINSEE (DDR)	46370
RHINSEE (DDR)	47070
RICHARDAS BUKAUSKAS (Ru)	67010
RIEMS (DDR)	39300
RIESA (DDR)	48240
RIFT (Ru)	21945
RIGA (Ru)	25840
RIGA (Ru)	38530
RIKHARD MIRRING (Ru)	23480
RILA (Bu)	77080
RILA (Bu)	80000
RIMNICU VILCEA (Rm)	82110
RIONI (Ru)	08846
RISTNA (Ru)	15460
RIURENI (Rm)	61020
RIYEKA (Ru)	60620
RIYEKA (Ru)	62580
RIZHSKIY ZALIV (Ru)	61100
RIZHSKOYE VZMORYE (Ru)	93820
ROBERT EYDEMAN (Ru)	12380
ROBERT EYKHE (Ru)	93820
ROBERT KOCH (DDR)	22550
ROBERT (Pd)	33015
RODINA (Bu)	51672
RODINA (Bu)	73290
RODINA (Ru)	17500
RODINA (Ru)	24310
RODINA (Ru)	39450
RODLO (Pd)	72115
RODNA (Rm)	13751
RODONIT (Ru)	07470
RODONIT (Ru)	11800
RODOPI (Bu)	77080
RODOPI (Bu)	80000
ROJEN (Bu)	48383
ROKISHKIS (Ru)	35310
ROLNIK (Pd)	78290
ROLNIK (Pd)	80020
ROMAN KARMEN (Ru)	47674
ROMAN PAZINSKI (Pd)	14480
ROMAN ROLLAN (Ru)	07900
ROMAN (Rm)	60978
ROMAN (Rm)	86170
ROMANKA (Pd)	52466
ROMNY (Ru)	67350
ROMNY (Ru)	71360
RONNEBURG (DDR)	03870
RONNEBURG (DDR)	04423
ROSA LUXEMBURG (Ru)	05620
ROSA LUXEMBURG (Ru)	14450
ROSA LUXEMBURG (Ru)	62701
ROSITZA (Bu)	88885
ROSLAVL (Ru)	12230
ROSLAVL (Ru)	67350
ROSLAVL (Ru)	71360
ROSOMAK (Pd)	33015
ROSSOSH (Ru)	85895
ROSTA (Ru)	26210
ROSTOCK (DDR)	03870
ROSTOCK (DDR)	04423
ROSTOCK (DDR)	19985
ROSTOK (Ru)	67350
ROSTOK (Ru)	71360
ROSTOV NA DONU (Ru)	80052
ROSTOV (Ru)	51212
ROTALIA (Bu)	23440
ROVINARI (Rm)	82220
ROVNO (Ru)	51212
ROYA (Ru)	89515
RUBEZHNOYE (Ru)	67350
RUBEZHNOYE (Ru)	71360
RUBIN (Ru)	12380
RUBIN (Ru)	22173
RUBINOVYY (Ru)	11800
RUBTSOVSK (Ru)	24030
RUCIANE (Pd)	75327
RUDI ARNT (DDR)	23410
RUDNYY (Ru)	67350
RUDNYY (Ru)	71360
RUDNYY (Ru)	85320
RUDOLF BLAUMANIS (Ru)	12380
RUDOLF BREITSCHEID (DDR)	15410
RUDOLF BREITSCHIED (DDR)	06380
RUDOLF DIESEL (DDR)	46370
RUDOLF DIESEL (DDR)	47070
RUDOLF LEONHARD (DDR)	10250
RUDOLF LEONHARD (DDR)	12630
RUDOLF SAMOYLOVICH (Ru)	93268
RUDOLF SCHWARZ (DDR)	23410
RUDOLF SIRGE (Ru)	23480
RUDOLF VAKMAN (Ru)	23480
RUDOLSTADT (DDR)	50128
RUEBELAND (DDR)	80109
RUEN (Bu)	55410
RUEN (Bu)	78850
RUGEN (DDR)	32890
RUHLAND (DDR)	80109
RUKHULLA AKHUNDOV (Ru)	53160
RUMB (Ru)	01736
RUMB (Ru)	22327
RUMBALA (Ru)	70760
RUPEA (Rm)	47540
RUSALKA (Pd)	87740
RUSHANY (Ru)	67350
RUSHANY (Ru)	71360
RUSLAN (Ru)	12230
RUSNE (Ru)	23480
RUSSE (Bu)	37310
RUSSOYE POLYE (Ru)	13751
RUSTAVI (Ru)	12230
RUTSAVA (Ru)	22327
RUZA (Rm)	13850
RUZA (Ru)	12230
RYAZAN (Ru)	67350
RYAZAN (Ru)	71360
RYBACHI (Ru)	33035
RYBACHIY (Ru)	11580
RYBACHKA (Ru)	23410
RYBAK BALTIKA (Ru)	93820
RYBAK CHUKOTKI (Ru)	45270
RYBAK KAMCHATSKIY (Ru)	45270
RYBAK LATVII (Ru)	93820
RYBAK MORSKI (Pd)	22350
RYBAK PRIMORIYA (Ru)	45270
RYBAK (Ru)	23410
RYBAK VLADIVOSTOKA (Ru)	45270
RYBAK ZAPOLYARYA (Ru)	26210
RYBATSKAYA SLAVA (Ru)	93780
RYBINSK (Ru)	67350
RYBINSK (Ru)	71360
RYBNIK (Pd)	82260
RYBNYY MURMAN (Ru)	93870
RYLYEV (Ru)	17500
RYSHKANY (Ru)	67350
RYSHKANY (Ru)	71360
RZHEV (Ru)	11300

Name	No.	Name	No.	Name	No.	Name	No.	Name	No.
RZHEV (Ru)	67350	SALEKHARD (Ru)	24030	SARYCHEVSK (Ru)	22327	SEDA (Ru)	11800	SERGACH (Ru)	22327
RZHEV (Ru)	71360	SALISTE (Rm)	82110	SASCUT (Ru)	82110	SEDANKA (Ru)	45715	SERGEY BOTKIN (Ru)	34240
		SALKHINO (Ru)	11800	SASHA BORODULIN (Ru)	15510	SEGARCEA (Rm)	82110	SERGEY BURYACHEK (Ru)	49240
SAADYARV (Ru)	13650	SALNA (Ru)	85320	SASHA KONDRATYEV (Ru)	15510	SEGEY LAZO (Ru)	93680	SERGEY	
SAATLY (Ru)	50770	SALOMATINSK (Ru)	22327	SASHA KOTOV (Ru)	15510	SEGEZHA (Ru)	15460	EYZENSHTEYN (Ru)	15120
SABARENI (Rm)	82110	SALONTA (Rm)	82110	SASHA KOVALYOV (Ru)	15510	SEGEZHALES (Ru)	24030	SERGEY GRITSEVETS (Ru)	50730
SABIRABAD (Ru)	50770	SALOS (Ru)	33198	SATINO (Ru)	22327	SEGOZERO (Ru)	22327	SERGEY GUSEV (Ru)	03770
SABUNCHI (Ru)	44100	SALVA (Rm)	77080	SATOW (DDR)	50440	SEIMINI (Rm)	82110	SERGEY GUSEV (Ru)	04010
SABUROVO (Ru)	22327	SALVA (Rm)	80000	SATOW (DDR)	52000	SEJNO (Pd)	33193	SERGEY KANDACHIK (Ru)	11800
SABURSK (Ru)	22327	SALVADOR ALLENDE (Ru)	03690	SATU MARE (Rm)	47540	SEJWAL (Pd)	10810	SERGEY KIROV (Ru)	58995
SACELE (Rm)	82110	SALYUT (Ru)	11610	SATURN (Pd)	11700	SEKSTAN (Ru)	13751	SERGEY KIROV (Ru)	86220
SADGORA (Ru)	22327	SAMARA (Ru)	23480	SATURN (Ru)	12230	SELEMDZHA (Ru)	15460	SERGEY	
SADKO (Ru)	11800	'SAMARA' class		SATURN (Ru)	22173	SELENA (Ru)	13751	KORSHUNOVICH (Ru)	34872
SADKO (Ru)	22220	(modified) (Ru)	08849	SAVENI (Ru)	82110	SELENGA (Ru)	06795	SERGEY KRAVKOV (Ru)	02417
SADKO (Ru)	33015	'SAMARA' class (Ru)	01736	SAVINESTI (Rm)	82110	SELENGA (Ru)	36235	SERGEY LAZO (Ru)	33910
SADOVA (Rm)	82110	'SAMARA' class (Ru)	04068	SAVINO (Ru)	22327	SELENGALES (Ru)	24030	SERGEY LYULIN (Ru)	13650
SADOVSK (Ru)	22327	SAMARGA (Ru)	12380	SAVINTSY (Ru)	22327	SELENUR (Ru)	22327	SERGEY	
SADRIDDIN AYNI (Ru)	50763	SAMARKAND (Ru)	39290	SAVRAN (Ru)	22327	SELETS (Ru)	22327	MAKAREVICH (Ru)	34872
SADU (Rm)	82110	SAMARKAND (Ru)	51212	SAVVA LOSHKIN (Ru)	79340	SELIGER (Ru)	11610	SERGEY SMIRNOV (Ru)	50763
SAFONOVO (Ru)	22327	SAMARKAND (Ru)	51212	SAYAK (Ru)	22327	SEMENIC (Rm)	11670	SERGEY TSENSKAY (Ru)	20790
SAGAYDAK (Ru)	22327	SAMBURG (Ru)	70020	SAYANI (Ru)	85320	SEMIGORSK (Ru)	22327	SERGEY TYULENIN (Ru)	60373
SAGITA (Bu)	23440	SAMOTLOR (Ru)	22327	SAYANLES (Ru)	24030	SEMILUKI (Ru)	22327	SERGEY VASILISIN (Ru)	93870
SAGITTA (Pd)	10540	SAMOTLOR (Ru)	70020	SAYANOGORSK (Ru)	22327	SEMIPALATINSK (Ru)	10610	SERGEY VASILYEV (Ru)	15120
SAJO (Hu)	50909	SAMSHIT (Ru)	23480	SAYANSKIE GORY (Ru)	91910	SEMIYARSK (Ru)	22327	SERGEY VAVILOV (Ru)	17560
SAKARTVELO (Ru)	11800	SAMTREDIA (Ru)	85970	SAYMENSKIY KANAL (Ru)	75400	SEMLOW (DDR)	50440	SERGEY YESENIN (Ru)	14370
SAKHALIN (Ru)	22173	SAMUIL MARSHAK (Ru)	07900	SAZHINO (Ru)	22327	SEMLOW (DDR)	52000	SERGO ZARIADZE (Ru)	80010
SAKHALIN (Ru)	22720	SAMUR (Ru)	08834	SAZHINSK (Ru)	22327	SEMYON		SERNOVODSK (Ru)	83680
SAKHALIN-1 (Ru)	20310	SAMUR (Ru)	76945	SAZONOVO (Ru)	22327	CHELYUSKIN (Ru)	22180	SEROGLAZKA (Ru)	12380
SAKHALIN-2 (Ru)	20310	SANDOMIERZ (Pd)	34360	SB-365 (Ru)	23665	SEMYON		SEROV (Ru)	02670
SAKHALIN-3 (Ru)	20310	SANGAR (Ru)	22327	SB-406 (Ru)	09035	CHELYUSKIN (Ru)	22220	SESTRORETSK (Ru)	33015
SAKHALIN-4 (Ru)	20310	SANGARLES (Ru)	11430	SB-408 (Ru)	09035	SEMYON DEZHNEV (Ru)	12380	SESTRORETSK (Ru)	79550
SAKHALIN-5 (Ru)	20310	SANGARSKIY PROLIV (Ru)	58510	SB-921 (Ru)	09035	SEMYON DEZHNEV (Ru)	22180	SETUN (Ru)	92160
SAKHALIN-6 (Ru)	20310	SANGARSKIY PROLIV (Ru)	71820	SB-922 (Ru)	09035	SEMYON DEZHNEV (Ru)	22220	SEVAN (Ru)	02670
SAKHALIN-7 (Ru)	20310	SANGERHAUSEN (DDR)	03690	SCAIENI (Rm)	82110	SEMYON		SEVAN (Ru)	11460
SAKHALIN-8 (Ru)	20310	SANOK (Pd)	34360	SCHILUTE (Ru)	13650	LAPSHENKOV (Ru)	34872	SEVAN (Ru)	20790
SAKHALIN-9 (Ru)	20310	SANTIAGO DE CUBA (Ru)	02520	SCHKOPAU (DDR)	52070	SEMYON MOROZOV (Ru)	79340	SEVAN (Ru)	85970
SAKHALINLES (Ru)	24030	SAPFIR (Ru)	12380	SCHKOPAU (DDR)	75170	SEMYON ROSHAL (Ru)	89250	SEVASTOPOL (Ru)	45110
SAKHALINNEFT (Ru)	33015	SAPUN GORA (Ru)	11800	SCHOLLAR (Ru)	86170	SEMYON RUDNYEV (Ru)	79340	SEVER (Ru)	01733
SAKHALINNEFT (Ru)	70760	SARAN (Ru)	22327	SCHONWALDE (DDR)	46370	SEMYON VOLKOV (Ru)	23305	SEVER (Ru)	22235
SAKHALINSKIE GORY (Ru)	91910	SARAPUL (Ru)	22327	SCHONWALDE (DDR)	47070	SENEZH (Ru)	23860	SEVERLES (Ru)	24030
SALAJ (Rm)	01380	SARATA (Ru)	83680	SCHTORM (Ru)	21260	SENFTENBERG (DDR)	79730	SEVERNAYA	
SALAJ (Rm)	01640	SARATOVSK (Ru)	07947	SCHWARZBURG (DDR)	03870	SERDEZH (Ru)	22327	PALMIRA (Ru)	12380
SALANTI (Ru)	13650	SARDINELLA (Ru)	22327	SCHWARZBURG (DDR)	04423	SERDOLIK (Ru)	07470	SEVERNYY DONETS (Ru)	88920
SALAVAT (Ru)	10610	SARGAN (Ru)	22327	SCHWEDT (DDR)	53190	SERDOLIK (Ru)	11800	SEVERNYY POLYUS (Ru)	93820
SALAVAT YULAYEV (Ru)	89250	SARGUS (Ru)	22327	SCHWIELOSEE (DDR)	46370	SEREBRYANKA (Ru)	17950	SEVERNYY VETER (Ru)	91224
SALAVATOVO (Ru)	22327	SARICH (Ru)	01960	SCHWIELOSEE (DDR)	47070	SEREBRYANKA (Ru)	79945	SEVERO-KURILSK (Ru)	22327
SALDUS (Ru)	11490	SARMA (Ru)	85320	SEBES (Rm)	82110	SEREBRYANSK (Ru)	02670	SEVERODONETSK (Ru)	02670
SALEKHARD (Ru)	23480	SARNY (Ru)	02670	SEBEZH (Ru)	22327	SEREBRYANSK (Ru)	85320	SEVERODONETSK (Ru)	93884

Name	No.	Name	No.	Name	No.
SEVERODVINSK (Ru)	25840	SIBIR (Ru)	22720	SINEGORSK (Ru)	34470
SEVERODVINSKIY (Ru)	89680	SIBIR (Ru)	91224	SINEGORSK (Ru)	36890
SEVEROURALSK (Ru)	93800	SIBIRLES (Ru)	06795	SINEGORSK (Ru)	43790
SEVERYANIN (Ru)	11610	SIBIRNEFT (Ru)	70760	SINITSINO (Ru)	17637
SEVKAR (Ru)	22327	SIBIRSKIY (Ru)	04080	SINOE (Rm)	11700
SEVORODVINSK (Ru)	15460	SIBIRSKIY 2101 (Ru)	73997	SINYAVINO (Ru)	23480
SEVRYBA (Ru)	93870	SIBIRSKIY 2102 (Ru)	73997	SIO (Hu)	74000
SHADRINSK (Ru)	24030	SIBIRSKIY 2108 (Ru)	73997	SIRET (Rm)	11800
SHAKHTERSK (Ru)	17637	SIBIRSKIY 2109 (Ru)	73997	SIRIUS (Pd)	11670
SHAKHTYOR (Ru)	33015	SIBIRSKIY 2113 (Ru)	78041	SITNO (Cz)	15090
SHAKOPOVO (Ru)	13751	SIBIRSKIY 2114 (Ru)	78041	SIVASH (Ru)	11800
SHALVA NADIBAIDZE (Ru)	93800	SIBIRSKIY 2116 (Ru)	78041	SIYANIE (Ru)	11580
SHAMKHOR (Ru)	50770	SIBIRSKIY 2117 (Ru)	78041	SKADOVSK (Ru)	22327
SHANTAR (Ru)	11800	SIBIRSKIY 2118 (Ru)	78041	SKAGERRAK (DDR)	18720
SHAPOSHNIKOVO (Ru)	13751	SIBIRSKIY 2119 (Ru)	78041	SKALAT (Ru)	22327
SHARAF RASHIDOV (Ru)	00965	SIBIRSKIY 2123 (Ru)	73997	SKALISTYY BEREG (Ru)	62701
SHATURA (Ru)	24030	SIBIRSKIY 2124 (Ru)	73997	SKALISTYY (Ru)	11800
SHEDAR (Ru)	12230	SIBIRSKIY 2125 (Ru)	73997	SKAP (Ru)	22327
SHEKSNA (Ru)	95015	SIBIRSKIY 2126 (Ru)	73997	SKAZOCHNIK	
SHEKSNALES (Ru)	11490	SIBIRSKIY 2127 (Ru)	73997	ANDERSEN (Ru)	09360
SHENKURSK (Ru)	22840	SIBIRSKIY 2128 (Ru)	73997	SKOCZOW (Pd)	03230
SHENKURSK (Ru)	34470	SIBIRSKIY 2130 (Ru)	78041	SKOCZOW (Pd)	03620
SHEPETOVKA (Ru)	13751	SIBIRSKIY 2131 (Ru)	78041	SKOLE (Ru)	22327
SHEREMTYEVO (Ru)	11720	SIBIRSKIY 2132 (Ru)	78041	SKORODUM (Ru)	22327
SHEREMTYEVO (Ru)	34610	SIBIRSKIY 2133 (Ru)	78041	SKRYPLEV (Ru)	09380
SHESTIDESYATILETIYE		SIBIRTSYEVO (Ru)	06795	SKRYPLEV (Ru)	45715
SSSR (Ru)	78060	SIBIRYAK (Ru)	12380	SKULPTOR	
SHILKA (Ru)	15460	SIBIU (Rm)	41310	GOLUBKINA (Ru)	80260
SHIRVANNEFT (Ru)	44100	SIDOR KOVPAK (Ru)	03950	SKULPTOR	
SHIRVINTA (Ru)	33198	SIEKIERKI (Pd)	59220	KONENKOV (Ru)	80260
SHKVAL (Ru)	21450	SIEKIERKI (Pd)	74540	SKULPTOR	
SHKVAL (Ru)	34290	SIEMIATYCZE (Pd)	03230	MATVEYEV (Ru)	80010
SHOTA RUSTAVELI (Ru)	04215	SIEMIATYCZE (Pd)	03620	SKULPTOR TOMSKIY (Ru)	02847
SHTURMAN YELAGIN (Ru)	12380	SIENKIEWICZ (Pd)	24560	SKULPTOR	
SHURA		SIERADZ (Pd)	50460	VUCHETICH (Ru)	80260
BURLACHENKO (Ru)	49240	SIGHISOARA (Rm)	81305	SKULPTOR	
SHURA KOBER (Ru)	15510	SIGULDA (Ru)	22840	ZALKALNS (Ru)	80260
SHUSENSKOYE (Ru)	07550	SIGULDA (Ru)	34470	SLANCHEV BRIAG (Bu)	91224
SHUSHENSKOYE (Ru)	79340	SILESIA (Pd)	08170	SLANIC (Rm)	82110
SHUSHVE (Ru)	33198	SILVER PIT (DDR)	18720	SLANTSY (Ru)	22327
SHUYA (Ru)	22173	SILVET (Ru)	85970	SLAPY (Cz)	59230
SHUYA (Ru)	22290	SIMERIA (Rm)	47540	SLATINA (Rm)	81555
SHUYA (Ru)	66380	SIMFEROPOL (Ru)	10610	SLAUTNOYE (Ru)	83680
SHVENCHENELYAY (Ru)	17637	SIMFEROPOL (Ru)	45110	SLAVA	
SHVENTOY (Ru)	11800	SIMON BOLIVAR (Ru)	80052	SEVASTOPOLYA (Ru)	10880
SHYAULYAY (Ru)	12380	SINEGORE (Ru)	22327	SLAVGOROD (Ru)	11610
SIARKOPOL (Pd)	73550	SINEGORSK (Ru)	15460	SLAVIANKA (Bu)	77080
SIBIR (Ru)	02415	SINEGORSK (Ru)	22840	SLAVIANKA (Bu)	80000

Name	No.	Name	No.	Name	No.
SLAVSK (Ru)	10610	SOLCA (Rm)	82110		
SLAVUTA (Ru)	22327	SOLIGALICH (Ru)	22327		
SLAVYANKA (Ru)	25550	SOLIKAMSK (Ru)	22327		
SLAVYANOGORSK (Ru)	22327	SOLNECHNOGORSK (Ru)	13010		
SLAVYANOSERBSK (Ru)	22327	SOLNECHNOGORSK (Ru)	22327		
SLAVYANSK (Ru)	02670	SOLNECHNYY			
SLAVYANSK (Ru)	93800	BEREG (Ru)	62680		
SLAVYANSKIY (Ru)	11333	SOLNECHNYY LUCH (Ru)	71670		
SLIVEN (Bu)	28980	SOLNECHNYY (Ru)	85970		
SLOBOZIA (Rm)	81555	SOLNTSEDAR (Ru)	11800		
SLUPSK (Pd)	34360	SOLNTSEVO (Ru)	22327		
SLUTSK (Ru)	10610	SOLOMBALA (Ru)	89200		
SMELA (Ru)	28060	SOLOVEVSK (Ru)	22327		
SMELYY (Ru)	22135	SOLOVIETSKIY (Ru)	11720		
SMIRDAN (Rm)	82110	SOLOVIETSKIY (Ru)	34610		
SMOLENSK (Ru)	71530	SOLOVKI (Ru)	01960		
SMOLENSK (Ru)	80200	SOLVYCHEGODSK (Ru)	22327		
SMOLNY (Pd)	10570	SOMES (Rm)	11800		
SMOLNY (Pd)	15340	SONDERHAUSEN (DDR)	03690		
SMOLNYY (Ru)	11610	SOPKA GEROYEV (Ru)	11800		
SMOLNYY (Ru)	53537	SORGU (Ru)	33017		
SMOLYANINOVO (Ru)	22327	'SORMOVSKIY' class (Ru)	79340		
SNABZHENETS		SORMOVSKIY 2 (Ru)	79340		
PERVYY (Ru)	12380	SORMOVSKIY 5 (Ru)	79340		
SNAGOV (Rm)	82110	SORMOVSKIY 6 (Ru)	79340		
SNEZHNOGORSK (Ru)	83680	SORMOVSKIY 7 (Ru)	79340		
SNEZHNOYE (Ru)	22327	SORMOVSKIY 9 (Ru)	79340		
SNIARDWY (Pd)	33193	SORMOVSKIY 12 (Ru)	79340		
SNIEZKA (Pd)	76665	SORMOVSKIY 14 (Ru)	79340		
SNOROVISTYY (Ru)	22173	SORMOVSKIY 17 (Ru)	79340		
SOBOLEVO (Ru)	22840	SORMOVSKIY 18 (Ru)	79340		
SOBOLEVO (Ru)	34470	SORMOVSKIY 19 (Ru)	79340		
SOCHI (Ru)	02670	SORMOVSKIY 22 (Ru)	79340		
SOFIA (Bu)	91700	SORMOVSKIY 27 (Ru)	79340		
SOFIYA		SORMOVSKIY 28 (Ru)	79340		
PEROVSKAYA (Ru)	06770	SORMOVSKIY 29 (Ru)	79340		
SOFIYA		SORMOVSKIY 30 (Ru)	79340		
PEROVSKAYA (Ru)	07550	SORMOVSKIY 31 (Ru)	79340		
SOFIYSK (Ru)	83680	SORMOVSKIY 33 (Ru)	79340		
SOGDA (Ru)	22327	SORMOVSKIY 34 (Ru)	79340		
SOHLAND (DDR)	80109	SORMOVSKIY 40 (Ru)	79340		
SOKOL (Ru)	03950	SORMOVSKIY 41 (Ru)	79340		
SOKOLICA II (Pd)	68920	SORMOVSKIY 42 (Ru)	79340		
SOKOLINOYE (Ru)	11800	SORMOVSKIY 43 (Ru)	79340		
SOKOLOVKA (Ru)	22327	SORMOVSKIY 44 (Ru)	79340		
SOKOLOVO (Ru)	11333	SORMOVSKIY 45 (Ru)	79340		
SOKRAT (Ru)	13751	SORMOVSKIY 46 (Ru)	79340		
SOLANO (Pd)	70955	SORMOVSKIY 48 (Ru)	79340		

SORMOVSKIY 109 (Ru)	79340
SORMOVSKIY 110 (Ru)	79340
SORMOVSKIY 112 (Ru)	79340
SORMOVSKIY 117 (Ru)	79340
SORMOVSKIY 118 (Ru)	79340
SORMOVSKIY 119 (Ru)	79340
SORMOVSKIY 121 (Ru)	79340
SORMOVSKIY 122 (Ru)	79340
SORMOVSKIY 3001 (Ru)	79340
SORMOVSKIY 3002 (Ru)	79340
SORMOVSKIY 3003 (Ru)	79340
SORMOVSKIY 3004 (Ru)	79340
SORMOVSKIY 3005 (Ru)	79340
SORMOVSKIY 3006 (Ru)	79340
SORMOVSKIY 3007 (Ru)	79340
SORMOVSKIY 3051 (Ru)	79340
SORMOVSKIY 3052 (Ru)	79340
SORMOVSKIY 3053 (Ru)	79340
SORMOVSKIY 3054 (Ru)	79340
SORMOVSKIY 3055 (Ru)	79340
SORMOVSKIY 3056 (Ru)	79340
SORMOVSKIY 3057 (Ru)	79340
SORMOVSKIY 3058 (Ru)	79340
SOROCHINSK (Ru)	22327
SOROKALETIYE POBEDY (Ru)	63975
SOSNOGORSK (Ru)	03950
SOSNOGORSK (Ru)	22327
SOSNOVETS (Ru)	83680
SOSNOVKA (Ru)	83680
SOSNOVOBORSK (Ru)	22327
SOUSA (Rm)	82110
SOVATA (Rm)	82110
SOVEJA (Rm)	82110
SOVFRACHT (Ru)	78520
SOVGANSKIY KOMSOMOLETS (Ru)	11720
SOVGANSKIY KOMSOMOLETS (Ru)	34610
SOVGAVAN (Ru)	12380
SOVIETSK (Ru)	09380
SOVIETSK (Ru)	10610
SOVIETSKAYA ARMENIYA (Ru)	92680
SOVIETSKAYA BURYATYA (Ru)	93820
SOVIETSKAYA BYELORUSSIYA (Ru)	92680

SOVIETSKAYA GRUZIYA (Ru)	92680
SOVIETSKAYA KALMYKIYA (Ru)	92680
SOVIETSKAYA KIRGIZIYA (Ru)	92680
SOVIETSKAYA LATVIYA (Ru)	85320
SOVIETSKAYA LITVA (Ru)	25840
SOVIETSKAYA NEFT (Ru)	63982
SOVIETSKAYA RODINA (Ru)	79340
SOVIETSKAYA RODINA (Ru)	85320
SOVIETSKAYA ROSSIYA (Ru)	93380
SOVIETSKAYA ROSSIYA (Ru)	93630
SOVIETSKAYA SAKHALIN (Ru)	25840
SOVIETSKAYA SIBIR (Ru)	93820
SOVIETSKAYA UKRAINA (Ru)	93860
SOVIETSKAYA YAKUTIYA (Ru)	50730
SOVIETSKIE PROFSOYUZY (Ru)	12380
SOVIETSKIY AZERBAIDZHAN (Ru)	20320
SOVIETSKIY DAGESTAN (Ru)	92680
SOVIETSKIY KAZAKHSTAN (Ru)	20320
SOVIETSKIY KHUDOZHNIK (Ru)	77080
SOVIETSKIY KHUDOZHNIK (Ru)	80000
SOVIETSKIY MORYAK (Ru)	50280
SOVIETSKIY NAKHICHEVAN (Ru)	92680
SOVIETSKIY POGRANICHNIK (Ru)	50280
SOVIETSKIY POGRANICHNIK (Ru)	85970
SOVIETSKIY SEVER (Ru)	79340
SOVIETSKIY TADZHIKISTAN (Ru)	92680

SOVIETSKIY TURKMENISTAN (Ru)	20320
SOVIETSKIY UZBEKISTAN (Ru)	20320
SOVIETSKIY VOIN (Ru)	50280
SOVIETSKIY ZAPOLYARYE (Ru)	93820
SOVIETSKIYE PROFSOYUZY (Ru)	48430
SOVIETSKIYE PROFSOYUZY (Ru)	49470
SOVIETSKIYE PROFSOYUZY (Ru)	49740
SOVIETSKOYE PRIMORYE (Ru)	93820
SOVINFLOT (Ru)	78520
SOYANA (Ru)	85895
SOYUZ (Ru)	11800
SOYUZ-9 (Ru)	22327
SOYUZ-10 (Ru)	22327
SOZOPOL (Bu)	79340
SPARTAK (Ru)	89250
SPASSK (Ru)	22720
SPASSK (Ru)	93800
SPASSK-DALNIY (Ru)	15460
SPIKA (Ru)	23305
SPLIT (Ru)	60620
SPLIT (Ru)	62580
SPRAVEDLIVYY (Ru)	04080
SPRUT (Ru)	09120
SPRUT (Ru)	17350
SPRUT (Ru)	34880
SPUTNIK (Ru)	12590
SREDETZ (Bu)	76865
SREDNA GORA (Bu)	49040
SREDNEKOLYMSKIY (Ru)	22327
SREDNEURALSKIY (Ru)	22327
SSV 464 (Ru)	12587
SSV 465 (Ru)	11995
SSV 472 (Ru)	33035
SSV-480 (Ru)	22159
SSV 501 (Ru)	12587
SSV 502 (Ru)	12587
SSV 509 (Ru)	33035
SSV 512 (Ru)	33035
SSV 514 (Ru)	33035
SSV 590 (Ru)	24145
SSV 591 (Ru)	24145

STAKHANOVETS KOTOV (Ru)	35150
STAKHANOVETS PETRASH (Ru)	35150
STAKHANOVETS (Ru)	04080
STAKHANOVETS YERMOLENKO (Ru)	35150
STALSK (Ru)	22327
STANISLAV KOSIOR (Ru)	79340
STANISLAV MONYUSHKO (Ru)	93870
STANISLAV YUDIN (Ru)	17327
STANISLAW (Pd)	33015
STANKO STAIKOV (Bu)	80052
STANYUKOVICH (Ru)	12380
STAR (Ru)	12380
STARA PLANINA (Bu)	49040
STARACHOWICE (Pd)	79870
STARITSA (Ru)	39290
STAROBELSK (Ru)	22327
STARODUBSKOYE (Ru)	22327
STAROGARD GDANSKI (Pd)	76220
STAROGARD GDANSKI (Pd)	76900
STARYY BOLSHEVIK (Ru)	01380
STARYY BOLSHEVIK (Ru)	01640
STASIS SHEYNAUSKAS (Ru)	22327
STASSFURT (DDR)	77105
STAVROPOL (Ru)	70165
STEFAN BATORY (Pd)	02180
STEFAN CZARNIECKI (Pd)	10350
STEFAN KARADJA (Ru)	47540
STEFAN STARZYNSKI (Pd)	12685
STEFANESTI (Rm)	82110
STEPAN ARTEMENKO (Ru)	48860
STEPAN KHALTURIN (Ru)	15460
STEPAN MALYGIN (Ru)	02417
STEPAN MARKYELOV (Ru)	78891
STEPAN RAZIN (Ru)	80171
STEPAN SAVUSHKIN (Ru)	06795
STEPAN VOSTRETSOV (Ru)	60620
STEPAN VOSTRETSOV (Ru)	62580
STEPANOKERT (Ru)	85970
STEPHAN JANTZEN (DDR)	22220

STEREGUSHCHIY (Ru)	22137
STOLETIYE PARIZHOSKOY KOMMUNY (Ru)	03950
STOLIN (Ru)	22327
STOLLBERG (DDR)	34960
STOYKO PEEV (Bu)	80052
STRADJA (Bu)	49040
STRALSUNDSKIY KORABEL (Ru)	13751
STRANA SOVIETOV (Ru)	79340
STRATOSFERA (Ru)	13650
STRAZAK-5 (Pd)	16000
STRAZAK-14 (Pd)	16000
STRAZAK-25 (Pd)	16000
STRELETS (Ru)	12230
STRELETS (Ru)	23860
STREMITELNIY (Ru)	22135
STREVE (Ru)	33198
STREZHEVOY (Ru)	22327
STROGIY (Ru)	22135
STROPTIVYY (Ru)	04080
STROYNYY (Ru)	22327
STRUMA (Bu)	60720
STUBNITZ (DDR)	17985
STUDZIANKI (Pd)	70540
STUPINO (Ru)	22327
STVOR (Ru)	23860
SUCEAVA (Rm)	39670
SUCEVITA (Rm)	82110
SUCIDAVA (Rm)	82110
SUDAK (Ru)	83680
SUDUVA (Ru)	23480
SUGAN (Ru)	13751
SUHL (DDR)	04910
SUKHANOVO (Ru)	22327
SUKHE BATOR (Ru)	70590
SUKHINICHI (Ru)	85320
SUKHODOL (Ru)	22327
SUKHONA (Ru)	35310
SUKHONA (Ru)	93800
SUKHONALES (Ru)	31890
SUKHUMI (Ru)	70610
SULA (Ru)	89460
SULAK (Ru)	76945
SULAK (Ru)	93800
SULEYMAN STALSKIY (Ru)	14370
SULINA (Rm)	82110

267

Name	No.
SULLEYMAN BAGIROV (Ru)	33527
SULOY (Ru)	11610
SUMY (Ru)	11800
SUND (DDR)	18720
SUNGARI (Ru)	24030
'SUPER ATLANTIK' type (Ru)	13650
'SUPER ATLANTIK' type, later (Ru)	13751
SUPUTINO (Ru)	22327
SURA (Ru)	88985
'SURA' or 'KIL' class (Ru)	23685
SURAKHANY (Ru)	44100
SURAZH (Ru)	22327
SUREN SPANDARYAN (Ru)	03770
SUREN SPANDARYAN (Ru)	04010
SURGUT (Ru)	83680
SUROVSK (Ru)	22327
SURSK (Ru)	22327
SURSKOYE (Ru)	22327
SURUGUTNEFT (Ru)	70760
SUSANINO (Ru)	22327
SUURLAID (Ru)	75640
SUVALKIYA (Ru)	13650
SUVOROVETS (Ru)	04080
SUVOROVO (Ru)	83680
SUWALKI (Pd)	79870
SUZDAL (Ru)	03950
SUZDAL (Ru)	93800
SVANETIYA (Ru)	02670
SVATOVO (Ru)	22327
SVENTA (Ru)	56270
SVENTA (Ru)	62730
SVERDLOVO (Ru)	22327
SVERDLOVSK (Ru)	51212
SVETLODOLINSK (Ru)	22327
SVETLOGORSK (Ru)	02670
SVETLOGRAD (Ru)	22327
SVETLOMOR (Ru)	48878
SVETLOMORSK (Ru)	22327
SVETLOVODSK (Ru)	22327
SVETLYY LUCH (Ru)	71670
SVETLYY (Ru)	17637
SVETLYY (Ru)	85320
SVIATOGOR (Ru)	25840
SVILEN RUSSEV (Bu)	48150
SVINOY (DDR)	18720
SVIR (Ru)	35310
SVIRSK (Ru)	15460
SVOBODA (Ru)	01560
SVORTSOV -STEPANOV (Ru)	03770
SVORTSOV -STEPANOV (Ru)	04010
SWIECIE (Pd)	14770
SWIETLIK (Pd)	87740
SYCHEVO (Ru)	22327
SYKTYVKAR (Ru)	15460
SYKTYVKAR (Ru)	22327
SYN PULKU (Pd)	70540
SYRENKA (Ru)	73650
SYRVE (Ru)	22840
SYRVE (Ru)	34470
SYZRAN (Ru)	02670
SZCZECIN (Pd)	48407
T BELLINGSGAUSEN (Ru)	22180
TADEUSZ KOSCIUSKO (Pd)	12685
TADEUSZ OCIOSZYNSKI (Pd)	14480
TADZHAKISTAN (Ru)	02350
TADZHAKISTAN (Ru)	35370
TADZHIKISTAN (Ru)	12380
TAGANROG (Ru)	11800
TAGANROG (Ru)	52304
TAGANROG (Ru)	52616
TAGANROGSKIY ZALIV (Ru)	61100
TAGIL (Ru)	45590
TAGIL (Ru)	76945
TAKELI (Ru)	86070
TAKHUNAAR (Ru)	89200
TALISMAN (Ru)	33015
TALLIN (Ru)	35370
TALLINN (Ru)	02350
TALNIKI (Ru)	07947
TALSY (Ru)	38530
TAMAN (Ru)	11460
TAMAN (Ru)	12380
TAMAN (Ru)	35310
TAMBOV (Ru)	62671
TAMPERE (Ru)	07550
TAMSALU (Ru)	86220
TAMULA (Ru)	13650
TANTAL (Ru)	11720
TANYA KARPINSKAYA (Ru)	67010
TARAKLIYA (Ru)	88920
TARAS SHEVCHENKO (Ru)	01750
TARAS SHEVCHENKO (Ru)	17500
TARASOVSK (Ru)	07947
TARKHANKUT (Ru)	47150
TARKHANKUT (Ru)	70810
TARKHANSK (Ru)	07947
TARNOBRZEG (Pd)	73550
TARNOW (Pd)	75770
TARPOL (Pd)	22330
TARTU (Ru)	86220
TARUSA (Ru)	11720
TARUSA (Ru)	34610
TASERGAL (Pd)	22330
TATARIYA (Ru)	02350
TATARIYA (Ru)	35370
TATARSTAN (Ru)	81195
TATRY (Pd)	67677
TAURAGE (Ru)	13650
TAURUS (Pd)	11700
TAUYSK (Ru)	00350
TAVDA (Ru)	02280
TAVRIDA (Ru)	11800
TAVRIYA (Ru)	79340
TAVROVO (Ru)	17637
TAYBOLA (Ru)	17950
TAYFUN (Ru)	21260
TAYGA (Ru)	23860
TAYGA (Ru)	24030
TAYGONOS (Ru)	24030
TAYMYR (Ru)	01733
TAYMYR (Ru)	04270
TAYMYR (Ru)	11430
TAYOZHNYY BEREG (Ru)	62671
TAYOZHNYY BEREG (Ru)	82651
TAYSHEN (Ru)	24030
TAYSHET (Ru)	12380
TAZAR (Ru)	23474
TBILISI (Ru)	12230
TCHAIKA (Bu)	12230
TEKHUMARDI (Ru)	23335
TELEGA (Rm)	82110
TELEORMAN (Rm)	47540
TELSHYAY (Ru)	13751
TEMRYUCHANIN (Ru)	13650
TEMRYUK (Ru)	85970
TENDRA (Ru)	39970
TEODOR NETTE (Ru)	12380
TEPLOOZERSKIY (Ru)	17637
TEREK (Ru)	76945
TEREK (Ru)	95015
TEREKHOVSK (Ru)	07947
TERIBERKA (Ru)	89250
TERMEZ (Ru)	86220
TERNEY (Ru)	06795
TERNEY (Ru)	12380
TERNOVSK (Ru)	07947
TERRAL (Pd)	70955
TESEY (Ru)	11800
TESSIN (DDR)	75330
THALE (DDR)	17329
THALE (DDR)	74820
THEMAR (DDR)	84940
THEMAR (DDR)	90600
THEODOR FONTANE (DDR)	11140
THEODOR KORNER (DDR)	34200
THEODOR STORM (DDR)	11140
TIBOR SZAMUELY (Ru)	00240
TIBOR SZAMUELY (Ru)	14975
TIERIBERKA (Ru)	17950
TIGIL (Ru)	23480
TIGR (Ru)	14962
TIKHON KISELYEV (Ru)	80100
TIKHON SYOMUSHKIN (Ru)	50763
TIKHOOKEANSKIY (Ru)	11720
TIKHOOKEANSKIY (Ru)	34610
TIKHORETSK (Ru)	11800
TIKHORETSK (Ru)	86070
TIKHVIN (Ru)	12380
TIKSI (Ru)	02724
TIM BUCK (Ru)	49342
TIMIRYAZEV (Ru)	17500
TIMIS (Rm)	87640
TIMISOARA (Rm)	41310
TIMOFEY GORNOV (Ru)	11800
TIMOFEY KHRYUKIN (Ru)	11610
TIMOFEYEVSK (Ru)	07947
TIMUR FRUNZE (Ru)	78060
TIORA (Ru)	24310
TIORA (Ru)	39450
TIRASPOL (Ru)	23480
TIRASPOL (Ru)	89200
TIRGOVISTE (Rm)	41310
TIRGU BUJOR (Rm)	78841
TIRGU FRUMOS (Rm)	78841
TIRGU JIU (Rm)	82110
TIRGU LAPUS (Rm)	78841
TIRGU MURES (Rm)	41310
TIRGU NEAMT (Rm)	78841
TIRGU OCNA (Rm)	78841
TIRGU SECUIESC (Rm)	78841
TIRGU TROTUS (Rm)	78841
TIRNAVA (Rm)	13650
TIRNAVENI (Rm)	82110
TITAN-1 (Ru)	17323
TITAN-2 (Ru)	17323
TITANIYA (Ru)	45210
TITOVKA (Ru)	17950
TITOVSK (Ru)	07947
TOBOL (Ru)	07550
TOBOLLES (Ru)	24030
TOBRUK (Pd)	59220
TOBRUK (Pd)	74540
TOKARYEVSK (Ru)	07947
TOLBACHIK (Ru)	23480
TOLYA KOMAR (Ru)	15510
TOLYA SHUMOV (Ru)	15510
'TOMBA' class (Ru)	04200
TOMIS (Rm)	77560
TOMSK (Ru)	93820
TONYA BONDARCHUK (Ru)	15510
TOPAZ (Ru)	12380
TOPAZ (Ru)	33015
TOPOLOVENI (Rm)	82110
TORGELOW (DDR)	50440
TORGELOW (DDR)	52000
TORMIDERAND (Ru)	23664
TORNADO (Pd)	70955
TOROS (Ru)	11610
TORZHOK (Ru)	11720
TORZHOK (Ru)	34610
TOUNDYA (Bu)	36820
TOYVO ANTIKAYNEN (Ru)	05620
TOYVO ANTIKAYNEN (Ru)	14450
TOYVO VYAKHYA (Ru)	79340
TRAKAY (Ru)	23480
TRALFLOT (Ru)	11580
TRANSSHELF (Ru)	17257
TRAPEZITZA (Bu)	93060
TRATTENDORF (DDR)	79730

TRENNTSEE (DDR) 46370
TRENNTSEE (DDR) 47070
TRETYAKOVO (Ru) 12380
TRINEC (Cz) 79230
TRINWILLERSHAGEN (DDR) 75320
TRIPOSFERA (Ru) 13650
TRITON (Ru) 13650
TRITON (Ru) 22178
TROCHUS (Ru) 24310
TROCHUS (Ru) 39450
TROPIK (Ru) 01736
TROTUS (Rm) 11800
TRUD (Ru) 37780
TRUDOLYUBIVYY (Ru) 84330
TRUDOVAYA SLAVA (Ru) 93780
TRUDOVYE RESERVY (Ru) 12380
TRUNOVSK (Ru) 07947
TRUSEVIK MORYA (Ru) 13650
TRUSKAVETS (Ru) 23480
TRUSKAVETS (Ru) 51212
TRUSKAVETS (Ru) 51212
TRUSKAVETS (Ru) 86070
TRYDAKNA (Ru) 24310
TRYDAKNA (Ru) 39450
TSEFEY (Ru) 13751
TSELINOGRAD (Ru) 45210
TSELINOGRAD (Ru) 86170
TSEMESSKAYA
  BUKHTA (Ru) 13650
TSENTAVR (Ru) 22173
TSESIS (Ru) 38530
TSEZAR KUNIKOV (Ru) 59890
TSEZAR KUNIKOV (Ru) 67650
TSIGLOMEN (Ru) 06770
TSIGLOMEN (Ru) 07550
TSIKLON (Ru) 18320
TSIKLON (Ru) 21240
TSIMLYANSK (Ru) 11720
TSIMLYANSK (Ru) 34610
TSIVILSK (Ru) 26210
TSKHALTUBO (Ru) 11800
TSNA (Ru) 35180
TSVETKOVO (Ru) 13751
TUAPSE (Ru) 67670
TUCANA (Pd) 11700
TULA (Ru) 02520
TULCHIN (Ru) 45715
TULEN KABILOV (Ru) 11800

TULOMA (Ru) 21580
TULOMA (Ru) 24030
TULSK (Ru) 07947
TUMAK (Pd) 33015
TUMAN-2 (Ru) 23480
TUMNIN (Ru) 17637
TUNEK (Pd) 23474
TUNGUSKA (Ru) 15460
TURA (Ru) 08849
TURAYDA (Ru) 13650
TURGAY (Ru) 67010
TURINSK (Ru) 76715
TURKMENISTAN (Ru) 81195
TURKMENIYA (Ru) 02160
TURKU (Ru) 06770
TURKU (Ru) 07550
TURKUL (Ru) 23480
TURMALIN (Ru) 12380
TUROSZOW (Pd) 60360
TUSHINO (Ru) 06795
TUTOVA (Ru) 94565
TUZLA (Rm) 94565
TYMLAT (Ru) 23480
TYMOVSK (Ru) 06795
TYNDA (Ru) 11720
TYNDA (Ru) 34610
TYUMEN (Ru) 24030
TYUMENNEFT (Ru) 36890
TYUMENNEFT (Ru) 43790
TZAREVETZ (Bu) 93060

UELEN (Ru) 55100
UGOLNYY (Ru) 11800
UKHTA (Ru) 85970
UKRAINA (Ru) 16140
UKRAINSKIY
  KOMSOMOLETS (Ru) 58510
UKRAINSKIY
  KOMSOMOLETS (Ru) 71820
UKRAINY (Ru) 05620
ULAN (Ru) 23305
ULAN-BATOR (Ru) 51212
ULAN-UDE (Ru) 24030
ULAN-UDE (Ru) 91224
ULBANSKIY ZALIV (Ru) 62671
ULBANSKIY ZALIV (Ru) 82651
ULYANOVSK (Ru) 70165
UMAN (Ru) 21580

UNAN AVETISYAN (Ru) 51672
UNAN AVETISYAN (Ru) 73290
UNIWERSYTET
  JAGIELLONSKI (Pd) 78680
UNIWERSYTET
  SLASKI (Pd) 65850
UNIWERSYTET
  SLASKI (Pd) 67690
UNIWERSYTET
  WARSZAWSKI (Pd) 79110
UNIWERSYTET
  WROCLAWSKI (Pd) 79110
UNZHA (Ru) 06795
UPITE (Ru) 33198
URAGAN (Ru) 18320
URAGAN (Ru) 21240
URAGAN (Ru) 22137
URAL (Ru) 17500
URAL (Ru) 52270
URAL (Ru) 76945
URALJSKIE GORY (Ru) 61270
URALLES (Ru) 24030
URALSKIE GORY (Ru) 81490
URAN (Pd) 12610
URANIYA (Ru) 13751
URENGOI (Ru) 90190
URENGOY (Ru) 70020
URGAL (Ru) 11720
URGAL (Ru) 34610
URICANI (Rm) 82220
URSUS (Pd) 14770
URZHUM (Ru) 70165
USHAKOVO (Ru) 33198
USINSK (Ru) 70020
USPESHNYY (Ru) 17637
USSURI (Ru) 15460
USSURIYSK (Ru) 52304
USSURIYSK (Ru) 52616
USSURIYSKAYA
  TAYGA (Ru) 62671
USSURIYSKAYA
  TAYGA (Ru) 82651
USSURIYSKIY ZALIV (Ru) 61100
UST-ILIMSK (Ru) 66380
UST-IZHMA (Ru) 66380
UST-KAN (Ru) 66380
UST-KARSK (Ru) 66380
UST-KUT (Ru) 66380

UST-LABINSK (Ru) 66380
USTOYCHIVYY (Ru) 17637
USTUPCHIVYY (Ru) 17637
UTENA (Ru) 17637
UTYOS (Ru) 22173
UTYOS (Ru) 22173
UVAROVSK (Ru) 24310
UVAROVSK (Ru) 39450
UZBEKISTAN (Ru) 02350
UZBEKISTAN (Ru) 35370
UZBEKISTAN (Ru) 81195
UZEIR GADZHIBEKOV (Ru) 79340
UZGORSK (Ru) 24310
UZGORSK (Ru) 39450

V KUCHER (Ru) 75320
VACHA (Bu) 85970
VADINSK (Ru) 26210
VAGA (Ru) 07550
VAGIF (Ru) 50730
VAGULA (Ru) 13650
VAKHRUCHEVSK (Ru) 22327
VAL (Ru) 21947
VALDAY (Ru) 11300
VALDAYLES (Ru) 24030
VALDAYSK (Ru) 22327
VALEA ALBA (Rm) 60978
VALENTIN
  KHUTORSKOY (Ru) 03950
VALENTIN
  KOTELNIKOV (Ru) 12380
VALENTIN SEROV (Ru) 91224
VALENTIN SHASHKIN (Ru) 92880
VALENTIN
  ZOLOTAREV (Ru) 56638
VALENTINA
  TERESHKOVA (Ru) 01560
VALERIAN ALBANOV (Ru) 02417
VALERIAN
  KUIBYSHEV (Ru) 03060
VALERIAN
  KUIBYSHEV (Ru) 03650
VALERIAN URYVAYEV (Ru) 93268
VALERIY MEZHLAUK (Ru) 03950
VALERIY VOLKOV (Ru) 15510
VALERIYA BARSOVA (Ru) 48430
VALERIYA BARSOVA (Ru) 49470
VALERIYA BARSOVA (Ru) 49740

VALKA (Ru) 23480
VALMIERA (Ru) 38530
VALUYSK (Ru) 22327
VALYA KOTIK (Ru) 15510
VALYA KURAKINA (Ru) 67010
VANINO (Ru) 52304
VANINO (Ru) 52616
VANINSK (Ru) 22327
VANKAREM (Ru) 21610
VANYA KOVALYEV (Ru) 67010
VARENA (Ru) 22327
VARNA (Bu) 50125
VARSHAVA (Ru) 36840
VARSHUGA (Ru) 17950
VASIL KOLAROV (Bu) 01980
VASIL KOLAROV (Ru) 01960
VASIL LEVSKY (Bu) 48430
VASIL LEVSKY (Bu) 49470
VASIL LEVSKY (Bu) 49740
VASILIY AZHAYEV (Ru) 47860
VASILIY BLUKHER (Ru) 93680
VASILIY BOZHENKO (Ru) 79340
VASILIY BURKHANOV (Ru) 02724
VASILIY
  BYELOKONYENKO (Ru) 69310
VASILIY
  CHERNYSHYEV (Ru) 45290
VASILIY DOKUCHAEV (Ru) 28980
VASILIY FEDOSEYEV (Ru) 21610
VASILIY FESENKOV (Ru) 10740
VASILIY FOMIN (Ru) 13650
VASILIY GOLOVNIN (Ru) 22180
VASILIY
  GRECHISNIKOV (Ru) 13751
VASILIY
  KALASHNIKOV (Ru) 75392
VASILIY KIKVIDZE (Ru) 59890
VASILIY KIKVIDZE (Ru) 67650
VASILIY KOSENKHOV (Ru) 11610
VASILIY KOVAL (Ru) 48650
VASILIY MALOV (Ru) 75380
VASILIY MATUZENKO (Ru) 47674
VASILIY MUSINSKIY (Ru) 54710
VASILIY PEROV (Ru) 91224
VASILIY POLENOV (Ru) 76580
VASILIY POLENOV (Ru) 79930
VASILIY POLENOV (Ru) 91224
VASILIY PORIK (Ru) 60620

VASILIY PORIK (Ru) 62580
VASILIY POYARKHOV (Ru) 22220
VASILIY
PRONCHISHCHEV (Ru) 22220
VASILIY PUTINTSEV (Ru) 93680
VASILIY REVYAKIN (Ru) 13650
VASILIY SHELGUNOV (Ru) 04010
VASILIY SHUKSHIN (Ru) 50763
VASILIY SOLOVYEV
SEDOY (Ru) 80010
VASILIY STRUVE (Ru) 10740
VASILIY SURIKOV (Ru) 91224
VASILIY YAN (Ru) 50730
VASILY GOLOVKIN (Ru) 11800
VASILY KLOCHKOV (Ru) 48430
VASILY KLOCHKOV (Ru) 49470
VASILY KLOCHKOV (Ru) 49740
VASILY SHELGUNOV (Ru) 03770
VASILY
VERESCHCHAGIN (Ru) 91224
VASILY VINEVITIN (Ru) 12380
VASILYEVSK (Ru) 22327
VASLUI (Rm) 41310
VASYA ALEKSEYEV (Ru) 11430
VASYA KOROBKO (Ru) 15510
VASYA KURKA (Ru) 67010
VASYA
SHISHKOVSKIY (Ru) 15510
VASYA STABROVSKIY (Ru) 67010
VATRA DORNEI (Rm) 89540
VATSLAV VOROVSKIY (Ru) 02120
VATUTINO (Ru) 08030
VAYDAGHUBSKIY (Ru) 51370
VAYGACH (Ru) 08849
VAYGACH (Ru) 11610
VAYGACH (Ru) 22173
VAZHGORSK (Ru) 22327
VEGA (Pd) 11670
VEGA (Ru) 12230
VEJEN (Bu) 55410
VEJEN (Bu) 78850
VEKTOR (Ru) 95043
VELEKA (Bu) 59890
VELEKA (Bu) 67650
VELIKIY OKTYABR (Ru) 59890
VELIKIY OKTYABR (Ru) 67650
VELIKIY POCHIN (Ru) 79340
VELIKIY USTYUG (Ru) 07550

VELIKIYE LUKI (Ru) 06060
VELIKIYE USTYUG (Ru) 06770
VELIKO TIRNOVO (Bu) 91700
VELIZH (Ru) 06060
VENERA IV (Ru) 11800
VENTA (Ru) 02105
VENTSPILS (Ru) 36250
VENTSPILS (Ru) 42800
VENTSPILS (Ru) 52304
VENTSPILS (Ru) 52616
VERA
KHORUZHKAYA (Ru) 78060
VERA LEBEDYEVA (Ru) 03770
VERA LEBEDYEVA (Ru) 04010
VERA MUKHINA (Ru) 76580
VERA MUKHINA (Ru) 79930
VERA VOLOSHINA (Ru) 79340
VEREYA (Ru) 06060
VERILA (Bu) 75790
VERKHOVINA (Ru) 11720
VERKHOVINA (Ru) 34610
VERKHOYANSKLES (Ru) 06795
VERKHOYANY (Ru) 11300
VERTIKAL (Ru) 21947
VESLETS (Bu) 75790
VESYEGONSK (Ru) 66380
VETER (Ru) 21260
VETERAN (Ru) 85320
VETLUGA (Ru) 26210
VETLUGA (Ru) 45730
VETLUGALES (Ru) 24030
VEVIS (Ru) 33017
VEZUVSK (Ru) 22327
VICTORIA (Rm) 39660
VIDEN (Bu) 75790
VIDNOYE (Ru) 66380
VIDRARU (Rm) 77080
VIDRARU (Rm) 80000
VIHREN (Bu) 77080
VIHREN (Bu) 80000
VIIRELAID (Ru) 75640
VIKTOR BUGAYEV (Ru) 02270
VIKTOR KHARA (Ru) 50763
VIKTOR KHUDYAKOV (Ru) 23480
VIKTOR KINGISEPP (Ru) 80010
VIKTOR KINGISEPP (Ru) 93870
VIKTOR
KURNATOVSKIY (Ru) 03770

VIKTOR
KURNATOVSKIY (Ru) 04010
VIKTOR LYAGIN (Ru) 91224
VIKTOR MIRONOV (Ru) 34872
VIKTOR
MURAVLENKO (Ru) 92880
VIKTOR STRELTSOV (Ru) 34872
VIKTOR TALALIKHIN (Ru) 78060
VIKTOR TARASOV (Ru) 60373
VIKTOR TKACHYOV (Ru) 49342
VIKTOR VASTNETSOV (Ru) 91224
VIKTORAS
YATSENYAVICHUS (Ru) 85320
VIKTORIO
CODOVILLA (Ru) 70590
VILCEA (Ru) 47540
VILIS LACIS (Ru) 93780
VILKOVO (Ru) 86220
VILNIS (Ru) 22173
VILNIUS (Ru) 26210
VILNYUS (Ru) 31185
VILSANDI (Ru) 86070
VILYANDY (Ru) 86220
VILYANY (Ru) 15460
VILYUY (Ru) 02105
VILYUYLES (Ru) 24030
VILYUYSK (Ru) 36250
VILYUYSK (Ru) 42800
VILYUYSK (Ru) 70020
VINNITSA (Ru) 51212
VINTSAS MITSKYAVICHUS-
KAPSUKAS (Ru) 93820
VIRBALIS (Ru) 33017
VIRTSU (Ru) 89200
VIRURAND (Ru) 23664
VISEU (Rm) 77080
VISEU (Rm) 80000
VISHNEVOGORSK (Ru) 79340
'VISHNYA' class (Ru) 11575
VISHTITIS (Ru) 33198
VISSARION
BELINSKIY (Ru) 14370
VITALIY BONIVUR (Ru) 12380
VITALIY BONIVUR (Ru) 85320
VITALIY DYAKONOV (Ru) 50763
VITALIY KRUCHINA (Ru) 69310
VITALIY PRIMAKOV (Ru) 79340
VITAUTAS PUTNA (Ru) 12380

VITEAZUL (Rm) 22178
VITIM (Ru) 89250
VITOCHA (Bu) 77080
VITOCHA (Bu) 80000
VITUS BERING (Ru) 09380
VITYA CHALENKO (Ru) 15510
VITYA KHONENKO (Ru) 15510
VITYA NOVITSKIY (Ru) 67010
VITYA SITNITSA (Ru) 15510
VITYAZ (Ru) 14905
VIYTNA (Ru) 13751
VIZIR (Ru) 23860
VLADAS REKASHYUS (Ru) 12380
VLADIMIR ATLASOV (Ru) 12380
VLADIMIR BRODYUK (Ru) 34872
VLADIMIR
FAVORSKIY (Ru) 76580
VLADIMIR
FAVORSKIY (Ru) 79930
VLADIMIR GAVRILOV (Ru) 46560
VLADIMIR ILYCH (Ru) 03060
VLADIMIR ILYCH (Ru) 03650
VLADIMIR ILYCH (Ru) 93380
VLADIMIR KALININ (Ru) 28600
VLADIMIR
KAVRAYSKIY (Ru) 23640
VLADIMIR KOKKINAKI (Ru) 51410
VLADIMIR
KOLECHITSKY (Ru) 59880
VLADIMIR
KOROLENKO (Ru) 14370
VLADIMIR KURASOV (Ru) 11333
VLADIMIR
LENORSKIY (Ru) 78891
VLADIMIR
MAYAKOVSKIY (Ru) 14370
VLADIMIR
MORDVINOV (Ru) 54710
VLADIMIR RUSANOV (Ru) 22220
VLADIMIR
SUKHOTSKIY (Ru) 02417
VLADIMIR
TIMOFEYEV (Ru) 54710
VLADIMIR
VASLYAYEV (Ru) 12680
VLADIMIR
ZATONSKIY (Ru) 79340
VLADIVOSTOK (Ru) 02070

VLADIVOSTOK (Ru) 92380
VLAS CHUBAR (Ru) 75350
VLAS NICHKOV (Ru) 54710
VNUKOVO (Ru) 11720
VNUKOVO (Ru) 34610
'VODA' class (Ru) 88985
VOGTLAND (DDR) 79315
VOINICUL (Rm) 22178
VOLCHANSK (Ru) 05410
VOLCHANSK (Ru) 45120
VOLDEMAR AZIN (Ru) 23480
VOLGA (Ru) 24030
'VOLGO-BALT' type (Ru) 79340
VOLGOBALT (Ru) 11300
VOLGOGRAD (Ru) 20745
VOLGOGRAD (Ru) 23664
VOLGOGRADSKIY
KOMSOMOLETS 22327
VOLGOLES (Ru) 24030
'VOLGONEFT' type (Ru) 67395
'VOLGONEFT' type (Ru) 90420
'VOLGONEFT' type (Ru) 92030
VOLGONEFTGAROZ (Ru) 44100
VOLKHOV (Ru) 38950
VOLKHOVSTROY (Ru) 11800
VOLNA (Ru) 02270
VOLNOMER (Ru) 11800
VOLNOVAKHA (Ru) 42960
VOLNYY VETER (Ru) 13751
VOLOCHAYEVSK (Ru) 45210
VOLODARSK (Ru) 17637
VOLODYA
SCHERBATSEVICH (Ru) 15510
VOLOGDA (Ru) 45120
VOLOGDALES (Ru) 04180
VOLOPAS (Ru) 11333
VOLSKIY ZALIV (Ru) 62671
VOLSKIY ZALIV (Ru) 82651
VOLZHANIN (Ru) 23480
VOLZHSK (Ru) 08030
VOLZHSK (Ru) 85320
VORKUTA (Ru) 24030
VORMSI (Ru) 88230
VORONET (Rm) 60978
VORONEZH (Ru) 06770
VORONEZH (Ru) 07550
VOROSHILOVGRAD (Ru) 13650
VOROSMARTY (Hu) 48430

Name	No.
VOROSMARTY (Hu)	49470
VOROSMARTY (Hu)	49740
VOSKHOD (Ru)	11430
VOSKHOD (Ru)	11580
VOSKHOD (Ru)	12380
VOSKHOD (Ru)	23664
VOSRESENSK (Ru)	24030
VOSTOCHNIY BEREG (Ru)	62671
VOSTOCK (Ru)	92150
VOSTOCK (Ru)	93660
VOSTOK (Ru)	33015
VOSTOK 2 (Ru)	11430
VOSTOK 5 (Ru)	11430
VOSTOK 6 (Ru)	11430
VOZNESENSK (Ru)	79340
VOZROZHDENIYE (Ru)	13751
VRANCEA (Rm)	25780
VSEVELOD KOCHETOV (Ru)	67680
VSEVELOD BERYEZKIN (Ru)	93268
VSEVOLOD PUDOVKIN (Ru)	15120
VSEVOLOD TIMONOV (Ru)	33305
VSPOLOKH (Ru)	11580
VULCAN (Rm)	82220
VULKAN (Ru)	22178
VULKAN (Ru)	23480
VULKANLOG (Ru)	93268
VYACHESLAV DENISOV (Ru)	50280
VYACHESLAV FROLOV (Ru)	93268
VYANDRA (Ru)	89200
VYATKALES (Ru)	06795
VYAZMA (Ru)	08030
VYAZMA (Ru)	66380
VYBORG (Ru)	08030
VYBORG (Ru)	33015
VYBORGSKAYA STORONA (Ru)	11610
VYBORGSKAYA STORONA (Ru)	50280
VYCHEGDA (Ru)	35310
VYCHEGDALES (Ru)	24030
VYMPEL (Ru)	11610
VYOVSK (Ru)	34610
VYRU (Ru)	15460
VYRU (Ru)	89460
VYSHINSKIY (Ru)	17500
VYSHOGOROD (Ru)	11720
VYSHOGOROD (Ru)	34610
VYSOVSK (Ru)	11720
VYUGA (Ru)	22220
VZMORE (Ru)	33198
VZMORYE (Ru)	06795
VZMORYE (Ru)	11800
WADOWICE (Pd)	79870
WALEN (Pd)	23440
WALKA MLODYCH (Pd)	65850
WALKA MLODYCH (Pd)	67690
WALTER BARTH (DDR)	23410
WALTER DEHMEL (DDR)	10250
WALTER DEHMEL (DDR)	12630
WALTER ULBRICHT (DDR)	03690
WARIN (DDR)	75330
WARKA (Pd)	75412
WARNEMUNDE (DDR)	17480
WARNEMUNDE (Ru)	03690
WARSZAWA II (Pd)	48407
WAWEL (Pd)	23710
WAWEL (Pd)	32715
WEIMAR (DDR)	70695
WEJHEROWO (Pd)	51260
WERBELLINSEE (DDR)	46370
WERBELLINSEE (DDR)	47070
WERNER KUBE (DDR)	23410
WERNER SEELENBINDER (DDR)	04230
WESTERPLATTE (Pd)	10350
WICKO (Pd)	33193
WIECZNO (Pd)	33193
WIELICZKA (Pd)	03230
WIELICZKA (Pd)	03620
WIELUN (Pd)	50460
WIGRY (Pd)	33193
WIGRY (Pd)	33560
WILANOW (Pd)	32715
WILHELM FLORIN (DDR)	04230
WILHELM PIECK (DDR)	08778
WILHELM PIEK (DDR)	62701
WILLI BREDEL (DDR)	17980
WILLIAM FOSTER (Ru)	03060
WILLIAM FOSTER (Ru)	03650
WINETA (Pd)	59690
WINETA (Pd)	81350
WISMAR (DDR)	31185
WISMAR (DDR)	34960
WITTENBERG (DDR)	34960
WLADYSLAW GOMULKA (Pd)	72115
WLADYSLAW JAGIELLO (Pd)	14910
WLADYSLAW JAGIELLO (Pd)	15720
WLADYSLAW LOKIETEK (Pd)	14910
WLADYSLAW LOKIETEK (Pd)	15720
WLADYSLAW ORKAN (Pd)	06090
WLADYSLAW ORKAN (Pd)	14800
WLADYSLAW SIKORSKI (Pd)	12685
WLADYSLAWOWO (Pd)	04400
WLOCZNIK (Pd)	11790
WOLGAST (DDR)	77398
WROCLAW (Pd)	80205
WROZKA (Pd)	73650
WYSZKOW (Pd)	50460
XI PYATILETKA (Ru)	79340
XV SYEZD PROFSOYUZOV (Ru)	23480
XVI SYEZD PROFSOYUZOV (Ru)	11720
XVI SYEZD VLKSM (Ru)	79340
XVII SYEZD PROFSOYUSOV (Ru)	11333
XVII SYEZD PROFSOYUZOV (Ru)	79340
XVII SYEZD VLKSM (Ru)	79340
XVIII SYEZD VLKSM (Ru)	11720
XVIII SYEZD VLKSM (Ru)	79340
XX SYEZD KOMSOMOLA LITVY (Ru)	26210
XXIV SYEZD KPSS (Ru)	79340
XXV SYEZD KPSS (Ru)	58510
XXV SYEZD KPSS (Ru)	71820
XXVI SYEZD KPSS (Ru)	11333
YAAN ANVELT (Ru)	03770
YAAN ANVELT (Ru)	04010
YAAN KALBERZIN (Ru)	03423
YAAN KOORT (Ru)	12380
YABLONOVSKIY (Ru)	22327
YAGUAR (Ru)	22160
YAKAN (Ru)	88130
YAKHROMA (Ru)	61840
YAKHROMA (Ru)	85895
YAKOB KUNDER (Ru)	50280
YAKOV ALKSNIS (Ru)	10720
YAKOV BONDARENKO (Ru)	48430
YAKOV BONDARENKO (Ru)	49470
YAKOV BONDARENKO (Ru)	49740
YAKOV GAKKEL (Ru)	93268
YAKOV REZNICHENKO (Ru)	50280
YAKOV SMIKNITSKIY (Ru)	04216
YAKOV SMUSHKEVICH (Ru)	12380
YAKOV SVERDLOV (Ru)	28980
YAKUB KOLAS (Ru)	50730
YAKUTSKLES (Ru)	06795
YALTA (Ru)	12230
YAMAL (Ru)	11430
YAMALSKIY (Ru)	22327
YAN BERZIN (Ru)	12380
YAN RAYNBERG (Ru)	13650
YAN SUDRABKALN (Ru)	67680
YANA (Ru)	90190
YANIS LENTSMANIS (Ru)	10720
YANIS RAYNIS (Ru)	10720
YANKA KUPALA (Ru)	50730
YANTAR (Ru)	12380
YANTARNYY BEREG (Ru)	62680
YANTARNYY (Ru)	07550
YANTARNYY (Ru)	45120
YARA (Ru)	33198
YARENGA (Ru)	08846
YARKIY LUCH (Ru)	71670
YARKIY (Ru)	17637
YARONIMAS UBORYAVICHUS (Ru)	12380
YAROSLAVL (Ru)	23664
YAROSLAVL (Ru)	45210
YASENYEVO (Ru)	49100
YASHA GORDIYENKO (Ru)	67010
YASHMA (Ru)	12380
YASNIY (Ru)	14962
YASNOYE (Ru)	46620
YASNYY (Ru)	17637
YASTREBOVO (Ru)	13751
YEGORLIK (Ru)	70810
YEKATERINA BELASHOVA (Ru)	76580
YEKATERINA BELASHOVA (Ru)	79930
YELAGIN (Ru)	23305
YELENA LITVINOVA (Ru)	79340
YELENA STASOVA (Ru)	04010
YELNYA (Ru)	44620
YELNYA (Ru)	70810
YEMELYAN PUGACHEV (Ru)	80171
YEMELYAN YAROSLAVSKIY (Ru)	03770
YEMELYAN YAROSLAVSKIY (Ru)	04010
YENAKIYEVO (Ru)	78891
YENISEY (Ru)	13590
YENISEY (Ru)	39290
YENISEY (Ru)	76945
YENISEYSK (Ru)	70020
YEOFIM KRIVOSEYEV (Ru)	34872
YERMAK (Ru)	20870
YEROFEY KHABAROV (Ru)	22220
YERUSLAN (Ru)	76945
YESSENTUKI (Ru)	44620
YEVGENIY BURYKHIN (Ru)	22327
YEVGENIY CHAPLANOV (or EVGENIY CHAPLANOV) (Ru)	06795
YEVGENIY LEBEDYEV (Ru)	45290
YEVGENIY NIKISHIN (Ru)	93680
YEVGENIY POLYAKOV (Ru)	13751
YEVGENIY PREOBRAZENSKIY (Ru)	24310
YEVGENIY PREOBRAZENSKIY (Ru)	39450
YEVGENIY VUCHETICH (Ru)	93380
YEVPATORIYE (Ru)	12230
YEYSK (or EYSK) (Ru)	11800
YEYSK (Ru)	22840
YEYSK (Ru)	34470

YEYSKIY LIMAN (Ru) 33620
YONAVA (Ru) 13650
YORDAN
  LUTIBRODSKI (Bu) 77127
YUBILEY OKTYABRYA (Ru) 12380
YUG (Ru) 23390
YUG (Ru) 23860
YUGANSK (Ru) 70760
YUGLA (Ru) 36890
YUGLA (Ru) 43790
YUKHAN SMUUL (Ru) 11800
YULIAN
  MARKHLEVSKIY (Ru) 93820
YULIMISTE (Ru) 11800
YULIUS FUCHIK (Ru) 00240
YULIUS FUCHIK (Ru) 14975
YULIY
  DANISHEVSKIY (Ru) 52612/1
YULYUS YANONIS (Ru) 87000
YUNOST (Ru) 01960
YUNOST (Ru) 12380
YUNYY LENINETS (Ru) 01560
YUNYY PARTIZAN (Ru) 67010
YUOZAS GARYALIS (Ru) 12380
YUOZAS
  GREYFENBERGERIS (Ru) 12380
YUOZAS VAREYKIS (Ru) 12380
YUOZAS VAREYKIS (Ru) 12380
YUPITER (Ru) 33035
YURBARKAS (Ru) 13650
YURIY ARSHINEVSKIY (Ru) 02724
YURIY AVOT (Ru) 78060
YURIY KLEMENTYEV (Ru) 75312
YURIY KOSTIKOV (Ru) 11610
YURIY
  KOTSYUBINSKY (Ru) 79340
YURIY KRIMOV (Ru) 50763
YURIY LEVITAN (Ru) 80052
YURIY LISYANSKIY (Ru) 22220
YURIY MAKSAYEV (Ru) 80260
YURIY MALAKHOV (Ru) 11800
YURIY SAVINOV (Ru) 54710
YURIY SMIRNOV (Ru) 78060
YURMALA (Ru) 13650
YURMALA (Ru) 63640
YURYUZAN (Ru) 22290
YURYUZAN (Ru) 89460
YUSHAR (Ru) 20738

YUSTAS PALECKIS (Ru) 78010
YUSTAS PALECKIS (Ru) 79990
YUSUP KOBALADZE (Ru) 52612/1
YUTA
  BONDAROVSKAYA (Ru) 15510
YUTNIEKS (Ru) 11800
YUZHNAYA ZVEZDA (Ru) 23305
YUZHNO-SAKHALINSK (Ru)93820
YUZHNOMORSK (Ru) 11800
YUZHNYY KREST (Ru) 12230

ZABAYKALSK (Ru) 24030
ZABAYKALYE (Ru) 09210
ZABAYKALYE (Ru) 22173
ZABAYKALYE (Ru) 45120
ZADONSK (Ru) 62460
ZADONSK (Ru) 78540
ZADONSK (Ru) 80130
ZADORIE (Ru) 17950
ZAGLEBIE
  DABROWSKIE (Pd) 75730
ZAGLEBIE
  DABROWSKIE (Pd) 88380
ZAGLEBIE
  MIEDZIOWE (Pd) 62460
ZAGLEBIE
  MIEDZIOWE (Pd) 78540
ZAGLEBIE
  MIEDZIOWE (Pd) 80130
ZAGLEBIE SIARKOWE (Pd) 73550
ZAGORIANA (Ru) 17950
ZAGORSKIY (Ru) 17950
ZAHARI STOIANOV (Bu) 47540
ZAISAN (Ru) 34470
ZAKARPATYE (Ru) 62460
ZAKARPATYE (Ru) 78540
ZAKARPATYE (Ru) 80130
ZAKAVKAZYE (Ru) 11300
ZAKHARIY
  PALIASHVILI (Ru) 59890
ZAKHARIY
  PALIASHVILI (Ru) 67650
ZAKHAROVO (Ru) 17950
ZAKOPANE (Pd) 81640
ZALAU (Rm) 48430
ZALAU (Rm) 49470
ZALAU (Rm) 49740
ZALESOVO (Ru) 17950

ZALIV (Ru) 23664
ZAMBROW (Pd) 81640
ZAMBRZE (Pd) 81640
ZAMOSC (Pd) 81640
ZANGELAN (Ru) 50770
ZAPOLYARNYY (Ru) 09380
ZAPOLYARNYY (Ru) 15460
ZAPOLYARYE (Ru) 01733
ZAPOLYARYE (Ru) 22173
ZAPOROZHY (Ru) 62460
ZAPOROZHYE (Ru) 78540
ZAPOROZHYE (Ru) 80130
ZARAYSK (Ru) 12230
ZARECHENSK (Ru) 62460
ZARECHENSK (Ru) 78540
ZARECHENSK (Ru) 80130
ZARNESTI (Rm) 82110
ZARNITSA (Ru) 11580
ZARNITSA (Ru) 23390
ZARNITZA (Ru) 17320
ZARYA (Ru) 23664
ZASLONOVO (Ru) 17950
ZASTAVNA (Ru) 26210
ZAVOLZHYE (Ru) 11300
ZAVYETY ILYICHA (Ru) 60680
ZAVYETY ILYICHA (Ru) 90720
ZAWICHOST (Pd) 81640
ZAWIERCIE (Pd) 81640
ZAWRAT (Pd) 68920
ZAYARSK (Ru) 86070
ZBIGNIEW (Pd) 33015
ZEFIR (Ru) 13650
ZELENETS (Ru) 11610
ZELENOBORSK (Ru) 09360
ZELENOGORSK (Ru) 21600
ZELENOGRAD (Ru) 90150
ZELENOKUMSK (Ru) 26210
ZELEZNOGORSK (Ru) 11720
ZELEZNOGORSK (Ru) 34610
ZEMLYANSK (Ru) 24310
ZEMLYANSK (Ru) 26210
ZEMLYANSK (Ru) 39450
ZENIT (Ru) 01736
ZENIT (Ru) 34710
ZENTA OZOLA (Ru) 10720
ZERNOGRAD (Ru) 26210
ZEULENRODA (DDR) 84940
ZEULENRODA (DDR) 90600

ZEVS (Ru) 22178
ZEYA (Ru) 02280
ZEYA (Ru) 22173
ZEYALES (Ru) 11490
ZGORZELEC (Pd) 50460
ZHADANOV (Ru) 48845
ZHALGIRIS (Ru) 70760
ZHAN GRIVA (Ru) 52612/1
ZHDANOVSK (Ru) 26210
ZHDANOVSKIY
  KOMSOMOLETS (Ru) 01380
ZHDANOVSKIY
  KOMSOMOLETS (Ru) 01640
ZHELEZHNYY POTOK (Ru) 23305
ZHEMAYTIYA (Ru) 11800
ZHEMCHUYNYY
  BEREG (Ru) 62701
ZHIGANSK (Ru) 44100
ZHIGULEVSK (Ru) 12340
ZHITOMIR (Ru) 39970
ZHITOMIR (Ru) 51212
ZHITOMIR (Ru) 51212
ZHIZDRA (Ru) 26210
ZHUKOVSKIY (Ru) 11300
ZHUPANOVO (Ru) 39290
ZHUVINTAS (Ru) 22327
ZIEMIA
  BIALOSTOCKA (Bu) 79640
ZIEMIA BYDGOSKA (Pd) 74660
ZIEMIA BYDGOSKA (Pd) 78140
ZIEMIA CHELMINSKA (Pd) 70698
ZIEMIA
  GNIEZNIENSKA (Pd) 70698
ZIEMIA KIELECKA (Pd) 74515
ZIEMIA
  KOSZALINSKA (Pd) 74515
ZIEMIA KRAKOWSKA (Pd) 62460
ZIEMIA KRAKOWSKA (Pd) 78540
ZIEMIA KRAKOWSKA (Pd) 80130
ZIEMIA LUBELSKA (Pd) 62460
ZIEMIA LUBELSKA (Pd) 78540
ZIEMIA LUBELSKA (Pd) 80130
ZIEMIA MAZOWIECKA (Pd) 74660
ZIEMIA MAZOWIECKA (Pd) 78140
ZIEMIA OLSZTYNSKA (Pd) 79640
ZIEMIA OPOLSKI (Pd) 79640
ZIEMIA SUWALSKA (Pd) 70698
ZIEMIA TARNOWSKA (Pd) 70698

ZIEMIA ZACHODNIE (Pd) 70698
ZIEMIA ZAMOJSKA (Pd) 70698
ZIGMAS ANGARETIS (Ru) 12380
ZIKONIYA (Ru) 11800
ZIMNICEA (Rm) 82110
ZINA PORTNOVA (Ru) 15510
ZLATNI PIASATZI (Bu) 91224
ZLATOUST (Ru) 12340
ZLATOUST (Ru) 62460
ZLATOUST (Ru) 78540
ZLATOUST (Ru) 80130
ZNA (or TSNA) (Ru) 02280
ZNAMENSK (Ru) 26210
ZNAMYA KERCHIL (Ru) 13650
ZNAMYA
  OKTYABRYA (Ru) 78060
ZNAMYA
  OKTYABRYA (Ru) 79340
ZNAMYA POBEDY (Ru) 11720
ZNAMYA POBEDY (Ru) 34610
ZODCHIY (Ru) 11610
ZODIAC (Ru) 23860
ZOLOCHYEV (Ru) 26210
ZOLOTITZA (Ru) 11430
ZOLOTOY KOLOS (Ru) 11800
ZOLOTOY ROG (Ru) 36250
ZOLOTOY ROG (Ru) 42800
ZOLOTOY ROG (Ru) 91224
ZOLOTYE DYUNY (Ru) 62671
ZOLOTYE DYUNY (Ru) 82651
ZONDA (Pd) 70955
ZORINSK (Ru) 62460
ZORINSK (Ru) 78540
ZORINSK (Ru) 80130
ZOYA
  KOSMODEMYANSKAYA (Ru)73290
ZUBARYEVO (Ru) 17950
ZUBOVO (Ru) 17950
ZUBR (Ru) 22154
ZUGDIDI (Ru) 70760
ZULAWY (Ru) 59690
ZULAWY (Pd) 81350
ZUND (Ru) 11800
ZUROW (DDR) 50440
ZUROW (DDR) 52000
ZUSSOW (DDR) 50440
ZUSSOW (DDR) 52000
ZVAYGZNE (Ru) 84330

ZVAYGZNE (Ru)	87950	ZVEZDA (Ru)	23390	ZVYEZDA		ZWICKAU (DDR)	36460	ZYGMUNT III WAZA (Pd)	15720

ZVAYGZNE (Ru) 87950
ZVENIGOROD (Ru) 62460
ZVENIGOROD (Ru) 78540
ZVENIGOROD (Ru) 80130
ZVEZDA KRIMA (Ru) 11800
ZVEZDA (Ru) 13650

ZVEZDA (Ru) 23390
ZVYAGIHO (Ru) 17950
ZVYEROBOY (Ru) 17950
ZVYERYEVO (Ru) 17950
ZVYEZDA
   ASOVA (Ru) 13751

ZVYEZDA
   CHERNOMORYA (Ru) 13751
ZVYEZDA
   SEVASTOPOLYA (Ru) 13751
ZVYOZDNYY BEREG (Ru) 62671
ZWICKAU (DDR) 36300

ZWICKAU (DDR) 36460
ZWICKAU (DDR) 43110
ZYEMCHUSNYY (Ru) 11800
ZYGMUNT AUGUST (Pd) 14910
ZYGMUNT AUGUST (Pd) 15720
ZYGMUNT III WAZA (Pd) 14910

ZYGMUNT III WAZA (Pd) 15720
ZYGMUNT STARY (Pd) 14910
ZYGMUNT STARY (Pd) 15720
ZYKOVO (Ru) 17950
ZYRARDOW (Pd) 07460
ZYRARDOW (Pd) 10740